*The Remarkable
Michael Reeves*

His Short and Tragic Life

The Remarkable

Michael

Reeves

His Short and Tragic Life

by John B. Murray

Foreword by Ian Ogilvy

Luminary Press
Baltimore, Maryland

Photographs courtesy:
BFI
Tom Baker
Bev Ferris
John Hamilton
Ernest Harris
Nicky Henson
Victoria de Korda
Robert Mackenzie
David Maxwell
Ian Ogilvy
Cherida Reeves
Virginia and Owen Scholte
Sue Sutton
Paul Vestey
Philip Waddilove

ISBN 1-887664-49-1
Library of Congress Catalog Card Number 2004109473
Manufactured in the United States of America
Printed by King Printing, Lowell, MA
First Printing by Luminary Press, a division of Midnight Marquee Press, Inc., July 2004

This book is dedicated to the memory of my parents,
John Murray (1914-1999) and
Ann Nita Murray, née Boland (1922-1989)
and to the memory of Michael Reeves' composer and close friend,
the late Paul Ferris,
whose music will never die

Table of Contents

Author's Note

It has not been my intention in this volume to attempt any critical analysis of Michael Reeves' films other than the circumstances of their making. For one thing, such an undertaking would probably require a volume in itself. For another, a number of other critics have already eloquently analyzed the recurrent themes and obsessions in Reeves' work.

Robin Wood noted "the obsession with evil and violence" and his oeuvre's "unpleasant aspect, its neurotic quality." David Pirie wrote: "In Reeves' characters, evil is inextricably intertwined with good, and their violence is circular and ambiguous." Iain Sinclair pointed out "the stock Reevesian preoccupation: the apparently decent, 'normal' citizen pushed to locate the evil within himself, to absorb and reciprocate all the venom of his oppressor," and "the bleakness... in his protagonists, the restless frigidity."

Bill Kelley has written that, in his first film: "Reeves suggests an idea that was to figure intrinsically in all of his features, building in prominence with each film: Aggression and violence are a contaminating force, a contagion that affects everything in the vicinity." Kelley saw these as "bleak spiritual views," Sinclair has described the films as "almost existential in their deadness and alienation," and other commentary has pointed out the "ambivalence" of Reeves' authorial voice.

David Robinson (*World Cinema: A Short History*) cited Michael Reeves' work as the fulfilment of French theorist Alexandre Astruc's call for a new type of cinema, the "Cinema-Stylo," which would allow films to be composed in the same way novels are, as Astruc wrote, "to become a means of writing as supple and subtle as that of the written language."

Michael's producer Tony Tenser explains at some length in this book what he later said in this vein to Pete Tombs: "When he made *Witchfinder General*, he wanted it to be so realistic that people who saw the film would be *enjoying* (if you can use that word) the violent aspect, the fear that was in the film, so much so that he would drive them over the top, that they would realize and feel a little bit ashamed. 'Well, why am I feeling enjoyment?' " Michael himself analyzed the anti-violence message of his films very lucidly, as revealed in this book.

I absolutely accept all of these interpretations, but my interest in this volume was more in knowing *who* Michael Reeves was and how he came to rise and fall so suddenly. From a critical standpoint, therefore, I have chosen to adopt the stance that they are simply *great movies*—highly entertaining, while also extremely interesting, and, as Iain Sinclair wrote of *Witchfinder General*, containing "several scenes, unassertively presented, that have the inevitability of the highest art." As I tend to agree with the above critics, it is superfluous for me to give a personal response to the meaning of the films and I have concentrated on biography rather than film criticism.

I am therefore most grateful to those of Michael's friends, colleagues and family who were prepared to submit to my enquiries, and in some cases offered hospitality above and beyond the call of duty, e.g., the late Paul Ferris insisting I stay the night at his house in Leamington Spa when our discussion went on too long, Tony Tenser driving me from Southport station to his house and back, Cherida and Zara Reeves for taking me to meet Mike's Aunt Joan, and so on. I wish to thank particularly the *great* actor Ian Ogilvy, who contributed so vitally to Reeves' entire oeuvre, without whose initial enthusiasm I would not have embarked upon this volume.

Researching this book, I personally interviewed (usually on tape) the following contributors: Tom Baker, the late Joan Bootle-Wilbraham, the late Paul Ferris, Jess Franco, Ernest Harris, Nicky Henson, Diane Ogilvy, Ian Ogilvy, the late Vincent Price, Cherida Reeves (now Cannon), Zara Reeves, Virginia and Owen Scholte, Tony Tenser, Kay Turvey (Chairman of the Seaford Museum and Heritage Society, who kindly took me to King's Mead School), and Paul Vestey. And I corresponded with and/or spoke on the phone with some of the above and also with the late Clive Baker (Cold Ash resident), Jane Barrett, Alan Bennett, the legendary Elmer Bernstein, the late Ken Brookman, Anthony Broom, Jeff Burr, the late Richard Coward, Randy Everts, K. Neill Fisher, Bryan Forbes, Duncan Forbes, Sarah Fox (Cold Ash resident), Peter Fraser, Mike Frankovich,

Jr., Richard Gordon, Beverly Gray, Charles B. Griffith, John Hall, Benjamin Halligan, Brett Halsey, John Hamilton, Pamela Hoare, Euan Houston, Miles Huddleston, Oliver Huddleston (original owner of Mike's scrapbook), Peter Jackson (Radley Archivist), the late Bill Kelley, the late Michael Klinger, Lucretia Love, Robert Mackenzie, David Maxwell (creator of the King's Mead School website), Judy Miller, Tim Miller, Tony Money (Radley Archivist), Frederick Muller, Nicola Pagett, Sarah Reeves (now Sesti), Alfred Shaughnessy, Tony Shellim, Gary Sherman (for contact information only), Dennis Silk (Radley Warden), Iain Sinclair, Bernard Stacey (Cold Ash resident), Ian Steel, Richard Steel, Donald Sutherland, Philip Waddilove, the late Alex Waye, Raquel Welch and

TONY TENSER presents

VINCENT PRICE
IAN OGILVY RUPERT DAVIES
WILFRID BRAMBELL

WITCHFINDER GENERAL

WITH
PATRICK WYMARK
AS CROMWELL

AND INTRODUCING
HILARY DWYER

Mel Welles. Thanks to a number of organizations for help: Association of Cinematograph and Television Technicians (Lynda Loakes), British Board of Film Censors (David Barrett), British Film Institute (especially Claire Thomas, Special Collections, and John Innes), Public Record Office, Seaford Museum and Heritage Society (Sue Sutton) and Westminster Coroner's Court.

Sadly, I struck out in contacting some vital people who either never received my enquiries or, if they did, were not able to be interviewed for a variety of reasons: Michael Armstrong, David Austen, Jack Cardiff, Sharon Compton, Roger Corman, Michael Culver, Patrick Curtis, Hilary Dwyer, Peter Fonda, Daniel Haller, Deke Heyward, Christopher Lee, Stanley Long, Paul Maslansky, Donald Pleasance, Jock Russell, Tony Selby, Don Siegel, Steven Spielberg, Annabelle Webb (although she did amend a couple of paragraphs in the text) and Christopher Wicking. Some of these people are no longer with us, such as Deke Heyward, Don Siegel and Donald Pleasance. I would be pleased to hear from anyone who may see this book who knew Mike Reeves and whom I failed to contact. And Irving Allen, John Coquillon and Betty Reeves died shortly before I started work.

I have therefore used secondary sources to quote from some of these people. The most important source is undoubtedly Bill Kelley's long 1991 article about Mike Reeves in *Cinefantastique* magazine. Bill, a long-time American Reeves admirer, was the only writer to get an interview with Don Siegel about Mike (apart from a comment Siegel made publicly at London's National Film Theatre), and I am grateful to Bill for letting me quote generously from that and other interviews in his article, including the Philip Waddilove material (Philip could not face going over it all again with me, though later kindly supplied lengthy extracts from the memoirs he is working on and chatted with me at length on the telephone), and his and Lawrence French's interviews with Vincent Price and Chris Knight's interview with Rupert Davies.

Pete Tombs' succinct 1999 television documentary about Mike was also useful for filling some gaps, and I have quoted some of the contributors' comments from that, such as Patrick Curtis (Raquel Welch provided me with an address for him which may have been out of date) and Paul Maslansky. Thanks to Pete Tombs for his permission. Apologies to various journalists and publications from which brief interview quotes have on rare occasion been excerpted without acknowledgment, because I have not been able to identify the source. A variety of horror film magazines were consulted (*Gorezone, Cinefantastique, Shivers, Starburst, Cult Movies, Filmfax, The Dark Side, Fangoria* and many others) to supplement original research.

The earliest critical writings about Mike, especially by Robin Wood (*Movie* 17) and David Pirie *(A Heritage of Horror: The English Gothic Cinema 1946-1972)*, were inspirational.

A particular thank you to Victoria de Korda for her support in this project, accompanying me to Ipswich Crematorium to find Mike's final resting place and helping me find Betty Reeves' house in Little Bealings, Woodbridge. She also drew my attention to Iain Sinclair's valuable book *Lights Out for the Territory*. Thanks to him for letting me quote from it and putting me in touch with the hitherto-elusive Tom Baker.

Photos courtesy of Tom Baker, Bev Ferris, Benjamin Halligan, Ernest Harris, Nicky Henson, Victoria de Korda, Robert Mackenzie, David Maxwell, Ian Ogilvy, Cherida Reeves, Virginia and Owen Scholte, Sue Sutton, Paul Vestey, Philip Waddilove (who opened up his marvelous photo album) and the BFI Stills Department. Thanks to John Henderson, Euro London Films and Jane Lawson of Metrodome Distribution for permissions and help. And to Gary and Susan Svehla and editors Linda J. Walter and Scott Nollen of Midnight Marquee Press for bringing this book to an American public.

Further thanks to that master of film publicity, Tony Tenser, for suggesting the subtitle of this book ("His Short and Tragic Life"). I would like to record the fact that Tom Baker did not like this subtitle: "Mike's life was not very long. But apart from the last six months or so, I'd say he lived the life of Riley." I do not dispute it in the slightest.

I never met Michael Reeves, so have kept all reference to myself out of the text, only referring to "the author" where necessary for factual clarity. (I had felt able to use such expressions as "told me" in my previous book on Robert Vaughn because I did meet him and have a fair amount of contact with him.)

On the other hand, several interviewees expressed curiosity why I was interested in writing about Mike Reeves when I never knew him and, although it may not be of much interest to the reader, I would like to briefly recount how I came to publish the first book to appear on the subject of this fascinating filmmaker.

As a young boy in the '60s, I lived around the corner from two wonderful West London flea-pit cinemas, the Essoldo on Great Western Road and the Prince of Wales on Harrow Road (where Mike's first film got its only original London screening, though I did not go...more interested then in Steve Reeves than Mike Reeves!). There I adored Vincent Price in movies like AIP's *Master of the World* and was terrified by the Roger Corman Poe films' stills and posters, though as I recall was too young to get in to see the actual films.

When *Witchfinder General* came out in 1968, there was a furor over the violence, but I paid some attention only because Vincent Price starred. I was still too young to go and see a Certificate "X" film. The furor died down; *Witchfinder General* disappeared from screens and I forgot all about it. I was not particularly into horror; I was increasingly interested in girls. I bought *Penthouse* magazine occasionally, purely for the girls. In one issue was a brief interview with Mike Reeves. Mike's comments disturbed me and I kept the magazine. (Strangely, this was one interview not in Mike's scrapbook; perhaps he did not read *Penthouse*.)

Witchfinder General turned up on London television in the mid-'70s, late one night. I sat down to watch another Vincent Price movie but was completely unprepared for what I saw.

Within five minutes I realized that Mike Reeves was a genius filmmaker and *Witchfinder General* was the most extraordinary piece of cinema I had ever seen. I found out what I could about him (precious little except that he was dead) while working at my first job for Rank Film Distributors on Wardour Street. I thought I would like to write something about him.

I was working on distribution contracts for films like Tony (son of Michael) Klinger's *The Butterfly Ball*. There was a *Butterfly Ball* film tie-in concert at the Royal Albert Hall in 1977 with stars like Twiggy singing and Vincent Price narrating the storyline. I approached him with a list of questions about Mike Reeves. He did read them before speaking to me. I was vaguely aware that

Vincent had not enjoyed working with Mike and was not very surprised when he, very politely but firmly, declined to answer any questions about Mike: "I'm sorry, I can't...I'm leaving tomorrow." I asked if he would be willing to send me written answers and he said, "Yes, I'll try and write to you," but he never did and he had a wary gleam in his eye as he said it that made me feel he was politely fobbing me off. I felt no sense of hurt, as I expected Vincent was constantly being harassed by fans. I learned years later he was very reluctant to talk about Mike with anyone.

Vincent Price

I determined to write something else and send it to him to win his confidence. I published a serious study of actor Robert Vaughn (Vincent had guested on *The Man from U.N.C.L.E.* and they had both been in De Mille's *The Ten Commandments*) in 1987 and sent it to Vincent. He wrote back "Thanks for Vaughn book. Good!" and made some comments about Mike, eventually answered two questionnaires about working with Mike, and spoke to me on the telephone, even inviting me to visit him in Beverly Hills. Though when I tried to take him up on this, his state of health made him reluctant and he made the polite excuse that he was going to be on his boat for a couple of months.

Other fans who have written about their contact with Vincent, such as Bob Madison, have revealed he had the same tactics of warding off over-keen fans, to be polite but refuse questions for lack of time. No matter. All the rest of my life I have been haunted by the image of this tall, sophisticated, elegant but vulnerable man, then 65, a Gothic horror star, walking off alone into the darkness of the South Kensington night in his tuxedo in 1977. An aging Hollywood legend, surprisingly without the minders, chauffeurs, limousines my naiveté expected. A kind man who smiled when someone else snatched a flash photo of him in his face without asking his permission. A giant among men. *Witchfinder General* is for me his greatest film performance (and Vincent agreed with me), and I bless Michael Reeves for it.

If Ian Ogilvy had not then been willing to cooperate, I would not have proceeded any further, but he was very keen. My thanks to him for setting me on a road that seemed to go on forever, as I became obsessed with digging deeper and deeper. All the people I interviewed were kind and wonderful and, if I had to single one out, I was particularly moved by Paul Ferris' candor and depth of feeling about Mike. Paul agreed to be interviewed, as he felt: "There *should* be a book about Mike." I only regret he did not live to see this one finished. I was unable to stay in touch with him and he sadly died far too young in 1995. I think of him from time to time and cannot listen to his film music without deep emotion.

Benjamin Halligan had been working on a book about Mike's life and films since 1998 and contacted me after the first British edition of this book in 2002. I am very grateful to him for supplying me with a copy of Mike's early film, *Intrusion*. His 2003 book is the first full-length critical study of Mike's oeuvre, eloquently and insightfully written, and also breaks new biographical ground. I have resisted the temptation to quote his findings (apart from a couple of significant observations and facts which are acknowledged in the text) and recommend his book, which is beyond question a very important milestone in helping to preserve Mike's reputation from such vandalism as the 1988 wiping of Paul Ferris' majestic score from all U.S. prints and videos of *Witchfinder General*.

This first U.S. edition corrects some errors of fact and omissions in the first British edition. Notably, there is now some coverage of Mike's time at prep school in Seaford, thanks to a wonderful website devoted to King's Mead School run by old boy David Maxwell, which became accessible shortly after the book was printed. By one of those ironic twists of fate, the ex-headmaster of the School died two days after my book came out and it is most fortunate that Benjamin Halligan managed to interview him before he died.

Critic Julian Petley has written about the censorship history of *Witchfinder General* in *The Dark Side* in 2003, and there is in production a book about Tony Tenser and Tigon by John Hamilton (which contains interviews with Christopher Lee and Stanley Long among others). These are welcome manifestations of the growing awareness of the importance of the work of Michael Reeves in not only British but world cinema.

—John B. Murray
London, England

Foreword by Ian Ogilvy

I knew Michael Reeves for about 10 years. We met in the late 1950s—when we were both in our mid-teens—and he died at the end of the '60s, when we were both in our mid-20s. For the last five years of his life, he was one of my closest friends. It was all a very long time ago.

John Murray's excellent portrait of Mike pretty much covers everything I might have to say about him. Over the intervening years between his death and now, I've had a great number of requests by students of film for information about the life and works of Michael Reeves and, on the whole, I've managed to avoid answering them all. That happy state of affairs lasted until John Murray turned up and he was so nice and so persistent that I told him everything I remembered, and he's put the whole lot of it into this book. So, whatever I write here is almost certainly reproduced somewhere in the following pages, which leaves me with not much to tell. However, at the risk of being repetitious, here are a few salient facts about the man I knew and worked with for 10 years.

Mike was rich and privileged. (This helps if you want to be a film director.) He was also friendly. Very generous. Slightly shy. Tall. Dark. Thin. He looked a bit like the French actor Gerard Philippe, in the role of Modigliani in the film *Montparnasse 19*.

Mike was obsessed by film. He knew just about everything on the subject. Bring up some obscure little 1930s second feature; Mike would know who the *cinematographer* was. In fact, his only topic of conversation was the cinema. He didn't care a jot about clothes, food, sport or politics, or anything very much, if it didn't flicker on a screen. If you weren't interested in the cinema, then frankly, Mike's conversation would bore you senseless. Luckily, most of us in Mike's small circle of friends were involved in making movies in one way or another, so boredom was never a factor.

Ian Ogilvy

Mike thought that Don Siegel's *The Killers*, starring Lee Marvin, Clu Gulager, Angie Dickinson and Ronald Reagan (the future President's last film) was the greatest movie ever made. It's essentially a B film with a fine cast. I saw it again the other day. It's good. Worth a look. But the greatest movie ever made? I don't think so. But Mike did. We all saw a lot of *The Killers*. Mike would run it often on his old 16-millimeter projector. We also saw Siegel's *Invasion of the Body Snatchers* rather more often than some of us would have liked. If you want to see what Mike admired in filmmaking—and tried to emulate—rent the collected works of Don Siegel...*but only the B movies*. Siegel hadn't yet made it big when we were doing our stuff.

Mike saw practically every movie ever made, with a few exceptions. There were several films Mike never saw. If he heard that there was a scene in the movie where a character had their facial features *completely* obscured in some way, he wouldn't go near it. It was a sort of phobia. For instance, he never saw *Ice Cold In Alex*, in which Anthony Quayle sank into a bog and was dragged out with his face covered in mud. It might be an interesting exercise to discover just how many films Mike *theoretically* refused to see on account of a muddy face.

Mike didn't like going to the theater. He'd go if pressed hard, but live performance wasn't for him. He was constantly on edge, worrying nervously that some awful accident, like falling scenery or a forgotten speech, was about to happen onstage and he liked actors and didn't want to be witness to their embarrassment, because that, in turn, would have embarrassed him beyond bearing, and Mike, like the rest of us, hated to be embarrassed. But with film, he felt safe; all the accidents had already been cut out.

Mike only made horror movies because they were more likely to see an easy profit—thereby giving him, the director, a reputation with producers for making sure-fire successes. He had no great affection for the genre and looked forward to the day when he could make a different kind of film. He said once that we were making crap, but it was going to be the *best-made* crap in the world. I like to think there are a few moments in the three films we made together where we came quite close to making the best-made crap in the world.

Making films with Mike Reeves was fun. We all laughed a lot. When Nicky Henson started filming *Witchfinder General*, the first scene he shot was toward the end of the script and contained the line, "Well, I'll see you in the tavern with the others, then," (or words to that effect—please, no letters telling me I've got it wrong). Mike found his delivery so hysterically funny that he immediately suspended shooting for the rest of the day because he was laughing too hard to continue directing. And later, when Nicky and I both fell off our horses at exactly the same moment, Mike had to lie down because hysteria kept buckling his knees. There was never much gravity on the set and it amuses me a little these days when movie buffs want to take the films of Michael Reeves too seriously. I know through experience that much of the best stuff in a film happens purely by accident, and these serendipitous little events occurred as much on a Mike Reeves set as on the sets of any other directors.

Mike and his films have become something of a cult. There's nothing wrong with this. However, I wonder sometimes what would have become of him and his movies if he hadn't inconveniently (or conveniently, depending on your point of view) died at such an early age. Dying young is, of course, the first step toward becoming a legend. It's almost an *obligatory* first step. I suspect that, had Mike stayed alive and continued to direct, the cult of Michael Reeves and his three films wouldn't exist. On the other hand, I think (in a long lifetime of directing) he would have made some monumentally important and memorable films—and that, I believe, would have been a fair trade-off for not having a cult devoted to him.

I want to thank John Murray—and commend him—for putting together such a thorough and detailed book about Mike, his films and his friends. If you want to know more about the guy, and obviously you do, otherwise you wouldn't have this book in your hands right now, then read on.

Just don't take any of it too seriously.

Prologue

He was a great film director.—Paul Ferris on Mike Reeves

Picture this for an extraordinary reversal of fortunes. Mike Reeves, a public schoolboy in the late 1950s, gets permission from his Housemaster to visit the local cinema every Saturday. There he worships Hollywood movies, especially those made by Don Siegel and Roger Corman, who become his idols. He dreams of emulating them. Ten years later, having directed only three films for a total budget less than £200,000, Mike Reeves is dead.

A couple of years later, Roger Corman comes to England to make a film. Actor Nicky Henson, who worked with Mike Reeves, is invited to an interview for a part in the film. As he walks into the room, Roger Corman says, "Tell me about Michael Reeves!"

Another couple of years pass. Don Siegel comes to England to make a film. Again Nicky Henson is invited to an interview for a part in the film. As he walks into the room, Don Siegel says, "Tell me about Michael Reeves!"

Of course, there's much more to it all than that!

Nicky Henson in *Witchfinder General*

The story of Michael Reeves must be unique in the annals of cinema history. Writers like David Pirie have had to invade the realms of Romantic literature to draw adequate comparison, referring in particular to Keats and Byron. Though close collaborators like writer Tom Baker prefer to stress Mike's attraction to "industrial cinema," to film as industrial process and craft.

So costly is the nature of film production and so few and far between are filmmakers of such phenomenal talent that the meteoric rise and inexplicable sudden fall of Mike Reeves must be without parallel. Not even the career of Orson Welles (who was once at a film party Mike attended in Rome) offers illuminating comparison, despite the fact that the Witchfinder himself, Vincent Price, once chose Welles as being the filmmaker Reeves most resembled of all those he ever worked for. Even if Reeves' one indisputable masterpiece, *Witchfinder General*, is a cinematic landmark in every way the equal of *Citizen Kane* (and there are those of us who find it superior as an aesthetic experience), the circumstances of their early flowerings and subsequent fates differ very considerably.

Reeves never had the option of working under the patronage of a Hollywood-style studio system and spent his entire career preparing projects independently, which makes the achievement represented by *Witchfinder General* in many ways more remarkable than that of *Citizen Kane*. Certainly for actor Ian Ogilvy, the "great, remarkable" thing about Reeves is that he managed to make three films at all for a total cost of less than £200,000. As *Witchfinder General* composer Paul Ferris said, it would never be allowed today, to have a director of 24, a composer of 26; it needed the heady, youth-oriented days of the '60s to give producers confidence in the relatively untried.

Furthermore, Welles went on to a long and often distinguished career, even if never at the same level of critical euphoria again, while the experience of making *Witchfinder General*—his mother told the coroner it had "taken a lot out of him"—appears to have been one of a number of factors that caused Reeves' tragic demise.

15

Chapter One: Beginnings

"My feelings about Reeves are hard to express in writing. I felt he had a great potential...I think it isn't always true that one's most pleasant working experiences in films are the best pictures. Many directors are difficult to work with, but the product they turn out can be far superior to any enjoyment in working with them."—Vincent Price (to the author)

The passage of time since the death of Michael Reeves in 1969 has only confirmed his status as the most remarkable English filmmaker since Michael Powell, despite the brevity of his career. The paperback *Time Out Film Guide* reckons his final film to be "one of the most personal and mature statements in the history of British cinema."

Michael Leith Reeves was born at Cedar Court Nursing Home, Cedar Road, Sutton in Surrey on October 17, 1943. He was the only child of Derek Leith Reeves and Violet Reeves, nee Kennard.

Derek Reeves was born in London at 36 Sloane Court on June 8, 1904. He was from a well-to-do professional family, but was to have health problems in his life and inherited a tendency to extreme mood swings, clinically known as manic depression (now bipolar disorder), from his father Hugh. It apparently went way back in the family, according to what Violet once told her relatives.

Derek's father, Hugh William Reeves, was born on December 21, 1866. He was the second son of Mr. and Mrs. Herbert Reeves of East Sheen, Surrey, and was educated at Merchant Taylors and Eastbourne Public Schools and, finally, Cheltenham College, which he attended from September 1882 to December 1884. At Cheltenham he was on the classical side, was a keen sportsman and was in the Hazelwell house, as was his elder brother Herbert from 1882 to 1883. Hugh was admitted as a solicitor in 1890 and entered his father's firm, Messrs. Herbert Reeves and Co. Solicitors.

In 1897, Hugh married Dorothy Leith, daughter of Mr. and Mrs. Walter Leith of Suffolk. Their first child was a daughter, Joan, born in 1899, followed by two sons, Derek, five and a half years later, and Ivor, another six years later. It was a large and happy family, Joan remembered: "I think we were all very close to my mother's family. She had three brothers and two sisters, so there were six of them. Basically, we were very close there."

Hugh prospered as a solicitor and together with his elder brother, Herbert began to build up a successful business as owners of property. Their business, the City of London Real Property Company Limited, would one day greatly benefit Michael. Joan recalled her father as "terribly interested" in the property business: "In fact, he always used to say he could smell out a good bit of land by looking at it. He was very, very lucky. He always used to be taken round properties. He knew exactly what ought to be done with it and therefore managed to buy it and did very well too, thank you very much!"

Hugh lived in Pont Street in London, though at the time of Derek's birth he was living at 6 Sloane Square. "He was very much a London solicitor," according to Joan. He was also able to rent Honingham Hall in Norfolk for the family. Joan recalled their childhood:

"We as a family used to spend every summer holiday in Norfolk, so we really didn't touch Suffolk at all. I spent the first 19 years of my life on a beach at Waxham, which was that way out, between Yarmouth and Cromer, wonderful bit of country full of those glorious sand dunes. Every winter the wind and rain used to alter the formation of these wonderful sand dunes, and we used to rush down and see whether our particular shanty had been moved, got blown away or swamped with rain. Derek was five and a half

16

years younger than me and my other brother was eleven and a half years younger. A tremendous gap, but we were tremendous friends, both as small children and as we grew up more and more and more."

Sadly, Hugh's wife Dorothy developed severe rheumatoid arthritis and was wheelchair-bound at a young age. Her daughter Joan married Evelyn (Lyn) Bootle-Wilbraham in 1924 and very soon after, Dorothy fell ill. She died in the spring of 1925.

Joan's husband was 30 years older and worked as a research scientist. He suffered in an explosion in a chemical research facility and had poor health thereafter; it was inevitable that she would end up a widow.

Hugh Reeves remarried in 1927. His second wife, Susan, would know Michael and he would holiday with his "Granny Susan," as he would with Lyn and Joan, who were very fond of him.

Derek went to a good preparatory school near Rottingdean and then he and Ivor followed their father to Cheltenham College. Both were in Christowe, Derek from 1918 to 1922 and Ivor from 1918 to 1928. Hugh Reeves thereafter became a College benefactor. He was a life member of Cheltenham College Council and, until the year of his death, never missed attending the annual Speech Day. He was also President of the Old Cheltonian Society from 1923 to 1924, Worshipful Master of the Old Cheltonian College in 1917, and Secretary of the College War Memorial and Endowment Fund. He was Captain of the Old Cheltonian Football Club in 1890 and rowed in the London Rowing Club Eight at Henley between 1889 and 1894. He made continuous benefactions to the College and the Old Cheltonian Society, to the College Mission, to the Old Cheltonian Masonic Lodge and to many funds inaugurated by the Council.

In 1922, when his sons were at the College, Hugh Reeves bought Charlton Park House and Estate. His purpose was to secure for the College new playing fields of 15 acres. He also helped the College find money to purchase a further 25 and a half acres of park land. This estate, within less than 400 yards of the College playground, was gratefully named by the College "Reeves field." He was additionally responsible for the acquisition of the College Boathouse. Hugh's sons followed their father in service to the College and to the Cheltonian Society.

Derek Reeves was always known as "Bungie." Some people assumed this was because his face creased readily. Virginia Scholte, a relative of Michael's mother, thought so: "It was a nickname, because when he smiled, his whole face looked creased. His eyes disappeared. He had a bungie face, a rubber face." Her husband Owen commented: "He was sort of boyish. He had a fatter, fuller face than Mike." However, Derek's sister Joan revealed how this nickname originated:

> "He was christened Derek. At prep school, in those days, boys and girls always used to call their India rubber bungie. One day there was a new issue of India rubbers at the prep school and, of course, they were Reeves' Artistic India Rubbers. They issued these India rubbers with Reeves all across them. Quite obviously, to every small boy holding one, Derek had to be Bungie. And it went right all through his life, even when he went off to Oxford. I met somebody and I said, 'Do you know my brother, Derek Reeves?' 'Well,' he said, 'I don't think so, but anything to do with Bungie?' That was because he never gave it up. My mother disliked it, so we never called him Bungie at home. Not in those days. We did eventually."

Derek went on to Wadham College, Oxford, where the family thinks he undoubtedly didn't work hard but "had fun." He was the more ebullient of the two brothers. Ivor Reeves became a career soldier, ending up Lt. Colonel Ivor Reeves, DSO, MC, until retiring to the life of a farmer in his early 40s.

Derek's heart was not in the Army, however, but in the Navy. His sister Joan explained:

"My mother had a brother in the Navy, who was a particular pal of us children. He and Bungie used to look like father and son, their hair was so alike. That's where it all came from. Unfortunately, just at that time, 1918, the Navy was axing people right, left and center, so Derek was rather pushed to one side. Quite incredibly, we were told afterwards it was simply an idea of his schoolmaster, who didn't think he was going to pass his entrance and didn't think it a good idea to let him go, which was maddening. It broke my brother's heart and mine, too, I think."

Derek went to work as a Company Director of the family firm, the City of London Real Property Company Limited, until the World War II broke out. Derek did spend World War II in the Navy, according to Joan: "The action wasn't so violent and he went in the Naval Supplementary Reserve and worked the first six months in the war underground at the Admiralty, which was all planning stuff. Then, from there, he went to sea and he was mine-sweeping during the War. His uncle, whom he was so devoted to, was mine-laying, so it was a rather interesting family we had. One generation mine-laying and the other generation mine-sweeping. Interesting!" He was a Lieutenant in the R.N.V.R.

It was probably at a wartime party that Derek, home from Harwich on leave, met Violet Kennard. According to Benjamin Halligan's book, it was at the Savoy Hotel, where she was a relief pianist for Carroll Gibbons and his Savoy Hotel Orpheans. They adored each other and married at the church in Woodbridge in Suffolk in 1941. Violet had no idea that Derek would suffer from manic depression and no inkling of the problems that this would bring for her husband and her son.

Violet Elizabeth Grace Kennard was born at the family home at 20 South Eaton Place, Belgravia, on March 6, 1902. She did not like her first name and so was always known as either Elizabeth or Betty. Her family could not recall anyone ever referring to her as Violet. Betty's father, Charles Heywood Kennard, was English landed gentry and worked as a Lloyds' insurance underwriter, but her mother, Mary Cleveland Channing, originally Mary Breamer, was an American, from Boston. It was this American blood in his lineage that led to published claims that Mike Reeves was part American or even an American living in England! One American magazine, *Gorezone,* even extravagantly referred to the U.S. as his native land! Betty did, however, often refer to herself as "a mongrel" because of this mixed blood.

Charles Kennard liked to go shooting and trained shooting dogs. He was apparently very good at it and adored his dogs. A sometime neighbor, Mrs. Pamela Hoare, recalled: "Charles Kennard used to shoot with my father, who was in the Navy and Captain of HMS Ganges at Shotley before the war, a sailors' training establishment." Mrs. Virginia Scholte, whose maternal grandfather was Charles' brother, said that Betty's childhood was not terribly happy. Charles was not wealthy and she was not terribly well-off when she was growing up. The family lived for a long time in a house called Cedar Lodge in Woodbridge and then they moved to London. Virginia thought Betty had "a ghastly upbringing" because her parents were "really Victorian" and kept her on a short rein.

And yet, although Betty married late in life, Virginia insisted that she had

"...a very swinging youth. She was quite wild; very good-looking and very witty. Tremendously witty and amusing, but I think lots of men felt she was just too much of a good thing to take on, and she was always very jealous of all my mother's boyfriends. She was my mother's first cousin. My mother was also very attractive and had lots of boyfriends. Aunt Betty said my mother used to take all her boyfriends away from her."

The impression of Betty as a glamorous and adventurous young woman is borne out by an elegant photograph of her in Tangier in 1929. She had gone to Egypt to stay with Virginia's parents and the photograph bears the inscription on the back in her own handwriting: "Me on my way home from Egypt—at Tangier." Pamela Hoare confirmed this impression of Betty in later years, too: "She was one of Suffolk's most glamorous spinsters, in her 30s, when I was about 19. Very elegant and sophisticated and good-looking, much admired by us young girls who were at least 15 years younger."

A main reason for her late marriage, according to Pamela Hoare, was that she was a devoted daughter and really looked after her parents, who were then living at Orchard House, back in Woodbridge. Her mother, Mary, died just before Betty married Derek Reeves. But it wasn't solely a question of looking after her parents, as Virginia already hinted in her observation that men found her too much of a good thing: "I think she just didn't find the right one. There were men who wanted to marry her but she didn't want to marry them, I think."

It was only when she met Derek Reeves that she decided she could now marry. Virginia met him many times and described him: "He was a really

Betty in Tangier in 1929, returning from her trip to Egypt.

kind man and great fun to be with when he was on his good times. I never really saw him when he was on his bad. Most generous, great fun, rather a sort of playboy-type, very attractive. Not classically good-looking like Mike, because Mike was more like his mother really, but very attractive and amusing." Mike's Aunt Joan said that, as a child, Mike looked more like Derek (for example, his nose), but "gradually, as he got older, he got more and more like his mother."

Virginia Scholte was sure that Betty had no doubt about marrying Bungie: "She adored him absolutely and he her." There is a 1941 photograph of Betty at Orchard House labeled "Bungie's favorite photo of me," which shows her holding a puppy called Rebel.

Virginia's mother attended the wedding, despite the ambivalent nature of her relationship with Betty, as Virginia described it: "It was a sort of love-hate thing, really. They were devoted in a way and yet they sort of sparred off each other tremendously. My mother wasn't witty like Aunt Betty was. Aunt Betty used to really take the mickey out of my mother and things like that, but they got on reasonably well." It was, of course, a wartime wedding and the war meant that they could not settle down into a normal married life. Bungie went back into the Navy and was mine-sweeping and in and out of Harwich a great deal, which left Betty alone. So Betty went back to look after her aged father, who was quite deaf and, according to Virginia, "a very difficult old man" who "never drew breath...like her!" He was very strict with Betty. Nevertheless, Betty was "very good to him always, most dutiful" until he died. As Pamela Hoare rightly pointed out, Betty only just managed to have Michael, as she was then 41.

Because of his parents' circumstances, the infant Michael Reeves could not grow up with them initially. It was decided it would be better for all concerned if he stayed with Derek's sister Joan and her husband Lyn, as Joan recollected:

Michael Reeves' birth certificate

"He lived with me for really two years when he first came out from the nursing home. He came to me when he was 10 days old and lived with me until he was not quite two. My husband and I had this house in Berkshire (Pyt House, Ashampstead, near Newbury) and we were always a second home for Betty. Everybody thought it was probably easier for Michael's father to get to my house, as Berkshire is not very far away from London. Betty really lived with us for the second half of the war."

Joan saw "quite a lot" of Betty, but stated, "I was never close." Betty would go for holidays to a house at Brancaster on the Norfolk Broads owned by Joan and Lyn. Mike used to call Joan "Aunt Jona," as did Zara (one of Ivor's daughters). Joan remembered: "Then, after a while, they disliked the name Jona. It didn't go on. There is still one family that calls me Jona, that's all: the Hardys." The Hardys were a vicar's family up in Norfolk near Joan, who had three sons all about Mike's age. They were great friends of Mike's. One of the boys became Joan's godson and his son became her grand-godson.

Derek did not ever discuss being a father with his sister Joan because she was older than he, but he was a proud father and, said Joan, would have been "tremendously" proud of Michael's fame as a filmmaker, even though he probably wouldn't have liked the films "any more than I did!"

It was only when the war was over that Bungie and Betty and Mike got a home of their own. It was Woodham Lodge, Woodham Ferrers, Bicknacre in Essex, near Chelmsford. Virginia and Owen stayed there in early 1951 and recalled that "they had a nanny and a cook and housemaids and all that sort of thing."

Derek left the Navy after the war and, for a short while, stayed at home. He then went back to work for the family firm but only for a short time, according to Joan. The Scholtes understood he had periods when he was not working, because after the war his manic depression began to manifest itself. Virginia explained: "I don't know really how much he did, but he was always on this awful business of being manic depressive, up and down. Six months of the year he was up and up and up, then down and down and down." It caused problems in the marriage: "There were terrible problems. She told me about them. But she coped with it and she was devoted to him always, manic or not. But it was difficult and he relied on her a lot."

Paul Ferris, who composed the stunning score of *Witchfinder General*, like many creative people of outstanding achievement, suffered from manic depression. This condition severely affected both Paul and Mike in later years and strengthened the bond of friendship between them. Paul, whose own father was a manic depressive, strongly believed that Mike inherited this condition from Bungie:

> "It's biochemistry and in the genes. We all suffered from it, Mike, myself, obviously his dad and my dad, which is why, in that sense, on that level, I understood Mike. You get inexplicable euphorias without any external reason for it. Beyond that comes the dark side that is in you. It was in Mike. It's in me. If you're manic depressive, you know it, because it's uncontrollable. It's not something you can talk yourself out of or be talked into, or talked out of by a psychiatrist who has never had that experience. When you go down, you go down, comprehensively, and you can't stop it. It's no good people saying, 'Cheer up. You had a lot of trouble lately?' "

Paul related an odd little story about Bungie, regarded by Virginia as not impossible: "One little thing that his mother told me about his father was that he used to carry cards around in his top pocket, and as he walked along the street, he'd take these things out and show them to you. They said 'Smile, damn you, smile!' It's not something you'd expect at all. I've never forgotten that."

Pamela Hoare's parents were friends of Bungie and Betty. Her parents bought a house at Melton, near Woodbridge, in 1946, where Pamela went to stay. She saw Michael a few times when he was a small boy up until the age of seven, sometimes went to see Betty and met Bungie two or three times. She described Bungie as "very well-off" and Mike as "rather spoilt." From an early age, Mike was given very expensive movie cameras by his father. His Aunt Joan observed: "At the slightest chance he'd have a camera and he'd get down to it."

He began on 8-mm and later moved to 16-mm and almost undoubtedly his father's generosity influenced Mike's future path. One might also wonder if being an only child caused, or at least affected, Mike's future obsession with movies, though Mike's star actor Ian Ogilvy refused to speculate over this: "I really don't know what effect being an only child has on *anyone*." Besides, Mike would visit his cousin Cherida, who was only three months younger: A September 1946 photo shows them and Kitti Cat, a pony, at Inwood in Shropshire. Surprisingly, Mike's earliest ambition was to be a tractor driver, but this swiftly took a back seat to show business. He knew, from a remarkably early age, what direction he wanted to go in, as Ian Ogilvy could confirm:

> "The story had it that when he was about seven, his mother took him to see *Ivanhoe* and he enjoyed it enormously, and he said, 'When I grow up, I want to be Ivanhoe.' And his mother said, 'You can't be that, dear, that's Robert Taylor.' So he said, 'Well, I want to be the person who tells Robert Taylor *what to do*.' That's the apocryphal story about Mike Reeves! No, he wanted to be a film director when he was about seven or eight. Before I knew him, he'd got a strange hand-crank projector. I never saw it. Literally a hand-cranked thing. And he was hand-cranking *Intolerance* and *Birth of a Nation* and things through this little projector!"

Tom Baker, Mike's future writing partner, confirmed this account to Pete Tombs: "He was very single-minded about wanting to make movies. He told me he'd decided to make films when he was eight. I didn't know him then, but he said something: When he was eight years old, he wanted to make movies."

Owen and Virginia Scholte observed Mike's development since childhood and Owen commented: "He was always very fascinated with the cinema. He'd show us his home movies when he was quite young." Family friend Tim Miller would believe that it was Mike's home movies that started the boy's obsession with the cinema. In other respects, though, he was a normal, boisterous young boy. Virginia could testify to this: "I do remember him being a thorough menace when Owen and I were courting and staying with Aunt Betty and he used to jump up on us. I suppose he was about nine. We were staying with Aunt Betty just before Owen went to Malaya and we were sitting in one of those garden *chaise longes* on a swing. We used to sit there canoodling or whatever, and he used to come up from behind and squirt water at us or something! We thought he was a real menace, I remember." His Aunt Joan described Mike as "tremendously" well-behaved but "full of fun and always ready for fun and that sort of thing."

The Scholtes did not see a great deal of him as a boy because he was at boarding schools all the time, but did see him odd times, said Virginia: "And he was a bit of a pain really, I suppose, as lots of schoolboys can be, and rather precocious and terribly bright and spoilt, obviously. He had to be, didn't he? But he was just a typical, lively, rather spoilt little schoolboy, sweet-looking always." The Scholtes did not think his being an only child was of great significance to his development. For one thing, Mike's school pal Paul Vestey has said that Betty was not demonstrative toward Mike but "they were very close" and Virginia's nephew Oliver Huddleston, who met Mike when he himself was six or seven, got the impression that Mike was a "mummy's boy."

For another, Ivor's three daughters, Sarah, Cherida and Zara, were close to Michael's age and he would see them in Gloucestershire, where Ivor was now hunting to hounds (according to Paul Vestey), or on holidays. Zara was a little too young to know Mike well, but he was very friendly with Sarah and Cherida. Cherida went on holiday to Italy with Mike and Betty and, when Mike was 14, his Aunt Joan took Mike and Cherida on a 10-day cruise to Majorca, as she wanted company on the trip. The Scholtes remembered that "there were always masses of photographs Betty had of the holidays that Mike had taken with his camera." (These photographs were sadly destroyed when Betty died.)

Mike reportedly did not get on too well with his uncle Ivor. Zara recalled that Ivor, a career soldier, was "slightly disappointed" with Mike for going into show business and Mike sensed this. Sarah recalled that Mike was "very sad" when Ivor said: "Why all this horror? Why all that talent on horror?" Mike was hurt because Ivor did not understand. Betty apparently did not get on very well with Ivor either, although she liked his wife. (Ivor died on February 6, 1986, and his wife in March 1988.) "She wasn't easy, Aunt Betty," said Virginia.

But also Owen argued that Mike's passion for cinema would have been there regardless of his family circumstances: "I think he would have done that whether he'd had brothers and sisters or not. It was just a natural inclination." Virginia agreed: "I think so, too. He was extremely bright and he just knew what he wanted to do. There was absolutely no question of ever doing anything else. It was *essential* to him."

Bungie and Betty now selected a prep school for Michael. They chose King's Mead School in Seaford, on the Sussex Coast near Eastbourne. Michael would be sent away as a boarder. King's Mead was established in 1914. It did not close until 1968, along with a lot of the prep schools in Seaford. According to Kay Turvey of the Seaford Museum and Historical Society, prep schools were Seaford's main industry in the first half of the 20th century. Filmmaker Val Guest went to one called Seaford College and other filmmakers who followed Mike Reeves at King's Mead were James Dearden and Hamish McAlpine.

King's Mead took boys aged 8 to 14 and had about 80 boys in total. It was a leading prep school, the most famous old boy probably being Sir John Nott, Margaret Thatcher's Defense Secretary during the Falklands War. It even advertised in *The Times* in 1945; this must, however, have been necessitated by the disruption caused by World War II.

Peter Barrett arrived as headmaster in 1951. His wife, Jane has explained that King's Mead did not usually advertise for pupils: "Under no circumstances did the private schools advertise—it would have been thought very non-U! We got our pupils through friends of friends, and sometimes

King's Mead School playing fields, which have now been built over

parents from abroad might contact Gabbitas Thring, the Scholastic Agency. We used them when we needed teaching staff and perhaps matrons."

The reason Betty and Bungie chose King's Mead was simply that they knew Peter and Jane Barrett as friends. Jane Barrett explained:

> "As to why Mike's parents chose a school so far away from Woodham Fer-rers, in this case it was because we were friends. But sometimes parents were keen to send their boys for sea air, or they thought they'd settle better if not too close to home. Parents didn't visit so often in those days, and visit-ing was so much easier without the modern traffic load. This hit the South Coast schools badly—later on, London-based parents found frequent visits very difficult. We had known Mike's aunt and uncle for many years. The Bootle-Wilbrahams were close friends of my parents. They lived near us and they used to go on foreign holidays in the winter together; therefore they knew the Reeves when they visited their relations. We knew Mike's parents, though not for so long. I got to know Mike's mother quite well but I never had more than a passing acquaintance with his father."

Unfortunately, Bungie died suddenly a few days before Mike was due to start his first term at King's Mead in 1952. He died at Woodham Lodge. This was shortly before his father Hugh, who died on October 15 at his home in Upper Hartfield, Sussex, leaving his widow Susan, his daughter Joan, son Ivor and four grandchildren. Bungie and Betty had only been married 11 years. It was the first of the major tragedies that befell Betty. Mike was only eight.

The cause of his father's death is slightly mysterious and, like so much to do with Mike Reeves' life, bedeviled by rumor. Mike's good friend Diane Ogilvy, for instance, long held the erroneous belief that Bungie died in a motorbike accident, possibly remembering that Mike had a fear of motorbikes. Pamela Hoare heard that he died of a heart attack, and Virginia Scholte con-firmed that this is what Betty told her: "The story she told me was that she just went to have her bath one morning and when she came back, he was dead. He had a thrombosis or something."

Derek's sister Joan denied he had had a heart attack: "He didn't, as a matter of fact. It was one of these sort of mysterious things. He all his life had suffered from circulatory trouble and

23

Mike and Betty with Gussie, Woodham Ferrers, 1953 (Photographer: Gray)

as he gradually grew up, we thought it was phlebitis. Finally, he was recommended to go and see a new specialist in London who had taken on this idea of trying to cure this frightful circulatory trouble and he had an operation and it wasn't phlebitis, it was Buerger's disease. He had an operation and they cut into all the small veins to make the blood flow into the arteries. He had this operation and he died very suddenly. Betty wasn't even in the room, she'd gone to her bath, came back and found him dead. Exactly the same as George VI. The footman had gone in with his tea and found he'd died in his sleep. Exactly the same. Fourteen months after the operation, exactly the same thing happened to my brother, Bungie."

Paul Ferris, however, was adamant that Betty once told him that Bungie had committed suicide. It is unlikely that this is correct. Most probably, Paul misunderstood what Betty meant. An acquaintance of his maintains he "often talked of suicide" and this was probably "fantasy." Benjamin Halligan heard Bungie died in the marital bed, which confirms the heart attack story. If it were correct, it would be an ominous foreshadowing of Mike's own fate, even if Mike's tragic death does not appear to have been a deliberate act of taking his own life. Certainly Paul and Mike would both experience suicidal feelings as a result of manic depression, so it may safely be assumed that Bungie did, too, though Virginia Scholte has pointed out that she never, ever, heard any suggestion of this. But, then, suicide in 1952 was not something it was acceptable to have known, and Virginia admitted: "Aunt Betty would hush things up if she didn't like to reveal them." The truth will probably never be known.

Virginia did not *see* any adverse effect on Mike from Bungie's early death and his Aunt Joan did not think it had one. She could not recall Mike ever talking about Bungie or about missing having a father to grow up with. Virginia opined: "Aunt Betty must have made up. With both her relationship with Bungie and with her relationship with her son, she was *battering,* in a way. She was a very dynamic person, tremendously fun. We used to talk about this, my brother Miles (Huddleston) and I, and we felt rather that she was an exhausting person to be with. I'm sure he adored her, obviously, but I think she must have been quite demanding to a relationship." Virginia was sure that Betty kept Bungie's condition a secret, especially from Mike: "She always told

King's Mead School photo, June 1953. Mike Reeves is in the middle row, extreme left; in the centre front row, left to right, Paul Holme and Peter and Jane Barrett

me she never, ever, told Mike that his father was a manic depressive. She didn't want Mike to know that his father was manic." At any rate, a photograph of Mike with Betty taken in 1953 with her dog Gussie shows him as a happy boy.

Mike's friend Paul Vestey confirmed that Mike rarely talked about his father: "I don't ever really remember him talking about his father very much. I once saw a photograph of him on a motorbike; it might be during the war. I don't know anything about him. Mike didn't seem to talk about him very much." Another school friend, Alex Waye, agreed: "I don't think Mike ever mentioned his father. As we were all war babies, a lot of our contemporaries had lost their father in the war, so it was a bit of a taboo subject." Paul Vestey speculated: "I think probably not having a father may have made him able to do and say more. He seemed to be more outgoing, more honest about his own feelings. He didn't have that sort of break that people have by having a father, particularly for a boy, who'll also push them in one direction or another. He was fairly free to do what he liked." Yet, despite this freedom, Paul thought Mike did have a good understanding of people: "He was quite sensitive. He had a lot of charm."

Betty and Mike remained at Woodham Lodge for another couple of years while Mike boarded at King's Mead. Jane Barrett recalled: "His mother bravely decided that it would be best for him to start school as planned. She was under considerable strain at this time and was in regular contact with us with regards to her son's welfare and his ability to settle into his first term." Mike attended from May 1952 to March 1957.

Mike's years at King's Mead were to be happy ones. With his family connections to the Barretts, he grew closer to Peter Barrett, who kept a fatherly eye on him. Jane Barrett observed: "As time went on and his interest in films increased, my husband's interest in acting—he had done some amateur dramatics as a young man—brought them closer. His mother found his interest trying!" Paul Holme was Joint Headmaster but not so close to Mike. One of Mike's closest friends at King's Mead, Tony Shellim, recalled Mike once telling him that Holme couldn't stand him. Another boy, Robert Mackenzie, an exact contemporary, remembered Holme as "an okay chap." When Holme died in 1975, Peter Barrett wrote in his obituary: "He treated all schoolboys as individuals first and members of the school second." Jane Barrett explained: "Mike saw more of my husband than Paul Holme. Paul Holme was more interested in sport and games and so he and Mike did not have so much in common. I have no reason to think he didn't get on with Paul Holme, though was obviously closer to my husband."

Perhaps Holme did not appreciate the fact that, from the time of his arrival, Mike was, as Tony Shellim recalled him, "an individual...a character." Tony arrived in 1954 and was best friends with Mike and two boys named Richard Campling and Chris Wakeham. Another of Mike's best

Mike Reeves at King's Mead in 1954

friends was a boy named Robert Armstrong (with whom he later shot the short film *Intrusion*). Tony recalled most strongly that Mike had "absolutely" developed an obsession with cinema: "He ate, slept, talked, dreamt films—even at nine he was very keen and knew a great deal about them. He would tell me at the start of a new term he had seen about 50 films in the holidays. I think he read a lot of books about films. He was always learning...about films." Robert Mackenzie confirmed this: "I can remember him with a huge almanac of facts on films, a mine of info. He was even in those days so mad keen on films that he could recite the names of producers and directors at the age of 12 or so."

Seeing films during term time was more difficult for Mike. In the King's Mead "School Customs" (revised March 1966) it says sternly: "At no time in the term are boys allowed into Cinemas or Theaters." Nevertheless, he did get to see some films at King's Mead. Films were shown during the winter on Saturdays and Mike got involved as cinema projectionist. This made an impression on a boy called Ian Steel: "My only memory of Michael at King's Mead was his involvement with the film projector—whenever we were lucky enough to be shown a film, Michael would set it up and change the reels, etc. He obviously got the bug at an early age."

It does not appear he started the film showings, but persuaded Peter Barrett to let him get involved in selecting the films, which Robert Mackenzie recalled as including Charlie Chaplin, Laurel and Hardy, documentaries on New Zealand and Canada and St. Trinian's films. Joyce Grenfell was in St. Trinian's films, which is interesting, as Robert Mackenzie testified to Mike's continuing amateur filmmaking in the school holidays: "I remember him saying during one of his holidays he made a little amateur film with Joyce Grenfell, who was a next door neighbor in Cold Ash, Newbury." (This was Mike's next home.)

At King's Mead, Mike was not mischievous, nor a rule breaker. The naughtiest thing he did was smoke with Robert Mackenzie behind the potting shed, "not real cigarettes, we made them out of grass and glue," Robert recalled. Tony Shellim and Robert Mackenzie both remember Mike as "very jolly," no sign of depression at all. "Mike was very popular," said Tony. Robert agreed: "He was certainly popular, it was his love of film which made him seem a bit eccentric." Ian Steel's brother, Richard Steel, recalled: "He was older than me—more my brother's age—but I remember him as a nice boy who did not use his seniority to boss about younger boys. I remember his floppy hair falling across his face. I remember his total enthusiasm running the school films and I think he was given quite a free hand to choose them."

In his leisure, Mike was occupied with sport and drama. He was in the Cricket First Eleven, the Soccer First Eleven, the Rugby First Fifteen. Mike was also a Patrol Leader in the Otters Patrol under Troop Leader Nigel Bannerman. Robert Mackenzie explained: "Everyone belonged to a Patrol, based on Boy Scouts, the team that got the highest score got a prize at the end of term." Mike was Joint Winner of the Green Cup for 1956/7.

Patrols sometimes did their own plays and Mike got involved with these, writing and directing a comedy *The Tragical History of Henry Homicide*, which as Benjamin Halligan points out may have been the forerunner of other serial killer projects like *The Sorcerers*. Mike's earliest exposure to acting seems to have come from his involvement in the annual King's Mead school play held in the school gym (each annual play was only performed once, not counting rehearsals). On November 27, 1954, Mike played "Frog-Footman" in Lewis Carroll's *Alice's Adventures in Wonderland*. A boy called Peter Bowles (not the famous television actor whom Ian Ogilvy replaced on the London stage in *Sleuth* in 2002) played Alice. Robert Armstrong played Magpie. The King's Mead Terminal Letter (end of term newsletter) did not single out Mike but wrote: "All the supporting roles were lively, audible and, as far as the audience could tell, word perfect."

" Androcles and the Lion "

A FABLE PLAY

by

GEORGE BERNARD SHAW

KING'S MEAD

26th November, 1955

On November 26, 1955, Mike played Centurion in George Bernard Shaw's *Androcles and the Lion*. Robert Armstrong played Ox Driver. This time the Terminal Letter named Mike's as one of the "outstanding performances" and praised "the clarity of the actors' diction, which even the late arrival of some of the audience failed to make inaudible right at the back of the Gym...It was obvious that the actors enjoyed themselves every bit as much as their audience." Tony Shellim drew the program cover.

Finally, on November 24, 1956, Mike played Alfred the Horse in A.A. Milne's *Toad of Toad Hall*. Euan Houston played The Back Legs of Alfred. He recalled: "He was a couple of years senior to me in the School and so I deemed my position as a follower a great honor! Frankly, all I can remember was that we formed a good team and had enormous fun." The Terminal Letter noted: "The standard of acting throughout was high." Robert Armstrong played Mole. Robert Mackenzie was Chief Stoat and confirmed Mike was only in it for fun: "It was certainly fun, we were all involved. All very enjoyable. I got the impression he was more interested in producing and directing rather than acting." Mike's acting certainly made no lasting impression on Jane Barrett or any of the boys.

Mike also began writing some very basic film criticism for the Terminal Letters under the heading *Film News*, basically just a plot summary but also trying to infect the other boys with his enthusiasm. He noticed forgotten films like *Fangs of the Wild, An Alligator Named Daisy* and *Sky Bandits*: "Renfrew of the Royal Mounted, played by James Newill, stars in this film about a doctor who invents a death ray which brings down planes carrying gold bullion. Renfrew finds this out, and takes a gold-carrying plane up himself. The climax will be found out only when the film is seen."

Betty certainly came to visit Mike at King's Mead. The "School Customs" noted a restriction: "Boys are allowed out with parents, friends or as guests of other boys two days a term on Saturdays or Sundays. This can be over one weekend or on separate occasions, whichever is preferred." Tony Shellim recalled: "I once met his mother. She took us out to a picnic in Seaford. She used to turn up and take Mike and his friends out to lunch." Robert Mackenzie recalled her taking him and other boys to Eastbourne or Brighton for lunch.

King's Mead 1956 Cricket Team

Mike was clearly content at King's Mead. He looks happy in surviving school photos and eventually presented the prie-dieu desk to the King's Mead Chapel. He stayed in touch for a while with some of his school friends there until their paths naturally diverged. He roped in Robert Armstrong to make *Intrusion*. Tony Shellim, after leaving, once went to the cinema with Mike and Betty and also went to a party at Mike's house in Cold Ash. Robert Mackenzie had once stayed for a week at Mike's house when Robert's parents were abroad, but when Mike went to Radley, Robert went to Eton and then spent a couple of years in Argentina, so they lost touch. He recalled: "Boys were aware of his going into films." Indeed, in the final Terminal Letter before the school closed in 1968, it was noted: "Michael Reeves continues to establish his reputation as a dedicated film director. Two films recently made are *The Sorcerers* and *The Witchfinder General*."

Mike clearly retained affection for the Barretts after leaving King's Mead and visited them while using the Seaford coast during filming of *Witchfinder General*. Mike most likely loved that stretch of coast from his days at King's Mead (boys were allowed walks to the seafront under supervision, either with parents or on organized school walks). Jane Barrett recalled: "The last time we saw Mike was when he dropped in one evening, out of the blue, and said he was filming up at Seaford Head and the Cuckmere and thought he'd look us up. I think he suggested that my husband should go up next day and watch what was going on. Whether or not he did, I cannot remember."

The affection was returned. Benjamin Halligan records some nice comments from Peter Barrett about Mike and the interesting observation: "He would be open to depression, I think." When Mike died, his death was inscribed in the register of old boys and the Barretts wrote a letter of condolence to Betty, but never got a reply from her. King's Mead closed in 1968 and the Barretts retired in 1972 to run a small restaurant on the seafront in North Wales. Peter Barrett passed away on August 17, 2002, two days after the first British edition of this book was published.

Mike was following the traditional English middle- or upper-middle-class route of prep school, to be followed by public (in England, this means private) school. In 1954 Betty and Mike had moved to Foxbriar House, Millers Lane, Cold Ash, Thatcham, near Newbury in Berkshire. It was a large stockbroker's type of house. Mike was to go to Radley College, so the move to Cold

King's Mead Chapel, the location of the prie-dieu desk Mike donated to the school.

Ash was "so it would be easier for Betty to visit him" according to Tom Baker, who now met Mike Reeves. There was another Baker, Clive, in the village who ran the Black and White Garage and who vaguely remembered Mike decades later, but he was not related to Tom. Another long-time Cold Ash resident, Bernard Stacey, recalled that Betty Reeves kept to herself and that is why they are only vaguely remembered in Cold Ash today. Tom's friend Iain Sinclair characterized Cold Ash in *Lights Out for the Territory* as: "civil servants, ex-colonials, widows living on their dividends. Detached houses with generous gardens, backing onto woodland."

His future great friend Ian Ogilvy doubted that Mike enjoyed his days at Radley: "No, I don't think so very much. I think he was an active member of the Film Society. I don't think he was a brilliant pupil. I think, rather like me, he wanted to get out and get on with life a bit. He drifted through his school days, rather like me, I would have thought. He wasn't a slouch at all, but his interests were primarily getting out." Ian did not believe that the all-male school environment had any effect on Mike creatively, though he agreed that Mike was clearly drawn to the arts and not interested in science: "Not as far as I know. I didn't see him at school. He couldn't *draw* or anything like that. I think he was rather like me. He slid through school waiting to get out. I always knew what I wanted to do and so did he. So it was a good partnership. We were both fairly obsessive about what we wanted to do."

Ian's ex-wife Diane had a story about Mike's continual rule-breaking at Radley: "Mike told me—I don't know if it's true, it's the sort of thing that one might possibly make up—that he used to be so bad (rule-breaking) at school that his mother had to give the school quite good presents for them to keep him!...He wasn't a student. He was a very intelligent man and he wasn't uneducated, either. He certainly wasn't educated beyond school. He had slightly different priorities from the ones they thought he should have, like going to the cinema and perhaps going out drinking." Owen Scholte recalled Mike did not excel at anything at Radley, even sporting activities: "I don't think he was an oar. He didn't row."

Tom Baker, also at Radley, was skeptical that Betty needed to give the school presents: "That's a good one! I can't imagine it, because he was very bright. I could stay. No one got thrown out of Radley for being stupid, absolutely at all. People didn't. I don't remember anyone being asked to leave because they couldn't pass exams. Life wasn't like that."

Mike's main friends at school were Mike Ball-Greene, Colin Wellwood, Martin Walford, and Paul Vestey of the famous agricultural family who had interests in Fray Bentos. And Tom Baker, who also lived in Cold Ash. It was more because they were neighbors than Radley boys that Mike and Tom became friends. Tom explained: "I didn't see a lot of Mike at school. We were just neighbors at home. I was a year senior to him, actually. He lived more 'cafe society' at school, where people like he and Paul and Mike Ball-Greene would spend the afternoon in the shop drinking Coke and chatting to each other, whereas I was too bloody poor to be doing that or I'd be doing something else. And people from one House to another didn't see a lot of each other."

Even in the hearty surroundings of public school, Mike pursued his passion for cinema, as Diane Ogilvy explained:

> "He used to go to the local cinema where there was a competition, a quiz on the cinema. If you won, you got two free tickets for the following week. Of course, Mike always won and would sneak off without permission the following week and get into trouble for it. Two of them, whoever wanted to go. That's what he told me. It would have been inconceivable for a movie to be shown and Mike not to have gone to see it."

Radley had to learn to accommodate this boy's extraordinary passion for movies. The American thriller director Don Siegel was his hero, followed by energetic horror/sci-fi director Roger Corman. It appears, from testimony below, that Mike struck up a correspondence with Siegel, which is of great significance in explaining the circumstances of his working with Siegel in Hollywood several years later.

Andrew Campbell was in the same House as Mike, Social B. At Radley, Houses are called Socials. Their housemaster was K. Neill Fisher, so it was known as Fisher's Social. Campbell knew Mike quite well, therefore, and told Pamela Hoare that Mike eventually got special permission from Neill Fisher to go to the cinema on Saturday afternoons, which was not generally permitted to Radley boys. He could remember that Mike was always off to the cinema. Mike also had with him at Radley the movie cameras his father had bought him, which meant he could continue to make movies as well as see them.

Mike obviously did make an impression at the school, for even a boy who was three years below Mike, a great gap in school terms, remembered him clearly in adult life. Duncan Forbes arrived at Radley in 1960, encountering Mike in Fisher's Social: "I remember him vaguely as a tall young man with a lock of dark hair which flopped over his forehead. A smoker, deeply interested in films, he was said to keep a detailed record analyzing all the many films he managed to see in Oxford or Abingdon. Since cinemas were officially out of bounds, he seemed to have some special privileges.

I suspect that Mr. Fisher turned a kindly blind eye to what was clearly an irresistible passion for the cinema. I think Mike Reeves was a contemporary of Chris Blackwell, John Haw and J.B. Whitefield. I don't know if Mike was a member of the Film Society at Radley, but it was run by a Mr. Brookman. Somehow I doubt whether it would have appealed to Mike Reeves." Tony

Clint Eastwood and Don Siegel on the set of *Dirty Harry*

Money, Radley archivist, explained: "Mike Reeves was not a member of the Film Society because membership was confined to seniors. Ken Brookman, the Physics Master who started and ran it with great enthusiasm, encouraged him in his passion."

Paul Vestey accompanied Mike on his sorties to the local cinema: "I remember after a year or so we used to go to the cinema, which was totally forbidden. We were both the same age, about 15. I never remember him not being interested in films. It wasn't a sudden thing. I think we used to go and see everything. I suppose the film changed every week and I'm sure we went every week. The one we went to most was in Abingdon, which was a circuit cinema. It was probably an Odeon. We went to all the usual releases. He used to write them all down." Paul could not recall Mike doing the quiz: "All I can remember is that he always used to go in the exit door because we didn't have any money. Knowing him, he would probably have done the quiz as well!"

Paul thought Mike got permission to go to the cinema eventually: "I think toward the end he did get permission because I seem to remember feeling rather jealous and wishing that I'd thought up the same story, but I don't think it made any difference. I think probably the last year or so, as he got more senior, they appreciated that he was genuinely keen."

An extremely valuable contemporary memoir of Mike at Radley comes in a letter of appreciation written by one of his close school friends called Alex J. Waye, whose father was a master at the school. This was written for the Radleian Society after Mike's death. The Society has kindly furnished this extract:

> "Although he was to me a really special person, none of his qualities were really on a par with those recognized at school. He was of course devoted to filmmaking—on his first day at school, he enthralled everybody by having been given a film title, reciting all the credits, from director through actors to technicians. This retentive memory gave him more time to avoid work and get on with the serious business of seeing films, 212 in one year when he was 16.
>
> "On the whole, he had no time for social graces, except in a business context where the situation deserved it. In fact, this applied with everything he did. He was devoted to anyone or anything that he felt merited it. He had a prolific interest and knowledge in English and was a profuse reader.
>
> "With regard to films, it is worth noting that he carried on a regular technical and critical correspondence with three top American directors, including Donald P. Siegel of United Artists, from 13, which they apparently found interesting and valuable. On being told that he was too young to join the Film Society, he founded a junior version which, showing his talent for organization, had 85% of the junior populace as members, financing incidentally his first horror film, which included a most dramatic and stomach-turning shot of somebody having his hands chopped off by a train—the driver of which must have had kittens.
>
> "A devilish laboratory was set up in one of the labs one weekend, with practically every conceivable bit of equipment in use, which when hooked up to a vacuum machine sent all the various bubbling tubes rainbow-colored. Charlie here had wrongly loaded the film and, as the authorities discovered what we'd been doing and refused permission for a rehash, that one was dropped.
>
> "Mike always showed terrific initiative, frequently channeled, I'm afraid, to such matters as cutting games, for which he had no time at all. However, he would only evade school duties because he needed the time to do something that was, to him, more important and not just from idleness, of which he was often unjustly accused. He was very sincere and always candid, sometimes with unfortunate consequences, and was a very true and generous friend."

Alex kindly expanded on this touching tribute for this book:

> "Mike did not fall into the category of the ideal student in an all-male boarding school catering to 13- to 18-year-olds. At school, Mike was no respecter of conventions. He didn't like sporting activities (obligatory every afternoon in

one form or another) and he only worked as hard as was absolutely necessary, except at English, at which he excelled.

"He was not very gregarious, was happiest when looking very scruffy, except at dances, when he used to like to cut a very flashy dash.

"The campus at Radley is something of a self-contained village within a 1,200-acre estate of rolling (mainly dairy) farmland about five and a half miles from the center of Oxford. The whole system relies on the pupils toeing the line and doing what they are told. Mike and I each had to fight our own battles for having serious interests which our peers didn't share.

"Mike was certainly not lazy; he spent a lot of time pursuing his passionate interest in films, the cinema, filmmaking and filmmakers. Michael was a voracious reader of novels. As far as I can recall, he would read anything—classics, modern classics, crime, romance, trash, sci-fi to ghoulish comics. He always had a large postbag and carried on a spirited correspondence with a number of directors and producers—Don P. Siegel was one. He was also mailed all the major film library catalogues.

"Michael had an astonishing talent for recalling facts and figures. By the time he arrived at Radley, he was already passionately interested in anything cinematographic. If you gave him the name of a film, he could instantly recite the whole credits, including distributors and running times. He used to regularly win free cinema tickets in competitions in the movie magazines.

"At Radley, during term-time, the unforgivable heinous sins one could commit were smoking, drinking, going out with girls, and going to the cinema. We were into all of them, booze being only a very rarely enjoyed one. One year, Mike saw 212 movies! We used to need a signed release from Neill Fisher, our Social Tutor, to leave the campus. Our only legal form of transport was a bicycle. As you can imagine, forging these notes was a vital skill to acquire! The only time we could get to see a film was on an afternoon three days a week between 2:30 and 6 p.m. Our circuitous route to avoid detection would take about 45 minutes each way, the other hazard being to manage to cut exercise without being detected. I think our record was seeing *Some Like it Hot* three times in a week.

"Radley always has a large number of formal 'societies,' with a master in charge (though not always present), to cater to all manner of extramural interests. When we were below the 16 age limit to join the Film Society, we decided to form a Junior Film Society and signed up 215 paying members in no time. It was only when we screened *War of the Worlds* in the Lecture Theatre/Cinema in the Science Laboratories (of which I had acquired the keys!) that anybody in authority twigged that we had no proper constitution or Don (Master) in charge. That was when Ken Brookman was co-opted to make sure, at least, that we didn't show any more 'unsuitable' films!

"Mike wanted to make a horror movie in 8-mm or maybe Super Eight. He had his own camera, projector and editer [sic]. Horror movies were always his favorite. I'm not sure he ever wrote down the script. The College is built around a four-story Queen Anne mansion, which has a more or less flat roof with a low parapet. Some of the bachelor Dons live on the top floor. We filmed some very hairy chase scenes up there, leaping over the parapet about 60 feet up and crawling along the lead gutters! (No safety nets or harnesses or anything!) Somehow, we got away with it without being rumbled.

"Mike had a pair of 'joke shop' ghoulish hands. One day we went down to the railway, where there is a bridge over the track. We tied up our hero and laid him beside the track with his arms up his sleeves, the tips of his fingers just holding these latex hands, filled with cotton wool and 'blood,' over the line. As there is a slight curve in the track there, we were blind to the Express Train driver until he was within about 200 yards of us. His panic and the sparks from the wheels as he tried to stop, to say nothing of his genuine horror as he watched his engine's wheels 'chop off' a small boy's hands and splatter him with blood, are engraved in my memory. Poor chap, I'm sure we took 10 years off his life! We certainly had to run like hell to avoid the consequences!

"The next weekend, I again used my spare keys to the Labs to gain entrance and set up hundreds of various flagons, tubes, coolers, retorts and suchlike filled with various different-colored chemicals, and with a vacuum pump on the end to make them circulate and change colors. Unfortunately, when we

33

processed the film, it turned out that we had turned it over twice in the camera and so had exposed the lab scene over the train scene. Shame, huh?

"I don't think we ever finished that film or, for that matter, any other one for the Junior Film Society. Although I did become a member of the Senior Film Society, I wasn't interested in the filmmaking side and cannot remember what part Mike took."

It is fascinating to learn that Mike's favorite movies were horror movies, since he later claimed to work in horror purely because it was an easy field to get backing in. Of course, he may have been affected by the negative reaction to his horror work by Ivor, Betty and Aunt Joan.

From his retirement in Oxford, Neill Fisher clarified the situation about permission to go to the cinema, which *was* unofficial:

"I did not give Michael Reeves permission to go to cinemas in Oxford but know very well that he did so. It seemed to me an entirely sensible thing for him to do, so long as he got back to the Social in reasonable clothing and time! I also hoped that he would not be too redolent of cigarette smoke.

"Michael was a most interesting and amusing person of considerable charm. It was a genuine charm and he was not at all a 'wicked' boy. He was just a gifted young man who did not bother all that much about the rules of the School. We all knew that he was a real enthusiast about the cinema and heard, after he left Radley, that he was most active and distinguished in the field of what I suppose might be termed 'horror films' in the Hitchcock mold.

"I'm afraid that I hardly ever went to the cinema after the war; I was too busy to do that and I have, in fact, been to about two films since I left Radley. Such evenings as my wife and I devote to entertainment are restricted to the theater and the opera, which are easily done here, what with Stratford and the Apollo Theatre in Oxford. I am sorry to say that I have never seen any of Michael's films.

"Michael's life after leaving school must have been a most interesting one and, sadly, a very difficult one in many ways. His mother was not at all well at that time and was a sad person in many ways. Michael's death came as a great shock to us and it is clear that he was a great loss to the film industry. His was a tragic story. My wife and I both had a very soft spot for Michael. He was pretty well liked at Radley and looked upon as something of an eccentric."

By contrast with this amicable account, Tom Baker testified that Mike paid a price for his rule-breaking, namely a beating:

"If you wanted to go to Abingdon or Oxford, you had to go to your House Master and ask permission. Mike was a thorough rebel and he gets on a bicycle and he pedals off toward Oxford. You're allowed to do that. You only had to get permission if you went into the town or toward the river. So, he's pedaling off toward Oxford and he meets Neill coming back from Oxford in the car. Neill, in effect, stops the car and says, 'Hallo, Reeves. What are you up to?' I can't believe it, but it's as though Mike says, 'Well, I'm going to the cinema, Sir!' You wouldn't even get permission for it, let alone do it without permission! In effect, Neill Fisher said, 'When you get back to College, come and see me, and I'll beat you!' So, Mike goes off to Oxford, goes to the cinema, pedals back to school and gets beaten...He was a very wry character, Neill Fisher, and he obviously suspected that is what

Radley College

Mike was off about, and so he might well stop and make some sort of slight remark about it. But he did, he got punished for it. He couldn't care, he *had* to go to the cinema."

Tony Money had another story: "Alex Waye told me that on one occasion he and Mike had gone to the cinema in Oxford without permission. As they sat in their seats, they heard the couple immediately behind them talking and realized that it was Neill and Lorna Fisher. They crept out unobserved...or perhaps not!"

Tom Baker doubted whether Mike really saw 212 movies in one year: "We did go to the cinema in Newbury but not a lot. I don't remember it being two or three times a week." He could remember Ken Brookman's Film Society: "He was an interesting man. There *wasn't* a Film Society at Radley. Radley was a completely philistine school in those days. In five years I was there, I don't know that I ever watched one film. Ken tried to make a film*making* society. Ken made a beautiful film of the 23rd Psalm. That was the first film anyone ever made at Radley. That knocked everyone out. It was a lovely film." Tom never saw any of Mike's Radley films, which reinforces the view that they were never finished.

Ken Brookman elucidated further:

> "*Witchfinder General* was a very good film, and there are others of similar genre. Like others, I am certain that had he gone on, he would have been one of the cinema's outstanding directors. At Radley he had a good deal of support from his mother, and subsequently encouragement to become a filmmaker. The school was allowed to have a Film Society, and I was its President. Michael's early interest in films ensured that he soon played a prominent part in the selection of film for viewing in an era of 16-mm copies and black and white TV without videos.
>
> "He sometimes skipped afternoon games to watch films in Oxford. Our society also made films from time to time, and two of our efforts were shown at the National Film Theatre. Occasionally Michael handled a camera, and we also talked about filmmaking. Unfortunately, his time at Radley did not

coincide with a major production. Nowadays, a proper course of Media and TV studies would allow him scope.

"He had good teachers, especially in English. Some of these were interested in the adaptation of texts for stage or screen. However, school was mainly a foundation for future progress for him, as it was for others like Peter Cook, who showed little sign of the genius he was to become. I once turned down a script of Cook's!"

Benjamin Halligan stated that when Mike was old enough to join the Senior Film Society, at 15, he urged the showing of films like *Kind Hearts and Coronets*. The rooftop drama identified by Alex Waye was called *Down*, featuring Ken Brookman as the villain, and was shown at the National Film Theatre in April 1959, having reached the finals of the National Amateur Film Festival. Mike would help Brookman with editing and sound on a film called *The Ballad of the Battle of New Orleans*.

Tom Baker was 12 when they met and recalled: "When I first met them, Betty seemed to have lots of money. She had a comfortable house with a housekeeper and a gardener."

Mike was a film buff "very early on," according to Tom:

"Even when I was going to have supper with him and his mum, you were allowed to watch a movie on television if Mike wanted to. That was a joy for me. We weren't allowed to do that at home. It was great, wheel the television in to the dining room...but, even then, he would be peering, wondering how Cukor had got some whatever. He always wanted to know how to *make* movies.

"He had a 9.5-mm projector when we were children. That was an alternative size to make home movies in and someone in Alaska or Canada, a logger in the Canadian outback...gold mining town or something...had given him a film. There was an aeroplane involved. An aeroplane crashes through this hangar. We spent *ages* trying to put a soundtrack on this film. It's a sort of a three-minute black and white adventure, it probably had a little board coming up with titles. As a 14 year old, Mike said, 'Oh, we must put a soundtrack on. What can I do?' Of course, the tape recorder would endlessly run to a different speed each time and the projector's not exact. As the aeroplane goes into this hangar, we would try the sound effects to get it and then we would go in and do the dialogue and then re-run it. And, of course, next time we played it, the sound of the aeroplane crashing into the hangar would come when it was still flying across the gray sky! But I remember that took us two or three afternoons really endlessly reworking it. We didn't know why the projector wouldn't synch, because when you turn it on, the music sounds right each time, you think they run at the same speed, then it began to dawn on us there are some fractional changes. So, even then he was trying to work out how films are made and how to make them. Endlessly.

"He must have had other films on 9.5. Otherwise, I just remember something like *Zorro* showing up at a birthday party. Betty hired *Zorro*. We were all knocked out. A film in the sitting room! We all sat on the floor and watched a film. That was *Zorro* (it wasn't *Birth of a Nation*!). He told Betty he was going to make films when he was eight years old. He told me that he chose to be a filmmaker. I don't know where it comes from at all. Lucky person at eight years old to decide what you're going to do."

Tom would observe that Mike's cinema-going was purposeful. He was, in effect, teaching himself how to direct: "He would *analyze* movies. He didn't just see films and say 'Well, that

Oil portrait of Michael Reeves at age 17 (Photo courtesy Virginia Scholte, Portrait owned by Cherida Reeves)

was a good movie.' He would try and work out where the camera had gone, *how* the director had produced the effect he had."

Tom soon got roped in to making amateur 8-mm movies with Mike outside Radley:

> "One of the earliest involved his mother's gardener and a bomb that was thrown over some blackberry bushes. By me? At me? I can't remember.

But there was a telling cut to close-up of the bomb on the ground waiting to explode. He used a green plastic picnic salt cellar. Lying there hopefully. (We didn't know how to make explosive, so that was that.)

"Next I was the reluctant star. I had a broken leg and had to get to a telephone to get help. Which entailed a lot of crawling through the woods dragging the broken leg. With an eye to production values, Mike had found a particularly wet and muddy stretch that I had to cross. On my stomach. I refused. But even as a teenager he could infect people with his enthusiasm for film and he soon had me flat on the ground and crawling through the 'swamp.' This film probably had a name but I cannot recall what it was.

"Next I think he shot something at school, at Radley. I remember his eyes lighting up when he discovered a water jump that was being dug for the cross-country running course. I certainly refused to get wet again, but he may have persuaded somebody else. We went location hunting at a big gravel workings down by the river. A classic Hollywood chase location. Great conical piles of gravel, being fed from conveyor belts supported on a tracery of steel girders. Running figures silhouetted against the sky. Or so we pictured it. I didn't shoot anything there with him, but he may have with other boys."

Paul Vestey had been at prep school with Ian Ogilvy and knew Mike right from the first of his four years at Radley. They were not in the same Social but were in the same Form. He recalled Mike's school career:

"Mike never stopped talking about films. I didn't know anything about them and wasn't all that interested but he was tremendously overkeen, really. The thing I remember strongest is how much he hated games—any form of physical exercise. He hated it so much he thought he ought to get off games, because he really didn't like it, so he thought it would be a good idea if he bashed his knee against the wall of his cubicle, the place you sleep in, until it hurt and then he thought it would probably swell up and he could go and see the Matron and be off games. Well, only trouble was, it worked rather too well. After a day or two smashing his knee against this thing, I think he did it quite a lot of damage and I think he was mildly injured for a time!"

Tom Baker agreed: "He certainly wasn't a games player at all. He played cricket. I remember him bowling somewhere in the team I was in on the edge. He quite liked cricket actually. He had a very wild bowling style. But I can't imagine him liking rugby or anything at all. He was pretty disorganized."

Despite this, Paul Vestey did not think Mike had a difficult time with the masters at Radley: "He was very intelligent and quite articulate, so I think they appreciated him in the end, anyway, for obviously being rather a character. He certainly had the capability of being quite academic if he was interested in something. If he wasn't interested, he just didn't do anything. He *was* very interested in films, but that doesn't do you much good. He certainly was interested in English." Tony Money taught Mike geography in a junior form and confirmed Paul's account: "All I can remember of him is that on several different occasions I asked him a question and he answered, 'I haven't a clue, sir.' Politely, but without interest. His mind must have been elsewhere." Mike's Aunt Joan confirmed that his academic achievement was "not very high": "He had tremendous friends and loved all these young people round about him."

Chapter Two: Getting a Foothold

"Too many people now want to be a film director rather than direct films. One's ambition should be to establish a reputation for professionalism and establish one's freedom that way."— Michael Reeves, *Vogue*

Mike Reeves already knew that he wanted to go into show business. The publicity material of Tigon, the company which produced the films that made him famous, stated: "He would have taken steps to become an actor if someone had not told him—quite wrongly, he later discovered—that all actors were conceited. At the time, however, he believed it, and so decided that producing and directing would be more in his line." Paul Vestey commented: "I never heard him suggest he was ever going to do anything else."

Ian Ogilvy, an actor remarkably modest about his own great gifts, expressed amusement at the idea that Mike might have liked to be an actor:

> "I think he probably would, but he just knew that he had no talent *at all*, not even a trace of talent! He would sometimes show you what he wanted you to do, usually in the physical side. He was uncoordinated, as well. Completely. He'd throw a blow and you'd say, 'You really don't want to do that, Mike!' And he'd say, 'No, no, no, but you know what I *mean!* I *mean* not like that, it's terrible, of course not, but that's the angle, you see.' So, no, he hadn't got a clue. But he was quite *flamboyant* on the set."

Mike's first meeting with Ian Ogilvy must be one of the most fortuitous encounters in movie history, in that this remarkable team of writer/director and leading actor worked so well together in all the films Reeves himself directed that each brought out the best in the other. Today it is impossible to imagine *Witchfinder General* being the masterpiece it is without the special qualities Ogilvy brought to it, and *The Sorcerers* is unthinkable without him.

Ian was a little hazy about that first meeting with Mike Reeves:

> "I suspect it was in one of those coffee bars in the Kensington High Street which used to be around in the late '50s. We were of an age, both 15, and we met through a mutual school friend. Mike was at Radley, I was at Eton, so I never knew him, but this boy called Paul Vestey, who was at my prep school—I remained in touch with him, I think, it's all a bit dim—said to me, 'Oh, you ought to meet my friend Mike Reeves, who's at Radley, because he's passionate about making movies and you want to be an actor.' In the holidays, Paul Vestey arranged this meeting and I was invited down to stay at Mike's house in the country with his mother. And we made a movie. It was the first movie I made with Mike. That's really when we met. We were both 15."

Paul Vestey thought it was 1960, when Mike would have been at least 16.

Ian and Mike hit it off from the very beginning, according to Ian: "We got on immensely well. We were contemporaries, we came from the same kind of background, he was passionate about making movies and didn't want to compete with me because I just wanted to be an actor." Interestingly, Ian's future wife Diane later said that Mike and Ian were temperamentally "totally different," but "Mike only had this one passion which was movies and Ian certainly had this passion for movies as well."

Paul Vestey could confirm that the first meeting was in a coffee bar: "I can remember where it was perfectly well, but now of course it's something else." He also explained why the location was Kensington High Street: "I think we were living in Sheffield Terrace, next to Bedford Gardens, which is up Kensington Church Street and therefore not very far from Kensington High Street where this famous meeting took place. You go down Kensington Church Street, turn right, it was just on the right. There's a church first, a little bit of garden, I don't think it's the first building, it's the next one, before the old Town Hall. I think it's a steak house now." (That would be an Angus Steak House.) King's Mead boy Robert Mackenzie lived nearby and has identified the coffee bar as the "Flamingo."

The location was also convenient for Ian Ogilvy, Paul explained: "I think he lived with his mother in Pembridge Villas, which was also that area as well. I can remember them meeting but I can't remember how it was arranged."

Paul agreed that they hit it off right away: "Yes, I think they did. They started talking about these damn films. Funny how I can remember the meeting perfectly well: Ian standing in a leather jacket, having arrived in some ghastly BMW three-wheeler or something, a peculiar sort of bubble car they had in those days."

Paul thought they had an inkling that they would work together: "I think probably quite soon, because they did hit it off very well." He doubted whether they immediately plotted the home movie they were to shoot together, though: "I think that would be apocryphal but, knowing Reeves, quite likely. They wouldn't have *plotted*. He'd have merely told Ian and Ian would have got enthused or not got enthused."

And so this phenomenal partnership—and friendship—began. Ian continued:

"We made two amateur movies together, when we were schoolboys. I went to stay down at his house in the country and he'd got an 8-mm film camera, and he'd written this little movie, a quarter-hour film called *Carrion*. I was the makeup man and star—I think that's why I was the star, because I was able to do the makeup. I was the beast. He played the hero. He was in it, I was in it, his girlfriend at the time was in it, there was another chap in it, and we stayed down there and we did the picture. I suppose it took about a week to make and we became great friends.

"And then, the following holidays, he invited me down there again to *remake* it, this time on 16-mm! He wanted to do it properly, and he'd also got himself a bit of equipment. He'd got a camera dolly this time and I think he'd got himself some better sound equipment. And he'd got himself some better lights. But I got sick with the flu about two days after arriving down there and really was actually quite ill and was nursed by his mother. Eventually, I ended up playing, I think, an Italian houseman or something in this...but it was a *remake!* I never saw the remake. Bits of *Carrion* do survive. It's black and white, it's very grainy and peculiar, there's no sound on it at all and I suppose only about four or five minutes of it still survive. I actually have it on videotape, but it's a peculiar little piece. I was a baddie in it, an invading wide boy or something."

This one was not a horror movie, as Ian explained: "No, violent! You know, innocent crippled girl in wheelchair, alone at night, escaped psychotic prisoner-rapist-murderer invades her house, boyfriend eventually comes around and rescues her...ha! Usual sort of thing! It wasn't a horror movie as such, no. It was a thriller, but a thriller in 12 minutes." Ogilvy had a photo of Reeves in a wheelchair: "He's taking a shot of her pushing the wheelchair or something. Subjective stuff, you see!"

The cast of the 8-mm version was Ian and Mike and Mike's then-girlfriend Liz and another friend called Chris. Paul Vestey was involved in the shooting of both versions:

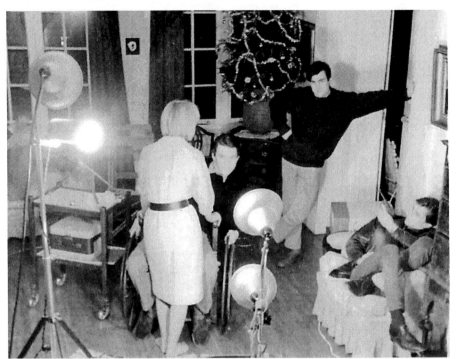

Liz, Mike (in wheelchair), Chris, Ian and the tea trolley camera dolly (photographer: Tom Baker)

"He really just made it for his fun and our fun, just for something to do, and then I think he thought it was such a mess really that he'd do the whole thing properly and do it all again. We made the same movie two years running. Only Reeves could have considered such an idea!

"The second time was much grander. We had Arriflexes. We had tremendous fun making it. I had to do something with the sound, pointing the microphone on a boom. Mike went quite mad and we hired all this equipment, great dollies. He had a great time. His poor mother, I think, nearly caved in under it all! We all stayed there for a week. I remember lots of snow. We hired the dolly, which is the thing the camera goes on, quite a professional thing, from Samuelsons. We had to hire a van to try to take it down. This is when he was living near Newbury, Cold Ash, and I had to drive it because I remember the snow on the ground getting down there and I thought we were going to get off the road with this thing. It was just after Christmas 1961. I was 17. That was the second, the grand version."

On the first shoot, Mike had used an 8-mm camera his father had given him. Paul Vestey was not in either version: "No, thank God I wasn't! Only on the second one, on the credits he had, over film of the people doing whatever their jobs were supposed to be. So I suppose there was a credit of me swinging my boom about or whatever." (This is not the case in the surviving print of the film.)

Tom Baker was roped in as cameraman on the 8-mm version of *Carrion* and recalled for Pete Tombs: "He didn't just want to make films. He wanted to make Hollywood movies, so we had to be able to track, things like that. It wasn't just 'point the camera.' And we had his mum's tea trolley with a little 8-mm Bolex on top on a tripod. He got me to do the camera and do the

Ian Ogilvy kills Michael Reeves in *Carrion* (photographer: Tom Baker)

Michael Reeves with the broken bottle used in the film to attack Ian. (photographer: Tom Baker)

lighting, so we had to practice tracking and focus-pulling and all this sort of lark on little 8-mm films."

Iain Sinclair has written of *Carrion*: "...there was no symbolism, no subtext, no homages. Straightforward action. An intruder breaks into a house and is hit on the head. That's about it. The quality lay in the *mise-en-scene*, smooth tracking shots, cuts on action, reverse angles properly worked out, dramatic night lighting. Hungry violence."

On a preferred diet of Westerns and Hollywood action films from the likes of Siegel, Mike was forming a conception of cinema based on action and violence to the exclusion of literary or philosophical concerns; later, the influence of Irving Allen's mini-epics would add an element of spectacle to Mike's conception of cinema. The ultimate irony is that his mini-*oeuvre* would prove so rich for analysis by heavyweight critics due to his innate ability to give personality to everything he filmed. Mike eschewed a pretentious "art" approach to cinema, but the complexities of his own personality—manic highs and depressive lows—are clearly mirrored in the exhilarating sequences and overall gloominess of his films. Perhaps it was this that has made his work stand out as unique in British cinema.

In some ways Mike's approach to cinema mirrored the beliefs of Spanish director Jess Franco, who also wanted to make films when he was eight and who would admire *Witchfinder General* and virtually remake it as *The Bloody Judge*. He explained to Kevin Collins (*European Trash Cinema* Special #1):

"...in Europe there's a mistaken belief that a film is a way to talk about politics or social problems or philosophy—and I don't think so. I think a film is a complete thing and when a film ends I think it is important enough, you know, to be just a show. Like a circus or a nightclub. But I don't feel (cinema) is so important that it has to be a representative of, or the master of, the deep culture of our age. A film is a distraction, it's a show. It has to be nice to take the people away from their own problems and not to put them in the middle of new problems."

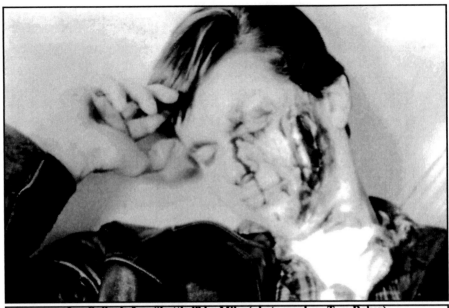

Ian Ogilvy's face "bottled" by Mike (photographer: Tom Baker)

Mike would surely have concurred.

Tom commented: "Up to this time, Mike had been director/cameraman, but now he was just director. And we took it seriously. Managing one or two creditable tracking shots I remember, with the camera and tripod mounted on Betty Reeves' tea trolley. Even some focus pulling."

After the 8-mm version of *Carrion*, Tom Baker persuaded Mike to shoot a story he had concocted, which was devoid of the usual Reevesian preoccupations. Iain Sinclair described it as "some romantic trifle about an artist and his model, canal bank walks, pigeons fluttering in church lofts." Tom recalled it:

> "Then the tale of the Artist. Which for my sins was my story. And with hindsight I can see it for a typical student film script. Love and angst and probably love triumphant. Pretty good tosh. And I can't remember what it was called. But there was our Hero, a regular upright sort of chap. And his Girlfriend, a clean upstanding English Rose type. And his New Love, an artist, living a much more interesting life of paint and disorder and hippieness in her studio.
>
> "So the English Rose turns up to win him back. And we have the great struggle between Creativity, witness dirty coffee mugs, disheveled bedclothes, half-finished canvases and possibly depression. And Home and Beauty, depicted by windy views enjoyed by lovers from the top of a church tower and cigarette advert-type walks along a river bank. That's why the film we failed to finish was just typical nonsense...couples walking along the riverbank hand in hand, what's the point of that? Except, I thought it was wonderful at the time, although it may have been an intentional joke, 'cos it was the time of Players' cigarettes having endless ads of people meandering along riverbanks hand in hand, so I think we were possibly taking the mickey a bit, but possibly not. Trying to be arty. And Mike was *never* like that, not an inch of it, except this one failed project, where he foolishly tried to follow me down the path of it. 'Got to have meaning, got to have stuff...' No, he wasn't involved in that.

"Anyway, when we were preparing this epic, one of Betty Reeves' friends hears of it and offers us the use of a 'studio' in her garden. We see this as our sound stage. Light and airy. A good place to build our set of 'chaotic artist's studio.' We both had driving licenses, so we must have been 17, 18 or 19 by then. And hauled a lot of stuff the 10 miles to Tidmarsh to dress the set...suitably subversive artworks, dirty coffee cups, disheveled possessions scattered about. The poor owner was outraged. We'd made it look too real. She thought we'd totally trashed the place and asked us to leave. So we had to repeat all the car journeys and haul it all back home. We ended up in the local Church Hall. Which was fine.

"And we had a good 'Hollywood incident.' The script called for our Hero to do a bit of kissing with the English Rose type. On a sofa I recall. And it wasn't going very well. The guy playing the Hero was thinking more of his real-life girlfriend than of the part he was playing. 'Hold on,' says Mike, 'let me show you what I want.' And he gets down on the sofa and he and the English Rose kiss. And kiss. And kiss. And go on kissing. And don't stop. And the rest of us have to leave the room. Leave them to it.

"It feels as though that was the end of the project. Perhaps we filmed some more, perhaps not. But I doubt anything was edited. Mike's new girlfriend, the girl playing the English Rose, whose name I cannot remember, went off to London to do The Season and have her own coming-out party. And Mike went with her and disappeared into high society for a while.

"The following winter Mike, having little faith in my literate story ideas, decides to return to action and drama and remake *Carrion*. Except this time on 16-mm and renamed *Intrusion*. He's discovered something called a crab-dolly and we have to experience the possibilities. Samuelsons in those days seemed to be a couple of sheds behind a shop in Cricklewood, or somewhere, in the snow and Mike persuaded them to rent him all this equipment and give me a two-minute lesson in how to use an Arriflex camera. We got it all back to Berkshire and even more surprisingly, into his mother's house. Where we crabbed and dollied and craned around the ground floor to our great amusement.

"Ian Ogilvy returned to replay his part from the original *Carrion* and the house party/film studio ambience reinstated itself. With the snow outside and us taking ourselves seriously inside, being well fed by the housekeeper and tolerated by Betty Reeves as we bumped and laughed our way round her living rooms with our movie equipment. My lighting arrangements were very primitive and I was rather surprised at the time that they survived being used outside without blowing every fuse in the house.

"I remember a man called Bob Armstrong, who had been at school with Mike when they were younger. I think he was grip and general dogsbody. His dad trained race horses and I remember he himself married Lester Pigott's daughter some years later. I don't remember the film being any better than the original, though we probably had properly synchronized sound. Maybe even a disappointment. I think it lost a certain taught edginess that *Carrion* had. But it showed how serious Mike was about 'making films.' The story, the acting, essential parts. But framing, lighting and above all moving the camera fascinated him."

The film starred a lovely girl called Sarah Dunlop. Tom recalled: "Sarah was my first girl-friend, for a few months when we were 16 and before she had discovered the joys of older boys with sports cars." *Intrusion* is notable for the professional look of Tom Baker's photography and

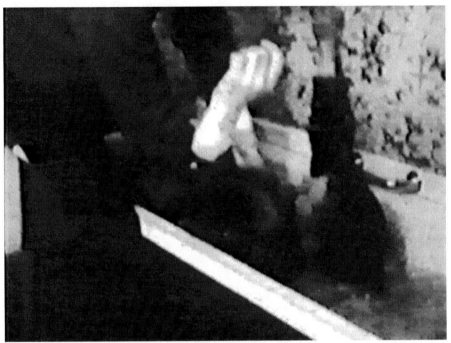

Mike Reeves is dunked in a tub full of water by Sarah's rescuer in *Intrusion*.

for Mike Reeves' charismatic performance as one of the sinister intruders in black sunglasses. So striking is Mike that it is hard to credit Ian Ogilvy's contention that Mike had no acting ability at all. Bizarrely, the film is dedicated to Jean-Luc Godard. This is a major surprise, as Mike did not seem to have any great sympathy for art cinema directors, and may be because Godard's *Breathless* was quite commercial in its subject matter despite its arty approach.

Sadly, the existing print located by Benjamin Halligan lacks the soundtrack, but the plot obviously follows the *Carrion* blueprint while differing in some ways. Mike Reeves is this time not a defender but one of two intruders menacing Sarah Dunlop (who disrobes for a bath in a very James Bond-like scene) and is defeated after a tussle when help arrives. Simple but very effective little thriller which in some ways looks even more professional than Mike's first feature film, *Revenge of the Blood Beast*, with beautiful scene setting in the Berkshire snow. (In the background one can see Betty Reeves' portrait of Mike at 17 on the wall; no one bothered to take it down even though Mike is in front of it as an intruder!)

For writers like Iain Sinclair, *Carrion* already encapsulated the vision that found its fullest expression in the shocking climax of *Witchfinder General* and which later led to an accusation that Mike had a "kink" about blood. Tom Baker was skeptical about that:

> "I don't know if he was obsessed with that. I suppose at the time I just thought that's a way of adding production value to make it saleable, to make it visible, except obviously if you start repeating these endings, you think, well there is something...Like in the very first *Carrion* we made, at the end the hero screws this bottle into Ian's face, because Ian is the baddie and he's up the stairs and the hero is down at the bottom. So we had to break a bottle. It's not very easy to break a bottle and make it all jagged. We broke quite a lot of bottles before we got one with a suitable spike and then it sort of screws up into Ian's face. Or, in this case, the camera lens. Scared the life out of me. So then there's a great deal of us trying to make little makeup on Ian's face,

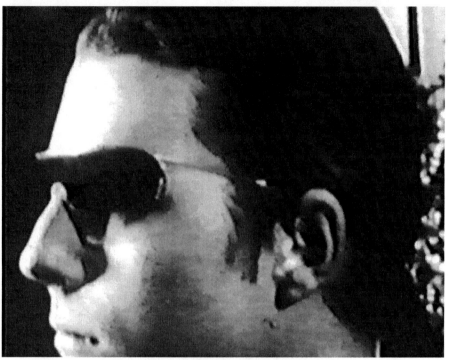

Mike Reeves acting in *Intrusion*.

pathetic bits of cellotape with bread dough underneath a little cut. That's the end of the film. Even then, Mike knew he wanted something very powerful at the end of the film. Whether it's to do with a kinky interest in blood, I've no idea, but he knew he wanted that really strong kind of effect. So there's Ian sitting on the stairs, his face in shreds, doing a Marlon Brando, thumping the stairs, moaning and groaning. I don't recall him having a perverse interest in blood particularly at all. No, I don't think so."

(And yet, the title sequence of a late, unrealized film, *Razor*, would feature a bleeding cut.)

Mike did not really do anything with *Carrion* or its remake *Intrusion*. It was never envisaged as any kind of calling card. "He played around with it, cut it, recut it and fiddled," according to Ian Ogilvy. Many years later, after Mike's death, the surviving parts of the original 8-mm *Carrion* were broadcast in England on BBC-2 Television as part of a short tribute to Mike by popular film historian Philip Jenkinson. When Mike died, Paul Ferris came into possession of the only copy of *Carrion*, so Jenkinson approached him and he agreed to make a copy for the BBC. He also made a copy for Ian Ogilvy.

It was during the making of *Carrion* that Ian got to know Betty Reeves:

"She was an English matriarch. Gray hair, very tall, thin. Patrician sort of woman. Very gracious, charming. Never *quite* knew what Mike was up to. She was the old school, rather patrician and regal. I liked her very much. I just lost all contact with her after Mike died because these things happen, but she wasn't a young woman when I knew her. She was alone, didn't have a chap or anything, and I think he was very fond of his mother, but I don't think she understood what he was doing at all and wouldn't have liked his movies."

Betty and Mike on holiday in Majorca; note Mike's camera (Photo: Cherida Reeves)

It is clear that she did take pride in Mike's cinematic achievements from the fact that she kept detailed scrapbooks on his career (passed after she died to a distant relative, film editor Oliver Huddleston). Ian Ogilvy pointed out that this pride was not overt:

> "She was the *kind* of woman who didn't impart that sort of knowledge. She was *extremely* English, extremely county. She certainly didn't say to me that she was proud of Mike's achievement, because it's not the kind of thing an English woman of her station in life would say. That kind of emotional side wouldn't come out particularly, but I would imagine she was proud, although I don't suppose she would have liked *any* of the pictures at all. I have vague memories that maybe she came to a press showing or something like that and shut her eyes a lot. I don't know, that might not be true."

But she did visit the set of *Witchfinder General* and must have seen it as she collected press cuttings about it and it caused such a ripple when it appeared, as Ian Ogilvy remembered: "I know Bernard Levin walked out within six minutes. Loathed it, loathed what he'd seen. Thought it was the most horrific, foul, beastly thing he'd ever seen!"

Paul Ferris recalled that Betty Reeves *seemed* to be about six foot three, although she wasn't, because she was so "imposing," but she did have a good sense of humor and was friendly. She used to say to Paul "Oh, call me Betty," but he never could bring himself to address her other than as Mrs. Reeves.

Ian Ogilvy certainly formed the impression of substantial wealth in Mike's background: "He and his mother were from a very good family. He and his mother lived *comfortably* in the country, but they were the poor relations of a large and immensely rich family." Betty always stayed in touch with the family. She was godmother to Virginia Scholte, who would see her regularly until her death. Betty would still have a lot of contact with Joan, who was widowed with no children, due to her fondness for Michael. Sarah, Ivor Reeves' daughter, explained:

"Being childless and we being three daughters, she adored Michael and the affection was more than mutual. It was she who was invited to see all the previews of his films, and she followed his progress minutely throughout his life."

After *Intrusion*, Ian Ogilvy and Mike Reeves lost touch for a few years, according to Ian: "Because we weren't at school together or anything like that, and we had exams and all the rest of it, I lost contact with him, but completely." They went their separate ways and each had a measure of success before their paths crossed again.

At about this time, something happened that was to alter Mike's life radically. He inherited a large sum of money from his father's side of the family, which meant he would be financially independent for the rest of his life and made possible the kind of film career that was to follow.

Ian told the story:

> I know that he came into his money at 16 and it took him by tremendous surprise. He was suddenly a very rich young man. It was extraordinary. His father had died and he and his mother were the poor relations and the way Mike Reeves told the story—this is only Mike Reeves' version—was that when he was about 15, when I first got to know him, the family solicitor told his mother he thought something could be done about this. They investigated and indeed they were owed by the family (this is again according to Michael) a very large sum of money, him and his mother. And overnight they won this amount of money. They didn't even have to go to court.
>
> "Mike found inherited wealth terribly hard to handle, having been fairly poor. He'd been to public school on the generosity of the rest of the family. 'The poor relations...must give the boy a chance!' So, they suddenly became terribly, terribly rich, although I don't think they'd ever been terribly, terribly poor, put it that way. Of course, it was all in trust. He could not actually get at the money and his expenditure was closely looked at. He had an income of about 60 pounds a week. Well, in 1962 that was a lot of money. He could have a nice house and a good car and change his car every year. He had long boring talks with accountants which he hated."

His Aunt Joan (whom Betty used to call Aunt Joey) revealed that the rest of the family had inherited their money just as unexpectedly:

> "The money came to us as a family when my father died and my mother died before. My mother died in '25 and my father remarried in '27 and it was very soon after that the money came to us. Nothing to do with women! It just happened. One of these mysterious things that happen overnight, one firm takes over another firm. That was very much the same with all of us, because we were allowed an allowance and that sort of thing, but then this extraordinary thing happened to us. One firm was taken over by another firm and you suddenly find that you, the members of the first firm, have got very much more money than you used to have. My mother had no idea that that money was coming to us, because it hadn't happened. It only happened quite a number of years afterwards."

Paul Vestey did not notice a great effect upon Mike other than surprise:

> "It came as a great shock to them all, I think, because I don't think they thought it would be quite that much. Perhaps it gave him a bit more confidence. I think he was quite pleased. I don't think he knew at that age how much he

was likely to get, because his mother would keep it fairly low-key. I always felt that none of them really knew what it was all about, because it was the Reeves' side it came from. City of London Real Property was where the money came from. One of Mike's uncles ran it. Certainly that was what Mike always said. I knew him well enough to know. That's where he thought it came from anyway."

Tom Baker said, "I didn't notice any change [in Mike]. Mike certainly didn't get his hands on the money until later, if he ever did, because there was this family solicitor he was always having to go off and see and ask if he would release money. I guess he was a trustee of his father's trust and Mike would have to go and pitch to him if money could be released from the trust. *The Sorcerers* was the biggest one he ever tried for but, just generally, there was always a break on putting money in films because you had to go and see the solicitor and get his agreement in some way."

Paul Vestey put the sum at about £250,000 for Mike and the same for his mother in the money of the time. Some of Mike's friends, such as Paul Ferris, thought it was considerably more than even that. Vestey thought he had an income a bit in excess of 60 pounds a week, but argued that Mike actually "spent more than that, on cars, hiring films and staying up all night."

Yet he spent little on clothes, as he had little interest in them, according to Diane Ogilvy: "Absolutely none at all. He took his jacket off and put it down, then he noted that it wasn't going to be hanging up when he got home and what a pity! He couldn't give a damn. I know once Annabelle (Mike's steady girlfriend) did manage to get him to go off somewhere frightfully smart and have some suits made, but he'd lost half of them within a week of them being finished anyway." Diane argued that cutting a dash sartorially "wouldn't have suited him." Paul Vestey felt: "I don't think he was very interested in general personal appearance. He wasn't dirty, but he just thought that was all rather vain and pointless." Yet Paul agreed that Mike was quite handsome: "Very good-looking. Very strong features. Very attractive to women. All these girls, I couldn't quite work it out what they did like. I think he was probably quite shy in a nice way. He was quite confident in himself anyway."

For Tom Baker, Mike's attractiveness to women was not necessarily connected to his wealth:

> "He was an attractive, interesting man anyway. Particularly by the time he was in Yeoman's Row—the dream house, clearly plenty of money—but even before. I remember years ago, when we were down in the village, we went to a friend's party. We were driving, so 17 or 18. I remember it was a friend of a friend. He went with a girlfriend, a tenuous girlfriend, to this party. And this girl called Liz, who's actually in one of the *Carrion* films, was staying with a friend of hers in the village, and she just walked over to Mike and sat on his knee and put her arm round him and wouldn't shift for the rest of the evening! The village community was just astounded at her brazenness. And she and Mike were together for a year...or six months...or two months. So he was attractive enough to make people do that, whether it was his money or his entertaining talk or his long hair."

Tom thought Mike was not particularly devoted to chasing girls: "I don't remember us ever talking about sex much. He spent too much time thinking about movies. He was too busy. Girls always pursuing him actually, more than anything else—not at the Annabelle stage—but generally."

Paul Ferris felt that the main first impression Mike made on people was "long hair" and denied that Mike resembled his so-called filmic alter-ego Ian Ogilvy: "Not at all. Ian's nose is totally different. Ian's got dark, straight hair, totally different. For me the incredible part of Mike were the eyes, the eyebrows and the nose. The eyes were deep dark brown and these most incredible bloody eyebrows and the forehead, literally Byronic, and this fantastic damn nose."

When Mike was 17, Betty Reeves had the oils portrait of him painted which one can glimpse in *Intrusion*. It is a large, beautiful painting, very romantic, slightly idealized (according to family friend Tim Miller) and decidedly Byronic. Paul Ferris commented: "I thought he physically was Byronic. For myself, he was incredibly beautiful, the face, the eyes, the whole. I found him fascinating—the actual face. You couldn't have failed to like Mike."

Virginia Scholte saw more of Mike as a young adult than she had as a child. She even taught him to drive: "When I left my first husband, I went to stay with Aunt Betty, taking my young son, and Mike was around then. I suppose he would just be leaving Radley, probably about 18. I stayed with her at Newbury most of one summer and he came and went. In fact, I remember he was dying to drive a car. He was learning to drive and I used to take him out in my car. I got stick from Aunt Betty because he wasn't supposed to, I think."

Ian Ogilvy characterized Mike as a very private man, and the Scholtes observed that he never volunteered much about himself. Virginia put this down to his vocation: "When you're in the films, you just talk about films, don't you? I don't remember him talking about himself or girlfriends. I seem to remember there were young women who went to stay at weekends and things but I don't remember whether any of them were serious. Aunt Betty was always saying 'He's coming with a whole lot of friends, young men and young women.' "

Judy Miller was a great friend of Betty from the time Mike was a small boy. Her son Tim was born in 1937 and saw Mike mainly when he came home from Radley. They were friendly because Tim was also interested in movies and was partner in a small film company set up in 1962 called Mithrash Films, which made documentaries. In the mid-'60s he became a Production Manager for 20th Century-Fox, MGM and other major companies. "Mike was rather impressed," he chuckled. He could recall Mike coming back to Foxbriar House from Radley with a large group of friends and, on a blazing hot summer's afternoon, drawing all the curtains and setting up his film projector. His friends all obeyed him without question, despite the weather, Tim recalled with wonderment. Mike was the leading light of the group and they willingly bowed to his dominant obsession with films, according to Tim. Paul Vestey found this unsurprising: "He had a very infectious sense of enthusiasm. He was great fun." Diane Ogilvy commented: "It wouldn't have been dominance that Mike did it. It would have been complete and utter lack of conception of anybody wanting to do anything else. And if there was a movie on television...You're kidding, be sensible, come on and watch the movie."

Aunt Joan never met any of Mike's friends: "I didn't live in London. He and his friends were basically London. His father Bungie used to come and stay with me a great deal, me and my husband, but I don't think he ever did." (She would visit Mike's house in Yeoman's Row once only.)

Showing movies and experimenting with cameras and tape recorders appear to have kept him going until he could leave school and get into the film industry. Virginia Scholte gave some examples:

> "I do remember the first time I ever heard my own voice on a tape recorder, it belonged to Mike. He said we all had to say something and then he played it back to us and did a commentary. It was the first time I'd ever heard my own voice and I thought, 'God, do I really talk like that? Awful.' Then he came and showed a Mickey Mouse film once for our children, when he was still at Radley. We had a party for the little things and 'What could we do for them?' Like you have a conjuror or whatever. 'Let's have Mike to do a film.' He came and did this film at Brunton Farmhouse in Wiltshire, where we first lived when we were married. I can't remember what it was about. It must have been Mickey Mouse or one of those sort of characters. He hadn't

made the film, he hired one and came to show it with his projector. Cartoons and things like that. And he spoke a bit or something."

Mike left Radley College after taking his A levels in July 1961. His family could not recall what he took. Paul Vestey said: "I'm sure he got English." Tom Baker thought "He probably did History and Geography. He didn't do Science, because I did Science and he wasn't down in the science labs at all, so I'm guessing at what else, and he didn't do classics at A level." Benjamin Halligan suggests he dodged actually taking A levels, telling the school of his ambition to be a film technician.

At a loose end, Mike flew to join Betty, who was visiting her relatives in Boston. There, he became so bored with what he later described as "an endless round of Boston tea parties" that he did an astonishing thing. He decided to seek out his pen-pal and idol, film director Don Siegel. Quite what his hopes were in doing this, other than to escape from noncinematic circles, is not clear. David Pirie, writing about this episode in his book *A Heritage of Horror*, assumed Mike was angling for a job with Siegel and argued that "Ten years before, such a method of breaking into features (for a director as opposed to a potential star) would have been not only impossible but unthinkable."

It is also possible that Mike simply took the opportunity, after several years' correspondence, to meet the director he most admired and seek his advice on how to become a film director. Actor and friend Peter Fraser thought Mike would have regarded himself as a friend of Siegel's after having a correspondence. So, on an impulse, Mike boarded a plane for Los Angeles and turned up, apparently unannounced and unexpected, on the doorstep of Don Siegel's Canyon home, although Iain Sinclair reckoned he called Siegel from a pay phone first. Mike later recalled that he virtually "barged into" the house. Benjamin Halligan writes that Siegel was out when he called and he had to be entertained by Mrs. Siegel, one of the many versions of this story.

Ian Ogilvy told Pete Tombs that Siegel answered the door in a vest and a pair of underpants and said, "What do you want?" And Mike said, "I've come all the way from England to see you, Mr. Siegel, because you are the greatest film director in the world."

David Pirie wrote that Siegel was impressed by Mike's bravado but was not aware that they had corresponded in the past. This does not detract from Mike's courage in approaching his idol. "Reeves wasn't short of bottle," wrote Iain Sinclair. But it makes the story, hitherto regarded even by Ian Ogilvy as "possibly apocryphal" because its only source was always Mike himself, a little less unthinkable. At least Siegel knew who Mike was, although he must have been amazed to have this 17-year-old English public schoolboy suddenly on his doorstep!

In an act of rare generosity, Siegel decided to give Mike not only advice but some practical experience with professional filmmaking. This would later prove invaluable to Mike in getting a foothold in the British industry. Mike later recalled: "Don was kind enough to give me some very temporary employment as dialogue director on some tests he was shooting for Paramount." Mike later told Paul Ferris that he was Siegel's assistant and the position was unpaid (but, of course, priceless to Mike).

There is no doubt all this happened, however extraordinary it seems at this remove of time. Virginia Scholte remembered Mike going to the States and Betty later telling her "He's got a foot in the door." The clincher is the fact that Siegel visited Mike in London after *Witchfinder General* and as Paul Ferris rightly pointed out: "For sure he did work with Siegel, otherwise Siegel wouldn't have turned up in London."

Furthermore, a later acquaintance of Mike's, Ernest Harris, reported that critic Barry Forshaw (of the *Islington Gazette*) went to a Don Siegel lecture at London's National Film Theatre some years after Mike's death and asked Siegel, "Can you tell us something about Michael Reeves?" Siegel reportedly confirmed that Mike showed up unannounced and said: "Michael Reeves was an extremely nice young man who turned up on my doorstep one day and said how much he admired my films." Paul Vestey commented: "He was quite capable of doing that. He wouldn't have taken 'no' for an answer."

Nicky Henson heard an alternative version of the story, which has now become a film industry legend and, like all legends, subject to variations in the retelling: "Mike wrote him a letter and Siegel sent him an air ticket back. He wrote him a letter saying, 'I think you're a genius, can I come and work for you?' And he sent him an air ticket and said, 'Come out on Monday,' which he did. That's as far as I know." This version had no support among Mike's friends such as Ian Ogilvy and also does not accord with Mike's own account of going first to Boston, and can therefore be regarded as apocryphal. It is recounted here as an example of the varying stories that circulate about Mike Reeves.

Paul Vestey recalled it this way:

> "I remember when he first went to America to see or meet Don Siegel. I think he'd written to him. I don't think he'd had very much back from him. He wrote and got just an acknowledgment more than anything else. I don't think it said 'Don't come,' but I don't know he got a vast amount of encourage-ment; I don't suppose he would have done as a complete stranger, because I expect Siegel had a lot of people writing to him. I think he stayed with him over there. He definitely went. He used to go on and on about it. He certainly did think that he was a genius. We used to hear about Don Siegel until it came out of our ears."

Ian Ogilvy had no difficulty believing Mike's account: "That was the kind of thing he did. He just upped and went. Because he was able to, lucky old bugger, he could do it." Ian was even unperturbed by the fact that knocking on Don Siegel's door was not a recognized route into the film industry:

> "No, it wasn't, indeed, but I wonder if Mike quite *knew*, you see. He'd been a public schoolboy. He'd not been to film school or anything. He didn't particularly *want* to go to film school. He felt that wasn't the right way of doing it. The way to do it was to go and work with somebody you admired a lot. And then Siegel, bless him, said, 'Okay, you can stay. Come and watch and observe.' And then he started giving him little running jobs. It went on from there. So he did start at the ground floor by being brave enough to go and do that. He didn't ever have to do that. He could have just said 'I'll make a picture.' He could have raised 20,000 pounds without any problem at all. But he didn't. And that's why I admire him so much. Because he said, 'It's just too easy.' I mean, he wasn't just 'Oh, I should be a film director.' He really worked at it. He was reputed to have hand-cranked *Intolerance* and *Birth of a Nation*. Done studies of them. And, give him his due, he could have gone off and made a movie immediately. Instead he went off, he was a runner, a fourth assistant director, working for idiots, working for marvel-ous people, and seeking out his hero and insisting that he was the greatest film director in the world. I mean, Siegel had never made any of these *Dirty Harry* kind of films. He'd just done things like *Baby Face Nelson* (1957) and all of those things, and to have Mike Reeves turn up on his doorstep and say 'You are the greatest film director in the world'...interesting! Mike said, 'The man's a genius. He makes small-budget pictures and they're all wonderful.' We used to have Siegel seasons in Mike Reeves' front living room. Endless showings of Siegel movies."

Paul Ferris thought Mike was wise not to go to film school: "It may have ruined him if he'd gone to film school." In any case, said Paul Vestey: "I don't know what there was in the way of film schools in those days; certainly there wasn't anything that appealed to him, I think.

But I think he was quite ready to get out of school of any sort and I think he'd had quite enough of education, shall we say. He didn't want to go to university. He wanted to make films." Tom Baker recalled there was very little in the way of film schools then.

Fortunately, an American show business writer, Bill Kelley, who was a Mike Reeves fan, got an opportunity to speak to Don Siegel and get his side of the story long before Don got cancer and died. Bill explained: "I sat down with him for a couple of hours in 1975, when he was still at Universal Studios, and ran a tape recorder while he told me everything he could recall about Reeves. Obviously, it was still all fairly recent history at that time (the interview was done in January 1975) and Siegel's memory was very sharp. He told me everything in anecdote form."

Siegel confirmed the truthfulness of Mike's account:

> "Michael showed up at my house, totally unknown, very brash—I think he was about 19—incredibly long curly hair for the time, which was certainly not the mode. He said, 'I think you're the greatest director in the world today,' or something like that. And because we're nuts, we let him come into the house, told him he could go up to the pool house, and live there if he wanted to. We didn't know him from a hole in the wall. I knew from his accent that he was well-educated, but I had no idea that he was a wealthy young man—au contraire, I thought he was really roughing it. I found out much, much later that he was quite wealthy.
>
> "He was a Siegel buff. He knew every film I'd ever done. And I remember I had a 101-degree fever, and Hal Wallis called and asked me if I'd shoot some tests on an Elvis Presley picture, to be called *Fun in Acapulco*. And there was Michael, so I asked him if he'd like to come down and help out. He said, 'Oh, God, I'd love to.' So I said, 'Great—you can be my dialogue director. It's nothing. You just take the script and go over the lines with the people we're testing. If they make a mistake, you make a note of it and come over to me later and tell me anything that occurs to you.' At the time, although I thought the script was an abomination, I was hoping to get the job because I needed the bread. Michael did that test with me, and then the next thing I hear, he's in England directing a few years later. And he got started by saying he was my dialogue director, which I thought took a wee bit of guts, and I sort of admired it."

The fact that Siegel described Mike showing up as "totally unknown" does not of course contradict the claims that they had corresponded in past; Siegel probably produced a lot of correspondence and would not necessarily be able to identify one fan from another when one turned up in person. Iain Sinclair has described the tests Mike worked on with Siegel as "a parade of jailbait ingenues and crooning models." He opined their friendship was enhanced by a shared fondness for poker and cigars.

Following his dream encounter with Siegel, Mike headed back home. Surprisingly, Mike's Aunt Joan claimed that Mike had gone to America and "disliked it rather intensely": "He liked the film part of it, that sort of thing, but didn't care for it very much. He wasn't there very long." This despite Mike's reported fondness for the vaguely American atmosphere of the Carlton Tower Hotel.

Elvis Presley and Ursula Andress in *Fun in Acapulco*, Paramount, 1963

Mike returned to Britain after his stint with Siegel all fired up to work in the British film industry, but had to spend periods just marking time, as an anecdote of Virginia Scholte's reveals:

> "I remember we went to Jersey. Aunt Betty took a house in Jersey called Mon Cochon and we took our sons Piers and Ivan, and Mike was there. He wasn't supposed to be there but he was obviously at a loose end, so he was there. It was the time of the Twist—1962—and I remember Mike trying to teach me how to do the Twist. He was so good at it and I couldn't do it at all. I think I was pregnant at the time! He certainly did the Twist beautifully. He had the figure for it, too."

Tom Baker then went off to Trinity College, Dublin, where Mike should have joined him. Tom explained:

> "Anyone could get into Trinity in those days. There was the lowest qualification for any university anywhere. We all went there, those of us who failed our A levels or marginally passed them went to Trinity instead. Betty did get Mike admitted to Trinity, but he chose not to go there. And so, in a sort of desperate attempt to have some further education, she sent him off to Switzerland for a finishing school. I think he lasted a term or so. He wanted to get on with getting into the movies in some form or other."

For the next three years, Mike shared a succession of flats in London with Paul Vestey, who was going into his family's agricultural business (they owned Dewhurst's, the butchers). Paul recalled: "We shared a lot of flats together round the place. Montpelier Street we had a flat. Rutland Gate we had a flat. We just rented things really, just me and him. Nobody else paid anything." During these years, Mike strove hard to get work as a director by writing endless treatments, as Paul Vestey observed: "I remember him pounding away at the typewriter. Mountains of stuff as I remember. He used to tap away."

As a flatmate, Paul affectionately described Mike as "completely chaotic," perhaps because he kept busy: "He was always off to these running jobs. He seemed to spend most of his time looking for jobs or trying to organize himself, which is normal." Paul remembered that Mike listened to "noisy music" as he typed his film treatment ideas: "For years before we'd had to listen to endless LPs of film music." He agreed that, as Paul Ferris would testify, Mike loved the score of *The Magnificent Seven*: "Yes, I think that's quite true. He always said he thought that film music was the classical music of the future. It saved him from having to learn anything about actual classical music."

There was also some Elvis Presley: "He liked Presley. We used to share Bedford Gardens

with his elderly Aunt Joan. We shared a double room with everything and there was quite a lot of Presley. I remember *G.I. Blues* particularly. It would only be Presley *film* music, I'm sure. That, and Westerns. A lot of Western film music." Ian Ogilvy pointed out: "Of course, Don Siegel had directed Presley in *Flaming Star*. I think it was his only non-singing role." Paul Ferris said Mike did not listen to pop music, only film scores; also, "he had some classical music, popular classical." Paul Ferris did not think Mike was that keen on Presley: "Not full of Elvis. Some. Most of them film scores."

At this stage, Mike was not writing full scripts, just story outlines or treatments, said Paul Vestey: "I think they were really treatments. I don't know how much anything was fully worked out or fully scripted and all the rest of it. It wasn't that I didn't pay much interest, but he'd always been the same, with fairly manic work going on." Mike was a nightbird even then: "It was the age we all were. There didn't seem to be a vast amount of work going on the next day early-ish. It tended to get pretty late. Lots of whisky used to be consumed and a vast amount of cigarettes. I think we were all the same. I don't think anything happened before 11 in the morning. So I think the whole day was moved on a few hours from the chap who had to go to the office."

Mike was already subscribing to the show business trade paper *Variety* and this probably helped him decide which people to approach, Paul thought: "He certainly seemed to have quite a knowledge of what was going on and who was doing what. He was very energetic, Mike. I mean his *brain* was energetic. He wasn't physically energetic. He didn't just sit around doing nothing."

Despite all this effort, it was very hard to make real headway and Paul felt this was why he eventually teamed up with Tom Baker to write together: "He did get fairly despondent. I think in a way that's why Tom Baker appeared. He probably thought it was easier or less depressing to have someone else to share the writing. I think you'd find that Mike would be very much a leader and Tom very much a follower. Mike had a fairly magnetic personality and always seemed to know what he wanted to do. I think he thought Tom had potential."

Tom Baker had stayed in touch:

> "He shared a flat with a man called Phelps-Penry, who was at school with us, who astounded us at school because he said he was going to be a film critic—that was his 'career choice'—and then Mike shared a flat with him for a while. I went there once or twice. That was somewhere north of Montagu Square. I remember going to film a little 8-mm film, or trying to, in this flat. The only reason I can remember that is because of this girl who had the kissing lark that I referred to, the English Rose from the Artist film. She and Mike were no longer a couple, like they ever were, she had another boyfriend. And he wanted to make a film with these two, and he must have contacted me to come and film them.
>
> "Because it was back on 8-mm or something, so it must have been quite early, but I remember there was this shot...he wanted me to film up with them standing up kissing each other and the camera was to be by their feet and I was to look up past their scantily clad (they *were* clad!) bodies to them kissing. The reason I remember that shot is because it was shot on Kodak 8-mm film, so you send it off, put it in an envelope and it gets developed... and it *never* came back from the processors. And we never knew whether it had just got lost or whether someone had censored it! I don't recall it at all being outrageous, but we just never knew. So that was another little film that nothing came of. So, it's possible that he may have rung me up and said, 'Look, I'm doing this, so will you come?' I stayed with him, once I think, there."

At this time, Mike's tendency to manic depression only manifested itself to people in a positive way, according to Paul Vestey: "He seemed to have the best sort of mania, he had high bits and he didn't seem to have low bits. That obviously was earlier on. He would get quite wound up. Quite opinionated too, I would think. Whatever opinion he had, he'd hold it quite strongly, and have some sort of argument to put forward."

In the difficult business of trying to get a foothold in the film industry, Mike took Tom Baker along for support on a couple of job interviews. Tom recalled: "First of all, we got a meeting at the Beaconsfield studio. In those days it was just a small studio and I remember we did go for an interview there with a man who must have been a producer with an office there. Asking for jobs, asking for work. Nothing came of that." Later, they went to an interview with producer Irving Allen and nothing came of that either, although Tom thought it was possible that Allen remembered Mike when *The Long Ships*, on which he employed Mike as an assistant, came up.

The interview was most likely at Allen's Warwick Films office in Mayfair ("perhaps South Audley Street" said Tom) and was "certainly Mike's idea": "I think he simply rang them up from home in Berkshire. And what jobs did we want? What was on offer? Obviously anything. Certainly no pretensions to being used for writing. Assistant director's assistant perhaps. Tea boy would have been good. I think it was left with Irving Allen that if anything came up, he would bear us in mind. But how that metamorphosed into Mike going to Yugoslavia on *The Long Ships* I don't know." Tom believed this was "perhaps 1963, possibly 1962."

Mike's refusal of further education paid off when a door finally opened into the film industry proper. It seems it was the experience of working for Siegel that opened a door for him with Irving Allen. Mike later claimed it was "just on the strength of that" that he got a job as a film-set runner—the lowest rung on the technical ladder—with the Polish-American film producer Allen. Allen founded his production company Warwick Films with Cubby Broccoli in London in 1953 and was about to make the mini-epic Viking saga *The Long Ships* for Columbia Pictures, with director Jack Cardiff and stars Richard Widmark and Sidney Poitier. Benjamin Halligan writes that Mike turned up every day at Allen's offices until a props man fell ill and Allen gave him a chance to see what he could do.

Ian Ogilvy thought it was not too difficult to get runner jobs in pictures in the '60s and Irving Allen (with whom Mike became friendly enough to refer to him as Irv in his diary) probably found Mike very engaging: "It was easy to be friendly with Mike because he was clearly such a lunatic about movies and also so knowledgeable." Paul Vestey backed up Ian's view that Mike wouldn't have found it too hard to get runner jobs: "No, I think that's probably right. I remember he always seemed to be off on something or talking about going off on something or other. I think probably on the foreign films they got paid very little and they didn't have to have union tickets or anything and as he had a certain amount of income of his own anyway, it didn't

really matter to him whether he was very well rewarded or not."

The producer Mike Frankovich was then the London-based world head of production for Columbia Pictures, and Paul Vestey commented: "There was a chap called Mike Frankovich, Jr. There was a dad who was the boss but there was a young Frankovich and I got the feeling that he had something to do with getting Mike. The young Frankovich had a sort of very junior job and I think Mike palled up with him to try and help things along a bit." Mike Reeves refers to Mike Frankovich, Jr., in very unflattering terms in a later letter.

Once again, Nicky Henson has recounted a version that diverges from Mike's account of persuading Allen to employ him. Henson's story, most likely untrue, is fascinating as an example of the legend that has grown up around Mike Reeves in the years since he died. Nicky himself appreciated this: "It is very weird for a guy to have become a legend like that, and all these really weird stories!"

Director Jack Cardiff on the set of *The Long Ships* (BFI)

Nicky's story of how Mike got a job on *The Long Ships* is one of the great film industry anecdotes: "I always heard this story that he was hanging around these pubs in Wardour Street. He was sitting in a pub in Wardour Street and he heard some guy say to another, 'Oh, I'm supposed to be going on *The Long Ships* tomorrow, but I've got a better job, so I'm not going.' He wasn't going to go on the picture and he didn't know how to tell them. Mike said, 'I'll go for you!' He found out this guy's name, actually picked up his work permit and turned up *as* this bloke! He'd been working on it for three weeks before they realized it wasn't him and that's how he got his union ticket. The union was terribly embarrassed! Now, that's again possibly an apocryphal story." Certainly the union ACTT (Association of Cinematograph and Television Technicians, now absorbed into the union BECTU) had no records of these events and could only confirm Mike was a member.

The story has also been belied by Mike's future producer Paul Maslansky, who claimed Mike got the job through family connections. It was on *The Long Ships* that Mike first met Maslansky, who was a production manager on that picture and would go on to give Mike his first really important break. Maslansky told Bill Kelley: "I met Michael in Yugoslavia in 1963, when I was Columbia Pictures' production manager for *The Long Ships*. Michael's mother was a friend of the producer, Irving Allen, and Allen gave him a job as an assistant on the picture." He later commented to Pete Tombs: "Michael came along, and he didn't last very long. He was there probably three or four weeks of pre-production and, as I recall, maybe four or five weeks of production. He used to sleep in late. I would have to get to his room and bang on the door, but he took care of business. Then he took off! I was really pissed off when he took off. I didn't *understand* it. I thought everything was going great, and it was, but it was something about a girl. Michael couldn't have been older than about 17 or 18 then."

Mike described his work on *The Long Ships* in the Tigon biography: "I was a 'runner'—something like a call-boy in the theater. I ran messages; called artistes on to the set; fetched the

Michael Reeves (in the white hat) stands beside director Levin on the set of *Genghis Khan*
(BFI)

tea and things like that. It was lowly, but I was in pictures. All I had to do was to keep my eyes
and ears open." Tom Baker noticed for Pete Tombs: "He was pretty pleased to have got that
close. Well, he was right in there, right in actually *making movies.*"

Ian Ogilvy confirmed all this:

> "I know he then worked with Irving Allen on two pictures, I think it was at
> least two, as a sort of third or fourth assistant. I remember long stories about
> the two Allen pictures. He was also asked to stand there with flags while
> cavalry charges came at him (on *Genghis Khan*). It was extremely frighten-
> ing, too, a lot of the time. They were just big-budget, rubbish pictures, but
> I think they must have been quite fun to work on and fairly uncomfortable.
> But he was just learning, learning, learning all the time. That side of his life
> I only ever heard of from him."

It is fascinating how much importance Ian Ogilvy attributed to Mike's experience on the
Allen pictures, despite Mike's devotion to the cinema of Don Siegel: "I think the great influence
on Mike's approach to cinema was not Don Siegel but Irving Allen. I think he learnt from the
sense of spectacle on the Allen epics. We didn't make an epic in *Witchfinder* because we didn't
have the budget, but there is a sense of spectacle." Mike was also roused by the sense of spectacle
in John Sturges' *The Magnificent Seven*, which Paul Ferris said Mike saw "300 times."

Actor Peter Fraser was then married to a lady called Pam, who worked on *The Long Ships*.
He recalled:

> "I spent some time in Belgrade, where it was shot, and we became good
> friends until Mike's unfortunate death. I was on the set every day. Mike was
> a fourth assistant. Derek Cracknell was first assistant. Mike was very gentle.
> I never saw him lose his head. He was always tidy, wore suits, no suede
> jackets, not flashy, a nice middle-class boy. He smoked, I don't remember
> him drinking at all.

"Mike was a young man then, and his knowledge of movies and movie-makers was amazing, but even more astounding was that he could re-tell the shots and framing in many movies—something I'd never come across before, or since. I don't just mean the obvious ones like Hitchcock's *Psycho* where he mixes from the drain into a close-up of Janet Leigh's eye and pulls back and *pans* and ends the scene on the handbag with the money, which caused her death. Or Welles' long opening shot in *Touch of Evil.*

"The most important thing about Mike was his knowledge of the business; I was *stunned* when he could tell me the framing, the camera angles, the close-ups, the position of the camera...this was before video and freeze-frame. At home he would put up his 16-mm projector. He often showed Don Siegel's *Hell is for Heroes.* I saw it there, but obviously Mike would watch and watch and watch. Mike thought Don Siegel was the best director around."

Peter recalled that living conditions were quite comfortable: "Mike stayed at the Metropol Hotel; everybody was bundled into it. It only cost £40 a week, it was a backward country economically. It was the best hotel in Belgrade. A sextet played music in the evening as you ate. I remember oysters."

Mike left *The Long Ships* before it was finished, possibly because he met and fell in love with the girl who would eventually live with him, Annabelle Webb. Paul Vestey said: "I kept going to South America for months on end in those days and I think she'd appeared during one of my absences." Tom Baker characterized her: "Annabelle fitted into the archetype of the 'dolly bird.' Annabelle was absolutely in that mold. She was very slim, she wasn't very tall, she had a good figure, she had some money, she could wear all of these clothes, her skirts could get shorter and shorter, and she was a girl about town. She fitted the fashion of the moment very much." It is clear from correspondence that Mike faced competition for her affections and it took him a while to make progress.

Meanwhile, Mike certainly used his money to gad about a bit. As Ian Ogilvy explained: "He used to jump about. He had the money to leap about. He would go off somewhere, frequently. He'd go off and have a holiday somewhere. Or go off and see something. A lot of it would have been setting up pictures or going to see people."

As Bungie Reeves had already provided a comfortable lifestyle, the fortune Mike inherited did not dramatically change his way of life, except for some initial excitement, recalled Virginia Scholte: "I think he did go a bit wild, I must admit, and bought expensive cars and things like that, which you would, wouldn't you? I think Betty was always worried about that, that it would make him change. But they lived very comfortably, and if they went to London for a few days, they used to go and stay at the Savoy. They'd take a suite at the Savoy! And if you went to see them there, he'd always pay the taxi as you got into it. So to me, at the time, it all meant opulence." Cherida and Zara Reeves remembered going for spins with Mike in his Lotus.

If Betty went to the Savoy when coming up to London with Mike, it would not be her usual style. Diane Ogilvy observed that when she was on her own, Betty would always stay at the less ostentatious Cadogan Hotel, where a single lady would feel more comfortable. As for Mike, Paul Vestey agreed that Mike indulged "in a normal sort of way" in expensive cars: "He had a fairly expensive career with his cars. He had an E-type Jaguar and he kept running into buses. I don't think he ever did anybody any harm, fortunately, but he certainly hit at least two buses! I think in the end they got fed up with him and he lost his license." Paul also commented that Betty did not often visit him in the various flats he had: "I don't think she came to London that much. I think she was a proper country lady. I think she only really came up because she was worried about him."

It is interesting that Vincent Price was to think Mike's enormous financial independence had affected his attitude toward people. He confirmed that he was aware that Mike was wealthy: "Yes, and I suspected that may have been the reason for his impersonal approach to people."

Vincent could establish little personal rapport with Mike, although some of that "impersonal approach" simply reflects Mike's overriding obsession with movies. Virginia Scholte maintained that view. In her opinion, Mike had inherited his mother's humor and vitality but was "so intense about films" that he "wasn't interested in you." She thought he was "egocentric" and "neurotic" in this obsession: "an intense, dedicated young man."

She did not mean egocentric in the selfish sense. On the contrary, she testified to the generosity he inherited from his mother:

> "I do seem to remember that he was very generous. He had one friend who was always on his uppers and Mike would come to his rescue. I think he was very generous, and rather concerned about the people who didn't have as much as he did. I think that was a sort of moral worry to him, in a way. He helped his friends out and he'd buy them things. Aunt Betty did that. She did that to all sorts of people. She was always buying people houses and paying for their holidays. They had a lot of money and, as lots of people with a lot of money aren't generous, they were really generous. I think Aunt Betty had been quite badly off in her youth. I don't think her parents were really well-off like she was and she had known what it was like to be a bit short of money, so when she got it, she loved handing it out and she did. To everybody. And to societies and children and all that sort of thing. So Mike obviously had all that and Bungie did too. They were both very generous."

Peter Fraser remembered an occasion later when Mike took 6 to 10 people to "some very nice restaurant in Wardour Street and Mike just paid for everyone."

Mike's cousin Sarah had been thrown out of school for smoking dope, and there was a furor with her family. She rang Mike, who was then living in a flat in Scarsdale Villas, and he said, "Don't be silly, come stay with me." So Sarah went and lived there for the whole of the Easter holidays with Mike and observed his early courtship of Annabelle: "He loved her so much." Annabelle was going out with someone Mike knew at the time, also called Mike, and Mike told Sarah of his feelings for Annabelle, belying Ian Ogilvy's observation that Mike was extremely private in anything to do with personal feelings, though one can put this down to his long closeness to Sarah.

Sarah recalled living with Mike:

> "We sat up playing poker and eating smoked salmon. Mike never ate anything else but smoked salmon, followed by grilled steak. He also insisted on Coca-Cola where I insisted on wine. When we went to the supermarket, he went one way, I went another. We went racing, to Brands Hatch every weekend. Mike was not so much keen on racing itself but he was of a delicate, nervous disposition, highly strung, and he found racing a tremendous release from the nervous tension of waiting for phone calls from film people.
>
> "He once took me racing in his Lotus Elan, which was as low to the tarmac as you could get. We were terribly late for a race as the traffic was ghastly. Paul Vestey was racing. Mike was furious to be late. There were flames pouring out from underneath the Lotus. The car had completely overheated. I was a young cousin, thrilled to be going racing, and didn't say anything. When Mike saw the flames, he said, 'My God, why didn't you say?' and pulled into a cafe to go to a tap for water for the car. When we got to the track, the race had started and he was furious. But he did teach me to drive. When he later lost his license for speeding in Cromwell Road, he said, 'I don't mind taking taxis, but I really mind not being able to burn it up.' He was very highly strung.

"Films were all he ever talked about. He said to me he was absolutely fascinated by the effect that cinema could have on a person sitting on a chair staring at a screen. One day he told me that in the States, they had invented this extraordinary three-dimensional combination of sound and vision that you couldn't look at in an abstract way. You would experience whatever was on the screen. He said it would be banned. We joked that it would give people heart attacks, even orgasms...there were all these things you could put people through. Then it *was* banned, so he was right. He talked about scaring people right into a horror film so they couldn't walk out at the end without talking about it."

Mike, of course, achieved precisely this effect with *Witchfinder General*.

During the time that Mike shared a flat in Rutland Gate with Paul Vestey, he first got the idea to form his own production company, Leith Productions Limited. He used the family solicitors at Lee Pemberton in Pont Street to have it incorporated in Jersey and act as company directors. It was only ever used to produce *Revenge of the Blood Beast* but allowed him to use impressive headed paper when writing to potential backers, though Ian Ogilvy said he used it all the time (and he did when writing to the Ogilvys with chit-chat). Paul Vestey commented: "I remember him talking about it in Rutland Gate days, so it was quite early. That was 1963 or 1964. I think at that stage it was just to think of a nice name. Leith was his middle name. I don't remember him using it. I don't know whether he wanted to make the whole thing sound more formal or more convincing."

Tom Baker, indeed, thought Mike might well have become his own producer after *Witchfinder General*: "He had a company, Leith Productions. He started that when we were children. He would call his little films Leith Productions, but it became a real company. Mike was rich enough, he was at ease in that world with people who had money and energy and he was able to pick up the phone and phone anyone in the world by and large and whatever it would take, so I imagine he might well have."

According to Tigon's brief biography of Mike, and the pressbook of *The Sorcerers*, there followed assignments as an assistant director on television commercials and television films, but Ian Ogilvy was dubious: "I don't think he did. After RADA, I really lost touch with him for a few years. I suppose he might have done before I re-met him. I don't know anything about television commercials. I never heard him mention them and, if I did, I've forgotten. I never heard him talk about television commercials or television films." Nor did Mike's friend Philip Waddilove, who thought this was probably publicist's hype.

Next came a very fruitful trip to Italy. Mike already knew Italy from holidays he had had there with Betty and his cousins. That Mike's career should begin not in the British film industry but in Italy is one of the interesting things about his career, and quite fitting in that his work would be quite un-British in many ways, owing more to a European conception of cinema, what Tom Baker called "industrial cinema" but imbued with a psychological element. The author sees Mike's work sitting more comfortably with the sophisticated artistic sensibility of European genre directors like Mario Bava (*Black Sunday*) and Riccardo Freda (*The Giants of Thessaly*) than more simplistic British horror directors like Terence Fisher and Freddie Francis.

Chapter Three: Italy

He had this ability to stick with the budget and "make do," and his "make doing" is possibly what makes his films so interesting; his "how to get over a bad situation."—Ian Ogilvy, star of Reeves' films

Paul Maslansky was about to produce his first film in Rome. Some writers have indicated that Maslansky invited Mike to Rome to do some rewriting, but Maslansky has told it differently. Once again, as with Mike's barging in on Don Siegel, his opportunity arose from bravado. He took Annabelle to Rome with him and sought out Maslansky, whom Diane Ogilvy remembered Mike always called Masloo because it was easier to say than Maslansky. Maslansky has stated to Bill Kelley: "He turned up in Rome with his girlfriend, when I was producing *Castle of the Living Dead*, and asked for a job. I hired him as an assistant director. I remember working with Michael as if it were yesterday. He was enormously talented. He directed all of the coach scenes on the way to the castle, a lot of the fights and the opening of the picture, with the hanging."

Castle of the Living Dead was written and directed by Warren Kiefer and has gone down in history as Donald Sutherland's first film. The film starred Christopher Lee and was an Italian-French co-production. It is intriguing that Mike's first experience of helping to direct a feature already put him at an established level of experience in the industry. The atmospheric cinematography was by Aldo Tonti, who had shot Fellini's *Nights of Cabiria*. (Interestingly, Diane Ogilvy was to say that Mike's only knowledge of Italian was for "Put the camera here!")

Christopher Lee was by now a well-established star. Future superstar Donald Sutherland played three parts, as a sergeant, as an old man and as a witch, and very good he was as a witch, although he later could not remember much about his involvement in the film, kindly writing to the author: "I am truly sorry, but it is a very long time ago, and I really don't think I can be of any assistance to you. But I do wish you well with your project." Philippe Leroy found greater fame as the husband in Jean-Luc Godard's *Une Femme Mariée*.

Donald Sutherland named his son "Kiefer" in grateful acknowledgment for his first big-screen appearance (he had done small roles on television in shows like *The Sentimental Agent*). Kiefer Sutherland went on to become a successful Hollywood actor. Warren Kiefer's credit for the film was somewhat diluted when it was credited to "Herbert Wise (Luciano Ricci)" for quota purposes, to make the film's director appear to be an Italian operating under a pseudonym. "Herbert Wise" had no connection to the Herbert Wise who later directed Ian Ogilvy in the BBC TV serial *I, Claudius*.

David Pirie has cleared up some of the confusion about Reeves' contribution:

> "Most writers have recorded that Reeves took over the whole production for about nine days because Kiefer fell ill, but Maslansky has informed me that this is quite untrue. Reeves remained on the second unit for the entire picture, but the work he was doing with a scratch crew turned out so much better than Kiefer's that his contribution was enlarged and he was allowed to make some additions to the script including the introduction of a rather Bergmanesque dwarf. None of the footage involving Christopher Lee was shot by Reeves."

Christopher Lee and Mike did not hit it off. Mike did not particularly like Lee, who was later privately disparaging of Mike, but he has generously been quoted as saying: "Michael Reeves was the first, second and third assistant director. He had incredible enthusiasm and imagination, loved movies, knew all about them and was very eager and full of energy. Michael was always scurrying about, a bundle of activity." On another occasion, he said to author Jonathan Rigby (*Christopher Lee: The Authorised Screen History*): "Reeves did everybody's job—he was producer, director, first, second and third assistants—or so it seemed. Full of enthusiasm, bright as a button, obviously totally dedicated to film—I liked him very much."

The film was shot at Odescalchi Castle with exteriors at Bomarzo Park, near Viterbo. Mike was pressed into service as an actor, supplying his hand doubling for Christopher Lee's hand, and appearing as a dashing mustachioed officer held in permanent suspension in a kind of waxwork museum of corpses. A major mishap occurred when Maslansky lost the film's entire soundtrack. Maslansky hired actor/director Mel Welles, who had been in Corman pictures and was a well-known "film doctor," to re-

Donald Sutherland holds the coffin in *Castle of the Living Dead,* **which was his first film. (BFI)**

voice the film. Christopher Lee redubbed his entire part. Mel has said: "I didn't meet Mike on *Castle* as the re-voicing took place well after he was off the pic and had returned to England."

Ironically, *Castle of the Living Dead* was not released in Britain until several months after Mike died and when reviewed by David Austen, who had championed all of the films Mike had directed, in *Films and Filming* magazine for July 1969, it got a thumbs down: "It rarely rises above the well-worn European formula of 'a stormy night at the evil Count's castle'...it can only be recommended as a curio-collectors item." The *Monthly Film Bulletin* found it "a very dull affair...conventional and visually unimaginative," which is about right.

Ian Ogilvy commented:

> "I must have seen it about the time he made the first movie *Revenge of the Blood Beast* and then it's disappeared forever. It's black and white. Donald Sutherland is in it playing a witch. It makes *Revenge of the Blood Beast* look really good. It is a real stinker. I don't even remember what it's about. Just awful. I've no idea which sections Mike directed. I think we ran it once and Mike laughed a lot and said, 'Isn't this terrible? Oh, I did that bit.' Literally static stuff, second-reel second-unit stuff, like shots of someone walking through a wall, an extra doing something. It would have been very minimal. There was a dwarf. I only saw it once."

Yet critic Robin Wood accorded it especial importance in his insightful analysis of Mike's oeuvre in *Movie* magazine: "The film...becomes extremely exciting: It might have been a minor masterpiece...I must confess to a special affection, within Reeves' work, for these later scenes of *Castle of the Living Dead*: the obsession with evil and violence that characterizes the subsequent films is here more muted and balanced, reminding us that there can be advantages, for an immature genius, in working from other people's material." These qualities led to Mike's first feature as full director (in addition to the fact that he could provide the funding!).

Robin Wood's suppositions about Mike's work on *Castle* seem to be wide of the mark, according to the testimony of the film's assistant director. The U.S. prints credit "Fritz Muller, Michael Reeves" as assistant directors. "Fritz Muller" was actually the future producer Frederick Muller, whose credits include *Don't Look Now,* which Mike Reeves once hoped to direct, and the original version of *The Bourne Identity* starring Richard Chamberlain. Muller used "Fritz" as his first name while his father, also "Frederick," was alive. Mike said in a letter that the film fell two days behind schedule. Muller shrugged this off. He could not agree with Christopher Lee's memories of Mike's contribution:

> "I don't think Christopher Lee's memory of the film is very accurate but I do remember the film very well, although it was a very long time ago. I was on the set for the entire shoot. The film cost very little, but even so, I believe it nearly bankrupted Maslansky. It may be true that the film fell two days behind schedule, as Michael said, but he should also have noted that it caught up. *Castle* cost so little that, what with continual reruns of the film, I would not be surprised if it actually made money, for somebody.
>
> "I was the first assistant director on the main unti and I had a second assistant, but I don't remember Michael Reeves being on the main unit. He was at a loose end and was just hanging around watching the shoot. I think he was a friend of Paul Maslansky's. I vaguely recall he did work as an extra on the set.
>
> "As far as I recall, Michael Reeves wasn't really assisting on set at all, unless he did some minor shots with a second unit after we finished shooting, which is possible. Sometimes in the editing you realize you need a shot or two for the sake of continuity, for example, of the coach driving along the road. It would only have been odds and ends. There was no second unit filming when I was there. The film was shot too quickly and cheaply to have a second unit."

Muller was sure that it is not true that Mike invented the character of the dwarf "Neep." "I don't think that is true at all. The script was all written by Warren Kiefer. I was at Warren Kiefer's house when we asked Donald Sutherland to be in the film. During the shooting, Sutherland and Kiefer became very close, which is why Donald named his son 'Kiefer'."

On such a low budget, the shoot was necessarily arduous. "We did extremely long hours. I did not socialize with Michael Reeves, if only because there was no time. There was only time to have dinner and go to bed. I remember him only vaguely because, as far as I could see, he was just hanging around."

Muller thought the credit given to Mike on the U.S. prints probably resulted from Paul Maslansky doing Mike a favor because they were pals and he needed to establish some experience. Muller observed Reeves and Lee were definitely friendly and remained so throughout the shoot. The coolness that seems to have developed between them by the time of *The Oblong Box* may have occurred as a result of various abortive projects along the way.

Today Muller is a little dismissive of *Castle*: "It's not really a very good movie. It was very quick and very cheap, though it had lovely locations at Bomarzo and at Bracciano in the Odescalchi Castle. It had a marvelous crew, including one of the greatest of all Italian cinematographers, Aldo Tonti, and camera operator Luigi Kuiviller, now one of the most important Italian directors of photography."

Paul Vestey saw Mike and Annabelle get increasingly serious about each other during 1964: "They nearly got married at one stage. We were living in Pont Street—yet another flat—and it was all a proper engagement and everything." Zara Reeves even remembered she was going to be measured for a bridesmaid's dress, and then suddenly it was all off. Mike got cold feet just days before the wedding and called it off, which is of course a terrible thing to do to a girl.

Mike found a permanent home by the end of 1964, but it was a small house rather than a flat as originally planned. It was bought by the trust and was ideally situated at 23 Yeoman's Row, a smart, modern cul-de-sac near Harrods in Knightsbridge. Mike's cousin Cherida had already bought number 17. Betty rang her and asked if Mike could come and live with her. She was not keen on having to entertain Mike's film friends and felt it was not done for them to share the

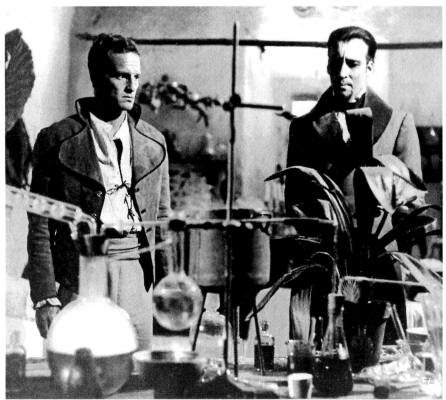

Philippe Leroy and Christopher Lee in *Castle of the Living Dead* **(BFI)**

house, so Mike bought the nearest one for sale. Whether or not this points up a certain fear of going it alone in London is impossible to say. In any case, Annabelle Webb soon moved in with Michael, so he was not alone for long. Mike and his mother still stayed in touch often, but began to lead more separate lives. Virginia Scholte commented: "I think he was a constant worry to her. He used to ring her up in the middle of the night and talk to her for hours and hours. She never knew where he was and, you know, being the only one, she worried about him all the time."

Paul Vestey eventually took up Mike's offer of a room and lived there until he bought a house at the end of 1965. He explained: "After I bought my house, I left Yeoman's Row and then I didn't see so much of Mike. I lived at Yeoman's Row for a year or so. I think Tom Baker lived there. I know Mike was certainly keen to have Tom there. I think he probably liked having someone he could bounce ideas off." Tom commented: "Paul lived just across the road. Paul and Mike saw each other a lot. They had the same sort of amount of money, so they could eat out together easily and he even went to watch Paul race a couple of times. He was trying to race Jaguars at the time, or a Lotus, and I think perhaps he didn't have a job."

Tom was not in the same financial league and felt a little discomfited in the atmosphere of affluence at Yeoman's Row. He left Dublin in 1966:

> "I used to go and stay there. He had a spare bedroom in Yeoman's Row and Jock Russell (a friend) lived there with him. If I went to stay, I would sleep on a camp bed in the study. I would just stay there short periods, odd holidays, or when I was coming up to London to get the train or plane back to Dublin. I was out of my depth financially, because I am not a financially flamboyant person and to some people, like Paul and Ball-Greene, I must

have been slightly 'the wretched Tom' sort of hanging around. 'Who's going to pay for Tom when we go to the movies?' Or 'Who's buying the drinks today?' I was always aware of that. We used to play poker and I used to think, 'How are we going to hold our own here?' Because Mike and Paul sat down to play poker. There seemed to be some tacit agreement that we would not make the stakes too high, not so I could stay, but just generally. I must have been a freeloader in a sense. You know, the gin and tonics came on. I wasn't going to go out to the off license and buy them, because I didn't have any money, but at the same time if somebody said, 'Do you want a drink?' I'd probably say, 'Yeah.' I was always aware of that tension there. Everyone else had a lot of money. Annabelle didn't, but certainly the men did. There was a group of men who were pretty wealthy."

Mike now, crucially, also had somewhere to screen movies, something he had been unable to do in the flats he'd shared with Paul Vestey. Tom commented: "We would go to movies, talk about movies, he would hire probably Don Siegel's *The Killers*, and we'd have to sit and watch that. I've seen that movie so many times it's just impossible."

Tom's aspiring filmmaker friend, Iain Sinclair, was a sometime visitor to Yeoman's Row: "The house was perfect for a serious filmmaker. It was as anonymous as a hotel room: a couple of Hopper prints, model cars on the mantelpiece, an active telephone...Mike was generous enough to allow me to project the rushes of the latest and last of the 16-mm films in his house. When he bothered to watch, he kept his comments to himself...undergraduate indulgence. There had been a more personal script...I'd shown the first quick draft to Mike Reeves...There probably wasn't enough pace, enough structured violence for Mike." Most writers, obviously drawing on Tigon's brief biography, have stated that Mike worked as a runner on *The Long Ships* and *Genghis Khan* and then went to Italy to work on *Castle*. However, two fascinating letters Mike wrote to Paul Vestey show this to be incorrect and, surprisingly, his work on *Genghis Khan* came after his work on *Castle*.

The first letter, well typed by Mike himself but unsigned, is dated May 1, 1964, and bears the address "c/o Paul Maslansky, Via Margutta 54, Interno 3, Rome, Italy." The fascinating things about the letter are Mike's then obsession with cars, the detail about *Castle*, the good humor throughout, and the moving final lines; when he typed these, he had no way of knowing, of course, that he would be a full-fledged movie director only a year later with *Revenge of the Blood Beast*. The full text is reproduced below, by kind permission of Paul Vestey.

Dear Paul,

Many thanks for your letter of some weeks ago. I did write you before this but lost the letter in the usual two-week interim between composition and posting.

I arrived in Rome about a fortnight ago to do this picture, now enticingly called Castle of the Living Dead. *In point of fact, it is not half as bad as it sounds; really quite fun as horror pictures go—in fact it is in effect a send-up of the whole genre. However, having now shot on it for only five days, we are already two days behind schedule! It looks as though I shall be here for some time...which I don't mind all that much as I am astonishingly enough getting quite fond of Rome. It is beautifully warm, without excessive heat, and as far as motor-car spotting goes it's bloody marvellous. The other night I saw a splendid cop-wagon; a 2+2 Ferrari, no less. The laws inside must have thought I was entirely loco, standing on a street corner gazing at them with my mouth open.*

I enclose a letter I got from our Len today. I thought it might amuse you. The Seven in question is owned by Ronnie, and he and Leonard are (were?) going to race it this season as a motorized ad. for Len Street Engineering Ltd. Before I left I drove it in London for a couple of days, and gosh almighty, is that car fun! Short of the fact that it boiled more or less continually at every traffic light, I have never enjoyed driving anything as much. It's 1340 with the Cosworth motor, and it goes. We had the mudguards off, which made it just like driving a Formula car. Great fun. By the way, by the time you get back to our fair isle in a jewell-ed sea (or whatever) I may be minus a license—I nearly killed a cop on a zebra crossing at about 80 in a 30-limit. Whoopee.

The Elan, now residing at Len's, was going well when I left. I took it, and the B-G took the Trev, down to Brands one Saturday, and we did laps in 65.1 and 67.4 respectively, which was reasonably pleasing. Even young Rick was not as unenthusiastic as usual, I think. Noncommittally impressed one might say. Anyway, I took about six inches of tread off and learned how to get round Druids in a hurry, though that self-education may have looked a bit tonsorial to some. And I did not spin at Paddock, which is a major break-through. Nor did Miguel, come to that, but then he is not quite as disaster-prone as me on that lil old turn.

Genghis Khan has been put back till August, so I shall be out of work again for about six weeks when I get back: but that will give me time to pursue the subject of Annabelle at my leisure. The situation looked not so discouraging when I exited a fortnight ago. Mike and she were cooling down, so unless there is some blue-eyed Maserati-sporting twerp in the offing by now, I could just get to the flag with any luck. If you see what I mean. As a matter of interest, and talking of girls, I believe we have Sammy Eggar in Genghis. Fun. Also bird-wise, I had a letter from La Belle Warman yesterday saying she had heard from you and that the slaughterhouse is not as unpleasant as any reasonable being might expect it to be. Can this be true??

I had a mention in the Daily American here a few days ago, under the heading of Via Venotopics...describing a film party I attended. It went through a list of names including Christopher Lee and Orson Welles and finished the list with "...and actor Michael Reeves." Oh well, such is fame. Hounded by the international press—I can't see myself having a quiet moment. If you see a blurred picture of your little friend kicking the camera of some luckless member of the paparazzi, you will now know what is happening...In actual fact, I am in this picture, or my hand is. Doubling for Chris Lee!

After Genghis finishes, whenever that may be, I intend to buy a flat in Kensington or Chelsea or somewhere. I really cannot stand another Golding type situation. (You, by the way, were not popular in that dept. Not because of your flit without supervising the repairs, or because the cheque you left only left about £20 over post-rent for them; but because you didn't say a nice good-bye to her. Most odd, that woman.) Anyway, I intend to pay around £10-12,000 for my place, for which I should get something pretty reasonable, and furnish it myself out of the multitude of meubles that Mother has scattered in various warehouses throughout the land. If you would like to have a room, all of your very own, in said castle, let me know. I figure a rent of about seven or eight pounds a week or less, perhaps, depending on how rich I feel. I want to get a place with at least two bedrooms, a good bathroom, a separate crap-house, a decent kitchen and a vast living room; and a garage if I can find a flat with one. I also intend to install double-beds in case any contingency should arise where they might add to the comfort and convenience of life!

I must go now and give the actors their calls for tomorrow morning. We are starting shooting at 6:30, which means de-slumbering at 5:30. If I ever do become a director, I just hope it will be worth all the effort. I think it will, though.

Don't get trampled in a stampede or anything,

Sorry, no pen to sign with.

Mike

Paul Vestey was in Fray Bentos, which Tom Baker recalled "freaked him out": "He went to Argentina and they put him in the slaughterhouse, and five minutes in the slaughterhouse he said, 'Christ, I'm not staying here,' and he got back on the boat or plane to England." The Leonard referred to in the letter was a mutual acquaintance, as Paul Vestey explained: "That was Len Street, who had the garage which kept your Lotus going, if you had a Lotus, and I think we both had Lotuses at that time." Paul agreed that, as he wasn't very interested in films himself, he mainly talked to Mike about cars: "He was quite keen, actually. Funnily enough. Quite keen for

On location with *Genghis Khan* (BFI)

a time. I don't think he'd started having his accidents at that stage, so I think he thought it was all pretty good stuff." The accidents apparently did affect Mike's enthusiasm, according to Paul: "I think so, because I remember in the end he had an old Rover which Tom Baker used to drive him around in, which was when he couldn't drive. It was a granny-type Rover."

The next letter is dated June 21, 1964 and contains interesting detail on the nature of his work on *Genghis Khan* (working title *The Golden Horde*). The address is "Hotel Metropol, Beograd, Yugoslavia" and one of the most interesting personal notes concerns his apparent abandonment at that point of the courtship of Annabelle. Once again, when he wrote these words, he had no way of knowing she would soon settle down with him for most of what remained of his life.

Dear Paul,

As you will probably have heard by now, I'm back in the Federal People's Republic, on a little £m6 job called The Golden Horde. *In fact, I was only back in England a couple of weeks after the Rome picture before I came out here, where I shall remain till September or October. We then go to Berlin for studio work. So I won't be back in London till around December, a fact which I am sure distresses everyone enormously. Anyway, I'm afraid this somewhat sudden change of plan pushed back the flat plan for a while. There was nothing I could do really—2 weeks is not really long enough to buy & furnish a large apartment. However, when I do eventually get back we'll see what we can do.*

The Carol rumpus had died down a bit when I left. But in any case, it's nobody's fault—certainly not yours. If anyone is to blame I suppose I am—shit—but not to worry, it'll all blow over. I hope.

I succeeded in mating the Elan with a rather solid bank the other day. A combination of loose gravel, Jinx Ward filming me, and misguided enthusiasm. Anyway, being in a hurry to get out here, I sold it damaged & bought a Cooper 'S,' which I brought out to Belgrade. The Greene came down to Zagreb as navigator (a job at which he hardly surpasses Henry Liddon!). But he's a nice bloke to have along. The trip was pretty uneventful, save for a moment when I got done by a Boche cop for overtaking him & a "NO PASSING" sign all at the same moment. Also, Ball-Greene was stung by a wasp in the middle of a tight left-hander on the Potschenn. I put him on a plane at Zagreb to seek first-aid in London, then came on down to Belgrade over 250 miles of what the Yugs. proudly call an Autobahn: an interminable stretch of potholes joined by crumbling concrete—and one lane only! However, the Cooper held together, though you could have cremated Nehru on the radiator after a couple of hundred kilometers. If that car survives 5 months in this sweet land, I'll personally write to BMC & say they can use my name to advertise on the backs of buses. The roads here are of such a standard, that when I arrived I had a vast boil on my butt*. (Footnote: *from bouncing up & down!) I'm getting a penicillin jab for it this evening, thank god!

I, too, intend to get an "E" when I return. I figure by December, they'll be going for around £900—and I'll be 21. I'm going to have it the fixed head coupe, in dark blue, and just use it on the roads. Then I can keep the Cooper for London or racing, or going off on locations.

I believe your father has written you about some cash he owed me, & for which both I & me solicitors had to ask several times over a period of three months. It was John's air fare to Stuttgart plus some rent for Scarsdale Villas that Mark- by Stewarts continued to pay into your bank after we had exited. Father was not very polite about it—slammed the phone down and so on. Is he being silly again, or have I really been "cheating" him out of £40? I'd be glad of comment on this one.

Mike Reeves (far left) behind Françoise Dorleac listens to the director on the set of *Genghis Khan*. (BFI)

Both Miguel and I have finally packed in the Annabelle stakes, much to everyone's relief. Mine included, to be honest. It was all really get- ting a bit turgid. She is now hooked up with some bloke who whisks her off to Paris at w/ends. Not in our league at all, I'm afraid.

You know, it is now the Monday after Le Mans, & I still can't find out who won the thing. Come to the Y.P.R. You'd love it.

Guess who else we have on this picture. Frankovich. And he's my boss, fuck his mother- sucking arse. This could mean war, to paraphrase Warner Bros.' rabbit. The only good thing about it is that he is so bloody incompetent that I will shine in comparison. Sorry, you don't like film politics, though. This picture, though, could be pretty good. In the cast we've got James Mason, Stephen Boyd, Omar Sharif, Yvonne Mitchell and possibly Jane Fonda, Sammy Eggar or Claire Bloom. And even the script is not too bad. We have some vast battle scenes, for which we are using a jet-powered chopper, and the company has bought (bought) six Mercs, an Impala, a Chrysler Imperial and eight of those big Land-Rover affairs. But even so, some of the locations are such that we get to them by mule. That, I suppose, indicates more boils on the butt. The money's good though!

Thanks, but I won't buy that Stuttgart station-wagon of yours. It would bore me rigid. By the way, how in hell did Jock do Stuttgart-Ostend in 7 hours? Coming the other way it took us about 3 days. But then, we never got started till about noon each day, & then had to drive with Economy-size hangovers. You will be relieved to hear that I have returned to normal and stagger through my days in a welter of alcoholic poisoning & quaking headaches. Such is the customary physical state of film technicians loaded into darkest Serbo-Croatia. But I'm still better off than you. At least I like the work. How is the bloodbath? I hear Fray Bentos is mixed up with this typhoid bit, via the dear old Food Ministry & their 30-year-old cans. I'll bet Father's happy.

Must now go down the canteen & top up. See you—
Mike
Sorry, I'm a bit pissed.

Mike Frankovich Jr., so rudely referred to in this letter, told the author: "I seem to remem- ber that he was hired as the third assistant director and I believe I had dinner once or twice with him in Belgrade but remember not much more, except his love for his Mini-Cooper in which he motored down to Yugoslavia." "Carol" was a casual friend of Mike's, who lived in Bywater Street, Chelsea and loved to listen to Joan Baez.

IL LAGO
DI SATANA

EASTMANCOLOR - SCOPE DELLA TECNOSTAMPA

BARBARA STEEL - JOHN KARLSEN

IAN OGILVY - MEL WELLES - JAY RILEY

Regia: MICHAEL REEVES

UNA LEITH PRODUCTION, realizzata da P.M. MASLANSKI

After *Genghis Khan,* it was probably inevitable that Mike would return to Italy, which was experiencing a phenomenal boom in film production. Expatriate actor Brett Halsey, then working in Rome, has commented in *European Trash Cinema*: "The time—the '60s—it was a real historical time. I remember one year we did like 450 films in Italy, and Hollywood was around 120, something like that. So when you say there were a lot of English and American actors there, people went because of the work."

At the age of 21, Mike clearly decided he was ready to go for broke. He had the experience of the amateur films, a brief stint in Hollywood, the Yugoslav epics and recognition from Paul Maslansky on his first production. He also had the advantage of having access to some of his money now. Jack Broom was a trustee of Mike's trust (and in that role later interviewed Raquel Welch, in connection with *The Sorcerers*). Jack's job was to administer Mike's finances. When he got to 21, Mike sacked all his trustees, except his Aunt Joan. He told Cherida Reeves: "She's marvelous, she'll listen to you, you can tell her anything you like." Mike took advice in this from his solicitor, Gerald Whately of C.R. Whately of Pont Street. This meant that he could free up some funds for Leith Productions Limited. Benjamin Halligan argues that some urgency came about when Mike had a health scare, a shadow on the lung, which turned out to be benign.

It was time to get started as a full-blown professional movie director. All he had to do was bring the money and Paul Maslansky together with an idea. Maslansky has recalled for Pete Tombs: "Michael reappeared in 1964. I get a phone call from him. He said, 'Look, I've got a script. I wanna make a horror picture. I've got £15,000 and I'd like you to produce it and I'm coming to Rome.' And he comes to Rome and we made the picture." This was *La Sorella di Satana* (literally "Satan's Sister"), released as *The Revenge of the Blood Beast* in the U.K. and as *The She Beast* in the U.S. The U.K. title dropped the definite article on the poster and is generally known as simply *Revenge of the Blood Beast.*

Debate raged for some years as to whether Reeves put any of his own money into the film, for it was credited as a Leith production. David Pirie wrote: "Reeves himself was so desperate to direct that he was prepared to put up a large amount of his own money to finance the film." Nicky Henson confirmed this: "He only ever actually used the money once to finance a picture. That was *Revenge of the Blood Beast.*" On the other hand, Paul Ferris totally refuted this: "No, he didn't. He didn't. That was the amazing thing. Absolutely amazing. He never spent any of the money that he inherited on anything. He told me that and I know it's true."

Ian Ogilvy tended to side with Paul's view but was less dogmatic that Mike did not put any of his own money into *Revenge*:

"That I honestly don't know. I have always assumed, because Michael always said, that he never put a penny of his own money into films. Ever. Because he said, 'That's too easy. Anybody can do that. If you've got as much money as I have, anybody can go out and make movies. I don't want that. I want people to think I can make movies and therefore offer me things to do. I *can* buy my way into movies.' Which was true, he could. But he always claimed he never did, so I don't know about that. He wouldn't invest the money in movies. That was too easy. I have great respect for a film-maker like Mike who could have bought his way into movies, but he didn't. He became a runner and an assistant and learnt his craft. He could easily have raised £20,000 and made a movie but he didn't. He wanted people to want him for what he could do. Anyway, the trust literally did not allow him to invest in films. Of course, although he claimed he never had and never would put any of his money into a picture, it did mean that, unlike a lot of film directors, people struggling to make pictures, he was able to live in between times. He never had to do anything else, that's the point. So, in a sense, he was lucky."

Ian's wife Diane did not think Mike had put money into *Revenge* either:

"No, he didn't. I would have said that that was absolute rubbish until this morning reading through these things (surviving correspondence) and there is some reference in there to somewhere where Mike said, 'and I wouldn't have to put any of my own money into it,' which makes me think just slightly that it might be right that he did. Certainly from when I knew him, which was *Blood Beast* onwards or before *Blood Beast*, he never put a penny into it. He wouldn't. I mean, he would bend a schedule to be able to get a piece of equipment that he wanted but he wouldn't put his own money into it."

It appears that Mike's script was little more than an idea and Maslansky commissioned a script from Amos Powell, American scriptwriter (Corman's *Tower of London* starring Vincent Price). Mel Welles acted in the film and has stated:

"The original script was written by Amos Powell, then rewritten by Chuck Griffith. Maslansky had the project from inception and commissioned both. Hired this young, passionate 21-year-old budding horror director and some rewriting took place during final prep. Mike was very familiar with my work for Corman and many of my other films. He met us all when he came down during the writing of the script which was supposed to be a Mack Sennett type of comedy-cum-horror film. Things changed radically once shooting began, hence the apparent unevenness of the structure. Maslansky wanted, in the beginning, to take advantage of Chuck's and my experience with *The Little Shop of Horrors* by making a horror farce."

Corman scriptwriter Charles B. Griffith was then living in Rome and wrote the script *Vardella* (the name of a witch) in three days for Maslansky in order to get an airline ticket for his girlfriend Sharon Compton to rejoin him. He said, "I vaguely recall Paul Maslansky telling me the idea or possibly handing me a treatment or synopsis. It's possible that Amos wrote a draft; I just don't remember. We were friends for many years. I have no idea how much of *She Beast* was written by anyone else. When I was given one of those impossible deadlines, I would read the original, then throw it aside and charge from page one."

Griffith pondered his years trying to survive in Rome:

"How did I live five years in Italy with almost no income? You know, I ask myself that question at least once a month and I have never figured it out. I did adaptations for dubbing and wrote vanity scripts for actors. Did some dubbing too. Mel Welles bailed me out frequently. Did some long-range stuff for Roger Corman. Did a *National Lampoon* horror-treatment, via interoffice memos, called 'The Mammal that Suckled its Young.' Wrote a lot of scripts that never got made, for which I would never get more than the first payments. Became a water deviner. But that still doesn't answer the question."

Mel Welles, who played the innkeeper; Lucretia Love, who played the girl he rapes; and Chuck Griffith, who was drafted in to direct second unit, were all friends. Mel Welles revealed his memories of Mike:

"Everyone was cast by Maslansky, we were all friends living and working in Rome at the time. I had handled the dubbing, re-voicing of Maslansky's first pic and he asked me to do this so that I could keep Michael straight and secure that the shots would all cut together. So, you see, I was kind of a watchdog to Michael. We all had a lot more fun making the flick than it was to watch it. Michael, at the time, was a sweet, nice free spirit who got along with everybody. Michael knew little of the acting and was completely absorbed by the Gothic formula for horror films, focusing on the visual more than on performance. I gave Mike oodles of specific advice...the use of a long lens when filming the kid running through the woods...constantly cautioning him on reverse shots where the actors flip positions (a major no-no) and he continually asked me what lens would be optimum for the given shot."

Chuck Griffith was not aware that Mike was wealthy:

"I didn't know anything about Mike's financial status. I can tell you he was a truly nice guy—never seemed rich or self-important, very ambitious, very excited about film, very eager to learn. I met him when he came on the picture. What I got from him was a little English film magazine with a rave review of *Bucket of Blood* and breathless expectation of *Little Shop*. I was enormously flattered, because it was the first time I'd ever been mentioned in a serious publication—and just about the last as well.

"*She Beast* was Michael's first time out. He plowed bravely through the beginner's mistakes, though he stuck to one or two misconceptions he held about photography, especially day-for-night etc., because British cameramen had been pulling his leg. I don't remember anything much about his directing at the time. *She Beast* was shot in a small town, but I only visited when they were at Lago de Vico, a wooded lake north of Rome. Hanging around the set is boring. I don't remember watching Mike work with actors. All our shop talk was about camera set-ups, lighting and Don Siegel. He asked a lot of questions about *Bucket of Blood*, etc. I went back to Lago de Vico in 1993 to house-sit (film producer) John Thompson's estate, just a few minutes' walk from where we shot Flash Riley, charging me with a burning torch and where we tied him to the ducking stool. Maslansky and Amos Powell were the two cops on bicycles.

"We certainly discussed direction—several times. I was into the Nouvelle Vague at the time—he was into American muscle directors. His hero was Don Siegel, and I was genuinely shocked when he told me that he copied Siegel's shots and patterns. I had never heard of such a thing before and

Ian Ogilvy and Mel Welles in *Revenge of the Blood Beast* (BFI)

believed that a director's style was mainly dictated by how best to display the moment and the mood and by what made him comfortable. The styling came from the producers through their power to distort and cripple the work of the writer-director team. But to Mike, it was a purely physical matter of dynamics.

"We got into some animated (but good-natured) debates about film aesthetics, etc. He could argue from history and I from experience. I think he was the first of the breed I'd met (except for Francis Coppola) and I wasn't used to their way of thinking, wherein old films formed a glossary of available moments, often directly quoted, moving toward the idea that the subject of a movie is Movie, as the subject of painting became Paint. Pictures had been shot by the seat of the pants and film theory had been left to the Europeans.

"I'm vaguely remembering the tenor of the debates I'd have with Mike. It was a young time, just before everything changed everywhere. Mike was on the new side of the change."

In his description of the subject of a movie is Movie, Griffith could be talking directly about Mike's next film *The Sorcerers*, deemed an allegory of cinema itself, not that Griffith saw it: "All I've ever seen of Mike's was a cut of *She Beast* during the editing."

He was certainly right about Mike's admiration for "American muscle directors," which remained consistent; even after *Witchfinder General*, Mike told *Vogue* magazine of his admiration of American action films, "the integrity of their directors, ignoring fashion and expressing a personal view through the tension of the film itself."

Mike now had a script and a producer but he needed a star. Barbara Steele was then the queen of Italian horror films and agreed to make a brief appearance in the film. It meant her name could be used to sell the film, even though she was really only a guest star.

Ian Ogilvy and Barbara Steele in *Revenge of the Blood Beast* (photo: Ernest Harris)

Paul Maslansky explained to Pete Tombs:

> "In order to sell the picture, I needed a name, and Ian Ogilvy wasn't a name
> at the time. John Karlsen, Mel Welles, wasn't. So, I had Barbara Steele, and
> I negotiated with (agent) David Niven, Jr. I paid Barbara a thousand dollars
> plus commission and she would work *one day.* I was a very clever producer
> in those days, and I didn't specify the number of hours that she'd work, and
> of course there was no great union there and Barbara wasn't SAG (Screen
> Actors Guild). Next thing you know, I worked her 18 hours straight, and
> she didn't talk to me for 27-odd years!"

Actually, Ian Ogilvy recalled she did four days' work on the film (Maslansky on another
occasion stated she was paid $5,000 overall): "She was making eight a year then. She was quite
pleasant, quite friendly. I suppose she was on it for four days. We compressed the whole thing,
did all those car scenes and all the rest of it. She was quite a *star* but was friendly and pleasant
and professional. I know she thought it was quite funny that the picture she'd just made was
called *Orgasm* and the one she was going to make just after ours was called *Climax.* Whether
that's true or not, that's certainly something she told us and she thought it was quite funny, really. She had a humor about what she was up to." Barbara could later only remember Mike as
"an enthusiastic film student."

Mike's friend Ernest Harris has told an amusing but apocryphal story to explain Barbara's
minimal presence in the film: "The story I heard about Barbara Steele on *Revenge of the Blood
Beast* was that one of the reasons why her character is replaced by this witch all the time was
that she was virtually uncontrollable—dope or something. This story came from David Austen.

He said this is why they got the character out of the way as soon as possible and put the double in wearing a mask."

Mike also needed a male lead and, as he didn't know any actors, he thought of his old friend Ian Ogilvy, who was now making a name for himself as a very promising young actor. Ian recalled: "I suppose I'd been to drama school, I'd done 18 months in Rep, I'd done my first little telly and everything was fine, and the next thing I heard was my agent at the time called me and said, 'Do you know somebody called Mike Reeves?' And I said 'Yes. Good Lord!' And he said, 'Well, he's just offered you a film. The lead.' So, the first picture I did was also his first picture. That was *Revenge of the Blood Beast*. I'd done that picture before *The Liars*." This was the popular British television series in which Ian first reached national prominence. "It was one of the first things I did, really, apart from Rep, was that movie."

Mike poured much of the budget into the impressive scenes of the capture and execution of the witch Vardella, clearly prefiguring the brilliance of *Witchfinder General*. Tom Baker commented:

> "He was very pleased with that, I remember him telling me about this. I don't know anything about witches, but just as an event, he was telling me we were going to have the dunking chair in *Witchfinder* in some form. I can't remember if we wrote it in the first draft but he was very keen on that chair. He was absolutely astounded, yes. If there's a chance of creating something on the screen, that's always appealed to him. The chair isn't just a toy, it's an effect. 'Hello, audience, wake up, something's going on in front of you.' "

Much of the rest of the film is played like a spoof. Paul Maslansky explained to Pete Tombs: "I think Michael's intent all the time was to make a horror picture that was scary. I think when we saw what we were doing, and all the actors, who were very intelligent people—we were all pretty bright people—when we saw what we were doing, that it wasn't quite that scary, so...we might as well play it for a little bit of camp, and we did."

Because the budget was so small, Mike was forced to use a second unit to save time. Chuck Griffith recalled: "I had directed second unit for Corman on several pics, and was given a car chase to do in second unit for Michael. Assuming we had a high-speed camera, I gave the Italian cameraman specific instructions on FPS as we went along. He concurred happily—and shot everything at 24 frames, giving us a stately, slow-motion chase. The picture came in short, but Paul asked if there wasn't a whole sequence we could take out. The whole operation was fairly amateurish."

Ian Ogilvy was not even aware there was a second unit and could not remember Griffith: "Second unit? I don't think we ever had a second unit. If we did, I don't remember. I suppose he might have done that. I don't remember him at all. I mean, I wouldn't know who he was. I suppose it's possible that we had a second unit. I wouldn't have thought we could have afforded to hire a second camera, to be honest. I mean it really was *cheap*." Griffith could remember Ian and said: "Ian seemed a bit high-strung in those days."

Mel Welles gave his view: "The second unit comic cop chase was done in keeping with how the script was to be done, until Michael veered to a more serious Gothic treatment. Michael changed his mind. The cop stuff was already in the can." So, the script went from Gothic, to comedy horror, to a curious blend of both which did not please Mike but, on a shooting schedule of only 18 days and a budget of about £14,000, he could not afford to reshoot. Later, he would only show potential backers "the good reels." The final credit is to "Michael Byron," which is *not* an example of Mike giving himself Byronic airs, Chuck explained: "Byron is my middle name, so I guess they whipped up a composite." Mel Welles commented: "I think it's unfair to even suggest that Mike completely rewrote the Griffith screenplay, and I am almost sure that the nom de plume was because Chuck did *not* want his name on the pic since he thought it was a debacle when they did a 180 on the comedy plan."

The situation still remains confused about Mike's intention to make a scary movie or a funny one. When looking back on *Revenge* during release of *The Sorcerers*, Mike told Tony Crawley (*Photoplay*) that *Revenge* "wasn't much better" than *Castle of the Living Dead*: "Though when I got home I found one London critic eulogizing over it! Actually I was rewriting the script every night, sending it up."

Ian Ogilvy has praised Mike's ability to "make do" on a tiny budget, and the derisory budget of *Revenge* forced him to make do more than on any subsequent film. The ducking-stool to which Vardella is affixed was in fact an abandoned siege catapult from a Roman epic, a good example of Reeves' ingenuity. The crew (and director himself) was pressed into service as extras for the mob in the witch's execution. Michael made very brief appearances in both *Castle* and *Revenge*; these were clearly not Hitchcock-style appearances, made out of vanity, but purely a way of keeping costs low; when he got better budgets, he made no appearance in *The Sorcerers* or *Witchfinder General.* In *Revenge,* there is a brief close-up of him reacting to Vardella's curse, in which he looks for all the world like a cross between a young Dirk Bogarde and a young Cliff Richard.

Sometimes brilliant, sometimes banal, *Revenge of the Blood Beast* is a fascinating early exercise of Mike's striking cinematic power. It is all the more interesting for being the only one of Mike's own films shot outside England. Ian Ogilvy agreed that it was very strange for them both to be making their first feature in a foreign country:

> "You must remember it cost about £14,000. Made it in 18 days and halfway through we suddenly decided it was going to be a send-up of movies. It started out as a sort of serious horror movie and then it got silly, and Mike started sticking lines about funny policemen falling off bikes! There you are, you see, you've got a star, Barbara Steele, who only appears at the beginning and end of the movie, and very much does her own thing anyway. You've got me, whose first picture it is, so I didn't know what the hell I was doing. You've got this strange man John Karlsen—I don't know what ever happened to him—and then you've got this idea that it's all set in an Iron Curtain country, so the policemen are all frightfully funny! The producer Paul Maslansky, who is now quite a respectable producer, played the funny policeman. That's Paul Maslansky, and very bad he was, too! But then we were all pretty bad. So it was peculiar. I'm sure it didn't work."

Mike had a number of problems to cope with, arising from the ad hoc nature of very low-budget filmmaking. Ian Ogilvy gave some examples:

> "We had a good crew, scratch crew, who'd line up at the end of the day to be paid. They weren't coming back unless they were paid every night in lire. Also, on the clapperboard we were making a documentary, because in those days—I don't know what it's like now—but in those days, a documentary license was half the price of a feature license in Italy, so on our clapperboard we had 'ruini Etrusci'—Etruscan ruins! It was literally like that.
>
> "It snowed one day! It was June in Italy and it snowed one day, so we would literally be rewriting as we went. 'Oh, it's raining, okay we'll set this scene indoors, let's find a barn, find a barn somebody.' You know, it was like that."

Mike had to work with an Italian lighting cameraman, one Gioacchino Gengarelli, but Ian said that language problems were minimal: "The whole crew was Italian. I can't remember who our interpreters were, but the Italian crews even then were pretty multilingual in that sense, so there wasn't too much of a problem as far as the language went. Also, a lot of our actors lived in Italy. It was the great heyday of the horror movies in Rome, Barbara Steele being the queen, so they all spoke fluent Italian. I think we got away with it all right. It was just a very fast shoot." Ian recollected that, on the whole, it was difficult.

He explained the slightly flat ending of the film:

"The film ends with Barbara Steele brought back from being a witch sitting in the back of a car, driving away from the terrible lake which she was dragged from and saying, 'I'll be back,' which is supposed to send a little *frisson* of fear down the audience's back. The original ending was a bit more expensive. We were to go back to London, a happily married couple. We're in bed together at night, the moonlight coming through the window, and I turn over and open my eyes and there is, not Barbara Steele, but the 400-year-old witch who's buried in the sulphur lake come back to life again! It would have been a simple matter to shoot that—just a couple of set-ups, really—but we didn't have the money."

Ian recalled the location:

"There was a small walled village which features strongly, I suppose about 15 miles outside Rome. I don't know what the name of it was at all. I remember that the man who plays the witch, a man called Flash Riley, black retired ballet dancer, in the lunch hour used to take great delight, because it was the main road to Rome just outside the walled village, in going and trying to hitch-hike like that! He'd stand by the side of the road. As a car came up, he'd lift his skirt and thumb for a ride. It was wonderful. He used to pride himself on how big the skid marks could be on the road!"

Chuck Griffith remembered him vividly, too: "Jay Flash Riley was an amazing character. A gay, middle-aged, highly talented, very funny, black entertainer, he produced and staged around Europe in a gospel road show called *Trumpets of the Lord*. He used to drive a VW camper around Rome, picking up Italian boys. He begged to play the witch and did a great job."

Ian first met Annabelle Webb on the making of this picture. She is credited as Set Dresser. She acted as a production personal assistant on this and on *The Sorcerers*. Ian described her:

"Sloaney sort of girl. She was his girlfriend then. He was pretty steady with Annabelle. She lived with him in his house in Knightsbridge. And she stayed his girlfriend all those years, with the odd walk-out and the odd rows and screams and yells. And she worked for him and kept his house and she was super. Quite good at her job, I believe. After Mike died, she went on and she worked on other pictures as a PA and things like that. She learnt it all because she worked with Mike, but afterwards she used it and did go on and worked in the production side. And, in fact, she's the only one I've ever seen since, really."

Chuck Griffith wryly observed: "His girlfriend Annabelle had the best body I have ever seen in this life."

Actress Lucretia Love, then at the start of a career in the Italian film industry, played the girl in the rape scene and has recalled: "Mike was funny and very quiet and sweet and just a shadow behind the camera crew. Annabelle was fun and *dependable*. Mel was my friend and work connection at the time. We were all hanging around in Rome that year, and there were *a lot of people* skate-boarding in the park (Villa Borghese) and drinking coffee on the Via Veneto. We were all sort of floating around." Two of Mel Welles' sons are also in the film.

Ian's living conditions were hardly to his liking:

"Oh, awful, awful, I was in a *pensione*. My expenses were 60 pounds a week. I had to pay *everything* on that, which meant that I lived in a small *pensione*. I had to *ask* to have a bath. I had to pay extra. I lived on oranges and spaghetti. I've hated Rome ever since. I was very lonely there. Mike was very, very busy writing at night. We were friends but he was so busy. I was very much left to my own devices on that picture. He was in another place, with Annabelle. I was left very much to my own devices, because he really didn't have time to entertain me in the evening. He had these people with him. I really should have taken somebody with me. I didn't have anyone to take at the time.

"And the other dreadful thing he used to do, which he didn't *mean* to do, because you wore a lot of makeup on film in those days, a hell of a lot, and my *pensione* was on the top of the Spanish Steps, was he'd drop me at the bottom of the Spanish Steps. The Spanish Steps around eight o'clock in the evening is a very gay haunt! I was covered in it. And I used to have to walk up these steps, running the gauntlet of all these kids, covered in thick pancake! It was very, very uncomfortable, but I wasn't there very long. Good God, we were there for what, three weeks I suppose. I did the whole picture in three weeks. But I remember it being very uncomfortable. I think Mike was living in a quite nice hotel. But again, it was a renewal of a relationship that had been lost for about six years. I hadn't seen him at all. In that time he'd done all these other things, so he used me because he knew me. He didn't know any actors."

Putting up his own money to achieve his ambition to direct paid off for Mike in that he impressed the men who would bring about his next production, *The Sorcerers,* Patrick Curtis and, eventually, Tony Tenser. Patrick Curtis was a young American entrepreneur. He had been in *Gone with the Wind* as Olivia de Havilland's baby and came to prominence as manager and boyfriend, then husband, of Raquel Welch. He recalled for Pete Tombs:

"I was involved in a little hamburger rib joint in Rome called *The Cowboy.* It was when I met Michael Reeves. He was doing *Revenge of the Blood Beast,* and I was just as fascinated by him as I think probably everybody has been. To me, he was the young Orson Welles of our generation. His love and affection and knowledge and effervescence about film were really greatly inspiring, I think, to all of us. We all [said], you know, 'Why not, why not? Let's go do it.' Which is exactly what he did on *Revenge of the Blood Beast.* I'll never forget that great scene where someone is wielding a sickle and it goes out of frame and they cut and it lands on a pile of hay on top of a hammer: you know, a hammer and sickle! 'Wait a minute, where did that come from?' "

Patrick Curtis was keen to get into film production and stayed in touch with Mike until a suitable script could be found.

Ian Ogilvy commented to Pete Tombs on the hammer and sickle joke: "He did it in one take and *he* threw the sickle. He said 'If this doesn't work once, we're not going to bother with it. It's just an idea.' So there's a hammer lying on the floor and he threw the sickle and it landed perfectly, and that's why it's in the film." Mel Welles claimed that he gave Mike the idea: "The shot at the beginning in the church of the sickle being thrown down on the hammer was all mine as I still thought we were making a comedy. It *was*, indeed, a spur of the moment idea, but by me (being an old avid Trotskyite). Ian's account of Mike's saying if it didn't work the first time they wouldn't bother is true though. However, it *didn't* work the first time but it was so close he tried it again and it was perfect."

The film is notably credited to "Mike" Reeves as opposed to "Michael." Journalist Tony Crawley explained that this was a clue to whether or not Mike was pleased with the finished film, quoting Mike himself: *"Blood Beast* was 'directed by Mike Reeves,' but when I'm pleased with the result, it says 'by Michael Reeves.' "

Revenge did remarkably well considering its modest origins. Ian Ogilvy stated: "It was apparently Italy's biggest-grossing picture for about three or four months, apparently very popular. They even made a comic out of it." The comic, issued shortly after the film's release in Italy, is called *La Sorella di Satana* after the film's Italian title, features a lovely color portrait of Barbara Steele on the front cover, and is an extraordinary and rare souvenir. Ian Ogilvy had a copy of it. Inside are dozens of what appear to be frame blow-ups with Italian dialogue balloons inserted.

In England *La Sorella di Satana* gained distribution by Miracle Films. The British release title was apparently the re-

Mike and Annabelle larking about in Woodbridge (courtesy Paul Vestey)

sult of a joke by Mike Reeves. A meeting was held to decide what to call the film for the U.K. market. Mike jokingly suggested, "Why not call it *Revenge of the Blood Beast*"? This was a throwaway reference to a 1958 AIP film *Night of the Blood Beast*. Paul Maslansky thought the title was quite commercial and so it stayed.

Mike did not seem too impressed with it as a title and, when interviewed after *Witchfinder General* by *Penthouse* magazine, did not even appear to remember his first film's title accurately, reportedly referring to it as "something about a blood beast terror," causing some confusion with the more widely seen Peter Cushing horror film *The Blood Beast Terror*, which Tigon had released as a support feature with *Witchfinder* (and which coincidentally was also scored by Paul Ferris). Mike described it to *Penthouse*: "It was quite possibly the worst film ever made. Everyone was in it—debtors, me, the producer."

The fact that the film was released by Miracle was to prove fortuitous for Mike, because the future producer of *The Sorcerers* and *Witchfinder General,* Tony Tenser, used to work for Miracle Films. "That's probably why I heard of it, but it must have been after I left," Tony commented. He first heard of Michael Reeves when he saw some of Miracle's publicity stills for *Revenge*. Tony never saw the film: "No. I'd heard about it. I'd seen stills from it. People who were releasing it sent them. But I'd heard and you don't have to see a thing, you get reports through the trade and I said, 'You know, he seems to be...' "

Ernest Harris, who would get to know Mike, later handled Miracle's publicity but somebody else had handled the job since Tony Tenser left and, although Ernest once spoke to Tony, it must have been that person who sent out the stills, as Ernest did not commence at Miracle until 1967.

Revenge of the Blood Beast was not widely seen in London on its release. Ernest Harris has explained: "It wasn't at all strange for a horror film like *Revenge* not to get a lot of London bookings (Bava's *Operazione Paura/Curse of the Dead* was another example), making its money on provincial booking. I believe Miracle were happy with the performance of *Revenge*."

Mike used to drop in occasionally to discuss how the film was doing with Miracle boss Michael Myers (whose name was appropriated for the *Halloween* film series) and would stop and chat about movies with Ernest Harris:

> "As far as I know, Mike got on okay with Michael Myers—if he didn't, he might have felt it undiplomatic to mention it to me, because of my job. I know he liked Dick Michaels, another of Miracle's executives, the third being Phil Kutner, and I certainly don't recall Mike ever seeming uncomfortable during his visits to the office. An awful lot of movies got discussed at Miracle! Besides myself and Barry Edson, who was in charge of Miracle's bookings during this period, there was John Pipkin (of Miracle Editorial), Ray Figgess (of Columbia), a guy named Pat from New Realm—all film buffs who used to be in and out of the office during the course of the day. Then there was Mike and David Austen and a girl named Tamara Lo.
>
> "I remember Mike talking a lot about Don Siegel and Roger Corman. I know he greatly admired Kurosawa and I recall talking to him about Anthony Mann...I know he would love to have directed a Western—he greatly admired Ralph Nelson's *Duel at Diablo*."

Ernest thought that Ian Ogilvy holding his horse in *Witchfinder General* was like a scene in Kurosawa's *Seven Samurai*.

Reviews were remarkably kind. Raymond Durgnat, the heavyweight critic, wrote in *Films and Filming*: "All in all the makers have clearly set out to make a rather jolly and soothing horror film. They've succeeded only too well." The *Monthly Film Bulletin* thought: "An engaging horror film...Although the beginning is a trifle comatose with its self-consciously stylish slow tracks and compositions (black-cloaked figures silhouetted against the skyline), it gradually gathers momentum while developing a nice line in comic grotesquerie...the acting in general is sound."

Around this time, *Films and Filming* writer David Austen became interested in Mike's talent and sought him out, starting a lasting friendship. It was Austen who would review Mike's later work for the magazine and defend *Witchfinder General* against its critics in the letters page of *The Listener*. Ian Ogilvy commented: "I think that's where David Austen got started with Mike, because they were great friends. He was one of the group toward the end." Austen, who once complained in the magazine that being a film critic was not a meaningful thing to do, later emigrated to Canada and wrote books and articles under the name David Wade. Ian stated: "I think he'd have loved to have been a filmmaker or a film writer. Certainly he'd have preferred that." Austen, one of the best film critics of the '60s, was one of the last friends to see Mike Reeves alive and was crushed by his death.

Revenge of the Blood Beast did actually play in London in November 1966, at the Prince of Wales cinema in Harrow Road, as a support feature to Riccardo Freda's *The Exterminators*, one of the "Francis Coplan" (French James Bond) spy films—a terrific double bill, typical of the Prince of Wales, which was actually a cut above being a fleapit and specialized in continental genre films of this type. Ian and Mike took Diane Ogilvy to the cinema that week to see it, so that she could catch up with Mike's little oeuvre. She recalled:

Ian Ogilvy and Barbara Steele in *Revenge of the Blood Beast*

"The only time I ever went to a fleapit was to see *Blood Beast*. I've never been there before or since. It would only have been because this was something before I came in on the scene and 'Here you are, catch up with this one.'" She quite enjoyed the film. Ian had already seen it on February 1 that year with his then-agent Aude Powell in a private screening laid on by Mike. Mike's diary entry comments: "Quite favorably received, I think." Ian agreed that was accurate. He explained he was looking at it, as all actors do, mainly from the aspect of judging his own performance, and found the film quite funny and quite good. As it was the first film he'd acted in, he thought he would have been quite pleased by almost anything.

Mike invited his Aunt Joan to see it. She liked it "in its own way" but did not see his later films. "Basically, I wasn't terribly interested in it. It wasn't me," she said. "I did just go to see it. But he promised me, 'I know you don't like it but one day I'll make you a very nice film.' And he was going to do it."

The film then disappeared from view for decades and was even slow to appear on video. Ian Ogilvy felt it was because it was "so obscure and peculiar really." When Ian was featured on Thames Television's *This is Your Life* in the '80s, host Eamonn Andrews screened a clip from *Revenge* and Ian was seen to grimace, but he explained to the author that this was no expression of disapproval for the film itself, but an unfortunate piece of editing by the program makers:

> "The bit you saw they actually cut on the transmission of that *This Is Your Life*. They *didn't* cut my grimace. Because what actually happens is, I come out of the water and someone comes running up to me and I collapse with the words, 'My wife!' Well, of course, in the full version of *This is Your Life*, that's in, and was deeply embarrassing because it's terrible. So I go, 'Ugh!' like that. Of course, in the final thing it was too long, so they thought, 'We'll cut that film clip.' All you see is the car going off. My grimace is in reaction to the fact that I had to say, 'My wife!' and fall over!"

A successful film career now seemed within reach, but Mike would first encounter more setbacks. He was beginning to become more depressed. Dr. Stephen Blaikie of Ovington Square, Chelsea had been treating Mike since 1964. The doctor respected the "great talent and purpose" in Mike's work. At the inquest he described Mike as "highly strung," with a tendency to get depressed if his work or life were not going according to his likes. Friend John Hall remembered that Mike was very prone to highs and lows and convinced that a film he was making would be a disaster. "He was never sure it was going to be good. If you told him it was good, he would say, 'you're only saying that to please me.' It wasn't that he was lacking in confidence, he was just prone to lows."

Chapter Four: London Projects

"I have the overall image of a maker of cheap horror films."
—Michael Reeves to John Trevelyan

Mike was now launched on a horror path and, because he died so young, his entire oeuvre loosely falls into this genre, though from the projects he intended to make after the success of *Witchfinder*, he clearly would have moved away from the genre, if only to please Aunt Joan. In any case, Paul Ferris said: "He never spoke of the future." For Ian Ogilvy, horror movies simply provided the easiest entry to the profession:

> "He used to say, 'It's easier to raise money on a small-budget horror movie than anything else, therefore let us make small-budget horror movies until such time as somebody wants us to make something bigger and better, but, given that, let's make the best horror movies that have ever been seen!' But when you actually analyze the three pictures, I don't think any of them actually *are* horror movies. What they do is, they use three horror stars (Barbara Steele, Boris Karloff and Vincent Price). Barbara is a sort of horror star, but the first picture is a joke picture. I mean, lines like, 'I think you've got my mother in there,' lines like that, it's a spoof. You can't call *The Sorcerers* a horror movie. It's a fantasy movie but there are no monsters in it or anything. And *Witchfinder General* is certainly not a horror movie. It's a sort of pseudo-historical piece with a lot of nasty things going on. In a funny sort of a way, I always think horror movies have got monsters in them. Mike didn't do that."

Of course, Mike did appreciate famous horror director Roger Corman. Tom Baker said: "He admired Corman, it's true. He admired Corman for his ability to get on and make movies, because he was obviously famous for getting on and making films like no one else but with a certain style and panache driving forward, but I don't remember him being obsessed in that sense like he was with Siegel." This was also Ian's view: "I think his attitude to Corman was that he admired the design, the way the pictures were made and all the rest of it, but it wasn't a field he terribly wanted to stay in. It's just that they were easy to get financing for."

Yet Robin Wood wrote that Mike's pictures spring to life in horror and violence. Ian disagreed: "I think they spring to life in action scenes, to be honest. You could broaden it to that. His visual sense was tremendous."

Ian thought it was fair to say that Mike was to some extent aping Corman, who began with monsters and moved into psychological horror with the Poe films:

> "Yes. Mike was rather like Stephen King in a way. Stephen King isn't passionately anxious to write horror. It's just he's terribly good at it. But he can write other things very well. Mike was merely aware of the fact that as a very, very young film director, untried and untested, horror movies was just the thing it was easiest to raise money on. I think he quite enjoyed doing them, but I know the project he was working on when he died was *All the Little Animals*. Charming book. That was very far from a horror movie."

It is a particular pity that Mike never made the film, as Betty Reeves would undoubtedly have liked it far more than his horror films. "Would have been fantastic," said Paul Ferris.

Mike's future producer Tony Tenser agreed with Ian that Mike had no obsession with horror as such: "No, no, he made the horror films because in those days—I believe even today, if they're made—it was fish-and-chips. There was a market for it, whichever way it came out, there was a market for it. Small, big, medium, or whatever. And he graduated from that—you know, *Witchfinder General* was *not* a horror film. It was a horrifying thriller. It was a period thriller."

Mike was now an experienced movie director ("Mike always called them movies, not films," according to Paul Ferris), and Ian an experienced movie actor, however modest the vehicle for their respective talents. This further collaboration ensured that they would not lose touch again, and theirs became a deep and lasting friendship.

Ian certainly regarded Mike as his closest friend, and Mike's surviving letter of September 1966 to Ian and Diane is very warm. Furthermore, Ian got on very well with Mike's girlfriend Annabelle, and Diane Ogilvy was very fond of Mike. Ian and Diane became fixtures in Mike's set, which congregated at Yeoman's Row.

The Yeoman's Row house in 2002

Ian characterized the Mike of this time as someone who was such a "lunatic" about movies that he "could tell you who was the third assistant on a '30s black and white Adolphe Menjou movie." In other words, said Ian, Mike was "deeply, oh enormously" cine-literate:

> "Mike was an absolute movie buff. He knew everything about movies, who lit them, who was the lighting cameraman, you couldn't catch him out. It was his only topic of interest. If you weren't interested in the cinema, you were a bore to Mike. It was the only thing he wanted to talk about. It was the only thing he *could* talk about, really. I happened to agree with him *at the time*. We were all movie-mad in those days. We went to see everything. I remember seeing with Mike probably five movies in one day, by going to a press show in the morning, then an afternoon show, then another one, and so on. We did five movies in one day at one point. We'd see everything. All of it. There was a great crowd of us used to go round to a film."

Diane Ogilvy was among them and concurs that it was five movies a day:

> "I've done it, yes. I don't think one could have done it without the Starlight Club at the Mayfair Hotel. You used to be able to get the extra one in that way, because otherwise it wasn't possible to see five movies. There weren't five showings a day. There was a period when Mike had been there tremendously. You could get sandwiches there. Absolutely compact little cinema. They were all good movies. Whoever was picking them knew what they were on about."

Diane recalled Mike raving about Kubrick's *2001* on one occasion. Ian recalled that Mike was not very selective in what he went to see. He went to:

"…everything, absolutely everything…what day is it today, Thursday? By Thursday we would have seen every movie in London. *All* the new releases. We would have seen them immediately. We lived in the West End not because we were going to nightclubs but because that was where the new cinemas were. I now go to my local cinema. Mike wouldn't. He would have seen all the pictures by now. Everything. The only films he couldn't see—and he had to have foreknowledge of this—was any film which involved somebody getting something on their face like mud. Anything that obscured the features he couldn't watch, like when Anthony Quayle sinks into the Qattara depression in *Ice Cold in Alex* and they drag him out by the help of a truck. Mike couldn't watch that. He had a thing about it, a psychological block about anybody having anything obscuring the features, so the features were not just visible and you couldn't see the nose."

Yet in *Witchfinder General* you see faces obscured by blood, but Ian commented: "Oh, no, that's all right, that's fine. It's just when there's so much stuff on the face that you can't see where the nose begins and ends. That was sort of a strange thing he had." Diane Ogilvy suspected there must have been a childhood experience behind this phobia and recalled also his phobia about being smeared in motorbike oil, which is what happens to Ian in the fight scene in *The Sorcerers*: "He hated that oil that Ian gets covered in. He made Ian do it because it frightened him so much that he thought it was going to be a scary thing. And I had always assumed that his father had died in a motorbike accident and Mike therefore hated motorbikes."

Mike's Aunt Joan threw a little light on this, recalling an accident Mike's father Derek once had:

"He had a motorbike as a young thing. In fact, he had a most unfortunate accident riding it. I suppose he was about 15 or something. Riding it down in Norfolk, he was run into by the local farmer, so that meant a month in hospital in Yarmouth. He didn't permanently have a motor-bicycle like so many of that generation but he did just at that time. The first day he went out, he was run into by this farmer who had already run into somebody before he hit Derek!"

Belgian poster for *The Killers*

This may well have led to Mike's fear of motor-bikes.

Mike's enthusiasm for film-going must have been very rare in somebody who was already in the film industry. "But he was very young, you see," argued Ian Ogilvy, "and he wanted passionately to make movies. And he loved them. He *loved* movies. He just adored films. He *could* be very scathing about them. It wasn't that he loved them indiscriminately. He just loved the whole business of going into a cinema with a bag of popcorn and sitting down there and watching them." Paul Ferris remembered that Mike insisted on the popcorn, the sweets and so forth and got very excited about the whole ritual. This, of course, did not apply when he saw movies at home.

Mike's favorite movie was released in 1964. *The Killers* was Don Siegel's version of the Hemingway story first filmed by Robert Siodmak in 1946 with Burt

Lancaster. This version starred Lee Marvin, Clu Gulager, John Cassavetes, Angie Dickinson and Ronald Reagan. The plot concerns the obsessive quest by two hitmen to discover why their target allowed them to kill him so easily. It all hinges on the fact that his life was destroyed by a woman he loved, a poignant situation that could perhaps be related to the poignancy of Reeves' work, although the film itself is "muscular."

Ironically, Mike's favourite movie was originally made as a TV movie but released to theaters when the network found it too violent; Paul Ferris, who met Siegel after Mike died, maintained Siegel *deliberately* made it too violent for television, as he felt it was too good to be a TV movie, and went over budget for the same reason, to ensure it got a theatrical release. (He added that Mike had said they all thought—all those making the film—that Reagan was "a prat.") Siegel did not admit this in his amusing memoirs *A Siegel Film,* writing simply: "The reaction to the violence in *The Killers* was one of shock in 1964, although later the film was considered to be quite tame."

One might have imagined other Siegel films being preferred by Mike, but Ian Ogilvy shook his head:

> "No, he thought *The Killers* was the best film ever made in the history of cinema, the Don Siegel version. He just loved that picture and he used to run it all the time. There was no video in those days. He had a fairly battered old 16-mm film projector and you could go off to Wallace Heaton in those days and hire a movie. He used to run *The Killers* all the time. One of those things he always used to run before he *made* a movie. He would run *The Killers.* I must have seen it 10 times at Mike's house."

Paul Vestey remembered that movies would have been on "at any time of day or night."

Clearly Mike had seen a number of Corman's early pre-Poe series B movies, though it is difficult to know how he got to see them as they were not that well distributed in Britain. Ian Ogilvy said:

> "Knowing Mike, he would have gone off and found them somewhere. They were much more difficult to get then, those movies. Wallace Heaton had a smallish lending library. *The Killers* was one of them. Quite a lot of the Siegel movies actually were on that list but it wasn't all that huge. He had all the different catalogues of all the different hire places, but now it would have been wonderful. But it's odd how important it was to him, that film, *The Killers.* And, although he ran all the others—he loved *Invasion of the Body Snatchers—The Killers* to him was the definitive film.
>
> "He said, 'Every element about it, the playing around with the time element, shuffling backwards and forwards, backwards and forwards, this extraordinary obsessive thing...' You see, there again, this obsessive thing. Those two men are *obsessed,* in a very laid-back way, with finding out *why* they were paid so much money to kill this guy who didn't run away. And it's the same thing in *Witchfinder General.* It's the same thing. This slightly obsessive chase, this man prepared to give up almost everything just to get this guy and stop him. *The Killers,* I think, is a wonderful picture but it is quite complicated. You find out just a little bit more about the John Cassavetes character as you go through it. Mike would have been a very happy man if he'd made *The Killers* himself. He couldn't fault it. I watch it every time it comes out almost for old times' sake. I know every shot of that picture. I know it better than *Witchfinder General,* much better. Because I've seen it more times!"

(Ian, many years after this interview, did a short scene with Clu Gulager in *Puppetmaster 5* for director and Reeves fan Jeff Burr and told Gulager how often he had seen *The Killers*!)

Paul Vestey concurred with Ian: "What did we used to watch? *The Killers,* which I liked because it had motor racing stuff in, because I was keen on motor racing." Nicky Henson revealed that Mike's obsession with *The Killers* even led him to play audio tapes: "He was encyclopedic on movies. He was unfortunate, in a way, that he was pre-video time, because he would just now be at home watching videos 24 hours a day. Because I remember he had 16-mm prints, obviously of his favorite pictures like *The Killers*. He was always showing the bloody *Killers*! But he also had audio tapes of *The Killers*. I remember sitting there one night listening to the soundtrack of *The Killers* while having supper!"

Nicky denied that people around Mike such as Annabelle got fed up with this, which would be understandable: "No, because he was so fascinating, and so fascinated, that he kind of pulled you in as well. And to hear anybody talk about something that they know a great deal about is fascinating, and if they're terribly, terribly keen, and he was. You could say the name of a picture and he'd say '1923, directed by...starring so-and-so...the lighting cameraman was...' He was just like a walking encyclopedia."

Paul Ferris would not put it past Mike to play audio tapes of *The Killers* during supper: "I didn't experience that. I believe it, yeah. He was *movie-mad*. It was his life, thoughts, dreams, the lot. Don Siegel-crazy." Diane Ogilvy defended Mike against the charge of obsession, however: "He very probably played an audio tape of *The Killers* to demonstrate a point or something. He certainly always showed anyone involved with a movie *The Killers* before they started shooting. I don't think he showed it any more often than that. I must have seen it four or five times. I don't think he was obsessed with it. He didn't even have a copy of it. It was just his idea of a very good, very cheap movie." She argued that playing audio tapes of the soundtrack of *The Killers* during supper was *not* typical behavior, and if there was intensity in Mike about his favorite movies, that was not his only trait, stressing his love of playing games: "His *only* conversation was movies, but not necessarily his own. Nobody would play the Movie Game with him, because he always won. He knew everything."

Ian Ogilvy said that *The Killers* made Lee Marvin one of Mike's favorite actors:

> "Marvin was in town one day and Mike introduced himself. Found him in a bar and actually brought him back. I wasn't there. He actually got Marvin back to the house. He said, 'Come on, tell me about *The Killers*, come on, come on.' In fact, if you were in a Don Siegel picture, you were terrific. Angie Dickinson, even Ronald Reagan, I suspect. And in fact he loved the story about the last shot where Marvin comes out wounded. He hasn't got the gun, he only uses the finger. The fact was that Marvin was absolutely blind drunk, bordered on *blind drunk,* and that's why he staggers all over the place and that's why he does this strange thing, and then the leg comes up, and of course Siegel was enchanted because it worked like a dream, but he couldn't understand why actors are blind drunk."

Tom Baker found Mike's behavior to be typical of the total film buff:

> "If he met someone in some small Siegel movie, they would be mates, because he would know them and he'd know who they were and understand what shot and how the camera had bloody well moved! He would tell you how the camera had moved. *I* don't know about that, I'm just paying attention to whether the guy's going to kill the girl or not, but *he* would, at the same time as paying attention to that, remember where the camera went and why the camera went. Very early on he was like that."

Diane Ogilvy remembered the meeting with Marvin: "It was in a pub. It was either in The Star, which is in a mews off Belgrave Square, or in The Grenadier, which is in another mews. There was a time, for a period of a few months, when Mike would have popped into The Star quite a lot." (This would have been when Mike moved on from Yeoman's Row and was living just around the corner from The Star.)

Nicky Henson thought it was a nightclub where Mike met Marvin, but said Mike was not interested in nightclubs very much:

> "No. We used to go occasionally. It just wasn't his scene. He liked to be in Yeoman's Row with a few mates, drinking and some pretty women and stuff like that. But basically he liked conversation and interesting people and he'd go out and find people. He found Lee Marvin drunk in a club one night and took him home. He rang everybody up and said 'Come and look. There's this drunken actor on the floor. Sit around and look at him!' "

John Hall confirmed it was the Grenadier: "Marvin was renting a flat in the mews and was so entranced by someone who knew every single shot of *The Killers*... they ended up back at Marvin's flat."

Mike never had any ambition to make "art cinema" (which makes AIP boss Jim Nicholson's condemnation of *Witchfinder General* as an art movie highly ironic). "Certainly didn't," confirmed Tom Baker:

> "He hardly *went* to it. That's one of the reasons I didn't do a lot with him in the early days. There am I, arty student, going to Dublin, the only films that are worth seeing are the Italian, French. Mike never went to any of these things. I remember stopping at a kiosk in Leicester Square, he wanted to buy the latest edition of *Movie* magazine and Hawks had just made *Hatari*, so Hawks is on the cover. I was all, 'What the shit's this? They're taking this American wild animal movie seriously!' So, I went off to Dublin and I was there for a while. Then I met Iain Sinclair and some of his friends and they were into *Cahiers du Cinema* and liking Hawks and Hitchcock and John Ford and stuff, so I began to pick up on that, but I was still interested in the foreign stuff.
>
> "I'd go to stay with Mike and I'd say, 'Well, why don't we go up to the Academy to see Godard or some Indian?' And he'd say, 'Oh, Christ, I'm not going to read subtitles all night, I don't want to see this stuff.' There was a bit of a split between us in that. I just gave up. He wasn't interested. He would see an occasional one, but hardly. American cinema! That's why I call it 'industrial cinema,' because it's not just the toys but the director's vision to frame things in a certain way, to do a lateral track across a hillside, to do that which Hollywood had the money to do, to create this ability to do those sorts of things, that was his fascination.
>
> "He loved to try these physical things, like in that opening of *Witchfinder* where the woman is pulled along the field and the gibbet is up the hill, one of the very first things he did—and that was shot at the very beginning of the shooting—was insist upon a lateral track as she is brought up to the gibbet and the goddamned hill is sloping. So, there is a lot of money going in, on a tiny budget, to build some level track on a sloping hill. It's a nice shot, but a lot of people would not spend the money like that, which wasn't necessary on one level. Someone else would have used a pan or whatever, but that's the world of cinema that he wanted to make and explore and understand. So

he would risk the money in there. It wasn't *that* difficult a shot, but just the fact that it's not level cost that much more in the chippies' time or whoever puts up the track, the camera crew or whoever, just that many more hours and pounds off Tony's budget to do that...and he would insist upon that, occasionally. That's what he wanted to do and that's good, really. No, he wouldn't see foreign films."

Ian Ogilvy thought Mike *would* see foreign films:

"Yes, he would see everything. The only thing I cannot overstress is that Mike was somebody who wanted to make movies. He didn't really want to do anything else. He didn't really want to think about anything else or have anything to do with anything else. He just wanted to make movies and he wanted to make entertaining movies. The only reason he did horror movies was that they were the easiest things to raise money on. And *if* there was a deep-seated psychological reason, which there probably was underneath all that, I didn't know about it. He was quite positive and definite it was a cynical decision to get a reputation for making good shit as opposed to bad shit. 'Let's make shit, but let's make really good shit, or make it interesting, or do something with it that's kind of fun.' "

Peter Fraser certainly discussed art cinema with Mike: "We would have talked about what was going on at the time, the Nouvelle Vague, Truffaut's *The 400 Blows* and so on." We know from the dedication of *Intrusion* that Mike admired the Jean-Luc Godard of the *Breathless* era. Mike seemed to be familiar with Ingmar Bergman's work, too. The dwarf he may have contributed to the script of *Castle of the Living Dead* has been described as Bergmanesque, and the climactic march up the hill to the castle in *Witchfinder General* has been described as an homage to *The Seventh Seal*. Peter Fraser was not convinced about this: "It *could* be an homage, but he could have said, 'That's the best way to get the shot.' These are the sort of things we discussed, Mike and me—what is the best shot to get across what I feel about the scene? We did talk about acting. Possibly Mike would talk more about the *shots*, the camera placement. Where the camera *adds* something to the script, *that's* Mike. As Alfred Hitchcock said, the purpose of the camera is to keep out of the frame what you don't want the audience to see, and include what you do."

The only kind of film Mike had *no* time for was the avant-garde, experimental, noncommercial or "underground" movie (an example might be Don Levy's *Herostratus*; ironic, then, that a couple of sources credit Mike with involvement, most likely erroneously, in another one, Peter Brooks' *Tell Me Lies*). Paul Ferris said: "He was dead against them. We had discussions about that. He was right. He had no time at all for them. Wouldn't even watch them." Ian Ogilvy concurred:

"Mike had no time for that at all. He didn't really. Because he said, 'These kind of things, nobody wants to actually see this kind of film. There's no point making movies without an audience. If you haven't got an audience, you haven't got a picture.' There was, as I say, this fairly strong cynicism about what he was doing. He was exploiting. He was exploiting the people who gave him the money, he was exploiting the audience, he wasn't exploiting the actors because he paid them, but he was exploiting those two sections. He said, 'Let us entertain people.' "

Ian did agree that Mike's work had a profoundly felt passion not found in the work of other "exploitation" filmmakers (of course, none of Mike's films really operate as exploitation films because, like the early Roger Corman, his genius lifts the movies to a higher artistic plane):

"No question about it, yes. He was passionate about making good movies. He liked good movies and he loathed and detested bad movies. When I say cynicism, I push that too hard. The cynicism was just about the subject, the *kind* of movie he was going to make, but he was determined to make it as *well* as he could, and to make it as good as he could. He loved his reviews, it's just that they started getting on top of him a bit. He loved all that. He thought it was great. It was just when John Russell Taylor wrote four columns about *Witchfinder General...*"

So when magazines like *Movie Monsters* have described Mike as "well on his way to becoming another Terence Fisher with a bit of James Whale thrown in," this was just a connection established through working in the horror genre rather than an essential psychological aspect of Mike Reeves' creativity. Or, as Ian Ogilvy put it: "If movie buffs want to put down the fact that Mike's angst was to do with the horror...Making horror movies was a totally *practical* consideration as far as he was concerned. He was cynical, he had a deeply cynical attitude to how to get yourself a reputation as being a man who makes good small-budget pictures that will really make a lot of money. He said, 'It's an easy genre to work in.'"

Ian was unsure what Mike's reading habits were: "He liked film books...He had a good collection of movie books. I have a feeling he preferred biography to novels. And I would also have imagined that anything he read was with half an eye to making a movie out of it." This was how *The Sorcerers* originated, "and certainly the *Witchfinder General* book by Ronald Bassett, and *All the Little Animals*. They were all books. I think he did read quite a lot, but that would have been something he'd do when I wasn't there, so my memory of him reading is nonexistent." Ian added: "There were periods when I was working when Mike and I would lose touch. When we were both back in London again, I'd give him a ring, so I never quite knew what he was up to."

Flatmate Paul Vestey commented: "I know he used to read quite a lot. Perhaps a bit more in the earlier days. It wouldn't have been anything heavy. Mainly American fiction." Benjamin Halligan cites a fondness for F. Scott Fitzgerald, to whom he was introduced by Miles Huddleston. An anecdote of Diane Ogilvy's shows that he was certainly keeping an eye out for likely movie material: "I remember him phoning me up one day because he'd just read the new Daphne du Maurier. He said, 'I haven't got time, try and get the rights for the Venice short story (which became Nicolas Roeg's film *Don't Look Now*).' They'd been got. Somebody had got them before. I was set to try and get that, so he must have read it. That was my chore for the day." Mike did not pay her for these little chores: "Certainly not. I wouldn't have expected it."

Revenge of the Blood Beast was of some value to Mike as evidence of directorial competence and experience when trying to set up future projects. For instance, Compton wanted to see it when they had a project of Mike's under consideration in January 1966. The film was called *Flame in the Blood,* originally titled *Blood Moon.* Mike submitted it to Tony Tenser and Michael Klinger, who were partners in Compton and had backed the low-budget horror films of the young Roman Polanski and others. Mike's diary for the week of January 31 to February 7, 1966, shows him anxiously awaiting Compton's decision. His January 31 entry muses that there may be two problems: The script may contain too much sex for the U.S. TV market, and Compton may be wary of young untried directors after Ian Curteis' flop *The Projected Man.* "I knew that bloody film wouldn't do us any good," wrote Mike.

Tony Tenser confirmed that he never saw *Flame in the Blood,* nor did he attend a screening of *Revenge,* although he was the person who usually made this kind of decision. At the time, his partnership with Michael Klinger had started to dissolve, although he didn't know it, and he thought that was why. Michael Klinger may have handled Mike's submission but, before he died, he denied any recollection of it or of Mike Reeves, so it may have been handled by a Compton employee: "While I am tremendously impressed by your research, I am afraid that I can't help you at all. Unfortunately I cannot recall Michael Reeves or the subjects you mention. Sorry to be of no help, but I wish you well in your endeavors."

One explanation may be that Tony Tenser recalled that Compton had lots of scripts sent in by people who didn't call in person, and if they weren't low-budget horror, they were sent back, as that was the field in which Compton was specializing. Tony thought Mike was wrong about Compton's possible reluctance to engage young directors, citing the example of Polanski. Compton had in any case only put some money into *The Projected Man* to secure the distribution rights, but it was actually produced by Richard Gordon and Gerald Fernback.

Mike had himself approached Gerald Fernback to get projects going, and he too wanted to see *Revenge*. Mike wonders in his diary if he can just "show the good bits." One project was *Crooked Cross*, to be shot in Yugoslavia on a budget of £70,000. Mike notes, "Meeting with G. Fernback, very hopeful." Elsewhere Mike writes, "Fernback likes *Manic Mind*, wants Jim to do masterscene script." Jim is a reference to screenwriter Jim Roberts, a friend of Mike's. His diary notes that Jim and he and Annabelle went to see all four hours of the revived *Batman* serial. Ian Ogilvy commented that these projects would have been simply treatments, not full-blown scripts, and Mike's comments about *Manic Mind* seem to confirm this. Actually, Peter Fraser has pointed out they were probably not treatments (10-12 pages) but synopses (two pages). In any event, it is most unlikely that they have survived in any form, apart from *Crooked Cross*, which was a full script by another writer.

However, Ian was clear that Mike did not have a pile of finished scripts he'd never filmed and also that he did not attach great importance to his scripts—hence even less to treatments. He thought that Mike would not have been happy as a screenwriter if he had had no opportunity to direct:

> "No, he wasn't proud of his scripts. His scripts were secondary. They were completely secondary. He didn't present you with a script proudly and say, 'How about this for a nice piece of writing?' He'd say, 'Listen, this is a kind of working script. Have a look at that and see if you like it.' 'Oh, it's great, Mike, yes...Don't like *that*.' 'No, no, it's terrible, isn't it? No, no, change all that. Shoot it.' To him it was the film mix with the cameras that was important, not the script. The script was merely the basis, the framework. Although he had worked very hard on it and it was structured and carefully done, but within it he was open to suggestions, from Coquillon (director of photography), from actors, from anyone. 'Why don't we do this?' 'What a good idea!' he'd say. 'Yes, why not? Let's do that.' He would toy with an idea and then throw it away. If he finished a script, I think on the whole he intended to make it. But they all went through tremendous amounts of changes, mainly because of the money side of it, because it was raining or he couldn't get Donald Pleasance. He was endlessly adaptable, but in making those kind of movies you have to be. You couldn't wait for a sunset. There was none of that David Lean and Freddie Young stuff. You shoot. Regardless of what the hell's happening, you shoot."

Mike always wanted to write his own pictures as well as direct. Paul Vestey remarked: "I always imagined it was because that was the only way he thought he'd ever be able to get started." Paul thought Mike would have been happy to direct others' scripts: "Mind you, he would then have wanted to kick the whole thing to pieces!" This was what happened with *Revenge*.

For all his energy and talent, Mike had to persevere in the face of much rejection, as Ian explained:

> "You see, *Revenge* wasn't really much of a calling card. It was just a sort of technical piece, inasmuch as he had made a movie. When they wanted to see it, he would think, 'Well, I wonder if I want to show this.' I never really knew of his difficulties. I suppose I did. I suppose he told me about

them. Again, I've forgotten really. But I think it must have been fairly easy with his financial cushion; and, secondly, he had enormous enthusiasm for other people's films, you see. So, if ever he felt down, he'd go off and see a movie or two or three or four. It was like a drug. And he'd then discuss endlessly.

"One of his great bete noires was, for instance, when everybody was saying what a great picture *Tom Jones* was, Mike was the only person who said this was the worst film he's ever seen, quite appalling. He said, 'How can Walter Lassally call himself a lighting cameraman when all he does is put green filters over the front of things and then pretend it's night?' He just loathed that picture. To him it was the end!"

Of course, there was some criticism of the day-for-night sequences in *Witchfinder General*, but Ian countered:

"Yes, but Mike insisted it was a damn sight better than *Tom Jones*, which was a very expensive, big-budget picture. That was what one did in those days. I don't think any more we shoot day-for-night. We shoot night-for-night now. I haven't been in a picture where we shot day-for-night for years. Just is not done any more, because it's too obvious. Any Western of that period, you see the total night shadows and things and all the actors will have their eyes screwed up. Doesn't make sense. But that was what one did in those days."

Critic Julian Bamford (*Films in London*) has claimed that the strong sun shadows in *Witchfinder*'s day-for-night sequences add an extra air of spookiness, but Ian disagreed: "That's reading something into it, isn't it? The fact is that we shot day-for-night. It's as simple as that." Nicky Henson commented that his children would delight in spotting day-for-night sequences in his '60s pictures.

Diane Hart was a model/actress when she met Ian Ogilvy in the lounge of Heathrow Airport as they were about to board a plane for Rome to test for the leads in Franco Zeffirelli's *The Taming of the Shrew*. Ian recalled: "We did a film test, Mike York and me and Diane, who was just a model, and Natasha Pyne. Diane and I failed. But that night we were in Rome and Mike was there and he said 'Come on, come out, we'll have dinner at Harry's Bar.'"

Diane, who became Ian's wife after a courtship of many months, was meeting Mike for the first time and they hit it off well immediately. Diane said:

"He was probably the closest man friend I've ever had. There was an incredible kindness in him and an incredible understanding about people. I don't know what I responded to. I believe that people can find each other and not have to talk about similarities in their past as children or whatever and there is an affinity because of that. Mike had a difficult childhood, perhaps because of the way his mother was—not that much affection. She adored him, he was the only thing in her life, but perhaps she came from a background where you didn't demonstrate it."

Paul Vestey confirmed: "I remember when Ian first started going out with her, Mike thought she was pretty special and Diane and he got on pretty well." *Revenge* was not out yet but would be soon.

Always eager to collaborate with established talents, Mike also worked with writer/producer Alfred Shaughnessy, later the script editor of the enormously popular television series *Upstairs, Downstairs* (in which Ian Ogilvy appeared for a while). Alfred recalled:

"Michael was indeed a colorful, talented character and, had he lived, must have become a very notable filmmaker. I can't be sure, but I believe I first met him through Matt McCarthy, who was a sound editor and friend working with me at Eyeline Films, a small company I formed in 1960 with Anthony Perry, Guy Hamilton, Charles Frend and Kenneth More, to make commercials and documentaries.

"As a screenwriter, ex-Ealing Studios, I was approached by Michael to work with him on an idea he had for a horror movie (I had directed one called *Cat Girl* for Anglo-Amalgamated), or maybe it was to rework an old script he had. I was amazed at the vast knowledge Michael had of movies; he knew every director, actor, cutter, and producer by name; the house was full of movie posters; and he was plainly a film buff, obsessed with the cinema. He told me the story of his hero-worship of Don Siegel and how he called on Siegel in Hollywood and talked his way into observing on one of his pictures.

"One charming thing I remember: He asked my wife and me to dine one night at Yeoman's Row—not a formal dinner but eating on the sofa—and told me he had a surprise for me. After food, he lowered the lights and switched on his 16-mm projector and ran a copy of a modestly budgeted thriller movie I had written and directed for Bryanston at Pinewood, called *The Impersonator*. It was a nice gesture and must have taken him trouble to get hold of a print.

"The project Michael and I worked on together was finally called *Crescendo*, and he tried to set it up with Compton Films and had casting agreements from Flora Robson, Christopher Lee and Susan Hampshire, who all liked my script and were willing to do it. At the last moment, Compton suddenly said they would not finance in full, although the budget was modest enough. I can never be quite sure, but I had a nasty feeling at the time that they knew Michael had quite a bit of money and I believe they wanted him to come up with the balance. Michael, quite rightly, refused on principle to invest his own money in the picture, so it fell through.

"Sometime later, the script fell into the hands of Michael Carreras of Hammer Films, who set it up with Warner Bros. and cast Margaretta Scott for Flora Robson, James Olson for Chris Lee and Stefanie Powers for Susan Hampshire. It was released as *Crescendo* and my script was altered slightly (not to my liking), but a fine musical score was composed by Malcolm Williamson. If Michael and I had made that movie together with proper control, it could have been a winner."

This is the only one of the unrealized projects that both Ian Ogilvy and Tom Baker could recall decades later. Tom said: "I remember this notion of *Crescendo*. *Crescendo* played a big part somewhere. It seemed to be hanging around for a while. *Crescendo* spans some months or years. It was certainly knocking around as a script in the house." It was then known as *Apassionata*.

Mike's diary from February 1966 reveals that he and Annabelle went to have dinner with "Mr. and Mrs. Fred," as he refers to them, and Paul Vestey could remember Alfred calling round to Yeoman's Row occasionally to bat ideas about with Mike. Mike was clearly excited about *Crescendo*, which was eventually directed by Alan Gibson in 1970. Stefanie Powers played a graduate student who goes to France to research the life of a dead composer and becomes involved with his family. The film was not a financial or artistic success. In a letter from Italy to Ian and Diane Ogilvy dated September 18, 1966, Mike wrote concerning *Crescendo*: "I can't go into it because those damned birds really are flying tonight." This meant it was a dead secret. Diane

Ogilvy explained: "It was that he wasn't even going to tell us any more about it. It was a subject that was talked about a tremendous amount."

A week of Mike's life in diary form has survived from February 1966. It only survived by pure fluke and is in the possession of Diane Ogilvy, who pointed out: "The only reason I have this is because obviously some years later he must have given it to my daughter Emma to draw in." Emma, indeed, stamped her initials all over the final day.

JANUARY 1966   31   MONDAY

Submitted final script of *Blood Moon* to Tenser & Klinger. Decided to retitle, possibly "Flame in the Blood." Maurice suggested a couple of minor improvements which will help a lot once we get them incorporated. But don't think their absence will affect Compton's yes or no. Personally a bit depressed. Despite good script, two things against us. 1. Too much sex for U.S. T.V. market. 2. Compton wary of young directors after Ian Curteis and *Projected Man*. I *knew* that bloody picture wouldn't do us any good. Nevertheless, Maurice optimistic, despite T & K's insistence on screening the *Beast*. Will only show them the good reels! Hope this doesn't throw them or make them mad.

Went to screening of Irv's new picture, *The Silencers*. Good film, & will make a bloody fortune.

FEBRUARY 1966   1   TUESDAY

Had idiotic sort of Board Meeting at Gilder at which Arbeid Hope & Maurice did the talking & I smoked their cigarettes. Screened *Blood Beast* for Ian and Aude Powell, his agent. Quite favourably received, I think.

In evening to Saddle Room, the sort of joint I detest, with Ian, John Hall and Isla and Annabelle. Became very depressed. Annabelle eventually went to sleep on me, lulled by the infallible lullaby of my neuroses. I can see her point.

FEBRUARY 1966   2   WEDNESDAY

Morning at Fred's house, mostly just chatting, but ultimately fixing how we will do the revisions suggested by Maurice. Had several good ideas; script will be yet better when all finally inserted.

In the evening, A. & self to dinner with Mr. and Mrs. Fred. Fun, but finally very drunken. Got to bed circa 3.00 a.m. Poor A. has to work tomorrow, God help her.

FEBRUARY 1966   3   THURSDAY

Meeting with G. Fernback re. *Crooked Cross,* Yugoslav project. Very amicable & hopeful. Picture to have £70g. budget, 50% of which Gordon has guaranteed already.

Saw *Batman*, all 4 hours, with A. & Jim Roberts, whose treatment Fernback has with view to doing it as a back-to-back deal with *Crooked Cross.*

No news from Compton on *Flame in the Blood*. Monday comes the crunch, I feel. Here's hoping. Let's just hope they haven't gone snob and are changing company policy from bosoms to Byron, or something equally disastrous for our picture.

FEBRUARY 1966   4   FRIDAY

Amos announces off to Rome to polish Brett's script. Possibly they may want me to direct. This would be fun, as I always wanted to do a big machinery epic, which this one seems to be.

Meeting with Ciga & Fernback re. Yugoslav project. Ciga has spoken with Avala, & in principle they are willing. Great, but let's not buy the champagne till the deal is actually signed. Fernback likes *Manic Mind,* wants Jim to do masterscene script to show Dick Gordon when he arrives. All this too easy for comfort. Where's the snag???

Again no news on *Flame*. We only sit and wait. I wish I had Freddy's calm; but then he's had 20 years in the business to formulate it, the lucky sod.

Saw *Return to the Ashes* with Ian & John. If J. Lee Thompson can get away with a plot like that on a $1m. picture, why shouldn't we be able to on a $140,000 job?

FEBRUARY 1966   5   SATURDAY
Slept till 5.30 p.m. Felt much refreshed on eventual arising...

FEBRUARY 1966   6   SUNDAY   *Septuagesima*
Lunch at Carlton. Met Andra & Angus. Spent afternoon constructing floor plan for house in *Flame in the Blood.*

FEBRUARY 1966   7   MONDAY
Still no news from Compton. There is nothing I can find to do, either with *Flame in the Blood* or *Crooked Cross.* Got well pissed in evening for want of anything better to do.

These diary notes, valuable for showing how difficult it was to set up projects and how hard Mike tried, refer to various industry figures and personal friends of the time. Arbeid was Ben Arbeid, a low-budget producer (*Children of the Damned*). Isla was actress Isla Blair, who was appearing in *The Liars* on TV with Ian Ogilvy. Amos was of course Amos Powell, who Ian Ogilvy said was "very nice." Brett is Amos' friend, expatriate Hollywood star Brett Halsey, who was starring in epics in Rome. Others are clearly film executives. Maurice is Maurice Foster, co-producer of Tigon release *The Projected Man.* Dick Gordon is producer Richard Gordon (*Inseminoid*). Avala is the Belgrade production company that co-produced *The Long Ships* and *Genghis Khan.* G. Fernback is Gerald A. Fernback, producing partner of Richard Gordon. Ciga is unknown but appears to be an agent. Mike was represented by the William Morris Agency in London, but all its records are destroyed.

John Hall was a social friend of Mike's, who had met him through mutual friend Mike Ball-Greene. Hall was working in the film industry as a technician when they met. He later worked for NBC. Mike was then working on and off in Wardour Street and looking for jobs. He asked Hall how he could get a union card. Hall said Mike went to the union office and said, "I'm Mike Reeves and I want to join the union." They looked at him like he was mad.

Producer Richard Gordon kindly recalled his contact with Michael over *The Crooked Cross:*

"Michael Reeves was referred to me when he visited New York City with a print of a film he had made in Italy called *She Beast*, which I believe starred Barbara Steele. He screened it for me and I was quite impressed by it. He was interested to know if I would consider helping to finance other projects that he had in mind or possibly employing him as a director for projects of my own. I had just made two films in England back-to-back, *Island of Terror* and *The Projected Man*, in which my partner was Gerald A. Fernback. *The Projected Man* was done in association with Compton Films (Michael Klinger and Tony Tenser), who provided partial financing and distributed the film in the U.K. For the record, I sold the two films as a package to Universal in the U.S.A. and they released them as a double-bill over here.

"Gerry Fernback and I had several other projects that we were developing. One was *The Crooked Cross*, an original screenplay by Peter Myers, which was a story of horror, witchcraft and devil worship among students at a University in an old German university town. An American actor, Bryant Haliday (who previously starred in two films I made called *Devil Doll* and *Curse of Simba* and who was also the star of *The Projected Man*) was envisaged to star in *The Crooked Cross*. We considered Michael Reeves to direct it. Unfortunately, the project never came to fruition.

"I have absolutely no recollection of a project called *Manic Mind*, nor of a writer called Jim Roberts. Possibly this was something that Gerry was developing on his own in England. We had meanwhile acquired half-a-dozen other properties in various stages of development. I can no longer recollect whether I met Michael Reeves again during one of my stays in England or not, but I remember him as very intelligent, very likeable and someone we felt would achieve success. Unfortunately, Gerry Fernback withdrew from further involvement in production because of ill health. I continued to produce other films on my own in England until 1980, when changes in the marketplace made it too difficult to continue as an independent.

"Michael had nothing to do with the writing of *The Crooked Cross*. Gerry and I commissioned Peter Myers to write it. I still own it! We were in discussions at the time with Avala Films in Yugoslavia, about the possibility of co-producing and co-financing several films with them. They owned a major studio in Belgrade, which I visited. I'm afraid I no longer recollect the reasons why we were not able to set up *The Crooked Cross* in particular.

"I should perhaps add that Boris Karloff (with whom I made two films in the 1950s) spoke about Michael several times when I saw him subsequent to the making of *The Sorcerers*. He had a very high opinion of Michael's talent but felt that he was (and I quote) 'a very disturbed young man' who needed to sort out his private demons."

Mike may not have had a high opinion of *Revenge of the Blood Beast*, but he still informed Don Siegel that he was now a credited director, and Siegel wrote to him on 20th Century-Fox Television, Beverly Hills, letterhead on March 11, 1966:

Dear Mike,

I'm not only amused, I'm very proud that you now have a chair with your name on it. The fact that you feel that the picture is "God-awful" places you in the company of most other directors, who have done many films that they feel are God-awful too. Certainly it's all important that you got the chance to show what you could do with the film.

I notice that Barbara Steele is in your movie. She's a very intelligent, nice girl. I worked with her briefly in a film I made with Elvis Presley.

Many thanks for the kind things you said about "The Killers." It was an exciting film to make and even though naturally we were handicapped by making it to be shown on TV, in the final analysis it didn't hurt us too much.

I may be going to Europe this summer and, if so, I'll make it a point to look you up. In the meantime, good luck.

Cordially,

Donald Siegel

Getting nowhere with *The Crooked Cross* was disappointing, but not the end of the world. The diary reveals many projects Mike was pursuing simultaneously. Diane Ogilvy observed: "There were always lots of projects on. It might have lasted three days or it might have lasted three months. They were going on the whole time. That's just a week you've got there." This probably helped him avoid getting discouraged by rejection, she thought: "He was blinded by everything except movies and that was all. He seemed always to have a lot of other things on the go that he could then put his energies into. He was determined to succeed...it seemed to be more *knowledge* than determination."

Yet Paul Vestey recalled that Mike did get a bit downhearted about not getting projects off the ground. Tim Miller commented: "I think that's typical of filmmakers, even ones with more films under their belts than Mike. I don't think he had any harder a time than any other filmmaker. He used to come to me and say, 'It's a bloody business.' I used to reply, 'It is, but carry on trying.' He would reply, 'I will.' He had the one essential ingredient, which was total dedication."

Ian Ogilvy explained that his experience as an actor was very different than Mike's: "In the '60s, when I was making movies, there was tons of stuff being made, everything from huge things to little things. I did big things, I did medium-sized things, I did little things. Most of it was awful, but where Mike was trying to set up a picture for 18 months, I might do three as an actor. Mike used to say to me, 'You know more about movies than I do. Because you've made many more than I have!' "

Ian thought that Mike's private means possibly contributed to the frustration he was experiencing, in the sense that without his means he would have done more:

> "I think he'd have gone off and done other jobs. If he hadn't been able to get himself a picture, he'd have gone off and been a first assistant on somebody else's picture. He'd have done all that. He'd got all his cards and tickets and everything, he'd paid all his dues. But what it meant was he didn't *have* to go off and do that. He could concentrate on putting a picture together and trying to raise the money for it. Whereas I, as just another working actor, would do a picture for Mike, but then Mike might be maybe 18 months to two years between pictures, and I would have to be working all that time. And I may not be available the next time round."

Ian stressed Mike did not flaunt his wealth: "With the money he had, he was very free to travel. He could move anywhere he liked. You would never have known he was particularly rich. He dressed very shabbily. He always ran a very ordinary car, never a Rolls Royce, all of which he could have afforded. He never did anything like that. He had quite a *nice* car. He had this very nice little house, which is the best thing he had, but you'd never have known it at all." Mike's friendly acquaintance Ernest Harris had no idea he was a millionaire and was shocked to learn this during an interview for this book. Paul Ferris and Ian Ogilvy both thought Mike's inherited wealth eventually caused him feelings of guilt and contributed to his depression. Nicky Henson agreed: "There was always that feeling. He was someone who shouldn't have been rich."

An example of Mike's freedom to travel was a trip Mike took to California to visit AIP after the completion of *Witchfinder General* and look up Chuck Griffith, who recalled:

> "The last time I saw Mike and Annabelle, they came to visit when I was holed up in La Jolla with Dan Haller, writing *Devil's Angels*. Danny was the director. Mike arrived, steered south by my grandmother, Myrtle Vail Damerel, creator of soap opera, who played Mrs. Swickart and Seymour's mum in *The Little Shop of Horrors*. Roger Corman was pissed with me for having written a 'better' Angels script for Danny than I had for him (*The Wild Angels*). Meanwhile, John Cassavetes was raving at me for not having produced a Tennessee Williams classic on that one weekend with Dan—heavily interrupted by Mike and Annabelle. Cassavetes needed a few bucks to finish one of his own pictures. It was, in fact, better than *Wild Angels*, which Roger butchered. We all went to Tijuana and observed some grotesquely vulgar displays in the bars. Mike thought it was a great subject for a picture."

Diane Ogilvy noted that Mike ate at quite ordinary places on the whole, though he did have a fondness for the Carlton Tower Hotel:

> "We went to the Savoy once, because there was a cabaret that we wanted to see. The place that we would eat at more than anything else was the steak house down the end of the road. Ian was a member of Gerry's, a theatrical

place in Shaftesbury Avenue owned by Gerald Campion (the actor who played *Billy Bunter* on television and did a small role in *The Sorcerers*), so Mike used to come there occasionally, but he didn't like it very much. No, it was all very much steak houses, down the bottom-of-the-market ones. Now, we frequently had lunch at the Carlton Tower, on Sunday only. The five of us, with Emma, Ian, Annabelle too. It was a special 'Let's go and be smart and have this wonderful roast beef and Yorkshire pudding,' because neither Annabelle nor I were about to cook it and, if one wanted it, go there."

Tom Baker used to go to Gerry's with Mike too and thought he loved going there: "After a movie, you would go in and there might be people he knew there. And he was moving in that world all the time, in the sense of the energy of making contacts." Tom noted a peculiarity:

"He had an infuriating habit of not finishing his food, Mike, one of those people embarrassing in front of company. Even when we were kids, he would come home and me and my mother would be horrified. Mike would eat half supper and just leave it. All right at his own house, because Betty doted on him and the housekeeper just cleared it away, but in our house it was excruciatingly embarrassing for me to see the food. In restaurants he would be the same. Betty would take us to the Carlton Tower sometimes, great big huge steaks and stuff, and he would eat *some* of it. Even if it was just potted shrimps in a bar, sometimes he would eat it all up, sometimes he wouldn't. He was very casual about that, pretty rude actually. But his own man, his own style. And he smoked a lot, so he probably didn't eat too much food."

John Hall observed the same thing at the Carlton Tower as Tom: "Mike would order beef with double onion rings and double potatoes and then leave it. I would ask him why he had ordered double portions. He had been thinking off on a tangent, about some shot in some film and forgotten to eat."

Of course, the Carlton Tower was close by, but so were other fashionable places of the era, such as Parkes in Beauchamp Place, habituated by celebrities like David Frost, but Diane said: "Mike wouldn't have gone. *Not because Frostie was there!* Only if there was a particular reason. Only once do I remember going to the Savoy. I think it was because there was some extraordinary cabaret, somebody singing or something, but that was only once." Paul Vestey thought it was the American flavor of the Carlton Tower that attracted Mike: "I think he liked it because in those days it seemed slightly American. Anything American was pretty good at that stage. He thought America was all right: modern, Hollywood, Siegel and all the rest of it. I think he thought it was all pretty good stuff. Most of his movie whatevers, Westerns, would have obviously been American."

Ian Ogilvy did not find Mike that interested in nightclubs and the Chelsea set: "Vaguely, but more as something to do after you've been to the movies, if you didn't want to go home. I suppose we did go off a bit to the odd place, but it wasn't a sort of endless round of Arethusa's or Annabel's or anything like that, no. It was much more 'go to the movies and then let's go home and have a drink and get pissed at home.'" Diane Ogilvy said that Annabel's "wouldn't have let him in, the way he dressed. He'd have lost half of the suit, if he'd got one!" Nor did he frequent the likes of Blaises, featured in *The Sorcerers*, which Diane said would have been chosen purely because they could get it at a cheap rate: "Mike didn't go to places like that. Maybe three times a year, unlike a lot of men in his position."

Mike did go to the Saddle Room, which was at 1a Hamilton Place near the Hilton Hotel and was frequented by people such as Ringo Starr, and which Mike said in his diary he detested. Paul Vestey described it:

"It was like Annabel's but not as grand. Just a sort of nightclub. It wasn't particularly sleazy, I don't think. I think he probably went there often for a short time. Knowing Mike, he'd have gone there every day for a month and then never go there again. I think it was just somewhere to go in the evening really, because in those days things weren't open for so much really. After about 11:00 everything shut, unless it was a club. I think it was really just somewhere you could go and get a drink and sit. Nightclubs are usually quite noisy and he did like to talk most of the time. I don't think he'd want to be drowned out."

Mike drank in clubs, as well as pubs like The Star in Belgrave Mews and The Grenadier in Wilton Row, but Paul Vestey said he was not obsessed with drinking: "I remember he used to drink in the evening but it just seemed perfectly normal. He wasn't a sort of drinker-type drinker. He didn't drink much in the daytime, I don't think." Ian Ogilvy suspected Mike did gravitate now and then to legendary clubs like the Scotch of St. James's, especially later on, but not often:

"I think he did a bit. I was a young married man with a young step-daughter, so I might go home fairly early and they might have gone on afterwards. There was a certain amount but not obsessive. Not terribly interested in it really. He was much more interested in going home and playing Monopoly. He loved games, board games, but he made up his own rules. So, playing Monopoly with Mike was absolute hell, because what would happen was, it would come to his turn and he'd look at the board and see where you all were and then he'd sell all his hotels and move them all over to his other properties, which you can't really do, and this would take 25 minutes to work out the sums if everyone waited!

"I remember he bought a game called Diplomacy. We were all going to sit down and play Diplomacy. When nobody was looking, my wife tore up the Rule Book and threw it away, because she was absolutely furious. She wasn't going to get involved in this bloody thing again! So we never actually did get to play Diplomacy at all, which hung about forever and he never really forgave her for doing that! But he loved all that."

Diane Ogilvy agreed:

"I got very bored with these games. They were Mike's particular house rules for Monopoly, which were frightfully complicated and always ensured that he won, because no one really was ever quite sure what they were, but a game would go on for a very long time! I remember he and Annabelle used to go away sometimes. I've no idea where they used to go. Two or three times they went away for weekends to play some beastly game that lasted all weekend. That wasn't Monopoly, that was some other game, which was frightfully devious and involved tape recorders in other people's bedrooms so that you could work out what their plans were."

Another game he played was the Truth Game, which Paul Ferris described as "a good room-emptyer." Diane recalled: "I remember it being played once at Yeoman's Row and I wasn't there. I was very cross about the whole thing. It was the night of the showing of the first rough cut of *The Sorcerers*. The showing was in a screening theater somewhere in Wardour Street. Poker used to be a lot played, too. We had a tremendous phase of that, after Monopoly. I got quite ruined."

Games were not the only manifestation of Mike's playfulness. Ian Ogilvy gave further examples:

"I remember he bought himself—purely for himself—a *frightful* gun called a Johnny Seven child's gun, which is an enormous great plastic thing about four feet long that shot grenades and bullets and lobbed things. It had seven different movements on it. He came over to our house and played with it in the garden! Half an hour later, he's bored with it, so he gives it to my daughter! But he bought it for himself."

Diane did not think so: "Ian and I would not allow Mike to spoil Emma with presents and I felt sure that this was just him finding a way round the rule—if he played with it first, he hadn't bought it as a present for her. He arrived with the gun still in its box and Emma and he unwrapped it together. I think it was a charade, an attempt to make us think that he had bought it for himself."

Ian also reflected: "I remember he did something once. I was working with wood and he came over and he saw a bit of plywood. He said, 'Can I have that?' I said, 'What do you want to do?' He said, 'I want to make something.' He sawed away for *hours*. He made a kind of cut-out car." This little wooden car with driver drawn on the side, a charming object, ended up in Diane Ogilvy's possession.

She commented: "Having never made anything *ever*, he sat with a saw between his chin and his knees and moved the wood up and down. And through the holes where the wheels are were pencils and, of course, film reels on the other side. It's lovely. It's a prized possession. It's all I have of him."

Ian did not think Mike's making a wooden car linked in at all with the description of him as a craftsman in the field of filmmaking: "No, I don't. He was an impulsive sort of person. He'd just go out and do that. He saw a bit of wood. He wanted to make a car. It was just an impulse. He then got bored with it and threw it away. I actually kept it. Don't know why. I had it for years. It was just an impulsive thing."

This might seem to be a surprising quality, given his long and steady relationship with Annabelle. His impulsiveness could easily have found expression in a long string of relationships, especially in the '60s. Ian explained Mike's steadfastness:

"It was this business about safety. Why did he always use me? It was safe. He knew what I was going to do. He knew I was fun to be with, cooperative, and didn't mind not having a caravan. Annabelle was safe. She understood him, she understood his moods, his difficulties. He wasn't easy, he was tricky, and moody. He was a bit moody and obsessive, and I think he loved women but he was slightly frightened of them, I think, in a minor sort of way. I don't suppose he was faithful to Annabelle particularly, though she was to him, but women and sex really didn't occupy a very big part in his life. He often used to say it was awfully messy."

Robin Wood has pointed out that the sex scenes in Reeves' pictures seem to be followed by retribution, as if there was a psychological guilt there, but Ian was dubious: "It's possible. I'm always slightly leery about reading too much into something which was merely Mike wanting to tell a story. I just don't think Mike was terribly interested in sex. I don't think he even *liked* it very much." Yet the love scene in *Witchfinder General* is quite lyrical, but Ian explained: "It's *very* lyrical, but I suspect Mike would always have liked it to have been lyrical and beautiful, but actually it was rather noisy and not terribly dignified. I don't really know, but he did say once to me he thought sex was seriously overrated and rather messy." Mike's cousin Sarah also

Annabelle beside Paul Vestey's Ferrari (Courtesy Paul Vestey)

remembered Mike confiding in her about his intimate life in a way that was quite frank and open for the time, even between cousins.

Diane Ogilvy disagreed that Mike was possibly ever unfaithful to Annabelle: "He had Annabelle and as far as I know he was never unfaithful to her. Never occurred to him to be. And there wasn't anybody else after Annabelle when they split up." In Mike's letter of September 1966 to the Ogilvys, he comments: "Patrick and I will be on the loose in Rome whilst the women in both our lives are making hay." Diane brushed this aside: "Pure joke. I spent a couple of months virtually solely with them. Ian was away, Annabelle was away, Raquel was away, and it was Patrick and Mike who were pretending to be two naughty young men in London. I was with them a heck of a lot and they did absolutely nothing at all. They looked at anything that went past but that was all."

Annabelle sometimes went away to work on films. In Mike's letter he states: "Annabelle's going to Malaga next week to work as Raquel's secretary while she's doing *Fathom*." Their relationship did blow hot and cold, though. Mike and Annabelle announced and broke off their engagement a second time. Even before the filming of *Witchfinder General,* Annabelle moved out and lived in her own flat on nearby Mulberry Close, sharing with actress and singer Dani Sheridan from *The Sorcerers.*

Diane could not recall women ever throwing themselves at Mike: "There were very few other women around. When we were out, literally there was Annabelle, me, Jock Russell's girlfriend, who was not there very often, and when we went out, we lived in our own little world round our little table. Ian was much better-looking than Mike, because I remember Annabelle and I having a conversation about it. I think that Annabelle actually said, 'I'd rather have Mike any day. That's just too good to be true,' or something, about Ian." Diane agreed to some extent with Nicky Henson's description of Mike as gawky: "He was gawky, he was skinny as hell because he used to forget to eat. If you think about it, he was too busy making movies. I wasn't aware of women falling over him at all until the last bit in Yeoman's Row, which was all very peculiar, with all sorts of strange people moving in."

However ambivalent his personal feelings about sex, Mike "was not even a little bit prudish," recalled Ian:

"For instance, the love scene with me and Hilary, which was the last picture we did. He knew my basic modesty and he was teasing me tremendously, saying, 'I'm sorry, you can't be under the sheets. We're going to have the full frontal, full back stuff.' I said, 'No. You know me well enough that long before I sign any damn contract, you know perfectly well that is not going to happen.' He said, 'Yes it is, yes it is, yes it is.'

"And, indeed, when it came to it, he did try and bully about it and I said, 'Mike, you know me, I wear gray flannel trousers and wellies.' That's what I did. I always do that. Not wellies, but I used to wear trousers, not just underpants. Trousers. When asked why, I'd say, 'Because that stops you shooting anything that I don't want you to shoot.' And he'd let me get away with it. So, I mean, he liked all that. He'd go out and buy *Playboy*, I think. I just think he was mildly disappointed in himself that he didn't enjoy sex more, that's all."

In fact, actress Hilary Dwyer was not too happy about the shooting of the love scene in *Witchfinder*, telling Pete Tombs: "I said, 'Do I have to take all my clothes off?' And he said, 'Well, it would be better.' And I thought, 'Oh my God, what's my mother going to say?' He said, 'Nobody will see a thing, it's going to be a very dark blue filter.' I said, 'Right.' So I did it and, when I saw it, I said, 'Mike, it might have been blue, dear, but it *wasn't* dark.'"

Paul Ferris mused: "Annabelle said to me about Mike that he was a voyeur, as a person. I can see that. What is a film director but a voyeur every day? Mike was forever looking through the film director's viewfinder, always, always, always."

In the September 18, 1966, letter from Italy to the Ogilvys, Mike reveals that he is within five days of starting work on a film called *Devil's Discord* starring Edd Byrnes (whom Mike identifies as Kookie in the television series *77 Sunset Strip*) and Peter Cushing. He laments that despite being the "presiding genius," he will not get a credit, for quota reasons. He also says he would like to use Kirk, a favorite assistant, on *Devil's Discord*: "I wish I could use Kirk on my masterpiece, but it's an Italian quota picture." This meant he would have to use an all-Italian crew. Diane Ogilvy has identified "Kirk" as a third assistant on a movie Ian Ogilvy was shooting and explained why his name arose: "Where there was a reference to us having written about somebody called 'Kirk,' it was talking about Mike's references to having been a third assistant, because Kirk was the third assistant and got thinner and grayer on this movie that Ian was shooting, so that would have been a reference to 'Yes, now we understand how hard you worked and how much you ran everywhere.'"

Devil's Discord was a horror film, a ghost story, and *Variety* reported on October 12, 1966, that Patrick Curtis would produce for Curtwel Productions (Curtis and Raquel Welch) and own 25% of the property, co-producing with Compton-Cameo (Tenser and Klinger). Byrnes and Cushing were confirmed as the stars, and Mike had been signed to a one-picture deal. The author was John Burke, who wrote the story behind *The Sorcerers*. John Hamilton, author of a book on Tigon films, came across this film in his researches:

"The script was included in a small pack of Compton papers I obtained some years ago. The script belonged to Harry Fine, a jobbing producer associated with Michael Klinger and Tenser throughout the '60s. It carries only the name of John Burke as writer, it has a hand-written reference to Harry Fine and a number of notes, changes, etc., in the same hand, which I am assuming to be Fine's writing. It's a draft script so there are no other credits given. At the time—1965—Compton had no producers under contract, but Fine had a desk in their office, having worked for Tenser on *The Pleasure Girls*. Tenser wouldn't have hired Reeves/Curtis without having his own man as co-producer. Fine would have fitted that bill for Compton. Plans didn't get very advanced. Fine has identified such things as second-unit footage but, to my knowledge, he was never paid for any work he did on it, so I am assuming that he was handed the script to review and asked for comments. The title continued to surface from time to time as a Tigon project but never progressed off the drawing board."

Mike's letter also talks about Sidney J. Furie's *The Ipcress File* and concludes with an invitation to meet up in Rome: "If you can't find me, ring our Production Manager or try Dave's Dive." Dave's Dive was a place in Rome frequented by filmmakers and actors. Actor Brett Halsey went there:

"The Brits would go to Dave's Dive. There you'd see Burton, O'Toole, all those guys. And then we'd all get together...As I recall, I did not meet Mike in Dave's Dive. Although I was a sometime regular there, I remember meeting Mike at the American Palace Hotel, where he and Annabelle had a small apartment. The American Palace was a popular stopping-off place for visiting Americans and Brits. Dave's Dive was in the basement of the Savoy Hotel, and was run by the late, well-liked Dave Crowley, who was a former middle-weight boxing champ in Britain. I didn't know Mike very well, but his dedication and knowledge led me to believe he was a coming force in the business. In later years I became better acquainted with his former life and business partner, Annabelle Webb."

Mike seems to have been flitting back and forth between London, Rome and Spain at this time. As Iain Sinclair has written: "At that time it was possible, if you had enough money, to take yourself over to Rome, there was so much going on, and talk yourself into doing a movie... Reeves entered into negotiation with schools of Soho sharks, happy to slap palms with a talented amateur who had the key to his own piggybank." It is surprising that he was so close to starting *Devil's Discord* before it fell through, and clearly he approached such projects with the greatest optimism that they would succeed. Many of his potential projects did not get beyond the idea stage, testified Diane Ogilvy: "Mike would have been quite capable of getting a treatment out the night before for something he was trying to get backing for the next day, if he had a meeting."

Mike's love of cars was diminished when he lost his driver's license for speeding in Cromwell Road. Diane Ogilvy recalled: "He lost his license just after I met him and I'm not sure he ever drove again; he took taxis." Tom Baker was around and came to the rescue, driving Mike around in a big Rover he had bought.

Mike then asked him to deliver the car to Rome and accompany him on a project that seemed to be getting the green light from producer Michael Klinger. Tom recalled the details:

"He went to Rome that autumn. *Blood Beast* had been made and that was shown and then he must have been negotiating with Klinger to make a film. There was some script and the notion was to go to Rome; Christopher Lee would star in it, Mike would make it, and Klinger's company would produce it. So he asked me if I would be his assistant. Indeed, he paid me £10 a week. And he bought this big Rover. By that time, Paul Vestey and Jock Russell had bought a garage in Holborn, a car saleroom-cum-garage, and he bought this car from them then. And I drove this car to Rome. He was also going in and out of Spain. Raquel Welch was filming in Spain, so Patrick Curtis was in Spain with her, and Annabelle was working for Raquel. Perhaps Mike was still trying to set things up with Patrick. So, he sent me off to Rome.

"He rented a flat in Rome, October 1966, that he and I stayed in. He just got it from somewhere, gave me the address and told me to get there. It wasn't smart, it wasn't one way or the other; it was just a flat. There was a hotel where Klinger's guy stayed, that was an Americanized, international hotel. We'd go round there and see him quite a bit. It wasn't a ritzy lifestyle. Klinger had a guy who was going to produce it out there, there was a real project, two or three people all staying, and a couple of offices in a little studio complex. I also think Klinger's boy was for *buying* films as much as anything. They would take us occasionally to see some dreadful Italian film.

"So we're in Rome and nothing happened. I spent two months there doing nothing, which was delightful for me, and he came and went. We ate some good meals. We would eat on the Via Veneto in little cafes there. We sat around mixing and met Paul Maslansky. There was no dealing with Maslansky at that time. He and his wife were someone to meet with and have a meal. We hired a guy to look for locations. I think Mike had used him on *Blood Beast* but he spoke English. We drove around. In fact, we went to see this little village where part of *Blood Beast* was filmed, which was an enclosed farm village, very strange place.

"Then we wanted a chateau or the equivalent, a palazzo, and he said, 'Oh, we know the place,' and he took us to this house up in the hills and there were people living in it in separate rooms, different families. It was a great, big Italian palazzo fallen on hard times. We march in the front doorway, there's no door in the doorway, and go up the stairs. It was like a National Trust or great baronial house, where the main rooms lead off one another. We went in there and there were partitions in the rooms and the families were peering out. Squatters, I suppose. Here's this guy marching us through, saying, 'Oh this might do, this might do.' We were surveying the backs of courtyards and we couldn't move them out of the way saying, 'Christopher Lee will look good, looking out of that window,' and we were wondering, 'How can we manage this?'

"Then Klinger or someone pulled the plug on that for some reason. Everyone back to London. I don't know what happened to that project."

After all this disappointment, Mike finally got a project off the ground and that got him his membership in the ACTT film union in 1966, without which he could not have worked as a director in Britain. Paul Vestey recalled: "I had a garage at the time, a commercial garage, and I remember him renting that, and I always associate that with when he'd got his ACTT ticket at that stage. It was probably the first time he'd worked in England I suppose, or worked commercially, which would have been about 1966." John Hall thought that Tigon got Reeves his ticket by pointing out he was a producer who wanted to direct—and so the rules should be bent for him. The project was his fascinating movie titled *The Sorcerers*.

Chapter Five: The Sorcerers

I'm interested in the depths of human degradation. Just how far you and I
can sink.—Michael Reeves, *Penthouse*

The Sorcerers, starring horror film legend Boris Karloff, came about when Mike Reeves
read a science fiction type of story by John Burke called *Terror for Kicks.* He could see immediately that the story was a virtual allegory of the experience of going to see a violent movie in the
cinema and was "determined, come Hell or high water," as he put it in Tigon's brief biography,
to get this one off the ground.

Tom Baker was drafted in to help with the script. He was living at Yeoman's Row. He
recalled:

> "*Sorcerers* was made in winter '66, early '67. The first thing I can remember
> of *Sorcerers* is a four- or five-page treatment, and I think Mike said, 'I've
> bought this treatment,' or 'I've got an option on it.' And I read it. I think he
> got John to write the script, but I can't really recall. It's certainly his story
> and he may well have simply written the first draft of the script. I remember
> we went to see him where he lived in Chelsea or Fulham, but it was pretty
> casual on my part. I was literally a visiting friend interested in the movies. We
> rewrote parts of *Sorcerers,* but it's John Burke's. We changed the ending.
>
> "I think Mike just got on this plane to Madrid and said, 'Mr. Karloff, here's
> a script I own.' Karloff said, 'I quite like it, but I won't do it the way it is,
> because it's thoroughly immoral.' The original is called *Terror for Kicks* and
> that's what it is. They are just sitting there, the old folks at home, enjoying
> this transmitted sensation. Karloff said, 'I'm not having that, that's just not
> good enough for my image. So, you've got to think of something that puts
> me in a good light, a more moral character.'

"So, Mike came back from Madrid and said, 'That's what the great man says, we can only get him if we can put him in a good light.' So we just rewrote the ending. It frees him up, it's him who pulls the plug on the system. It's his choice definitely to bring this whole deal to an end. And Karloff said, 'Oh, right, I'm on for that.' Karloff's pay was half the budget for that film."

John Burke returned to Ireland before shooting began. Iain Sinclair wrote in his book *Lights Out for the Territory* that Burke was delighted to find himself given an equal screen credit, but subsequently received an aggrieved letter from Burke, who felt his contribution had *not* been sufficiently acknowledged. Burke may have a point. The script is credited "Screenplay by John Burke, Michael Reeves & Tom Baker," but by the time the film was made, the credit had become "Screenplay by Michael Reeves and Tom Baker from an idea by John Burke," and he gets no mention on the cinema poster at all! This could have been because much was changed during the actual shooting. Certainly the script contains scenes that were never shot, such as Ian Ogilvy's character getting on a bus. (Diane said Ian himself never used buses.)

Mike had a promising script and agreement from a major star if backing could be found. His friends Patrick Curtis and Raquel Welch had gone into a film production partnership as Curtwell Global Productions and they agreed to put up half the £34,000 budget, if a distributor could be persuaded to put up the other half and distribute. It is interesting that Mike did not, in fact, need to screen *Revenge of the Blood Beast* (not even the good reels) in order to get this project off the ground, but then he had done much more preparation on *The Sorcerers* as a package and had the services of Patrick Curtis as producer.

It is unclear how many distributors Curtis approached, as it was he who made the initial approaches, before they—in every sense—struck lucky with Tony Tenser, now of Tony Tenser Films Limited. Tony commented:

"I wouldn't think at that time of my career that I'd have been the first person that someone would come to with it. Knowing Pat Curtis, I suppose he would have tried maybe Anglo-Amalgamated or MGM or Hammer. I don't know. I didn't *ask* who they'd been to. I assumed that they would have been to other people before they came to me. I'm not an extrovert type of person to think that people come to me because I'm the best and only one. They came to me because I was next on the list as a likely possibility."

Tony Tenser first made his mark on the film business as the energetic publicist of the distribution company Miracle Films. He invented the phrase "sex kitten" about the young Brigitte Bardot and first brought her to fame in Britain. His description of her hair as "carefully disarranged" and other gems became known to film reviewers as Tenserisms. He then went into partnership with nightclub owner Michael Klinger and started the successful Compton Cinema Club chain. Together they ventured into the production of modestly budgeted horror films like *The Black Torment* and struck gold when they backed the young Roman Polanski with *Repulsion* and *Cul-de-Sac*.

The partnership dissolved in 1966 and Tony decided to go it on his own. With £5,000 of his own money and an equal amount on overdraft from the local Midland Bank, he started Tony Tenser Films Limited in one room over a tobacconist's on Wardour Street. He bought and distributed foreign films, and the company expanded through an investment of capital by Norman Hyams, whose father was involved in creating Eros Films. Tony recalled: "I managed to rent out a tiny space, like a cupboard, on the next floor, which my secretary had a desk on and there were two chairs. She sat on one and the Sales Manager sat on the other, and that's how we got going." Eventually, he changed the company name to Tigon Pictures, after a little paperweight of a lion with stripes that someone had left in the one room over the tobacconist's.

For his first small production, *Mini-Weekend*, he used cameraman Stanley Long and line producer Arnold Miller, who had a small company making RAF documentaries. The film came about when its director, George Robbins, called to see Tony and show him the script he'd written. It only cost just over £11,000. Tony got it released, sold it in a few countries and made a handsome profit. It was just the right time for an approach by Michael Reeves. Mike already knew who Tenser was from pitching projects to Compton, and industry contacts of Mike's such as censor John Trevelyan would have been able to guide him to potential backers like Tony.

Tony continued:

> "The next thing I did was...I was sitting in this office, with the annex upstairs with a girl, and the Sales Manager sitting on the girl's lap. She had to go to the toilet if he wanted to use the desk! And I got a call from a chap. He said, 'You don't know me, my name's Pat Curtis. Somebody said to contact you because you've started up. What we're looking for is somebody to come into co-production with us and to handle the distribution.' So I said, 'Fine. Come up and see me.' Now this chap was then driving a Rolls Corniche. Charming young man. He was one of the quiet, unassuming types of American, except for the car. He came up to my office and he sat down and he brought out a script. He said, 'I've got the script here. I've got Michael Reeves who wants to direct it.' So I said, because in this small end of the market beyond the big end one gets to know, 'Didn't he make a film with Barbara Steele?' I got the script. He said, 'Boris Karloff and Catherine Lacey as the stars of it. We're going to call it *The Sorcerers*. It's going to come to £34,000.' Very, very low budget."

Iain Sinclair wrote it was £25,000. Diane Ogilvy was sure: "Mike was working to £40,000." David Pirie wrote the budget was "about £52,000."

Tony Tenser commented:

> "Fifty-two? Well, probably by the time you start paying for prints and things like that, you lose the cost of the film then. You shoot the film on your negative. From that, which is all pieces stuck together, put onto a track, then that has to be printed as a print, then that print is your master positive—that you keep. That's your Bank of England. From that master positive, you draw off a master negative from that, and from that master negative, you make all your prints from. If somebody wants to make a foreign version, they draw off their own master negative from that master positive, because the more copies you take off a thing, the less effective it is in clarity. So the cost of a negative, the cost of a master positive and a master negative, then we have to make an extra negative to send to America, so you add these things on, they cost half as much as the film again."

Hopefully, that clears that issue up.

Tony read the synopsis of the script and liked it. Mike came round to the next meeting at Tony's office with Pat Curtis and made a favorable impression on Tony:

> "I'd known of the film that he'd made and Pat Curtis had explained what was happening, what we were doing, and when I met Mike, he looked like what he was. He looked like a young man who came from a good family, who wasn't doing this for money or fame. He was a film *buff* to the *nth* degree, and he looked a very serious, very much a thinking young man and he looked and gave the impression of having a lot of talent."

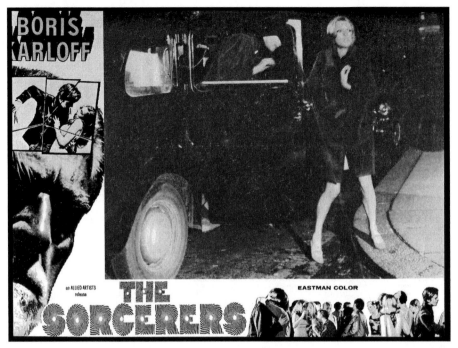

To his great credit, Tony Tenser was almost unique on Wardour Street in giving young talent a chance. Other beneficiaries included Stephen Weeks and Michael Armstrong. But it still seems remarkable that he backed a young director, then barely 23 years old. Tony did not see it that way:

> "Well, it wasn't that marvelous, because I'd only just started on my own at the time. I liked the script and I felt, even if he doesn't make it so well, it's saleable. It's fish-and-chips. It could be the best Dover Sole avec Pommes Frites, or it could be a Cod and Chips, whichever way it comes out the subject was commercial. The path was commercial, so I wasn't taking all that much chance, but I did *feel*, I must admit, that he was going to do a good job. He was really a *most* unusual young man, exceptionally talented."

Tony said, "Yes, we'll do it." Significantly (and possibly to Mike's relief), he did not ask to see *Revenge of the Blood Beast* because, with the sure-fire package he had been offered, he felt he "didn't need to see it." Tony was, incidentally, not at this stage aware how wealthy Mike was.

Thus, filming of *The Sorcerers* went ahead in January 1967. Tony noted: "We shot it in Barnes Studios. It was really like an oversized Anderson shelter aboveground in Barnes. There was a tiny little dressing room. You couldn't shoot the sound track. Most of it had to be redubbed because it was so near to the M4 [highway] and the studio really wasn't sufficiently muffled. There was a lot of studio work in it and the rest was location shots." Such a location was the well-known Blaises nightclub.

The Sorcerers is a very '60s movie, which is a large part of its charm today. Much of this atmosphere derives from the setting in Blaises nightclub, a swinging spot of the era, fashionably located in the basement at 121 Queen's Gate, South Kensington. The club was established enough to survive into the '70s, although the glamour had faded when *Time Out* magazine reviewed the place in 1974: "Full of tourists. Mainly foreigners—more male than female. Claims to play all types of music but definite West Indian influence when we visited. Very bad sound reproduction to anywhere except the dance floor. Decor unremarkable, unobtrusive, boring rather than seedy." The club later closed for good.

It was a different story, though, in 1967. Ian Ogilvy commented: "We thought that club, at the time, was very 'in.' We thought the atmosphere was very good. Of course, within a *year* it had started to date." It appears that the scenes in the club were shot during the daytime, as it would have been too expensive to close the club at night and pay overtime to the crew. Tony Tenser thought so: "I remember shooting in a nightclub. I think that Arnold Miller would have done that, and I think he would have negotiated. I mean, it wasn't shot [when] people [were] in the nightclub. It would have to be contrived. Or you tell the people, 'There's shooting going on, the camera is on, just act normal,' as is sometimes done. But I think in this case we got our own people in. It was good publicity for the nightclub, wasn't it?" Diane Ogilvy confirmed it was contrived: "I seem to remember Annabelle was responsible for an awful lot of the wardrobe, what the girls were wearing."

Diane, initially attending purely as Ian's wife, got roped in to help: "Anybody that was around always had to. There were no spare bodies ever to do anything. One could never tell whether it was go out and buy something for the wardrobe, or it would nearly always be me that would be sent off somewhere, because everybody else was busy doing something." Even Patrick Curtis was hands-on, as he told Pete Tombs: "On a film like this, everybody pitches in and does whatever, so I was lying on my back on the floor filming the kids on the dance floor dancing. And this is right at the height of the mini-skirt era, so the skirts are really quite short. Fortunately, I think they had matching knickers! Anyway, I'm looking through the viewfinder and I see the incredible face of my wife looking down at me, going '*What* are you doing?' "

Blaises may have been hip, but the music group playing at the club is quite conventional (the instrumentals and songs were theirs, not the work of composer Paul Ferris), considering Syd Barrett's Pink Floyd played Blaises! Indeed, in the scene where Ian Ogilvy goes to Elizabeth Ercy's flat, she puts on Cliff Richard's *In the Country*, a hit of the time but hardly representative of the psychedelic explosion that was imminent in contemporary pop music. Ian Ogilvy commented:

"I suppose that's the answer, it was just a hit of the time. I don't think music played a tremendously big thing in Mike's life. Conversation more than music. We went through the hippie era. Most un-hippie man you've ever met in your life. He wasn't a slave to the latest fashionable ideas and the closest he got to psychedelia was what plays on my face in the mesmerizing scene in *Sorcerers*, and that he was quite pleased with, because he'd got some special machine to do it with, but that was as close as he got to the flower power people. He was very unhippie-like. He was just interested in making pictures."

Paul Ferris shared Mike's love of film soundtrack music and said Mike was never interested in the music of groups like Pink Floyd. Benjamin Halligan writes that he had seen them play live, though.

Yet there was a small amount of dope-smoking among some of Mike's circle—nothing unusual about that in the late '60s among the well-to-do young—and Mike tried it a bit, but "wasn't a pothead," according to Paul Ferris, who said that Mike preferred drinking. Paul told a funny story of an unfortunate experiment in which they indulged: "We even tried to smoke banana skins! I remember it was in Mike's house. They're roasted and, smoked, they make you high. I remember nearly choking ourselves to death trying to smoke banana skins, which of course didn't get you high at all. They just made you sick and made you stink of bananas!" Tom Baker had memories of these experiments: "In the innocent days of the 1960s, banana-skin smoking was one of the most enduring urban myths. No one really believed it, but sooner or later everyone

Elizabeth Ercy, Ian Ogilvy and Victor Henry in *The Sorcerers* (BFI)

tried it. I certainly gave it a go. Rather baffled by what to do with what I remember as being something of a crispy, charcoally texture. Perhaps I had the recipe wrong."

Ian Ogilvy recalled the shooting of *The Sorcerers*:

> "Raquel came along and worked on the set several times, helping with wardrobe and things like that. That was rather nice. I remember Raquel phoning me one day and saying, 'Listen, I wonder if you can help me?' I said, 'What?' She said, 'Well, I want to take acting lessons, but I can't go off to a drama school, because I'm already a great sort of sex queen and everybody would laugh. Do you know of anybody who does it privately?' So I gave her a couple of names and addresses and she never took them up. But it was quite a nice relationship everybody had. She wasn't there very often, but she was around a bit. Arnold Miller was in the picture. There's a taxi driver in it, Arnold Miller also played that taxi driver! Everybody did get roped in. I'm surprised Patrick Curtis wasn't in the picture, frankly. I'm also surprised he didn't manage to get Raquel in there somewhere, but I suppose Raquel would have drawn the line at that."

In such a brief career, Mike certainly seemed to have a huge number of contacts in the business, even Raquel Welch! Ian reasoned: "On those Allen pictures and with Don Siegel, he'd picked up a lot of people on the way as a young kid, and he had an eye to the main chance. He knew who he admired and liked, so, before I knew him, he would have found a lot of these people out. And he had the time, you see. He had the time to go off and work on it."

A memorable moment in *The Sorcerers* is the zoom-in to the Wimpy Bar burger, and Ian agreed that it was unintentionally hilarious: "Yes, I think what he wanted there was to show that this is where this old boy thinks he'll find somebody who'll fit. The idea was that it should look fairly nasty, the 'Wimpy'...yeccchhh! So, I suppose Mike's view of a Wimpy Bar was somewhat jaundiced!"

One critic described Ian's character, Mike Roscoe, as a "mod," and it was the tail end of the mod era, but Ian said that was not what was intended:

"No, not at all. It was a word that never came up. Mike just said, 'Look, be yourself, but could you possibly do it just slightly *off?* As opposed to being Eton, could you be not-be-Eton? Could you be a bit grammar school?' Which I tried to be. I don't know if it works at all. It's slightly *off.* I was doing it a bit like *that.* That's all. That's all he said. No, there was no attempt at making it any one of a group. Would a mod be running a little antique shop? Probably not, no. The man's just a bit of a wide boy, isn't he, really? That's all. Jack the Lad, that's all Mike said, 'Just be Jack the Lad.' "

The Glory Hole, the antique shop in the picture, was not an actual antique shop: "I don't think it was an antique shop. It was in Lisson Grove. The stuff we had in there was pretty terrible and we were breaking it up, smashing things, and we had the door set specially done. It was just a nice little location, an empty shop that they managed to rent and set up. I don't think it was real."

But another location, the fur salon, was real: "That *was* a fur salon. In fact, I bought my wife a fur coat from there, fairly cheap one but I did. It was called Frank Cooney Furs and it was a real furrier." The salon was in Avery Row. Other scenes were filmed around Latimer Road.

Such locations contribute a nice London feel to the film. Another was in the swimming pool scene. Ian stated:

"That was Dolphin Square. Probably because he knew somebody who lived in Dolphin Square. You know, every shot is *stolen,* in all the pictures. We never got *permission* for any of these things. The blowing up of the car at the end of *Sorcerers* was absolutely illegal and we were very nearly arrested for it. Because we'd never asked permission for this. We'd just found this building site, dereliction site in Notting Hill, and we got a little bulldozer to push the car over, so that was that. Then the special effects man came in and rigged it all up with explosives and we had three cameras on it, including my 16-mm camera, and we blew it, and he'd left all the petrol in the petrol tank! He'd forgotten! So that explosion is *big* and the special effects man went white and got in his car and just drove away, leaving us there saying, 'Wa-hey, what a great bang!' Then 'ee-ee, ee-ee, ee-ee'...five fire engines, police cars, everybody's taking names, Mike Reeves was virtually arrested, certainly Arnie Miller had to go off to the police station. Oh, it was terrible! But all that stuff, we never got permission to shoot it. We just stole it. 'Anybody looking now? Okay, go and shoot!' All of them!"

Diane Ogilvy recalled: "There were stories of little old ladies' gas cookers leaping away from the walls in the local flats and things, because it was a very big bang. Patrick Curtis has a series of stills on this, where he was behind one of the cameras. It was probably the only occasion *ever* of a two-camera shoot. The camera running all by itself eventually, because the man had gone!"

Tony Tenser remembered the trouble with the police:

"Oh yes, there was. It wasn't so much trouble with the police. It was done on a Sunday morning, to do the car chase, and you could make it whatever time of day you can, but at that time in London on a Sunday morning—I don't think you can do it now—if you were there early enough, the streets were clear. Not necessarily the main roads, but the side streets were clear. What had happened was that there was an explosive device in the car, just to blow it up and set it on fire. The pyrotechnicians were involved in that—we got them in—and I think Mike wanted Ian to be seen at the controls, so we shot from the passenger seat looking up at Ian's face driving and took other shots from behind and from the side of the car. When the explosion happened, Mike wanted it to look as if Ian was in the car when it blew up. The car screeched to a halt and Ian got out before the explosion. I can't remember using a dummy. It was going to be more a matter of flames and less of a bang. We were going to expand the bang in the studios, but it was quite a bang and people phoned the police. They thought something real had happened. There was smoke coming out. And the police weren't happy about it. Arnold Miller had to go and explain it. There was an apology: 'It won't happen again.' "

Diane Ogilvy recalled there *was* a dummy in the Jaguar when it crashed, to give the impression of Ian being at the wheel. (Mike Reeves' hands, covered in blood, doubled for Ian's in the crashed Jaguar.)

Patrick Curtis suggested to Pete Tombs the size of the explosion was no accident:

"I remember it like it was yesterday—well, if we put maybe 10 gallons' worth of petrol at the bottom of this pit and when the Jaguar goes over the cliff and it hits the bottom, we can explode the 10 gallons, and it was, 'Well, 10 gallons is good, 50 will be even better.' And it blew the hell out of all of us. It shattered windows for blocks around. Our concern was that if we didn't get the shot and didn't get it finished within *minutes*, the police would arrive and we'd all be in jail for sure. And so we left this burning Jaguar at the bottom of this pit and we all took off for nine different directions. We figured, 'Well, they'll catch one of us, but we'll all keep our mouths shut.' "

Arnold Miller made himself useful, according to Tony Tenser:

"A London taxi is used for a couple of scenes in the film. It was also used as a camera car when we were doing moving shots. It was also used to carry the equipment in. It was used for a number of purposes. Arnold Miller—I think he knew people in the business—bought the taxi, which was no longer operating as a taxi. I think the police were informed that we'd be shooting a scene with this thing that looked like a taxi but wasn't really a taxi, but we put the taxi thing on it when Karloff hails it and Arnold had to drive it. All he had to say was 'Evening, guv,' and 'Thank you, guv,' or 'Half a crown, guv,' or something. I said, 'Well, it's a good idea, keep the costs down, such a low-budget film.' I think he paid 60 pounds for the taxi and when the film was over, I think he sold it for 65. Made a profit out of it!"

Ian confirmed they rarely had two cameras:

"That was very rare. Couldn't afford two cameras. But on an explosion you've only got it once, so you'll cover it with as much as you possibly can. They were all deserted cameras, too. Every single one of them was set running and we all scampered because nobody quite knew how big it was going to be and they were all very close to the car. There were three cameras all by themselves, all with different lenses in. No, he would very rarely do that. Apart from anything else, he would naturally have objected to the style of doing it. He was very sparing with his coverage. He didn't shoot endless stuff. He was quite cut-inside-the-camera. He knew exactly what he wanted to make. As far as I know, in no Mike Reeves film was an entire scene ever deleted. In terms of film *structure,* no scene was ever deleted because it was superfluous. All right, he wasn't cutting to television timings, he was very free, but at least from the point of view of the structure of the original script, he would maybe cut within the scene, but no way the total scene was ever dropped."

Ian testified that, although they could only afford one camera most of the time, the films were fully crewed (unlike some of Roger Corman's early films):

"Oh, they were fully crewed. Well, as a minimum, what we could get away with. We didn't break any union rules. I suspect we broke every Equity rule in the book, but in those days we didn't really care, you see. Using non-Equity actors, shooting far too long, not having proper doubles—we never had stand-ins, we had stuntmen. Alf Joint was a favorite. Alf Joint was in both *Witchfinder* and *Sorcerers.* In fact, he had a part in *Sorcerers,* he was the boss of the garage, and then he plays the guard at Orford Castle in *Witchfinder,* and was a great favorite, and did all the stunt arranging on both those pictures. Mike was very fond of him. But I'm sure we broke all sorts of rules."

Mike would not be upset by little accidents like the unexpectedly large explosion. On the contrary, as Ian explained:

"Mike did love accidents. The chase scene in *Sorcerers* toward the end when the police are chasing me and the police car spins was total accident. And I was in the car: I was in the police car! The reason was that Mike was in the boot. He always shot from boots of cars. He said, 'It's the best camera platform in the world.' So open up the back of a car, lie in the boot and shoot from the back of the car. And I was there that day, because I'd been shooting stuff of me being in the leading car, and Mike said, 'Listen, we need another face in the back of that Jag, Ian, you wouldn't go in and pretend to be the other policeman, he's not here today?' And I said, 'Fine, fine, fine.' And that spin was a *complete* accident. But then, you see, having got that spin, he then cuts to Ivor Dean grimacing. Because he said, 'We've got it, it's absolutely wonderful, we've got the whole damn thing, all right. Now we need a cut of you, Ivor, just grimace.' So all that kind of thing Mike loved. Anything that happened."

If making the film sounds rather dangerous on occasion, Ian confirmed to Pete Tombs that it was: "I was driving this motorcycle down the M4 at about 100 mph with no helmet, no protection of any kind, with Mike Reeves in the trunk of a car. 'Come closer,' he'd say, and I was only about inches away from the back of this car!" This motorcycle scene has clear parallels with scenes of Ian running through countryside in *Revenge of the Blood Beast* and riding on horseback in *Witchfinder General*: All three scenes show Mike's affinity with recording movement onscreen. He never forgot that these were *motion* pictures, which is what makes his work more cinematic than Hammer's horror output; for Paul Ferris, most English movies were in fact "*stillies*."

Julian Bamford (*Films in London*) wrote that Mike nearly abandoned production of *The Sorcerers* at one stage because of the difficulties involved, but this was refuted by Ian Ogilvy. Diane Ogilvy commented: "I don't think it's true. He wouldn't have let go. He wanted it. He wanted it very much. He could have been having a horrid day and said to someone, 'I've got a good mind to chuck it in,' as we all do." These problems seem to have arisen from the low budget, making Mike's perfectionism and ambitions almost impossible. Director of Photography Stanley Long protested that the schedule proposed was not achievable and as a result, Tony had to cut costs by shortening the script and shooting schedule. Benjamin Halligan writes of the frustration this caused Mike and the tension with Stanley Long.

Tony Tenser thought:

> "I don't know of that, but if I was asked to have a guess, I would say that if such a thing did manifest itself, he may have been in a down mood. He would never say, 'I'm fed up with this' and go off. He wasn't that kind of person. He wouldn't speak like that. He would go off to his room and he would be silent and lock himself in his room for a while. Now, knowing that he had this depressive illness—I didn't realize at the time he had that—that could have been blown out of proportion."

On the whole, *The Sorcerers* was a happy shoot and Tony Tenser in part attributed this to the cooperative temperament of its star, Boris Karloff:

> "*The Sorcerers* was a small picture and it was shot in a very short space of time and we didn't have actors of the type of Vincent Price. Now, Boris Karloff was a quiet, modest horror man. He wasn't ranting and raving. Vincent Price was the big...you know. They're both excellent actors but I don't think Boris Karloff could play a Vincent Price part, and vice versa, good actors though they were. They *could* play the part, but it wouldn't be convincing enough. Mike Reeves, he was a quiet person, he didn't show himself like Vincent Price."

According to Ian Ogilvy, Mike got along well with older people like Arnold Miller and the various backers he went to see: "Mike got on fine with the older generation. Remember, he had been to public school. Whatever you think of the morality of a two-tiered educational system, the public schools do train you in the social graces, of which Mike had an abundance. I remember my mother being very fond of him. He could be charming and attentive when he wanted to be." This was undoubtedly a help when it came to working with the elderly Boris Karloff.

Karloff posed Mike none of the problems he would later encounter with Vincent Price, recalled Ian:

> "That was extraordinary. I remember shooting the scene in the Wimpy Bar late at night and I arrived and Boris had been there for quite a long time, because he had to do the entrance and the coming in, all this stuff. I got there. It was about eleven o'clock at night. He was just sitting in a corner. Suddenly I said, 'Boris, have you had anything to eat?' I said, 'Nobody has

Boris Karloff in *The Sorcerers*

thought to ask you if you shouldn't have some dinner? It's terrible.' And he said, 'Wait, wait, wait, by all means go and make a little row if you like, but don't tell the young director. He's got quite enough on his plate as it is without all that.' That was remarkable.

"And Mike had him doing all sorts of things like falling over. But he was very solicitous of Boris and adored him. Boris was not like Vincent. I mean, Boris had long ago decided that he was just going to keep working and do anything anybody offered him. He got a standard rate whether he had one line or whether he was in the whole picture. He had a standard rate of pay, didn't argue about it. You wanted Boris, you got him like that. Of course, he was uninsurable at that age. You couldn't get insurance on him.

"I remember the best and most extraordinary thing that happened was that the sound man quite early on in the picture went to Mike Reeves and said, 'Listen, Mike, I don't know what it is, but every time Boris moves, we're picking up a squeak. We're going to have to do something about it.' Mike went to Boris and said, 'Boris, it's very embarrassing, but apparently every time you move, we're getting a terrible squeak. Could you tell me what that might be?' Boris laughed like a drain. He said, 'Oh!' He called for the props man and said, 'Got any Three-in-One?' 'Huh?' Really like the Monster, you see. He pulled up his trouser leg and he had had an accident which had bowed one of his legs badly and he had a brace that supported his leg, fitted to his shoe and jointed at the ankle and the knee, and he just oiled himself like that! He thought it was terribly funny.

"And Boris also carried a tiny cylinder in his pocket, probably a preparation for asthma relief. Going up stairs, he'd suddenly stop and breathe in heavily. So it was really rather odd, because it was very like the Monster in many ways. It was almost like a fabricated man, but he was the most charming man in the world, and he and Mike adored each other. I remember I had my little girl who was five and Boris was sitting there with that awful black burn makeup all over his face. He was sitting there like that and my daughter Emma was looking at him and he said, 'Come here.' She went over, sat on his knee, they were chatting away like that, and her reaction was, he was just a funny old man with black stuff on his face. There was no connection at all. Just a man with black stuff! But he was a very charming man and most delightful and game for anything. 'What do you want me to do? You just tell me what you want to do, I'll try and do it.' There was great affection for him."

Boris sent Mike a Christmas card, which Mike pasted into his scrapbook, reading "Here we are—Good Luck to us & heaven help us!"

Ian Ogilvy was unsurprised that Karloff went on working literally until he dropped:

"There was no reason for him not to. He enjoyed it. He used to think about it, talk about it, and he was very pleased to play a goodie. He liked that. He thought that was a nice part. He also was *overjoyed* when it played at the Carlton cinema in the Haymarket. He said, 'I haven't had a movie of mine played here in the West End in 15 years. They don't get West End releases.' This is before *Targets* and this sort of thing...He was frightfully proud of the fact that it was playing at the Carlton cinema. This enormous great star was proud of the fact that it was playing at the Carlton."

Ironically, the support feature to *The Sorcerers* was *Tower of London*, directed by Mike's hero Roger Corman, written by *Revenge*'s Amos Powell and starring Mike's next leading man, Vincent Price! Mike kept two color snaps of the front of the Carlton advertising *The Sorcerers* in his scrapbook.

Boris Karloff, then still very active in low-budget horror films, must have been an obvious choice for Mike, but the choice of an actress to play his wife was more difficult. It was Alfred Shaughnessy who came to the rescue: "Michael looked on me as a sort of father figure, who had been in films since 1946, and we used to discuss casting and technical matters. He was stuck for an elderly actress to play a sinister part in one of his films and I suggested Catherine Lacey. Michael Reeves was delighted with her performance and thanked me for the suggestion."

Except in the case of Vincent Price, Mike generally did not get much involved in an actor's performance, as, like Roger Corman, he felt that was best left to the actor himself, unless of course he was way off track. Ian Ogilvy explained:

"He was in awe of actors and respected them because he didn't understand what acting was. He never understood actors at all and always said that. He never directed you, you see. He would say, 'Could you do that a bit quicker?' That was about the limit of Mike's directing. He always said what Don Siegel said. Apparently Don Siegel said, 'I wouldn't presume to direct an actor, but what I will do is cast it right.' When asked why he got such great, lovely performances, Don Siegel said, 'I cast it right. I don't presume to tell an actor what to do. I don't *know* what to do. It's a mystery to me.' Mike always felt the same. He said, 'I don't know what you do. Absolute mystery. I know if you're a bit slow or if you're going too fast, but the rest of it really is up to you. That's why I cast you.'

"I think there were only two times Mike ever did really get involved with an actor's performance. First of all with Vincent, which was a great bone of contention, and the other time was with Catherine Lacey, because she begged him to. She said, 'I can't work like this. You've got to tell me what to do.' And he said, 'But you're a wonderful actress. You should know what to do.' And she said, 'But I need the reassurance of you telling me.' Mike said, 'Listen, Catherine, you're just perfect.' 'I can't be, I must be doing something wrong.' 'Well, maybe you could go a little faster!' That's about all he could say! What she was doing was wonderful. She was a wonderful actress, a great stage actress. So he kind of made up a few things for her to do...Catherine hated her part, and it worried and depressed her. She didn't really like having to do these things at all. But they got on well. It was actually a very happy shoot. Everybody was nice on that picture."

Mike even used his friend Peter Fraser in the small role of the detective. Peter had achieved success on stage at the Royal Court under Lindsay Anderson and was in *Dr. Who: The Dalek Invasion of Earth*, which drew the highest-ever Saturday evening viewing figures. "He gave me a lick and a spit," he noted wryly.

Ian Ogilvy's work in *The Sorcerers* is especially intense, particularly by comparison with his later film *No Sex Please, We're British*. Where most casting directors have considered him what he called "a lounge lizard, relaxed sort of character," Reeves in *The Sorcerers* and at the end of *Witchfinder General* brought out something very dark in his persona, something unique in Ogilvy's work and even in the British cinema generally (only echoed by Michael Powell's once-vilified film *Peeping Tom*).

However, Ian denied that this was something Mike deliberately encouraged:

"I just wonder whether it wasn't the nature of the movie we were making? Actors, if they have any pride at all in what they do, will adjust what they do to the atmosphere of the picture, and both those movies had dark and black sides to them. There weren't many jokes in Mike Reeves' pictures. So I suppose you simply adapted to the mood of the movie, because the mood of the movie between that and *No Sex Please, We're British* was enormous. So really I think it was just a general adaptation of what we were doing, but without any thought behind it really."

A couple of moments in *The Sorcerers* reveal the atmosphere of intense violence that dominates *Witchfinder General*, but Ian Ogilvy confirmed that there was no violence at all in Mike's own personality: "I never saw signs of violence, incipient or otherwise, in Mike. He was the kind of person who would walk away from trouble rather than stay and watch or even become embroiled. Sensible chap." Tom Baker spoke about Mike's attraction to violence onscreen: "Mike and I had no experience of violence, but you think what would be quite strong stuff, or what would work? What the hell did we know about violence? Sheltered public school life, we didn't know about these things. But you think what would look good onscreen and what would work, so it seems a reasonable idea."

Stanley Long, who photographed *The Sorcerers*, was less convinced about Mike's motives, years later complaining in David McGillivray's book *Doing Rude Things* that Mike had a kink about blood: "He was flinging blood about on the set like it was going out of fashion, I mean gallons of it...He had this obsessive thing about throwing it up the walls, and when Susan George was stabbed with a pair of scissors, it was going all over the cameras and all over the crew and everybody's clothes, and I said, 'Really, you know—come off it!' But he loved it. He seemed to revel in it. He definitely had a kink about blood."

Elizabeth Ercy as Nicole and Ian Ogilvy as Mike Roscoe in *The Sorcerers*

This compares with Nicky Henson's memory of shooting *Witchfinder General* quoted by Jonathan Rigby in *Shivers*: "I remember on *Witchfinder* he used to walk about with a viewfinder and a blood squirter; he'd just come up and squirt it over you. He had it with him all the time to avoid constantly giving orders to the costume people. He'd also come at you with scissors and cut your clothes so that there were proper bullet holes in them."

Robin Wood has suggested Ian was Mike's alter ego in films, but Ian rejected this: "It was just safe. He knew what I would do. He knew I'd be okay. I could sort of vaguely do it and it was safe. And he always threatened that he didn't want me at all in any of the pictures, you know. He always said, 'I'm going to get John Castle in the next one or I'm going to get so-and-so,' and I'd nod and think, 'Well, poo on you!' But he'd always end up with me because he'd like having people he knew around him." Ian did not feel he looked like Mike facially: "I'll tell you who he really looked like, I thought, was that very romantic French actor who died in the 50s, Gerard Phillipe. That's who he looked like, Gerard Phillipe. Well, a bit."

A beautiful photo of Mike was taken on the set and described by Betty as Mike eating a spoon of ice cream. Diane Ogilvy was responsible for the photo being taken and has explained this was not what Mike was doing:

> "No way was it ice cream. It was chewing gum. Mike was playing straight into a super 8 camera lens. Betty Reeves probably knew exactly what it was but preferred the ice cream image. The photograph was taken by Tony Boase, a photographer friend of mine. 30 Bourdon Street was his studio. With Mike's permission, I had asked Tony to come on location and take some

much needed photographs of Ian. It was taken outside of the Glory Hole. I seldom pointed a camera at Mike for fear of breaking his concentration. Nearly all of the shots that Ian took of Mike were of him talking quietly to the actors or crew (in other words, directing) or of him being totally absorbed in a thought process. I am sure that the chewing gum and other playful actions were only him acknowledging, for just a few seconds, that the camera was on him. Then he could return to his thinking process."

Mike Roscoe's pal in *The Sorcerers* is played by the late Victor Henry, whom Ian remembered fondly:

"Victor was a great, great friend, because he and I were at drama school together, but he's dead now. Victor was one of the great wild men of his day. He did a picture called *All Neat in Black Stockings*, he was king at the Royal Court, he was kind of the Kenneth Branagh of his day, I mean he was the most exciting young actor in town. Everybody was after him. He just did this picture right in the *height* of his career. He was a great drinker and boozer, a mad, crazy little guy from up north, and a *wonderful* actor. And not long after he got knocked over by a bus and remained in a coma for *17 years* until he died. Nobody had ever heard of him, apart from in the business, and Simon Callow wrote this wonderful obituary which was published in the *Evening Standard*."

Ian recalled a minor problem Mike encountered with Victor:

"Victor was a great, great drunk, a *terrific* drunk, on beer, and there's a scene just outside a pub where I say, 'I'm going off,' and that's where I go to the Wimpy Bar, at the very beginning of the picture. It was a very cold night and they were setting up outside this pub, this real pub, and Mike stupidly said to us both, 'Go in, you know, keep warm.' So I had half a lager and Victor starts on the pints. He's absolutely fine. He can hold his drink perfectly well. He's perfectly fine. And then we get called out. We go outside and the temperature is below freezing, and it hits him, and he does his scene. He's trying to find his pocket and he can't find it, so it looks like he's masturbating! I mean, it's absolutely extraordinary!

"And Mike's sitting there, and he doesn't know whether to laugh or cry, because it's unusable. Victor's slurring his speech like this and what happens is, the next day up at rushes, Mike says to him, 'Victor, I want you to come to rushes today, and I want you to bring your agent please.' And I go there because I'm riveted, and I sit behind Victor and Victor's agent. His rushes start and Victor, who's sitting right in front of me, sinks lower and lower like this. It's unusable. This agent said—this is how much it cost in those days—'Listen, take it out of his salary, we'll reshoot it, we'll pay for it.' So what you saw outside that pub was a reshoot because Victor was so drunk. Mike was *amused* by it, but not to the extent of letting it go. You couldn't actually show that scene. It wouldn't have made sense. You had a totally drunk actor. But Mike used to get drunk himself. He was quite a drinker. If it got in the way of a movie, he would be really angry, but if it didn't get in the way of a movie, he'd laugh."

Ian Ogilvy's girlfriend in the picture was played by French actress Elizabeth Ercy, whom he described: "She'd done one of those *Doctor* pictures the year before, one of those 'Simon

Mike on the set of *The Sorcerers* playing with chewing gum. (Photographer: Tony Boase)

Sparrow' things. She was a lovely looking girl, but very inexperienced. She just looked pretty and that's all Mike wanted, really. I think he'd seen her in the picture and just asked for her." Diane Ogilvy recalled that Mike had a problem with the getting of her union ticket and that Elizabeth was then Michael Caine's girlfriend. Patrick Curtis met Michael Caine socially at this time. Nothing became of Elizabeth Ercy in British films thereafter, but there were rumors of an attraction between her and Mike.

The Sorcerers is also famous for being Susan George's first film. Ian Ogilvy explained how she was chosen:

Ian Ogilvy and Susan George as Audrey in *The Sorcerers*—her first film

"I claim to have discovered Susan George. Totally. In *Sorcerers*. She was 15 years old. And that picture's never on her CV. She was absolutely enchanting. I remember the interview. We had three girls. I was in on this interview. Three girls. One girl came in and she was terribly wrong. Frightfully wrong, awful, glasses, miserable, boring and ugly. And then another girl came in who was foreign and kept saying she had to go to three more interviews and she really couldn't spend too much time with us.

"And then this girl Susan bounced in. She came bouncing with all her hair flying, a little mini-skirt, she was so pretty and she was such fun, we said, 'Ah!' So I claim to have been instrumental in starting Susan George on her career. And she was lovely in the scene, I thought. Charming. She looked sweet. An absolute natural. At the interview, we just fell in love with her. We just thought she was wonderful. She's always nice to me when I see her. She does remember the picture, it's just that she wants her name taken off!"

Some of the critics who reviewed *The Sorcerers* found the color uneven and the photography not particularly good. Stanley Long went on to direct his own sex films for the British softcore market in the '70s. Ian Ogilvy commented: "We didn't have Johnny Coquillon on that picture. Stan Long, I think, was very B or C team, frankly. He was part of the production thing as well, really. It was all a bit scrappy. I think we did have problems with matching. No, I don't think *The Sorcerers* was particularly interestingly shot, but we tried. Stan was game. He'd allow himself to be tied onto the top of the endless Jaguar with the blue light in the foreground. He was only tied on with bits of string! Whirring round! He was game, but..."

Diane Ogilvy agreed: "There wasn't the incredible group of very keen movie-makers on *Sorcerers*. Stan Long was a brilliant hand-held cameraman but not the most inventive. Johnny Coquillon was out to make his name. They're not in the same class at all."

Tom Baker agreed that he wrote "not so much" of *The Sorcerers*. Mike was supporting him financially during this period, as he had no other employment. In a letter, Mike jokes about employing Tom as "my butler, my chauffeur." Ian Ogilvy said: "I was always very dubious as to what exactly Tom's involvement was. I think he did co-write. Tom and Mike were great, great friends. Tom wanted to be a writer. We were all very young and at the start of our careers. I think probably he was a rather good writer and indeed they did work together but, for instance, Tom was never on set or location. When the script was finished, that was the *beginning* of the script. After that, it was torn about and fiddled about with and rewritten according

Paul Ferris during his modeling career

to circumstances. Usually, writers are quite often there watching their work being done. Tom never was, not as far as I remember."

Mike was encountering one of his most important collaborators when he first met composer Richard Paul Ferris (he did not like the name Richard and was known as Paul). Paul was from a working-class family, had "no money at all," was briefly a civil engineer, became a male fashion model, went to drama school, acted on stage in *Camelot* at Drury Lane, landed a role in the television series *The Baron* as Steve Forrest's assistant, and eventually gave it up. He said: "*The Baron* was such crap." He stopped acting and turned to music, teaching himself how to score for films. His ambition was to write film scores like Maurice Jarre. He and actor Nicky Henson, who had been in *Camelot* with him, had a contract to write for Cliff Richard and the Shadows. They had already written the theme for a minor Gene Barry movie, *Maroc 7*.

Paul remembered his first meeting with Mike:

> "I first met Mike in the Shadows' office. Before the contract with Cliff and the Shadows, I'd done a slow song called 'Visions.' Anyway, Mike had heard that. The tie-up was through the office. They had the publishing on the *Maroc 7* music and the Shadows did a single of the theme from the movie. It was an awful movie, but the Shadows did a single from it, and it got to number 70, only because it was the Shadows, so it wasn't very good. But Mike had heard that and wanted the tie-up or liked it somehow, and I seem to remember meeting him first in the Shadows' office: a fellow called Harry Walters who was looking after their music side.
>
> "I liked Mike immediately. I knew we could do good stuff together. I felt it instinctively. He didn't bullshit. That was the great thing about him. No bullshit. That's worth its weight in gold in itself. That plus enormous talent is one hell of a combination, isn't it? It does spoil you—instead of enormous bullshit, no talent, like most other people. He said he wanted me to do the music for a movie. That was *The Sorcerers*. It *was* because he knew what I'd done."

Tom Baker commented: "They were quite drawn to each other. Mike was very struck when he found Paul and Paul was keen to get into the movies and Mike gave him the opportunity." Paul's enthusiasm was not dimmed even when he eventually saw *Revenge of the Blood Beast*, of which he said: "I thought it was awful...no, not *awful,* I exaggerate."

Paul's *Sorcerers* score was underrated, even by Paul himself. The mood of the music is often calming. When Ian Ogilvy goes to Boris Karloff's flat, there is just soft piano tinkling. Later on, in the more dramatic parts, there is a harpsichord. Paul himself regarded his score as "bad" and "awful": "There's only one moment—I can't even remember the music for it now—which isn't bad. When Boris is walking along the road." Paul was trying to make the music creepy in that scene and succeeded, but overall still deemed his work "Not good, not good. Not bad. Not as good as it could have been. I didn't like the film either. The music's the worst aspect of it."

Paul attributed the fact that it was a low-key, unobtrusive score (unlike the stunningly notice-able *Witchfinder* score) to "mostly incompetence." Mike Reeves was satisfied, however:

"He liked it, I think. You know, unless the music's awful, almost all direc-tors are delighted when the music's added, because they've had this awful silence watching rough cuts, you know, final cuts, thinking, 'It's awful, this, and terrible, that,' and suddenly the music lifts it. Of course it does, unless it's absolutely useless, because you've agreed that that's where it's needed, so just somebody playing a violin is a plus. But, not a good score, no."

Paul attended the shooting.

There are long stretches of *The Sorcerers* where there is no music at all. Paul said this was not for budget reasons but simply due to "all of our incompetence." For instance, there is a long dialogue sequence between Boris Karloff and Catherine Lacey which is only dialogue with no music. Paul commented: "And it needs it. I saw it once. I was wincing so much, I could hardly take it all in, I thought it was so bad. I thought it had good moments but certainly not what we were all aiming for, which was a complete good movie. I wasn't happy with what I did and I'm sure Mike wasn't. I don't think he thought it was *very* bad." Paul did agree that it was a remarkable achievement for the tiny budget, however: "For 5 million pounds, there have been worse ones than that!" (On the debit side, Diane Ogilvy pointed out: "I'm frightfully aware of a very bad continuity on Ian's trousers in *Sorcerers*, where he goes up to the door on one side and comes out the other side with different trousers on.")

Nicky Henson came to know Mike through Paul and also through Ian Ogilvy. Nicky ex-plained:

"I knew Mike as a friend of Ian's, because Ian is one of my oldest mates, and also I knew him through Paul, because Paul and I were writing music together. We had a three-year contract writing for Cliff Richard and the Shadows, writing songs, and Paul wanted to get into movie writing and we actually wrote a film score together for an extraordinary movie called *Maroc 7*, an extraordinary movie with Gene Barry and Cyd Charisse, produced by John Gale and Leslie Phillips, really bizarre thing. That's how Paul got into film writing and he fell in love with it. Then we had to make a choice. Paul and I were both in *Camelot* together in 1964 at the Lane and he was an actor. We just played guitar together and we just started to write songs together, and then we did this movie score, and then that's what he decided he wanted to do. So he gave up acting, he locked himself away and he taught himself to score properly. He wrote about 13 film scores over the years. I knew Ian terribly well, Paul got to know Ian and then obviously we both got to know Mike through that. Then Mike got Paul to write the score for *The Sorcerers*. So that's where we knew Mike, as a mate. Socially."

Tony Tenser kept a benign eye on the progress of shooting:

"We used to go see the rushes in one of those little preview theaters on Wardour Street and there was Stanley Long and Arnold Miller, who again were brought in as lighting cameraman and in-line producer, both very good at it, and Michael Reeves, Pat Curtis, Raquel Welch and myself. We used to sit there and watch the rushes. And it was a very nice business scene. We'd just discuss business. Raquel Welch didn't get too much involved with the business side but, on the aesthetic side, she'd discuss things with Pat and she was a very charming lady. She seemed to know what she was doing and was very interested in it. There was no part for her in it. It was too small a film and she didn't need it.

"In that film, they used to come to me for clearance on all the main items, to make sure that I'd approve of them. My approval was there because I was concerned not so much with the artistic side, because it was in the very capable hands of Mike Reeves, but with the commercial side of it. I just didn't want people to come to me to ask my permission and discuss with me just because I happened to be the boss of the distribution company or because I wanted to be in some kind of senior position. I wanted to make sure that, when I marketed it, I'd not say, 'Oh, wish we'd have done that, it would have been much easier to sell.'

"So I had the decision on the main actors, apart from those two (Karloff and Lacey) whom I agreed with and one or two of the other main actors. Ian Ogilvy was brought in. He was a friend of Michael Reeves. I hadn't met him before and he was very good. There was a situation whereby I said, 'You have got all the cast now?' They said, 'Well, we've got a young girl to take the part of Ogilvy's girlfriend in the film. She's only just turned 16. We're not sure, so we don't want to make too much of a thing about her age.' I said, 'I don't need to see her.' They said, 'She's pretty cute, she knows what she's doing.' They took her on. That was Susan George.

"Whenever I could, I went onto the set and on location to see how things were going and chivvy things up a bit. I met her two or three times. As a result of that film, she became known, because she was quite good at it. About five or six years later, I went to one of these charity functions, the Film Ball, and I was there with my wife Diane and she was on the floor dancing with her boyfriend. I smiled and I said, 'Hello, how are you?' She just turned her head away, either didn't know me or didn't want to know me. I don't get peeved with things like that. I just thought, 'Well, it's a shame, really. She should have recognized me.' I didn't expect her to come over and say hello to me, but she could—even if she didn't know me—have just smiled and said 'Hi,' as most people do who don't know you. It was the last time I saw her. But *The Sorcerers* is what got her started. Now she's quite a talented actress. She was very, very good in the film.

"The film became 'a Tigon-Curtwell Production.' They put half the money in. I put half the money in. All that side got paid. I don't think Pat Curtis or Raquel got paid, but Mike got paid. My company Tigon handled the distribution at a certain fee which was agreed, and then producers' fees were accounted for and shared out, by which time I had acquired a book-keeper/accountant, who used to work for me before. He was looking for a job. He came to see me. I said, 'Well, if you can squeeze up here...' So we had to find a space for him, until, halfway through the film, Pat Curtis phoned me up and said, 'We want to talk to you.' About the location or something.

He wanted to come and see me to discuss these things. He told me, 'I hope you don't mind, but I can't sit in that goddamn box of an office of yours. Can we meet in a cafe or something like that? And why the hell don't you move to a bigger office?'

"It prompted me. I didn't want to expand too fast, you see. I'd only been going less than a year and all this had happened. So I had to find premises and I found a suite of offices at the top of Wardour Street (number 205). Then once I started distribution, I needed a logging clerk, by which time we had seven or eight people working for us full time.

"The film was made. We were all very pleased with it. I was very impressed with Michael Reeves. We sold it outright to America for a fixed amount. I'd always found that, if you'd take a percentage of the profits, the profits come after all overheads connected with the film and, in general, they can be quite astronomic. And then, after that, the distribution fee, the cost of prints, etc., you may not be left with very much and you may have to wait a long time for it. So, unless you've really got a blockbuster, then you go for a good sale figure. If it did well in America, we were pleased, because then you didn't have someone looking upon you as having sold them a pup. I sold it in a few more countries. It didn't get a circuit release but it was nicely released in the U.K., by which time we had 12 people working for us, and I bought a couple of films."

The film made a lot of money in America.

The Sorcerers at script stage faced some censorship difficulties with the British Board of Film Censors, who were unhappy with the portrayal of sadistic pleasure, but Mike convinced chief censor John Trevelyan of his seriousness.

Ian Ogilvy commented: "They liked each other very much. Trevelyan took his job very seriously, and he always had enormous sympathy with Mike. He always said, 'I know what you're trying to do, but we can't quite get away with *that*, we've got to do *this*.' And Mike would say, 'Okay, John, if you insist.' Trevelyan was always regarded as being very unbending, but he would allow Mike to get away with just a bit more, because he knew Mike was very serious about what he was doing." As a result, *The Sorcerers* got through without damage, unlike Mike's next film, which he once commented was "nearly burnt."

Reviews helped establish Mike's growing reputation. David Robinson (*Financial Times*) found the film "quite evidently the work of a director of invention and authority." John Russell Taylor (*The Times*) wrote: "Last year one of those Italian-made horror-films, *Revenge of the Blood Beast*, showed a particularly lively talent...Again the subject is horrific, but the film is written and directed with quite remarkable intelligence and economy."

The *Monthly Film Bulletin* noted: "Reeves manages to build a considerable charge." Not everyone raved though. Ann Pacey (*The Sun*) thought: "It is a remarkably bad film." *Kinematograph Weekly* wrote: "It's hokum all right, but it's showman-like hokum."

The Sorcerers was invited to the Trieste Science Fiction Film Festival in 1968 and got the Grand Prix there in July, by which time *Witchfinder General* had already been released. Ian Ogilvy went to collect the award.

It had been a happy team on *The Sorcerers*. "We were all good friends," said Tony. However, the Reeves-Curtis partnership ended because Pat Curtis married Raquel Welch and returned to America. Mike, Ian Ogilvy and some of Mike's friends attended the quiet wedding in Paris. Paul Vestey recalled: "I remember him going over to their wedding in Paris, and coming back in some open Rolls Royce and all sorts of things. I wasn't seeing that much of him by then, so it was rather random what I saw him doing. Mike and Patrick were very friendly at that time. Patrick was here more than Raquel was, but I certainly remember her going round to the house and meeting her there. She was obviously around."

Ian Ogilvy and Dani Sheridan as Laura in *The Sorcerers*

Revenge of the Blood Beast had been credited as a Leith Production. The script of *The Sorcerers*, interestingly, is credited to both Tony Tenser-Curtwell Productions Inc., 72 Wardour Street, London W.1 and to Vardella Film Productions Ltd., 6 Stratton Street, London W.1, the latter clearly a company set up by Mike to establish rights in the movie. Indeed, Diane Ogilvy believed Mike said he had done a deal with Tony: "Nearly all of *Sorcerers* reverted to him after seven years." This does not seem to have happened in the end. Tony had no memory of this and the film print bears no mention of Vardella Film Productions. Jack Broom's son Anthony has been able to shed some light on this:

> "I was an Articled Clerk at the time Vardella Film Productions was in existence. Vardella Film Productions Ltd. was indeed a stand-alone company set up by Michael Reeves, initially with his own money, to shoot a picture called *The Sorcerers*. From my memory, whilst he backed the initial work on this film, he was seeking funding from the Royal Bank of Canada. There were two other film companies involved, one was called Leith Investments and the other Leith Productions, although I am afraid now I cannot recall their linkage to Vardella Film Productions Ltd. Neither my father nor I have knowledge of whether the rights to *The Sorcerers* would revert to him after seven years. The films were all carefully budgeted and Mike Reeves was given an allowance from a Trust in order to cover his living expenses. The Trust also had a professional lawyer as a Trustee and his name was Gerald Whately."

Mike at the knee of Boris Karloff on the set of *The Sorcerers*

Mike kept in touch with Tony, though. Tony realized that Mike was "a young man who wanted to have connections on Wardour Street" and that he was really his main connection now, so their relationship was business, but even so he remembered Mike with great warmth: "Mike used to come and see me occasionally. Occasionally I'd go to his house and have a drink with him there, or he'd come to the office. And we had I suppose a father-son or uncle-nephew relationship."

Tony only now became aware how wealthy Mike was:

> "I'd heard that he was from the Reeves paint family, Reeves' artists' paints.
> Somebody said that and I put two and two together. He inherited when he
> was 21 a quarter of a million pounds, which was a lot of money in those
> days, but I didn't know that until after we'd made the film, until we were on

to the next film, and it made no difference as far as I was concerned. But he bought himself a camera and a projector and he used to make little movies at home since he was nine years old. He really was a *most* unusual young man, exceptionally talented."

Strangely, Tony did not reckon Mike as a writer and assumed he relied heavily on collaborators: "He had ideas. He couldn't write. But he had people who could work with him on the scripts. The scripts were good. He had the right kind of people." Of course, Mike's friends argue that his was the main creative input into his scripts, although the situation is complicated by the distinctive contribution of Tom Baker to *Witchfinder General*, and further complicated by the consistency of Reeves' vision whether working with Tom Baker or Amos Powell or Alfred Shaughnessy or Jim Roberts and so on.

Tony was so impressed with Mike's directorial talent that he decided to sign him up to a five-year contract, as he explained:

"He came up. We agreed that we'd have a five-year contract where he would make a minimum of one film a year. That was to protect *him*. He was under contract to me. As long as he had a minimum of one film, if anybody else wanted to make a film with him, they'd have to do it through me. I didn't do that to make money out of him but to help his career. I was going to make more than one film a year if I'd get the scripts in, get the finance and get the release done."

Ian Ogilvy said that Mike did not take an undue interest in the exhibition of his films: "I don't think he did any research on it. I don't think he would go along and sort of sit in the audience and wait for their reactions. No, I don't think he'd do that." Mike was not terribly interested in the marketing side of making films. Ian Ogilvy thought that the friendship with critic David Austen had nothing to do with considerations of getting good reviews in *Films and Filming* magazine:

"No, I think he was entranced by somebody who loved his movies. He became friendly with David Austen because David Austen told him he was a wonderful filmmaker. It's not hard to believe, it's quite easy to believe somebody who tells you you're wonderful. So they are instantly attractive. And David indeed believed all this. David was passionately a champion of Mike. That's very nice, to have someone who's influential, who's got a column in a big film magazine, who likes your work. And they were able to talk movies. That was the other thing. Mike was able to talk movies with David. Great joy."

Although David Austen cited Bertrand Russell on the nature of fear when he reviewed *Witchfinder General* in *Films and Filming,* Ian believed that when Mike was fashioning a script, he would have eschewed abstract concepts in favor of concrete scenes that would generate pace and drive:

"I have a feeling that he thought David Austen's article was quite funny. It did always amuse him tremendously that this picture was looked upon as being so marvelous. It did amuse him that the more intellectual critics read things into his pictures and he said, 'If only they knew *why* that was there! If only they *really* knew!' He thought that was terribly funny, and he didn't disabuse them ever of their attitudes. No, why should he? But he did find it slightly funny. And, indeed, if you over-intellectualize his contribution, he was going to sit there and think that was funny too!"

Of Robin Wood's analysis of Mike Reeves' films, Diane Ogilvy laughed: "I find some of it terribly funny. Fancy seeing deep psychology in that! Rubbish! He'd got 10 minutes to get it in."

Mike's ready capacity for friendship is again demonstrated by Ernest Harris, later a columnist for *Shock Express* magazine, who described Mike there as "a fascinating artist at the beginning of what should have been one of the most exciting careers of its generation." Ernest, who was two years younger than Mike, recalled:

> "From 1967 until 1969, I was in charge of publicity for Miracle Films, the company that handled the British distribution of Michael's Italian horror film *Revenge of the Blood Beast*. It was during this period that I got to know Michael, who used to drop into the office to see Miracle chief Michael Myers and check on how his film was doing. Being fellow film buffs, Mike and I soon struck up a friendship of sorts. Mike had great enthusiasm and he always had time to stop and talk to anyone about films. We were about the same age but, to me, he was someone who had directed Boris Karloff!"

Ernest's early meetings were generally in the company of David Austen, who was a mutual friend, and he recalled Mike's deep appreciation of his leading actors in *The Sorcerers,* so very different from his experience with Vincent Price on his next film: "He used to rave about how good Catherine Lacey was in *The Sorcerers* and his great admiration for Karloff."

At Miracle one day, Ernest was talking with two associates about an episode of *The Invaders* on television the previous night, which began with a brilliant armored car robbery. Mike overheard them and asked who directed it. They said they didn't know. Mike said, "It was probably Don Siegel, he's great on armored car robberies."

On another occasion, Mike mentioned an actress. Ernest misunderstood whom he meant and made a remark about her being gorgeous, whereas Mike was talking about her acting talent. About three sentences later, Ernest realized he'd made a mistake and that Mike had realized but not deemed it worth correcting. Ernest said, "I made a fool of myself over that, didn't I?" Mike said, "Yes, rather." Ernest recalled having lunch with Mike on one occasion and going to a pub with him on Wardour Street. He even introduced Mike to his mother once, outside the Rank building in Wardour Street.

Ernest noticed at such meetings that, friendly as Mike was, he would be perpetually looking over Ernest's shoulder "to see if someone more interesting was coming along" and sweeping his hair back. This eye to the main chance goes along with Tom Baker's description of Mike as perpetually active:

> "Mike was such a busy person. He was always doing something. At night-time, he would settle down in the evening and play cards or something, but he was always doing something, ringing people up. He was very rarely by himself, although he could be by himself. He'd always be, 'If I'm going out for a meal, who would come with me?' He'd go to a film by himself happily, but first of all find if anyone else wanted to go and take a gang of people. So it was always busy."

In 1966, Betty Reeves moved from Cold Ash back to Suffolk. Joan Bootle-Wilbraham recalled Betty's love for Suffolk: "As a girl, the summer holidays were always spent in Suffolk, so she loved it, Woodbridge. So it was always arranged that when Derek retired from the city, that's where they would like to go and live." Now that Mike had flown the nest, Betty returned to Woodbridge. Virginia Scholte commented: "She had more or less grown up in Suffolk, so she was back amongst all the people that she'd known and she had a lot of friends. Up till the last few years of her life, she led a very busy life really, with friends and things. She was pretty lonely toward the end, but then she was 84."

Her new address was Galleon House, Little Bealings, a quiet village outside Woodbridge. Galleon House was another enormous stockbroker's style of house. Virginia used to take her sons there over the years: "Our boys loved her. We used to take them up to stay with her in Little Bealings, because she had a lovely sort

Ian Ogilvy accepts the Grand Prix award for *The Sorcerers* **at Trieste**

of villa-type house, great lawns, and a swimming pool. They loved going to stay there. She had all manner of things. They could play on swings, so it was always a treat to go and stay with Aunt Betty."

Despite the size of the house, Betty and Mike (who was only there some of the time) were the only residents. There was a staff, recalled Virginia: "Aunt Betty had a couple called Richings who had an annex at one side. He was the gardener and she was cook and housekeeper. She always had staff. She used to entertain a lot and have people to stay. Then Mike used to go with his friends and fill the house at Christmas and so on."

Mike had his own sitting room and Virginia remembered that it was full of books and records. Paul Vestey went there once or twice and found it very like Foxbriar House: "It was extraordinarily similar, inside anyway. The houses were remarkably similar because the staircases and the rooms and everything were all in the same place. It was odd." Of Mike's mother, Paul said: "She was quite a sort of grand lady, I suppose, and there seemed to be enough money around to look after things."

Betty did apparently contemplate remarrying after Bungie died. She saw a couple of gentlemen ("old boys" Virginia described them) and did think of marrying at least one, but when Mike died in 1969, she could no longer face the prospect.

Pamela Hoare told a story that illustrates Mike's impatience with worlds other than creative: "A friend of mine in Little Bealings was at a party once there and went to get her coat from Betty's bedroom and Mike was on the floor telephoning and didn't see her. He was talking to some London friend and saying how awful and boring all Betty's Suffolk friends and people were, and he was going to make an excuse—it was Christmas—and get back to London as soon as he could!" No great significance should be attached to this amusing episode, however. As Pamela commented: "I expect a lot of us found our parents' friends boring." Nevertheless, Diane Ogilvy has said there were no tensions with his mother's world: "He would go home weekends."

Mike's relationship with Annabelle was not going well now and they would split up and get together again. Tom Baker never saw them have rows when he was there, but thought she might have "got a bit bored" by Mike's obsession with films. Philip Waddilove told Bill Kelley that, though they broke up before *Witchfinder* started, Mike "still cared a great deal about Annabelle and when she was injured in a car accident in London during production of *Witchfinder General*, he drove all night to visit her in hospital and then get back to the location. He couldn't have gotten more than a couple of hours' sleep." Annabelle had been hit on the head by the wing mirror of a truck and Tom Baker recalled Mike "got himself a speeding ticket for his pains."

Chapter Six: Witchfinder General

I think violence and murder (in film) are quite justifiable. All you have to do
is bring it down to an acceptable level. Then you can make points about the
aggressiveness inherent in everybody.—Michael Reeves, *Penthouse*

Matthew Hopkins Witchfinder General (to give it its full title from the print; on the poster it
was simply *Witchfinder General*) is the crowning glory of Mike Reeves' brief career, the film on
which his enduring international reputation is based. It would also be the highest achievement
of almost everyone involved in the film, including Vincent Price and Tony Tenser.

Tony Tenser related the sequence of events at Tigon British Film Productions Ltd. that
brought about this cinematic classic:

> "By this time, I had people come to see me, agents for writers and things like
> that. A chap phoned me up and said, 'I'd like you to read a book, Mr. Tenser,
> a galley proof of a book that's coming out. It's something you'll like.' It
> was called *Witchfinder General*. I got the book. I read the book. I took an
> option on the rights and discussed it with Mike. He read it. He flipped for it.
> A chap called Philip Waddilove was brought in by Michael Reeves as one of
> his friends. He was involved in pop music publishing with an older partner
> and had said he'd put some money into it and he acted as an in-line location
> manager. I saw quite a bit of Philip Waddilove, but we financed it. It was
> going to come to about £120,000. We were in the big time now.
>
> "In order to finance the film properly, I contacted Sam Arkoff, the boss
> of American International Pictures. Arkoff was the archetypal American
> Lew Grade with the cigar, before Lew Grade was that well known. They
> had a man in this country called Deke Heyward, because he took a part of
> a Deacon in a play once in America and he got called that. His name was
> Louis B. Heyward, same as the actor. He was a man I had a lot of affinity
> with, a good character, and he was in London representing AIP. I contacted
> him and said, 'We're doing this film. Read the book.' It was he who came
> up with Vincent Price for the part."

Tony gave Mike the book because he felt only he could make it on the kind of budget that
was envisaged and he also thought: "It was right up his street, that kind of film. It had some scope
to it, had some breadth to it. There was some canvas to this film." Mike was principally excited
by the chance simply to make another film. The book's author, Ronald Bassett, had no involvement at all with the making of the film and Mike turned to Tom Baker to prepare the film script.
Tom's brilliant contribution was largely downplayed until Iain Sinclair's 1997 book argued that
the film's bucolic and meditative aspects came largely from Tom. This is undoubtedly correct.
Tom said: "I wrote every bloody word of *Witchfinder*, of the original draft, I should think."

He literally wrote it—he operated the typewriter—and he researched it. The shocking
violence of the film came from the research Tom did, although he was personally averse to
violence:

> "I don't think we cooked up any of that to be shocking. We may have, but
> I just thought, 'If we're going to have a bit of violence, let's have a bit of
> violence, let's get on with it.' Certainly when I researched the witchfinding
> business, which was pretty real to a certain extent, I was pretty horrified. They
> were put in the impossible situation where they were damned if they did and
> damned if they didn't. It didn't happen a huge amount, but it happened. We

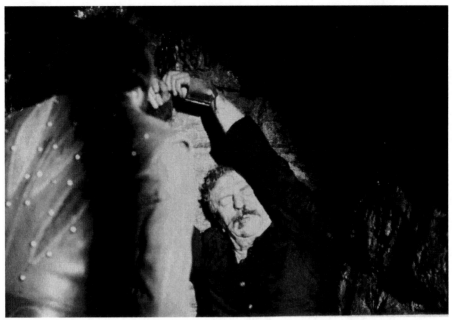

"If we're going to have a bit of violence, let's have a bit of violence.." *Witchfinder General*

wrote it in because it clearly did happen and you put yourself in their place. It was a bit of a predicament to be in, when you're suddenly tortured in that sense...also, half that, half production values."

Tom has credited Mike with "very considerable" input to the script: "I think a lot of the styling comes from our concentration, working with each other on what kind of movie we were trying to make. I think it's a valid thing to do. Though it's *his* movie, there's no question it's his movie, although a lot of work goes in to creating the vehicle for the director to work with." They largely eschewed the element of psychological motivation for Matthew Hopkins in favor of making an English Western, a revenge Western. What explanation there is for Hopkins' vindictiveness is simply pecuniary, and Tom Baker later regretted there had not been more:

> "We tried to suggest that, as I recall. He seems keen on the money at one stage. There is a suggestion that he's enjoying it. I read a quote recently to do with the character, which I rather wish I'd read before. I think it said there was this Witchfinder in the 17th century, but if you give somebody the title 'Witchfinder General,' you shouldn't be surprised if you find some witches! And I thought, 'Oh, I could have run that around a bit...who called him "Witchfinder"?...and how did that affect his thinking?'"

According to Ernest Harris: "I remember when I first was talking to Mike about *Witchfinder* when it was just going into production. I'd just read a book called *Witchfinder General*, not the Bassett one, another one, and I had assumed his film was based on that, and I said to him, 'Oh, the book's awful.' And he said, 'Oh, I know, we've thrown it away!'" Tom Baker agreed: "I think that's what struck us. It was the possibility to make a film partly to do with English landscape but also to do with *movement* through the geography of England and the landscape."

Mike's love of Westerns dovetailed neatly with Tom's interest in history and landscape, and it is likely it was this combination that made the final film somewhat unique in British cinema.

Iain Sinclair was the first critic to identify this: "I believe that the film's success lies in the tension between Baker's Utopian permissiveness, his feel for the countryside, and Reeves' demonic fatalism." Tom expanded on how this actually shaped up:

"Tony Tenser produced the book and said, 'I've bought this book, I think it'll make a great movie.' I read the book. I don't like it very much, but then I'm not particularly into violence. There's discussion about how to make the movie, what the budget is and stuff, but basically Mike and I just stood around wondering how to try and make the book into a film, how to fit it all together.

"My interest in that was in the history and the landscape. And though we never emphatically sat down and said 'Let's make a Western!' one way or another we knew that that was a shared ambition, to try and create a movie in a landscape in Britain...not literally, but somewhat. That's just one of the many elements. Mike would say, 'If you're going to steal from anyone, you might as well steal from the best.' He always liked that phrase. So, if you're going to make moving through landscape, you might as well copy Anthony Mann. So, we'd spend a long time trying to work out how to fit the story into a film and anything he was interested in, any changes in the story, or maybe I tried a few things.

"At that point, Tony said, 'That's fine, let's go ahead with it.' That's when we went off to try and find the locations. Because we didn't *write* the script until we'd found the locations, or a big chunk of the locations. I don't know why we felt that was necessary, but it just seemed so. We knew on the budget we'd have to find real places anyway. There was no question of creating it, so we by and large had to say, 'Where can we find that will allow us to actually write the particular scenes?' So then we set off to look for places. I don't know what we'd put down on paper. There's an awful lot of coming and going, so we must have somewhere written down on paper who was going where and who was meeting who and who was dashing off again, and who was passing each other in the night and not seeing each other, and roughly tried to work that out. And then we had to go and find places to do it in.

"But we didn't actually write the script until we'd found enough places to make sense to us and, I say, I wrote every word. I certainly worked the typewriter and wrote most of it, and we would agree on it, and I would write it, and then we would read it and change bits and Mike might write some of it. I'd like to think the lines that aren't to do with violence come from me. I'd give Mike his due, if they're about shocking violence, then I'm sure he wrote them or spoke them, and if they're not, then I'd like to think they're mine."

The location hunting proved to be one of the great creative forces in the film, contributing such stunning scenes as the pre-credits sequence of the execution of the witch, filmed in Kersey in Suffolk. It was Mike and Tom who found Kersey:

"Yes, we did. That's down the road from Lavenham. We went to Lavenham because I saw a postcard. I remember we just saw a postcard near Woodbridge, where Betty's house was, stopped to buy some cigarettes and there's a picture of Lavenham, and we thought, 'That looks a good spot.' So we drove over there and we were just driving away from Lavenham and—it doesn't show in the film—but there's a gable end of a house onto the road with a track down the side. Black and white house, onto this road as you come down, but

One of the magnificent locations for *Witchfinder General* (photo: Philip Waddilove)

there is this track running from the road past the house onto the landscape beyond. So we thought, 'Oh, that looks possible.' So we peered around and poked about, and then, when Philip Waddilove was put on location finding, it actually turned out this house belongs to Hammond Innes, the writer. So he gave permission to film there. In that sense, we found the location, and wrote the little scene round that.

"Philip came literally a week or two later. Mike and I spent one weekend just the pair of us looking round and went to Lavenham and went back and found the place where the priest lives at that house, that house with the church at the end of the drive, just driving around: 'That's great!' We were delighted with that. Mike already knew Philip. We went to show Philip these, but he's done his own research and he's discovered that there's this Army land in Norfolk by this time. He got permission from the Army to show us round and we went a week or two later to a Captain or someone who took us in.

"It was *written* to fit some of these locations. They didn't use all the ones we wrote. Orford Castle, where the end takes place, was added later. We did write it around places. We were trying to stretch the landscape a bit.

"There's a quote of Mike's I've been trying to remember, this weekend we first went out to find the locations just the pair of us. For some reason, Mike didn't want to take a car. He was like that every now and again. He just didn't want to drive to Suffolk or something. Very peculiar. Anyway, so we'd get on a train from Liverpool Street, wander off to Woodbridge on this Friday evening, quite late, and we're ticking along in some local train and, in effect, he said to me, 'This is what it's all about.' The point of the tale was, we were in this rather scruffy train late on a Friday night, ticking along, not because we were being paid £10,000 a week to make a movie, but because what we wanted to do was *make movies*.

"I was very struck by this, and that was our agreement, really. He was rich, I wasn't, but we were there not because we were trying to make a great financial career in the movies but because, suckers that we were, we were hooked on this idea of trying to make a film, so there we were! I mean, we

133

could have actually been driving in his Jaguar E-type, so we weren't driving, we were clicking along in this little train late at night. That's what puzzles me why later after *Witchfinder* he came off the rails. That's the big change, from the man who saw the pleasant reality of doing something for nothing, in effect, on the way to writing a script.

"The irony is that actually when we then went to Philip Waddilove—his wife Sue picked us up the next day—Philip was quite the reverse. He had this huge American car in a country where there were no American cars. Philip somehow had huge great big fins, weaving around Suffolk and Norfolk! Philip had worked on one of the pirate radio ships. On the day we were driving around with him, for that scene where they go to the coast to see if King Charles is down there, we're on the coast and on the car radio we're listening to the first broadcast of *Sgt. Pepper*, which was being broadcast by one of the pirate radios, but Philip knew this, which was why he turned the radio on, so he had worked on one of those ships.

"So Philip is brought in and we go round together and we see the Army land and we show him the other places that we've found and then we digest the Army land. How can we fit this in to this rough outline of who's going where? And then we sat down and wrote the script from getting all those places in as best we could with the storyline we'd chosen. The story's crazy, really, so much coming and going in the bloody thing. I'm sometimes embarrassed by it."

Iain Sinclair wrote of the Kersey opening sequence:

"Reeves liked strong openings. He amazed me once by declaring his admiration for Michael Winner's *I'll Never Forget What's 'Is Name*; Oliver Reed smashing up a desk with an axe. The freshness that is still to be felt, even viewing *Witchfinder* on television, comes from this reversal of standard industry procedure. Reeves and Baker didn't write their script and then hand it over to location finders, they made a journey, allowing the spirit of place to enter the dictation."

Mike originally had Donald Pleasance in mind for the role of Matthew Hopkins, Witchfinder General. Philip Waddilove claimed to Bill Kelley: "Michael had got Donald Pleasance interested in the script." He recalled that when Pleasance was ruled out by AIP, "Michael very nearly walked off the picture at that point." Ian Ogilvy, who was once again, through his close friendship with Mike, involved in pre-production and post-production, explained:

"The original casting we wanted to play Matthew Hopkins was Donald Pleasance, and Mike told Vincent Price this. My understanding of it was that shortly after Vincent began, Mike *told* Vincent Price, which didn't really help Vincent's attitude to the picture very much. I do know that Mike originally wanted Donald Pleasance, which would have put a very different slant on the picture. He had a scene where Donald Pleasance got onto his horse and fell off the other side! The big man getting onto his horse...he'd fall straight off and all the villagers guffaw. Fascinating stuff! Making him out to be a nasty little drip. A man driven by his own smallness and ugliness and nothingness. *Driven!*

"Mike wanted an explanation of this man and he felt that if Donald Pleasance had played him, rather than Vincent, this elegant, rather handsome man, it would have explained the obsessiveness of trying to be the big man. But

I think, like a lot of happy accidents, it worked very well. Pleasance would have altered the whole atmosphere. Pleasance didn't play it because I suspect that AIP had never heard of him. Pleasance was only the ideal in Mike's mind. AIP simply called the tune and forced Vincent onto the project: in the long run, rather a happy 'force,' I would suggest."

Paul Ferris commented:

"What Pleasance does now is mostly caricature stuff, but then he was very threatening, and not just silly-threatening, but *very* threatening. Which is what Mike wanted. He wanted to make an absolutely *realistic* film of that period, in so far as that is possible. It's all true, that's the point. It wasn't bullshit. And it may have turned out weaker, you don't know. You never know. It may be that it was a good stroke of fortune that Pleasance couldn't do it. If Vincent had been allowed to get away with doing the full panoply of effects, it would have been disaster."

It was unfortunate that Mike told Vincent early on in the shooting that Donald Pleasance was first choice for the part of Hopkins. Vincent confirmed to the author that this did not help his attitude to the film. Tony Tenser agreed that Mike should have been more diplomatic, especially with a star actor. The ironic thing was that Deke Heyward had written to Vincent before he even started the picture to enthuse him about the project (letter dated August 12, 1967):

"We work together again...and I must confess, I think this will be the happiest experience we have had together so far...I think it is a hell of a well-constructed piece...the director. He is a young British talent, very much like Jeremy Summers, only far his superior as a picture maker and personality. This is his fifth picture...at the age of 23. His last one received brilliant directorial reviews, *The Sorcerers*, starring our old buddy Boris Karloff. I believe you will find young Michael Reeves one of the most inspiring things that has happened to you as an actor in a long time. He is not only bright, imaginative, and well-organized, but he has the *cujones* to force a crew through to doing things the way he wants to...He was a sort of protégé of Roger Corman, who schooled him in the care and treatment of Vincent Prices. He wafted off in a faery-like cloud of ecstasy when he heard we were casting you in the lead... Seriously, much happiness on my part to be working on a *good* production with you. I think it has got to end up a hellofa picture."

In hindsight, it is clear that Deke realized the project would be difficult because Mike did not want Vincent and was simply flanelling Vincent to cast a positive light on the situation.

Mike might have been reluctant with Vincent, but Tony Tenser was delighted: "Mike may have had Pleasance in mind to start with, but the Vincent Price casting came in when I got tied in with AIP. He was their name for America and, of course, he was ideal. If they'd have come out with 'George Doates,' I'd have said 'Forget it. We'll do without your money.' But Vincent Price, he *was* the Witchfinder General, wasn't he?" (Deke had told Vincent that Tony was "second vice president of the Vincent Price fan club in London.")

Although Vincent Price was under contract to AIP, who did not have another of the highly successful Edgar Allan Poe adaptations to offer him, he confirmed to the author that he was not simply assigned to *Witchfinder General* (which was eventually released in the States as a supposed Poe adaptation!) without knowing anything about it. Indeed, it seems he had the discretion to refuse it: "I knew what it was. AIP had every intention of putting a Poe title on it anyway. I had read the book and the script. I liked the script; that's why I did it."

Vincent Price as Matthew Hopkins

Vincent was to lend great dignity to Hopkins and confirmed that he found the role attractive. On another occasion, he told fan Lawrence French: "Matthew Hopkins was a really evil person, and it was a true story. He wasn't just a sadist though! If he were I wouldn't have wanted to play him."

Tony Tenser confirmed that AIP arranged for Vincent to agree to the film:

> "They got him. They said they liked the book, they liked the script and they were interested. They said, 'Who are you going to get for the part?' We chose names. Amongst them, I presume, would have been Donald Pleasance. Then they came back and said, 'We'd like Vincent Price and he's read it and he likes it.' So, fine, because it suited me then. He was the man for the job and

that's how he got it. And they paid for him to come over. That was part of the deal. Part of their money was him. We knew what it was costing etc., but whilst he was here, we'd look after him, all his hotels and all the rest."

Tony also scotched the persistent idea that AIP was the major investor in the film:

"Deke said, 'Yes.' He got the okay. They put half the money up but wanted the Western hemisphere for that. The final budget was £120,000 and they put £60,000 in and I put £60,000 in, and it went over budget because of something we had to do. I didn't ask them for the extra. It went a few thousand over budget because of something we had to do. Sam Arkoff was no fool, a very tough cookie. I didn't ask him for his share of it. I said 'It's my fault, my responsibility.' And he knew. They'd told him that. He made some remark about what a wonderful guy I was. He'd never met anybody like me! So, it was worth it to hear an American praise a British producer for a change! Normally they pick holes in the thing."

Philip Waddilove pointed out that AIP got a good deal: "The final budget was £83,000. AIP put in all of £32,000 for their half interest in the picture, and part of the deal was that we use Vincent. He was under contract to AIP. Vincent's salary came out of AIP's contribution, so they got quite a deal. In fact, I think they only paid Vincent £12,000, which would have lowered their contribution below what's in the official contracts."

Deke Heyward was given an executive producer credit and looked after AIP's interests during production, recalled Tony:

"He had his sixpenny-worth of say here and there, from the point of view of the American market. This was why. He was only interested in the distribution side and we got on well together. I did spend quite a lot of time on location, mostly in Norfolk, some in Suffolk. Bury St. Edmunds is where we based ourselves for a while. Sam Arkoff only came on the set once. Deke used to go on location when I didn't go. We didn't often go together. When he went, I used to say, 'Just talk to Vincent Price. Don't get involved with anybody else. Let *me* know if anything goes wrong.' I didn't want a strike on my hands! He didn't do the amount of work that I did. He wasn't expected to. He wasn't asked to. He was looking after Sam Arkoff's interests. He was also interested in the film. He had some knowledge about films."

Ian Ogilvy remembered Deke's involvement quite favorably. Deke is also credited with writing additional material, but Ian thought his input was very minor and Philip Waddilove said it was limited to adapting the Poe poem Vincent Price reads on the American prints to justify selling it as a Poe film. Deke did not come up with any of the sensational scenes AIP wanted, according to Ian:

"Because Mike flatly refused to shoot them and Deke used to come along and sort of agree with Mike. Deke Heyward had his heart in the right place. I later on did an awful remake of *Wuthering Heights* under Deke Heyward, which is an AIP thing, and Deke Heyward managed to sell the movie, so the story goes, to Sam and Jim Nicholson of AIP by telling them it was a dirty movie and telling them a totally ludicrous plot, nothing to do with *Wuthering Heights*. 'Sounds really good, sounds a really dirty movie, yeah.' He was fairly cynical, Deke Heyward. I don't think he worried too much what Mike was doing."

The *Witchfinder General* Michael Reeves/Vincent Price match was not made in heaven.

Philip Waddilove has said that Deke Heyward appeared on location only once, when some nude scenes he had contributed for foreign versions (particularly Germany's) were shot in a tavern set. (These scenes, which were not in the U.K. or U.S. theatrical versions, have crept back into the videocassette and DVD releases.) Ian Ogilvy commented to Bill Kelley: "Deke Heyward said, 'Let's have a scene here, and a scene here,' and Mike, because he wasn't looking to make trouble, said, 'OK, Deke, we'll shoot the scenes.' We shot them and put in 'Additional Scenes by Louis M. Heyward,' which the film industry would recognize as a dig by the director at the producer in question...That was a joke entirely designed by Michael."

Ian gave an example of what AIP really wanted: "On *Witchfinder General* Sam Arkoff and Jim Nicholson used to send directives. They used to see rushes and they'd say, 'We want a reshoot. In the pub scene we want the girl to have her tits naked and blood on the tits.' I saw some of these telegrams. Mike used to show them to me, saying, 'What rubbish is this?' and tear them up and say, 'Listen, we're 6,000 miles away, let them do what they like.' "

Mike Reeves was clearly unenthusiastic about the casting of Vincent Price as Matthew Hopkins. Deke Heyward commented to Bill Kelley: "Reeves did not feel Vincent could do the acting job necessary. He felt that Vincent was having too good a time at whatever part he was playing, and however horrible the man he was portraying was, there would be an overtone of, 'You and I both know we're kidding,' which Michael didn't want."

Yet Paul Vestey confirmed that Mike had screened Vincent's pictures at Yeoman's Row: "I remember the original *Fly* and *The Pit and the Pendulum*—oh, we certainly had to have that!" There might have been more of Vincent's films screened but for the fact that the Wallace Heaton library was not all that comprehensive, said Paul, who was sure that Mike was impressed by screen legends like Price and Karloff: "I think he was. He had great respect for them. I don't think 'impressed' is quite the right word. He was a proper movie-groupie, really, and they were stars. I think he thought Price was quite difficult."

Unfortunately, Mike may have been under the impression Vincent was forced to do the picture without any real enthusiasm. Diane Ogilvy explained: "It was a contract movie for Vincent. He had no choice about doing it. We were all under the impression that it was a contract picture."

According to Tigon's brief biography publicity sheets, Mike accepted "without surprise the fact that he finds himself, at so early an age, in control of veteran actors like Vincent Price. 'After all,' he asks, with perfect justification, 'in this age of Youth, when young actors and actresses are coming forward in such great numbers, why not directors too? There is no mystique about making films, just know-how, plus ideas and enthusiasm.' "

EDGAR ALLAN POE'S
THE CONQUEROR WORM

With the star part cast, Mike was left free rein with the rest of the casting. Ian Ogilvy, always so good in costume roles, was a natural for the part of the young trooper Richard Marshall, who becomes obsessed with wreaking vengeance on the Witchfinder. The third most important role to cast was that of Sara, Marshall's beloved, whose violation by the Witchfinder so outrages the young trooper. Ian Ogilvy suggested the young Nicola Pagett, who of course went on to become one of Britain's most important actresses but was then in the early days of her career. Ian had been her boyfriend in the past. They had been at RADA together and he said:

"I wanted her in *Witchfinder General* because it would be fun. And Mike said, 'Sure, I think she's very good.' She came along and she was very suspicious. We interviewed her in my flat in the King's Road. There was no script. We explained the part to Nickie. Here she was presented with a young director and an old boyfriend. She thought it was an amateur job and she was very tricky and not easy in the interview at all. She was beady-eyed and apprehensive when we mentioned the love scenes. Probably a lot of people were trying to get her to take her clothes off for films. I don't think we even offered her the part. She left and Mike said, 'I don't want to use her. She's got no enthusiasm at all.' "

Nicola Pagett graciously commented: "I don't remember the interview, but I probably was unforthcoming because I would have thought it was indeed not strictly professional—not having heard anything about it from my agent. It has such a wonderful reputation as a film that the whole thing is very much my loss. It just goes to show that one should always be pleasant and positive." She confirmed the part was never offered to her.

The role eventually went to an actress, Hilary Dwyer, who was new to films (she had done tiny roles in such television shows as *The Avengers* and *The Prisoner*) and in this part gives one

Hilary Dwyer in her astonishing debut as Sara Lowes in *Witchfinder General* (BFI)

of the most astonishing debut performances in cinema history. Ian Ogilvy thought that Mike discovered her simply by seeing a lot of actresses: "I wasn't necessarily in on this. I wasn't a producer or anything and although in many ways I was involved in pre-production and post-production and decision-making quite a lot, I have to admit that there were great *chunks* where I had nothing to do with it at all. Didn't want me around." Diane Ogilvy remembered Mike and Ian and Philip poring over *Spotlight*, the trade directory of actors and actresses.

In any event, Ian found Hilary to be such an excellent actress that he overcame his disappointment about not working with Nicola Pagett: "In fact, I was quite pleased because Hilary was wonderful, because she was much more English rose, sort of vicar's daughter than Nickie Pagett would have been. She was *terribly* good in it. Everybody commented what a lovely performance she gave. She was dead right for it as well, I thought. Slightly sort of gauche English lady. I did enjoy working with her because she was so good."

However, he admitted he found the love scenes did not come naturally because Hilary looked rather too like his sister: "It's hard, when you're supposed to be playing great love scenes!" Diane Ogilvy thought Mike did not need to give Hilary any help in her debut film role: "I think she knew exactly what she was doing." Sadly, like many of those who worked with Mike Reeves, Hilary would never again embrace work of such quality and, after some undistinguished films and the Gerald Harper television series *Hadleigh* in which she became nationally well known, she ceased acting and became a successful film producer.

One cast member who recalled Mike being helpful to Hilary on the set was Nicky Henson. Casting Nicky Henson in the role of Marshall's close friend, the Cockney Trooper Swallow, was logical, as Ian and Nicky were close friends in real life. Nicky observed: "I knew Mike and Mike said, 'There's a part for you in the next picture,' and I was terribly excited, because I hadn't done many pictures, and it was a lovely part actually. He's a kind of licensed fool, isn't he? I remember ringing my agent and say-

Nicky Henson was the star of *Number One*

ing, 'He'll ring up and he'll offer me the part and he'll offer no money. Take it. I want to do it. I'm desperate to do it.' "

Nicky had not seen either *Revenge* or *Sorcerers* at this time. The role helped to establish him as an actor: "It started me off on a period of playing the 'erstwhile friend of the hero,' like Ian always calls me. I'd say, 'I've got a picture.' 'So who are you going to be the erstwhile friend of this time?' I played everything Cockney in those days. I was known as a Cockney actor, all-usage Cockney actor. I only played Cockney roles."

Ian Ogilvy recalled that Nicky appealed strongly to Mike's sense of humor right from the start:

> "He loved laughing. The number of times I've seen Mike just rolling on the floor, not being able to *speak* because he's laughing so much at something one of the actresses has done, supposing to be serious. It's like that Nicky Henson problem on being in the tavern with the others. We'd already shot a fortnight before Nick came up and his first line in the picture was when I return to Lavenham and see my girlfriend in the bedroom. Nick's standing outside the door and he sees that I'm about to embark on a love scene with my girlfriend in the bedroom. He puts his head through the door and says, 'Well, I'll see you in the tavern with the others.' This is the end of a long shooting day and Nick had been hanging about quite a lot and this was his first scene, and Mike said, 'Let's not rehearse this, it's only one line, it's just a big close-up, we haven't got time to rehearse this, come on. We'll finish in a second. Just do the line.'
>
> "So, Nick went, 'Well, well, see you in the tavern with the others, then,' in a deep Cockney accent! Mike fell on the floor, he laughed so much. He

said, 'That's the funniest thing I've ever seen in my life.' Nick said, 'Wha, wha, what's the matter?' Mike said 'We're going to shoot this tomorrow morning. I can't, I can't. If you try to do that again, I'll have a heart attack.' Nick said 'What do you mean?' Mike said, 'Well, it's a bit 1965, Nick, could you kind of tone down the Cockney cheeky chappie a bit!' But instead of being mad with Nick or anything, he just instantly fell in love with him and thought, 'Oh, this is wonderful, I love him.' "

Nicky recalled he had to learn to ride for the film, unlike Ian Ogilvy, who could ride already:

"I did 25 pictures in the old days, but all the way through the '60s I was always going up for pictures and they always said, 'Could you ride?' I always used to say, 'Yes.' Thank God I never got any of them! *The Charge of the Light Brigade*, stuff like that. I'd have been in dead trouble! But he said, 'We're doing this *Witchfinder* film, which I want to shoot as an English Western.' He said, 'I want to shoot it as a Western. Real horses.' I said, 'I don't ride, Mike.' He said, 'Right, we'll send you off and teach you.' So I learned to ride for the film, which was really nice. I picked it up very fast and it's a wonderful skill, very useful thing to have, to be able to ride. I've kept it up ever since, for movies. And we went out there and found those Army ranges. Those extraordinary ranges let you do those wonderful tracking shots with Paul's brilliant music. Paul's score was absolutely stunning."

Swallow is the only cheerful and completely amiable character in *Witchfinder General* and Nicky said this was only partly his doing:

"It was very much in the script, but also he *allowed* me...The first scene that I shot was when I say, 'I'll be in the tavern with the others.' It was right at the end of a day's shoot and I arrived out in this aircraft hangar where they were shooting those scenes in the hotel. I walked in and I said the line and the whole unit fell in and he said, 'I think that's a wrap, we'll start again in the morning.' He just said, 'It's great, Nick, but much, much *less*. Take it right down.' Because I'm a very over-the-top kind of comedic actor, anyway, except now I've started to play uncles, but in 1967 I'd hardly made any pictures at all, and I'd already done 10 years of going right over the top in the theater, so he just had to pull me right back down. Then, of course, I was up every night in the hotel in Bury St. Edmunds anyway, playing guitar and telling stories all through the night, so that quietened me down as well."

Mike's relations with Vincent got off to an inauspicious start when Mike refused to go to Heathrow to greet his star. Philip Waddilove has explained in his memoirs:

"The evening before Vincent Price's arrival from the U.S.A., Michael Reeves and I were having dinner again and I asked him if he'd arranged a car for himself to meet Vincent. 'I'm not meeting him,' Michael replied. 'You're the producer—you're meeting him!'

" 'Michael,' I responded, 'you're 24 years old, directing your third movie. Vincent is 56, appearing in his 75th. Don't you think it would be wise to meet him?' But Michael was adamant in his refusal to do so.

"At eight next morning I stood in the arrivals hall at Heathrow waiting for our star to appear. I didn't have long to wait before Vincent swept down

Vincent Price on the set of *Witchfinder General* with "your god-damned young genius." (photo: Philip Waddilove)

the elevator. Greeting him, I introduced myself and apologized to him on Michael's behalf for not being there to meet him: 'He's tied up with the screenplay,' I explained, 'but he's asked you to have lunch with him at one o'clock.' 'Of course, dear boy,' Vincent retorted. 'Just take me to your god-damned young genius!'"

Philip had come into the project to scout locations and help with the production side. Mike and Annabelle had met Susi Waddilove when she was a secretary at the William Morris Agency in Rome and fiancée of Philip, a former A&R man at Pye Records and pirate radio and music producer. She had mentioned her future husband had begun a company to find film locations.

Philip recalled:

"My wife-to-be Susi had known Michael Reeves in Rome since 1963 when they were both working in Italy. She introduced me to him in late 1966 at a Sunday lunch party given by mutual friend Amos Powell at his cottage in Sussex and, during the ensuing three years, Michael and I became close friends. He had just finished editing his second movie, *The Sorcerers*. At the time I was running Locations TV & Films Ltd., a company founded and owned by myself and my friend and colleague John Whitney. Over the years John and I had been associated on numerous radio or television productions and now, as our new company name implied, we were providing location research for film and TV companies, often from Canada or the U.S.A. We also arranged the location filming permits and even the catering and hiring of crews for our clients. As Michael immersed himself in work on the screenplay of *Witchfinder General*, he suggested that Locations TV & Films—meaning myself—did the preliminary location research for the movie."

This photo, taken by Philip Waddilove, shows the beautiful locations he discovered.

Philip came on board, putting up £5,000 for Associate Producer billing (eventually upgraded to full producer status). He helped Mike with his script and took location stills in East Anglia, recalling to Bill Kelley: "Tony showed those photographs to AIP and that helped induce them to put up the completion funds." Tony did not like Norfolk and was busy in London, so Philip found himself drawn in on the production side.

Philip has written:

> "During principal photography, Michael said that I should become the de facto location manager and, as John and I had recently appointed a full-time manager for our company, I had John's wholehearted encouragement to take on the assignment. At the time, John himself was fully occupied in writing for the highly successful ATV television series *The Plane Makers*. In July of 1967, Susi and I took off for East Anglia on a preliminary location hunt. After a week of driving mile after mile and consulting numerous maps, we found all the primary locations that were featured in the screenplay to date.
>
> "We were also able to make preliminary enquiries regarding hotels, local catering services, availability of equipment, etc., before we took off for a few weeks' vacation at our villa in Spain. However, after we'd been there for nearly a month, we began to wonder if the movie would ever happen. A few days later when we'd just about given up hope, a cable arrived from Michael saying the project was a 'go' and that I was to return to England immediately for pre-production work.
>
> "At dinner with Michael on the evening of my return from Spain, he told me it was essential that I now tie up all the locations I had found in July, plus more to come. He also said that Tony Tenser had agreed with him that, as opposed to being 'location manager,' I was to be 'associate producer' with a 'single card' screen credit. I asked Michael who was actually going to be the producer. 'Well, you are, really,' he replied. 'But Tony will eventually be bringing Arnold Miller on board to look after the hiring of equipment and some of the other logistics. However, Arnold's on another movie at the moment.' So I was given a room down the hall from Tony Tenser with a desk and telephone at Tigon's Wardour Street offices, and was instructed to 'just get on with it!'

The witch-burning sequence, which was shot from a cherry picker in the town square of Lavenham. (photo: Philip Waddilove)

"Thrown in at the deep end as I was, my experiences with Locations TV & Films had been an enormously helpful preparation for dealing with most of the basic problems facing me. Significantly, I was able to persuade Tony we couldn't afford to use a conventional film studio for interiors. I'd found three old aircraft hangars on an abandoned World War II RAF airfield near Bury St. Edmunds, where our unit would be based at the Angel Hotel. Equidistant to most of our locations, the hangars would be our studio and weather cover. The rent of the hangars for an entire month was £80, as opposed to £1,000 per day at a conventional studio.

"My other coup was to arrange for the witch-burning sequence (our biggest) to be shot in the town square at Lavenham for a token donation of £30 to the local school playing-field fund, plus £15 to rent a cherry picker and operator from the Electricity Board in place of an expensive camera crane. I also arranged for entire families of the United States Air Force stationed at Lakenheath airfield to work as extras at the ridiculously low rate of £1 per day per man, woman or child—and they brought their own paymaster and catering with them for free!

"Frighteningly, three weeks before the first day of principal photography, other than for John Coquillon and his camera crew, we didn't have a film unit. I knocked on Tony Tenser's door and he invited me in. As I entered, he was holding for someone on the phone, so I quickly explained my problem to him: 'I don't know whether you realize it, Tony, but we haven't got a unit yet.' In his strong Cockney accent, he replied, 'You know the trouble with you is, Philip, you're always worrying. Just stop fucking worrying. We'll get a unit in time!' But it so happened that in 1967 the British film industry was busier than usual and there were very few technicians available. Extremely luckily for us, a Columbia Pictures movie called *The Ski Bum* that was about to go into production was cancelled two days later and we inherited their crew—most of them in their '60s."

Production Manager Richard (Ricky) Coward joined later on in the production. He also worked on Tigon's *The Blood Beast Terror* and, although he did not work closely with Mike, assisted the author with some contact information before he died in 1990.

The first meeting between Vincent Price and Mike Reeves took place at the Pastoria Hotel in St. Martin's Street, off Leicester Square in London. Tony Tenser was there and recalled:

> "I was there because I booked Vincent into the Pastoria. He wanted to be somewhere central in the West End and he didn't want to be in a big, noisy hotel and I'd had one or two meals there and I'd had people stay there before. I phoned up and said, 'We don't want to make a fuss.' They said 'Yes,' and Vincent Price was given the room. And we met in the hotel. We were there when Vincent Price arrived with his bags and I saw him into his room. He came down and had a drink with us and met Mike there. Everybody got on well, but we seemed to get the impression that he liked Mike. I mean, he'd met me for the first time. He said, 'Hi, Tony. Great here...' But with Mike, the feeling was that he'd known him for a long time, or maybe known him somewhere, which he hadn't done. There was that sort of feeling. Like father and son. But Mike wasn't interested. Mike was not cold but a bit impersonal. He often quarreled with Annabelle because he was married to his work. He could never have been married to anything else. We used to say, 'Be nice to him, Mike. Say hello to him. The guy is upset. Just be nice to him. Just say good morning, Mike.' "

Vincent could not recall that meeting for the author but refuted the suggestion that he had personal feelings toward Mike: "It is false. Our relationship—as were my feelings—was entirely

actor/director oriented." Interestingly, Victoria Price revealed in her book *Vincent Price: A Daughter's Biography* that Vincent "was emotionally drawn to both men and women" and suggested he may have wrestled with feelings of bisexuality throughout his life; in a discreet way, Tony Tenser was alluding to this element of Vincent's character. It was Philip Waddilove's impression that Vincent was drawn to Mike and Mike did not want to know. And Ian Ogilvy was aware that Vincent expressed admiration of a good-looking young male film technician. Ian said: "If Mike had been aware of that, he couldn't have handled it. He would have run a mile from it." On the other hand, Vincent's college roommate and friend of 60 years reportedly said there was no way Price was bisexual. Vincent was the very model of the aesthete and it may be he simply appreciated beauty, male or female.

But clearly Vincent came to be offended by what he too described as Mike's "impersonal" relationship with him, blaming as we

Philip Waddilove took this photo of Mike Reeves, in which he appears even younger than 23.

have seen the fact of Mike's inherited wealth and its supposed effect on Mike's approach to people.

Mike, of course, was still only 23 at this time and, in addition to Mike's coolness (not helped by the fact that he didn't want Vincent in the part in the first place), the question of his youth dismayed Vincent. Matters were exacerbated by Mike's lack of diplomacy about Vincent's acting style and it all led to a stormy working relationship. Vincent confirmed that his director's youth dismayed him from the very beginning of their association: "Yes—but only because I thought if he was that young, he needed more knowledge of how to handle actors. Youth is no excuse for incivility."

Unfortunately, Vincent had not seen *The Sorcerers* (and still had not when writing to the author in 1988—he probably never saw it before he died in 1993), even if Deke had enthused to him about it. Perhaps if he had, he'd have had more faith in Mike Reeves, especially as Boris Karloff was a good friend and he'd have seen how well Mike used him in that picture.

Ian Ogilvy later expressed no surprise that Vincent had not seen *The Sorcerers*:

> "I don't think Vincent went in for that kind of research! In terms of investigation of unknown directors for whom they were about to work, Vincent was like Karloff (otherwise, they were chalk and cheese). Boris didn't really ask questions. Boris certainly didn't say, 'Well, what have you made before?' Boris said, 'How much? Where?' That's what most actors do. 'How much? You know I earn 11,000 pounds for a picture whether I've got only one line or 20 lines?' 'Yes, Boris.' 'Will you pay me that?' 'Yes, Boris.' 'Where have I got to meet you? How long is it going to be for? I'll do it.' *Then* they say, 'Show me the script.' An awful lot of that goes on. It's a lovely *idea* that we all study our scripts and wonder whether or not, but an awful lot of the fact is, 'How much?' *I'm* perfectly prepared to do a whole lot of rubbish if I need the money. Beggars can't be choosers, that's the thing."

Vincent, though, did not agree with the author that seeing *The Sorcerers* would have altered his misgivings about Mike's directorial expertise, however good he might have thought it. Part of the problem that arose between Vincent and Mike was that Mike, although he much appreciated working with real Hollywood movie stars like Vincent Price, was too single-minded about what he wanted to achieve to be very respectful. Clearly Vincent was offended by his directness, as exemplified in Ian Ogilvy's account of why Vincent was so unhappy on the picture:

> "You must remember he had this contract with AIP to do these Edgar Allan Poe films. They'd run out. He had one more picture to do. So they said, 'OK, we're going to lend you to this guy in England.' That's why they called it *The Conqueror Worm*—ridiculous title. And he'd never heard of Mike. He was faced with a 23-year-old director who kept telling him not to roll his eyes. It's only bit of direction Mike ever did with Vincent, was 'Vincent, I really don't want one of these Edgar Allan Poe performances, I actually want a *real* man.' Vincent resented all this bitterly. He also resented the fact that he wasn't in a nice comfortable studio, and of course the Corman movies were all done in the studio. We were in a *hangar* out in Norfolk. The only fun Vincent had was to go out and look for antiques. And he didn't understand what was going on."

Vincent explained his growing disillusionment with the film to Lawrence French and Bill Kelley (this account is an amalgamation from three different sources):

"I had a lot of difficulty with Michael Reeves. He did not want me in the picture. I did it to fulfill an obligation. I had read the script and was terribly excited and really interested in this young fellow, but he was a man who really did not know how to handle actors. There are certain directors who affect this kind of disinterest in actors and think that it's a director's medium. We did not get along at all. Well, he hated me. I didn't like him either, and it was one of the first times in my life that I've been in a picture where really the director and I clashed, like that. He didn't know how to talk to actors, he hadn't the experience, or talked to enough of them, so all the actors on the picture had a very bad time. I knew though, that in a funny, uneducated sort of way, he was right, in his desire for me to approach the part in a certain way. He wanted it very serious and straight, and he was right, but he just didn't know how to communicate with actors.

"Actors are very sensitive people. I'll never forget one time he came up and said, 'Don't shake your head.' I said, 'What do you mean? I don't shake my head.' He said, 'Yes, you do.' So we didn't get along at all. He really got all our backs up. He'd come to you and say the one thing you shouldn't tell an actor that gives him no security at all. Afterwards, I realized what he wanted was a low-key, very laid-back, menacing performance. He did get it, but I was fighting with him almost every step of the way. Had I known what he wanted, I could have cooperated. He was so talented and had such a bright future, but he was a deeply troubled young man. I realized only after I saw *Witchfinder General* finished how talented he was. He was brilliant. I think it's one of the best performances I've ever given."

Matthew Hopkins tortures Sara as John Stearne (Robert Russell) looks on. (BFI)

Vincent is quoted in *Classic Images* (June 1992) as saying that working with Mike was "a very sad experience...He was very unstable...difficult but brilliant."

Nicky Henson got on very well with Vincent socially. Clearly he was more respectful, but then he did not have the whole weight of the film on his shoulders as Mike did. In any case, he testified in *Films and Filming* that Vincent was "lovely": "Michael introduced me to this man who'd been a legend to me for years and I said, 'How do you do, Sir. Very pleased to meet you.' The Legend replied, 'Don't push it, Alice,' and I never stopped laughing for seven weeks after that—an extremely amusing man. Vincent and Michael fought a good deal on the picture. Michael was young and Vincent didn't trust him very much because he *was* so young and Michael wasn't very polite to him, either, which is difficult for those kind of caliber stars."

Nicky later expanded on this for the author:

> "We had a very happy, jolly time with him. I don't think he had with Mike. At that time, he was the highest-paid lecturer on art and antiquities, and acting by that time was a hobby. He used to like to come on and raise the cloak and give it all that, and Mike wasn't going to let him do that. Then he learned he wasn't first choice for the part. It affected his attitude to the whole picture.
>
> "He thought, 'I'm not first choice and I'm not going to be allowed to do what I usually do, and this young lad who's never directed a picture as far as I can tell is telling me how to act.' Now Mike knew pictures inside out and bloody backwards, but he didn't know a lot about actors. He knew a few of

Michael Reeves confers with some soldiers on the set of *Witchfinder General*. (photo: Philip Waddilove)

us. His first note to me the first day was, 'Listen, I know when you're do-ing it right and I'll know when you're doing it wrong, but if you're doing it wrong, I won't be able to tell you how to do it right. So just do it a different way and when it's right, I'll tell you.' That's the way he worked with actors and that's why he *needed* mates round him in terms of actors, because actors are funny people. He was a bit shy and had tunnel vision a bit. The group of us got on terribly well, but he left that side of it up to us. He would just say 'Do less,' or 'Do more,' or 'More of that,' or whatever."

Diane Ogilvy commented: "He always used to quote Don Siegel: 'If you cast it right, all you ever need to do is say "better" or 'faster".' "

Interestingly, Nicky Henson wasn't even aware of the conflict between Vincent and Mike until after the filming was finished, so the conflict was low-key for the most part:

"Absolutely, because Vincent was wonderful in the hotel at night. We were all up every night, drinking, telling stories, singing. I was still playing guitar a lot in those days and Vincent was about to go back to New York and do a musical with Pat Routledge (*Darling of the Day*) and he was playing the songs. He was playing the demo tape that they had a lot. I had no idea of this clash. I only did one scene with Vincent, so I wasn't around Vincent when he was working, but I was around him every night, where he was just

**Vincent Price enjoys some goodies while still costumed as Matthew Hopkins during film-
ing of *Witchfinder General*. (photo: Philip Waddilove)**

> wonderful. He was just the funniest man in the world and I don't think I've
> ever laughed so much. Lovely, lovely fellow."

Famously, on one occasion on location in Bury St. Edmunds, the catering truck did not arrive, so Vincent went into town, bought fresh vegetables, pasta and shrimp and prepared lunch
for the cast and crew in the hotel kitchen. Vincent later had his own cookery series on BBC
television.

Ian Ogilvy did not tend to socialize with Vincent in the evening, explained Diane Ogilvy:
"The chances are that Nicky would have spent more time with Vincent in the evenings than we
would have done. It would have far more likely have been cast, and Ian wouldn't at that particular
point have been cast, he'd almost have been on the production lot because he was spending a lot
of time with Mike, much more than any of the other actors."

The fact that Mike did not join in with the socializing because he was so dedicated to the
film undoubtedly worsened his relations with Vincent. Asked by the author to describe Mike's
personality, Vincent could only sadly reply: "There was so little rapport between us it was difficult to form an opinion of his personality." Tony Tenser, who found Mike Reeves and Roman
Polanski the two most dedicated film directors he ever worked with, confirmed that Mike did
not mix much:

> "Polanski would work out the next day's shooting. He'd work out all the
> angles, exactly what was to be done. Although Mike didn't actually do
> that—he didn't need to do that—he'd sit up in his room on his own after
> the day's shooting and he would go through all the next day's work, as
> meticulous as Polanski. He wasn't even much of a drinker. When I was
> there, we used to dine together. He'd dine with me or sometimes he'd dine
> with Annabelle, but he didn't spend much time in entertaining at all. When
> we were out on location and they were setting up a scene, I might be sitting
> there with Vincent Price and Tony Selby, a very good raconteur. He and I
> and Vincent would sit down and I'd be telling him the Jewish stories, and
> Selby telling his story, and Vincent would have a really good laugh and drink
> a glass of wine. Vincent was a mixer. He mixed with people and chatted
> away. People all called him 'Vinnie.' "

Vincent Price socializes with other cast members during filming of *Witchfinder General*. (photo: Philip Waddilove)

Philip Waddilove could not recall Annabelle ever visiting the location, so Tony may have been thinking of *The Sorcerers*.

Ian Ogilvy's first meeting with Vincent Price illustrates Vincent's dry, sarcastic (though not malicious) humor. Vincent had already done two days' work when Ian arrived and was given his horse named Captain. He did the scene where he is cantering to the rectory to see Sara. Ian recalled: "I was cantering and I saw what I thought was a bundle of black clothes lying in a ditch. Then this voice emerged and the line was, 'Oh, my God! She's so pretty, and she rides that fucking horse so well, I hate her!' *Her*—feminine, you see! And that was my introduction to Vincent Price!"

Clearly this was a favorite line of Vincent's. Paul Ferris, who was only there for a couple of weeks, said:

> "He was very funny at night. We had dinner one evening in the hotel dining room. Vincent's there, I was there. I think Nick was round the table as well. They had these two swing doors where the waiters go one side. I thought there must be some slapstick. The fellow comes out with a plate of stuff, and whoosh! Straight over Vincent. Anyway, he then walked back and tripped over and banged his head into one of the doors. It was like a full slapstick. They're all nervous. Anyway, Vincent did say to me at the table, 'That young Michael Reeves, he's so young, so handsome, so talented, and I *hate* him!' "

Price fan Bob Madison, an aspiring young writer when they met, has recalled Vincent saying to him: "Someday, you will write a bestseller, and I'll hate you forever!"

Mike tended not to socialize with Vincent, but Diane Ogilvy explained this was not a snub: "He was working. I think most of the time when that would have happened, it would have been because Mike would go straight into the office, and Philip would probably have been there as well, and then get into the dining room at the very last second." Diane agreed Mike pre-planned the shooting meticulously: "I don't remember things being pasted all over the walls, but Mike knew every single camera angle and every shot that he was going to do."

Things got serious between Mike and Vincent on set, however. One of the worst moments occurred on location in Lavenham for the witch-burning scene. Tony Tenser observed it:

"Vincent was supposed to come out to the crowd around the witch and speak his lines. It was only a short track, but Vincent did not feel like being serious and started moving his head from side to side. Mike said, 'Vinnie, could you please not move your head?' Vincent replied drily, 'Very well. Not moving head.' Then Vincent threw his voice as if on stage. Mike asked him not to throw his voice. Vincent said, 'Very well. Not throwing voice and not moving head!' Another problem arose, I can't remember what it was, and Mike said, 'Please don't do that.' At which point, Vincent rose to his full height of six foot four. He towered two inches over Mike, who was six foot two, and said, 'Young man, I have made 94 pictures in Hollywood. How many have you made?' Mike replied, 'Two *good* ones!' And everybody fell about. Even Vincent fell about. It was such good repartee. Vincent's attitude was only on the surface."

Vincent confirmed this for the author: "My displeasure was mock serious." He could not remember throwing his voice out of fun.

Ian Ogilvy was not around at this point. Although his character is in Lavenham in the film, Ian did not film there. Diane Ogilvy observed: "That would have been one of the early happenings, and Ian wasn't around in Lavenham. We did go up for the day sightseeing, but that was all. The way Mike told that, though, Vincent wasn't doing anything except the acting *he* wanted to do. The way Mike told the story was he had to put so much energy into pulling Vincent's performance down, away from the great Shakespearean-type performer. Mike was definitely pulling up Vincent all the time."

Deke Heyward rejected for Bill Kelley the theory that Mike was deliberately rude to Vincent to provoke an angrier performance: "I do not believe Michael would go to the point of being rude. I know he had a capacity of sitting down and talking to people to get a better performance from them." Catherine Lacey was, of course, an example of this.

Paul Ferris was in no doubt:

"It's all good fun in retrospect, but at the time Vincent wasn't at all amused. And all this thing of saying, 'Vincent, down, down, down.' All the time it was 'down.' Vincent had had so many years of the outlandish horrors, great fun but nothing in it, and Mike brought him up short because Mike didn't want him. He wanted Donald Pleasance and he was pissed off because he was saddled with Vincent Price. Mike had no option. In came Vincent with a totally different approach and they started changing lines already, just softening it. That's when the tension started. Because Mike originally wanted sackbuts and Donald Pleasance—*dead real*, not a laugh anywhere. I don't know which lines were interfered with, but Mike was saying 'They're trying to change this and that and soften this.' Vincent mainly. AIP behind it, but mostly him, because it was the most realistic part he had attempted for years and years. He thought he was just going to waft into another horror part and Mike wasn't going to have that."

Philip Waddilove recalled that Vincent was so disaffected with Mike that he refused to attend the daily showing of rushes at the local cinema before the evening's public performances for the first week:

Mike Reeves wanted a dead on serious performance from Vincent Price.

"During the rest day, I was also able to spend time with Vincent, whose mood throughout filming had been variable but never less than professional. I suggested he should watch our dailies (rushes) that we'd arranged to have screened every day at the local cinema before the evening's public performances. I said he might then see that Michael was getting a wonderful performance out of him and that the entire film was looking great. Vincent replied: 'I never see dailies, dear boy. I can't bear seeing myself on the screen.' Finally, he crept in one day, looked at the screen, and sniffed, 'Ohh, well...' "

Benjamin Halligan writes: "Had Vincent Price seen, in the Vincent Price up on the screen, something that he had not quite seen before in himself either?" Quite likely, it seems.

Ian Ogilvy gave an example of the realism Mike was aiming for:

"One of Mike's original ideas, which he was very overexcited about—we never did it, I suspect because he was talked out of it—was that he wanted, as we were riding down a road in *Witchfinder General*, to have *dead rotting bodies* in the ditch, and nobody to say anything about it. He wanted that. He said that was what it was like. You know, you'd get the odd body from a battle lying in a ditch. Nobody would take any notice. That's what he wanted, but he never did it. That was the kind of thing he wanted."

Of course, Don Siegel had brought realism to the crime movie and Mike seems to have applied that realism to the fantasy of the British horror movie, which is perhaps why his work is unique. Ian commented:

154

"Yes, he wanted the realism. He didn't want the staginess of the Poe movies. He wanted it total realism, which is why he wanted these rotting bodies in ditches and things. He just wanted to do it and not comment on it. And he loved and was frightfully proud of the fisherman scene, because he loved what the man said. 'I didn't even know there was a war on.' Because he'd done his bit of research and that was true. He said, '*That's* what this picture is all about.' The place was being torn to pieces but outlying places were completely untouched by this. Then you get people lying in ditches."

Tom Baker disagreed with Ian about this scene:

"Actually, that's a shocking bit of writing. They're talking to that fisherman and he hasn't even heard of a civil war. I suspect that's Mike. That's a sort of a Mike joke, I think. Mike liked jokes about history. I was much too serious about history, or trying for realism, so I suspect that's a Mike joke. Then, about two lines further on, the fisherman has heard that a Witchfinder has showed up in a village 20 miles away, and you think, 'Well, if you know that, how have you missed the last three years somehow?'"

The attempt at realism also determined Mike's technical approach to direction, as Ian explained:

"Mike detested shots like those taken from inside a fireplace with flames in the foreground. He said, 'Whose point of view is this? Who is this sitting in the fireplace?' He did regard the camera as a character. It very much was somebody's point of view, which is why he wouldn't allow shots taken above chandeliers looking down. He would say, 'Who *is* hanging up here on the chandelier?' The camera had to be in a logical place. If the camera *is* another character, an observer of the scene, then everywhere the camera is *must* be logical. And Mike, I think, doesn't break that rule ever. All right, occasionally, from the top of a police car, yes. But that's fun, and again you could have somebody lying on the top of a police car. You just can't have them in the fireplace, that's all. So logic was kind of important to him. Mike was kind of keen on those sorts of things. He learned a good lesson from people like Don Siegel. It's not necessarily how much you see, it's where the camera *is* that allows you to see it."

When one looks back on *Witchfinder General* from the viewpoint of cinema history, one can see that it was virtually unique of its type, but Nicky Henson said they did not fully realize this at the time they were making it:

"Yes, I don't think we looked at it as a *genre* picture when we were making it. There was no way we thought, 'Gosh, this is a tremendously violent, unusual, historical *horror* film or whatever.' We looked on it very much as a *historical* film in a way. We were terribly aware it was the first time that an English Civil War picture had been made where the Roundheads were the heroes. Is there any other film where the Roundheads are the heroes? So we were trying to get it historically correct. It was just after *The Charge of the Light Brigade*, so there were people from that: the guy who plays one of the troopers with me has still got all his mutton chop stuff from *The Charge of the Light Brigade*. It's *completely* wrong for the period! He's one of the two guys that I ride with all the time."

John Lowes (Rupert Davies) is brutalized by John Stearne in the infamous drowning scene in *Witchfinder General*. (photo: John Hamilton)

No one, least of all Vincent Price, realized during the making what an extraordinary film would result (even Mike was surprised, writing to the film censor: "I think the end result is pretty powerful, as you yourself said—more so even than *I* thought it was going to be"). Most of Tony Tenser's other horror pictures were comedy-horror or otherwise good-natured. Diane Ogilvy commented: "I don't think he quite knew what hit him. Neither he nor AIP knew what they had got in their hands until they saw the rough cut. They had no idea that they had a very, very good film."

Mike was therefore determined to achieve realism in Vincent's performance and was prepared to be rude if he thought it necessary, according to Ian Ogilvy: "He was fighting to get a performance out of him. I think Mike thought he'd got the basis of a very good picture here, which could have easily been ruined if Vincent had been allowed to get away with his rolling eyes and his high camp."

To be fair to Mike Reeves, he was also under great pressure of time, as Ian pointed out: "It was hard work. For the first time, he was faced with a difficult leading actor. And he wasn't a great diplomatist, old Mike. He wasn't a great man who was going to shout and scream at you by any means, but he couldn't understand why Vincent didn't *want* to do what he wanted him to do. Vincent didn't understand what he was doing out here in the wilds of Norfolk in this uncomfortable bloody horrible hotel, with this young snotty kid who told him not to roll his eyes!"

In fact, Vincent told the author he enjoyed the hotel in Bury St. Edmunds and summed up his memories of the main physical discomforts of the filming: "The most uncomfortable thing

Mike Reeves takes a break on the set of *Witchfinder General*. (photo: Philip Waddilove)

was the fact that the horses were not used to camera and crew noises, and sooner or later each of us was thrown. I was thrown onto the ground...flint stones! I was badly bruised, but accommodations were very pleasant. The hangar where we shot was down wind of a mushroom factory and there was a constant stench. That was the worst of that."

Diane Ogilvy commented: "It was a wonderful old English hotel, four-poster beds and things. I don't think Vincent disliked it at all. And he loved showing people round the local museum, because he was a great expert. He had an enormous budget from Sears at the time (to buy antiques for mail order)." Nicky Henson agreed about the accommodation: "I would have thought from an American point of view it would be rather lovely. I was terribly impressed. It was the first proper picture I'd ever been on, because it was a *big* unit. I knew it was a cheap film, but for *those* days, it was like a great big trundling unit. Lots of trucks which would go the night before, I suppose, when they changed locations. Lots of trucks and unit caterers and, of course, horse boxes as well. I think the vans would stay out there, probably sleep in the cabs and stuff like that."

Tom Baker observed Vincent's behavior on set:

> "Once I had a meal with him on location. It was a most entertaining evening. He was across the table and that voice he had! I'm not a great Price fan particularly, but I've seen a few films he's in, and it's just amazing when the guy talking to you about passing the butter has got the same voice and the same eyes, the same sort of semi-quizzical and semi-amused, semi-suspicious voice! I did spend a day shooting when they were burning the witch, having a great deal of hanging around for that, like all filmmaking. All day long that he was around. Actually, he spent a great deal of time asleep or lying down in some room that we were all sheltering in to be out of the camera's eye, on the square at Lavenham. I remember him in his great leather boots and hat, just going, 'I'm going to just lie on the floor here for an hour or two until they want me.' "

Paul Ferris recalled that Vincent was reading a tome on the history of English crystal between takes.

157

Vincent at this time was 56 years old, and riding was his least favorite activity. Nicky Henson commented to Jonathan Rigby in *Shivers*: "He rode very strangely in any case, because he insisted on having his Western saddle flown across from America, which was kept covered all the time because it was completely out of period." On the very first morning of shooting, September 17, 1967, Vincent had his fall onto the hard flint stones and had to spend the remainder of the day in bed. Mike refused to visit Vincent but sent Philip Waddilove instead, to satisfy insurance requirements. Victoria Price has written: "Though some felt that Reeves chose not to check up on Vincent in order to goad him into anger and thus a more menacing performance, Vincent himself simply felt it was a matter of poor communication skills and lack of experience on Reeves' part."

Again, alas, Mike offended his unwanted star. Mike Reeves fan Randy Everts has stated that Vincent actually blamed Mike for his fall, when he once asked him about Mike:

"I had known in advance about Vincent Price's hesitancy to discuss Michael, so could kick myself when I had the chance to tape record his comments and he admitted that Michael was right, and he was not, about his acting in *Witchfinder General* and it was his greatest performance ever in a horror film. He did say that he was upset because Michael did not know how to direct well, and did not know at all how to direct him on a horse. Result: The horse threw Price on his coccyx, causing him much pain and much adverse commentary directed at Michael."

Tony Tenser said he never knew Vincent was ever thrown: "He wasn't deliberately thrown

Vincent Price's wild ride

from a horse, not in the film. He may have fallen off, I don't know. I wasn't told about that. Perhaps they kept it from me in case I would worry about it. I wouldn't have him on a horse then. I'd have a double on it. I wasn't there all the time. I was making one or two other films at the time, as well as dealing with distribution and other things." Tony's memory must have failed him over this, as Philip Waddilove's full account of the incident reveals that Tony was informed and that Vincent had no justification for blaming Mike for the fall.

Philip has written:

"Prior to Vincent signing his contract, when he was asked if he could ride a horse, he said that he'd been riding horses all his life. It was then explained to him that there were a lot of shots in which he would have to ride because we couldn't use a stunt double in those shots. He agreed happily to this. Indeed, Vincent's very first shot in the film for the opening credit sequence was of him in his big black cloak, sitting on an especially chosen docile gray horse. From the pre-credit witch-hanging sequence in a hilly field, the camera zooms to Vincent on his horse outside a village church as he watches the hanging. As my on-set tranquilizer, I was taking stills photos of Michael as he directed the hanging sequence. Some 200 yards away across the field, Susi—herself an experienced horsewoman—was helping the wrangler to familiarize Vincent with his mount.

"Suddenly, I heard a cry from her and I looked in her direction. She was waving at me frantically to come over. I could see that Vincent's horse was now riderless, with Vincent nowhere to be seen—only a mound of black cloak on the ground. Unaware of the real-life drama in progress, Michael continued to shoot as I ran across the field to the black heap and gingerly lifted the edge of the cloak to reveal Vincent lying stoically on the ground. 'Are you all right, Vincent?' I asked him anxiously as I helped him to his feet. 'I'll be perfectly all right after getting a good night's rest, thank you dear boy,' he responded. 'But I'm not getting back on that damn horse!' Susi had already summoned Vincent's limousine driver while I persuaded Vincent that he should at least return to the hotel and rest.

"As Vincent's limo departed for the drive into Bury St. Edmunds, I hurried over to Michael to tell him what had happened. He said that I must get a doctor to see Vincent immediately, if only for insurance purposes. Driving as fast as I dared, I arrived at the Angel Hotel a short time after Vincent and immediately went up to my suite to put through a call to Tony Tenser in London. Tony repeated Michael's instructions to me: 'Tell Vincent he's got to see a doctor immediately. Immediately, you understand, Philip?'

"I went down to the first floor and knocked on Vincent's door. He was in the Dickens Suite—the best in the hotel. 'Who is it?' he enquired. 'It's me, Philip. I must talk with you, Vincent.' Through the door he replied, 'I'll be fine by the morning, I'm perfectly alright.' Still at his door, I resumed: 'Well I've just talked to Tony in London, Vincent, and he says you must let us have a doctor examine you, if only for insurance reasons.' Vincent responded: 'I'm not seeing any goddamned English quack!' Hurrying upstairs to my suite, I got back on the phone to Tony with latest report. Tony's response was to announce that he would call Sam Arkoff in Hollywood for support, even though it was the middle of the night there. Minutes later, the switchboard girl called me: 'There's a Mr. Arkoff on the phone from Los Angeles. He wanted to be put through to Mr. Price but Mr. Price won't take the call, so Mr. Arkoff's asked to be put through to the producer—will you take the call, Mr. Waddilove?' I took Sam Arkoff's call and, after some opening pleasantries, he said that I must tell Vincent officially that it was essential for him to see a doctor, that he was contractually bound to do so and that's all there was to it!

"I called the switchboard and asked to be connected with Vincent. 'But Mr. Waddilove, Mr. Price says he's not taking any calls from anybody,' she said to me. 'OK, Alice,' I replied. 'It's not your fault.'

"I hurried back downstairs to the Dickens suite and knocked at the door. 'Yes?' came the familiar voice. 'It's me, Philip,' I said. 'Please let me in, Vincent. Sam Arkoff's just called and he says that you're contractually bound to see a doctor in case there has to be an insurance claim.' 'All right, come in' he replied. 'The door's not locked.'

"I entered the room to find him seated upright in the four-poster bed, wearing an old-fashioned night shirt and a pointed woolen night cap, reading a large volume of Dickens that he'd found in the suite. 'Vincent,' I said. 'If you won't see a doctor, at least let me find out if there's any visible injury to your back.' He got off the bed and, kneeling down, leant over the bed with his back facing me. I pulled up his nightshirt and began to feel his nether regions, pressing gently to see if there were any painful places. 'How does that feel?' I said. 'Wonderful, dear boy!' he responded.

"At that moment the door opened and, not realizing that Vincent had returned early from the location, our young wardrobe mistress Jill Thompson swept into the suite carrying Vincent's costume for the next day. The expression on Miss Thompson's face when she saw the two of us was a picture I won't forget.

"As Jill left the room, Vincent climbed back into bed without registering the slightest concern, picked up his book and addressed me. 'Now, if you'll just leave me in peace, Philip, I'll be on the set in the morning—ready for work.' Nevertheless, the next morning we called in a doctor and Vincent finally agreed to be given a check-up."

Nicky Henson commented:

> "We all got thrown. Ian's actually a very good horseman, but there were some of us who just weren't, and there were an awful lot of molehills. We were lucky we didn't lose any horses. It was low budget and that was the one area where they skimped. Maybe it wasn't skimping, but the film horses weren't very good. They weren't used to camera noise. They used to shy. It used to spook them all the time.
>
> "They weren't movie horses and they gave my horse a Pentathol jab for that fall. They didn't have a proper falling horse and I did it with me on it. Then I think, eventually, they shot it again with a stunt man and a falling horse, some few days later. The first time we did it, we did it with a Pentathol jab, which was awful. He didn't know what he was going to get and he could have broken his leg on it."

Paul Ferris observed: "Mike wanted the horses to be real, instead of these beautiful race-horses you see in Westerns. I'm sure they didn't have them. They didn't shave their horses, they used racehorses. He wanted to use the big shire horses. What Mike wanted was big bloody clod-hoppers, big, long-haired, as horses were." Virginia Scholte later recalled that Mike hated the way the horses were treated on the film.

Nicky Henson remembered another unfortunate incident:

> "There was a guy in it who did what I did, and said that he could ride, and he fell off every time. Every time! Every shot he was in, he fell off. There are lots of the still shots where you see a stray horse with nobody on it, which he's fallen off, and Mike couldn't be bothered to go back shooting those long tracking shots. He fell off once when the clapperboard came in, and Mike kept a shot in of him falling off. It's when we all wheel round and Vincent rides away from me when I rush to him. Just as I turn my horse to go after him, you see these two feet come up the bottom of the frame. That's this same guy. Every fucking time he fell off, and Mike left that one in."

Paul Ferris was amused by this, too: "Wonderful one. The feet come up. Casting sessions, he said, 'Do you ride?' He'd never seen a horse in his life. They put the helmet on this guy, it was too big and it rolled round. He was screaming his head off." Nicky himself had a problem "trying to keep your boots up and stuff like that."

It is a tribute to Mike's directorial skill that none of the funny side of making the film transmits into the final product, even though Ian Ogilvy remembered that Mike found the scene of the feet appearing upside down "hysterically funny": "Mike loved that. He thought it was hysterical. He used to run it again and again. He used to say, 'Look, look, here are his feet, here they come!' So all that went on. There was an enormous amount of *fun* in the making of a picture. He loved the sort of little accidents that were happening."

Mike did not have fun with Vincent Price, however, and things got so bad that Vincent tried to walk off the picture twice. Paul Ferris confirmed this: "It was all off at one point. Vincent had

Vincent Price was extremely unhappy during filming.

said 'Adios.' He was going to leave a couple of points there." Ian Ogilvy agreed: "Vincent was a *personal* production difficulty. He was found two or three times sitting at Bury St. Edmunds railway station. 'Who do I have to fuck to get off this goddamn picture?' All of that was going on. It's true, he wasn't happy." Paul Ferris actually heard Vincent say this ('Who do I have to...') but thought Vincent had used the phrase 'sleep with.' Paul found it quite witty and it can be assumed that it was an example of Vincent's dry, ironic humor.

Diane Ogilvy also confirmed that Vincent was found one time at least at the station:

> "Vincent was running away. I mean, to be found at the station. I only re-
> member once. Definitely, very early on in the movie. I'm sure Tony wouldn't
> have been told. I remember leaving the location one day in the car and there
> was a very, very dejected Vincent sitting in a ditch. He seemed to spend a
> lot of time sitting in a ditch—nothing to do with the shot—and I just wound
> down the window and said, 'Can I give you a lift?' And he said, 'Are you
> going past California?' And he meant it, he really did."

In fairness to Vincent, it should be recorded that he denied to the author that he ever tried to leave the picture (though Ian Ogilvy predicted he would deny it), and Tony Tenser's argument that it is not likely that he did is compellingly logical. Of course, as emotions do not obey logic and as there is so much other evidence of Vincent's general dissatisfaction, it is hard to see how much store can be set by this. Tony's argument is at least useful in highlighting that Vincent's attempts to leave were probably a demonstration that he was not being treated properly and not a determined effort to escape:

Vincent Price has Michael Reeves to thank for his brilliant performance.

"He'd had enough and he'd go off and sulk a bit. But it didn't happen very often. He may have been found at the station whilst I wasn't there; they didn't tell me about it, but I can't imagine that. I think he *wanted* to be talked out of it. He didn't want to go off and leave. He knew he couldn't. He'd ruin his career if he walked off a picture before it's finished. But he wanted somebody to say, 'Look...' Because Mike wasn't a director who ever flannelled people. He never said, 'Now look, darling, you do that. You're going to be fine.'

"It was left to me to do that. *I* would flannel them and people wanted *directors* to do that. Directors in the main don't do that. You don't find many directors that treat people like that. They're indifferent. They want to see the thing done. Vincent was frustrated. He wasn't happy with his relationship with Mike. That's how I saw it at the time. But it was all right. And I thought, 'He's the main star of the film. He is the Witchfinder.' He *was* the film. The film was really the work of Mike Reeves, but he was the film, and I feel at times he was entitled to act the prima donna, as he *was* the prima donna. And that's what happened. So I had to treat him as one treats a prima donna: 'Oh, come on, Vinnie, take no notice. You know how we feel about you. You've made all these films. I've always watched your films. Are you gonna let your fans down? You're doing a wonderful job.' 'Oh,' he said, 'it won't work.' 'You wait. You wait.' That's how he went on."

Indeed, after Vincent saw the film, he wrote to Tony to say he had been right. Tony replied on April 24, 1968:

Dear Vinnie,

Thank you for your most marvellous note—I think it's the first time somebody has ever said I was right—very nice of you to take the trouble to write.

I knew you would love the film when you saw it. I think it will do us all a power of good and although it may sound corny, I really did enjoy your company on the occasions we were together at Bury St. Edmunds.

If you weren't so damned expensive I would give you a four-picture-a-year contract!

Love to you and your wife.

Yours,

S. Tony Tenser

Asked by the author why he was particularly unhappy during production, Vincent confirmed, from an actor's viewpoint, the gist of what Tony has said and also greatly flattered Mike: "Michael didn't know how to work with actors, but his filmmaking ideas were very good—rather like Orson Welles." Paul Ferris remarked: "It's extraordinary he should say that, because that's what I feel about Mike, too. The same kind of maverick. He didn't want to meet other filmmakers. Orson Welles didn't want to meet other filmmakers: He said he never *watched* other movies. A virgin eye. That's what Mike was preserving, I think. It's not a conscious thing at 24, it's just a passion. Watching rubbish, that's all right. It fires you up." Of course, we know that Mike would watch things like the original *Batman* serial.

Some critics thought there should have been a bit more development of Hopkins' psychological motivation but, as David Pirie has argued, the film "does not work on the basis of profound psychological insight." It is a Western, and Hopkins' motivation is summed up as purely mercenary and opportunistic in the voice-over spoken by Patrick Wymark at the start of the film. Ian Ogilvy commented about the voice-over:

"You know what that's a take-off of, don't you? That's a straight steal from *The Third Man.* Do you remember how *fast* the voice-over is at the beginning of *The Third Man*? It's very fast and almost like the person's making it up as he says it. It almost doesn't sound scripted. And Mike said, 'I very much want to try and get that.' He never quite succeeded, but the idea was that it shouldn't be portentous. It should be very much 'The year is 1650 and Cromwell's army ...(rapidly spoken).' He wanted that. He nicked that very much from *The Third Man.*"

The voice-over makes some people feel as if they are in for a history lesson, which then does not happen. Ian said:

"In which case it failed; he wanted very much *not* to have a history lesson. He wanted very much to have an almost contemporary attitude toward it. You know, 'The year is 1650 and it's pretty nasty around here.' That was the idea. He very much wanted that kind of loose, freewheeling kind of voice-over. I think he got as close to it as he could simply by the speed that it's said. Usually it's, 'The year is 1650...[slowly spoken].' He didn't want all that. He wanted very much like *The Third Man.* It *was* a Western. Course it was. Horses, revenge, the goodie and the baddie and it's all very clear-cut. To him, he wasn't making a Civil War movie at all. He was making a cowboy movie with the Civil War in the background. It's exactly the same as saying a revenge movie during the Civil War in America. So you might have the odd

A tracking shot is filmed on the set of *Witchfinder General*. (photo: Philip Waddilove)

> passing bluecoat and the odd passing graycoat, but actually you're following
> this damn cowboy who's furious with somebody else."

It is Mike Reeves' use of the camera that is especially interesting to many admirers of his directorial skill. Ian commented:

> "I have a feeling that Mike was one of the early exponents of the track-and-
> zoom shot. I know he *talked* about it. I learned about it *from him*. I know
> he wanted to do it somewhere in that picture. I'm not sure he ever got round
> to it, and if he did use it, it's too dark really to notice. I know Mike *knew*
> about it and he wanted to try it. He'd never done it before and it's a hell of a
> set-up. It takes quite a lot of time to get them equal, because you must keep
> your central character the same size, he mustn't vary. It's what happens to
> the background. It makes your stomach lurch. And you can only use it once.
> I know Mike wanted to use it and I always thought he put it in the nighttime
> scene when Vincent realizes that Hilary is only screwing him because of
> what she wants out of him. But I may be wrong. He may not have done it.
> I always thought he did. I know he wanted to."

There is no apparent track-and-zoom in the released version.

In the pre-credits sequence which Tom Baker has explained was inspired by the Kersey location, there is very intelligent film direction where Mike Reeves focuses on the mob coming up the hill, pulls back to set them in perspective with the gibbet, then tracks round to the side to observe their progress. It establishes the scene and gives you the context and has emotional pull toward the center of action as well. Ian agreed: "And it gives you the geography. That's quite true. To establish how things worked and where everybody was. Again, I think his great strength was pictorially. He wasn't *really* happy in dialogue scenes. He was all right but...he used to play jokes in dialogue scenes. He knew I *loathed* Brussels sprouts and in *The Sorcerers* somewhere along the line I have a lunch with Elizabeth Ercy or someone. He ordered piles of Brussels sprouts! All that kind of thing went on. It was all very friendly and fun. A lot of laughs. We had a lot of laughs with him." Indeed, Tom Baker characterized Mike at that period as "a perfectly cheery chap, lively and busy and interested."

Patrick Wymark as Oliver Cromwell gets a touch up as producer Philip Waddilove, in a bit part as a solider, waits for Reeves' action.

In that pre-credits sequence, Mike seems to be tracking sideways and zooming out. Ian confirmed this: "Yes, I think he absolutely is. It's not a difficult shot to do, of course, but you have got to have a very good *reason* for doing it. I remember seeing John Guillermin's *The Blue Max* and I thought, 'If this camera doesn't stop moving quite so much, I'm going to be sick.' The camera never stopped moving all the time."

One of the characters that critics of the film felt had been skimped was Cromwell, played in a small one-day cameo by Patrick Wymark (who went on afterwards to make the *Witchfinder* rip-off called *Blood on Satan's Claw*). Ian Ogilvy, however, argued:

> "It wasn't *about* Cromwell. It wasn't about battles. Mike said, 'We can't afford to shoot the Battle of Naseby. Therefore we *won't* shoot the Battle of Naseby, but we'll have them talk about it. We can't afford to do it. So what we're going to do is, make a very intimate, rather nasty little story about a nasty man. But we can't do crowd scenes. Can't do them. Leave that to *Cromwell* and Richard Harris.' "

Tom Baker did want to have the Battle of Naseby in the film:

> "I shoved the Battle of Naseby into the original script, because historically it's there, but I think we wrote it in a page of montage or half a page of montage, because we knew it was very unlikely that we'd have any money for a battle. It was one of the things that made the censor really bloody cross, that we're slicing people's arms off and stuff. He, or his underling who read it, said, 'I can't stand this. This is gratuitous, I won't have it!' What do we do? We've got about 30 seconds to put in one of the major battles of the Civil War! Pity we didn't get the battle in."

Rupert Davies endured many uncomfortable scenes in *Witchfinder General*.

When the censors objected to the first draft of the script, Tony Tenser got a revised draft off to them straight away. This quelled objections until they saw the assembled film.

Diane Ogilvy got involved in chauffeuring Patrick Wymark, whose television success (*The Power Game*, etc.) lent him a certain star status: "Patrick Wymark couldn't be taken out onto the set in case he had a tantrum before he was needed, so I would take him out, because there weren't the spare cars or drivers or anything like that. So, after eleven o'clock, one left. He was treated with kid gloves, not taken out at ten o'clock and made to sit around for two hours. I was told to stay home and look after him." Poor old Vincent wasn't treated with kid gloves, she thought: "I don't remember that, because I seem to have these extraordinary visions of Vincent spending so much time sitting in a ditch; he probably did it *once*."

It is not true that the film entirely neglects the psychology of its characters, of course. For instance, in the scene where Ian and Hilary leave the church after swearing the oath and they part, Ian hesitates to caress her. Robin Wood interprets this as Marshall feeling that Sara is degraded by having slept with the Witchfinder and having difficulty in bringing himself to touch her. This seems right, but when one looks at the scene specifically to see if that is the case, the playing is so subtle that one becomes unsure if that was the intention.

One may wonder whether Mike Reeves and Ian Ogilvy were consciously trying to convey the sense that Marshall is slightly revolted by his now-defiled girlfriend: It is slightly question-able in that Marshall is tender to her *before* and *after* this scene. Yet Sara's appalled reaction to Marshall's hesitancy does seem to confirm that she senses he thinks she is somehow degraded. Ian Ogilvy commented: "I *think* what was intended was this: that Sara believes Richard's hesi-tancy is because of feelings of temporary revulsion toward her, but that Richard is locked into a state of murderous revenge and that this is neither the time nor the place to show compassion to anybody—even Sara."

Rupert Davies, in his day a very popular British television star on the BBC's *Maigret* series, was given a rougher time during the making of *Witchfinder* than Vincent Price was, in the sense of enduring physical discomfort. However, unlike Vincent, he realized how talented Mike was and did not complain. In 1975 he recalled Mike Reeves for Chris Knight:

> "He was very good, but very exacting and very exhausting. He had a great belief in realism. I'm all for that myself, but I thought in some way he car-

ried it a bit far. Like in many shots, where a double would've been used in most films, he wanted the actual actor, even if the camera was on the back of his neck or he was too far away to be recognizable. For instance, I get dragged through the gravel, drowned in the moat, and hung on the tree, all wet, straight from the moat—and before that, I had spikes stuck in the moles on my back, screaming ad lib for hours on end—I believe the censor cut about nine of those stabs and just left a flash in.

"And then I was in a dungeon cell in the town, chained to the wall, blood everywhere. And he had four inches of specially smelly water put in as though it made a difference. But it did something for him, I think. Then, when the crew was finally ready, and the camera was pointing through the bars of the dungeon, I heard a voice say, 'Right—put the rats in.' Nobody told me anything about rats! They had a rat fancier and he put in three rats. They started crawling up me. Mike was saying, 'Don't move, Rupert. Don't move. Wait till that one starts nibbling your jaw, then you might move your head a little.' I said, 'I might, yeah!' The continuity girl who was sitting there with her knees through the bars and her work sheet shrieked and flew out. It was all that kind of thing.

"When I was hung on that tree, it really was straight after the moat-dunking scene and we really were wet. We had to go shivering into that house which had the moat around it and change into the harness, put the wet clothes on again, then go out and do this stuff in the evening gloaming. Michael had all this absolute realism going on the whole time. Very exacting, very impressive."

Ian Ogilvy recalled that Rupert's availability posed one of the frequent production difficulties on *Witchfinder*:

"There's always production difficulties on everything. I remember on *Witchfinder* out on the Norfolk flats, Mike had to have Rupert Davies for one more day and his contract had finished on that day. Mike still needed one more day, so he went to a phone box on the Norfolk flats, and called Tony Tenser. He said, 'I must have Rupert for one more day.' Tony said, 'You can't. Haven't got any money. You can't have him for one more day.' And Mike said, 'What do you think I am doing now, Tony?' Tony said, 'What do you mean?' 'Well, I am standing in a phone box and I'm not going to leave this phone box until I get Rupert for one more day.' Tony literally went into the 'I'll put my wife on the streets, sell my children...' All this went on. Mike said, 'The stage Jew is terrific, Tony, but can I have Rupert for one more day?' 'You're killing me, my boy.'...He got Rupert. Total blackmail. But he had production difficulties all the time."

Tony Tenser could not confirm this story: "I can't remember that."

Witchfinder General has been praised for making a positive virtue out of English landscape in a movie, whereas Hammer horror films, even when filmed in the countryside, never did. Ian Ogilvy commented:

"They were never prone to get that far afield. You saw the same old bits of wall, the same old houses in Hammer pictures. Hammer was very tied to its studio concept. Everything was inside, everything was studio, having spent all that money on the studio. Amicus as well. I did two Amicus pictures. They'd spend a fortune on sets. Mike didn't want to do that. He wanted to

Ian Ogilvy, shown in the film's climax, gives a fantastic performance. (BFI)

go to the real places, which meant that we found a central location at Bury St. Edmunds, where we lived, and radiated out from there. Anybody can use the Army ranges and they're an ideal location to shoot, no houses. Hammer was very studio-bound, frankly. So was Amicus."

Furthermore, none of the other directors of the time seemed very interested in English landscape. Ian Ogilvy argued that the reason for this was that they weren't making Westerns: "And Mike was making a Western. And landscape is everything in a Western, absolutely. And he wanted scenes of galloping horses, he wanted the motorcycle scenes (in *Sorcerers*) and the galloping horses scenes, gotta go out for that."

On the other hand, Mike Reeves used very studied compositions, like the fantastic natural cross of light in the trees, which is the first image in the film. It is a very striking beginning to the drama that follows. The question is whether, when Mike got to the location, he would have wondered, "How am I going to start it?" and then looked around, or whether that was already in his mind, to find a striking image like a natural cross of light. Ian thought:

> "He would look at the location and then work it out. He wouldn't build the location to his concept. He was, again, endlessly adaptable. He loved little accidents. There's a little bit with the shepherd and as I gallop my horse, the rump bumps the shepherd. A little tiny thing like that, but that's why he got the shepherd to spit, because as I ride off the horse bumps the shepherd. It's *corny*, the shepherd spitting, but Mike said, 'Okay, now we need another shot, sorry. Big close-up.' He would *use* those things, you see."

168

David Pirie wrote that there were some defects in the acting in the film. He would seem to be referring to characters like the shepherd, who are not totally convincing in what they are doing. Ian agreed:

> "No. What happens is, on a budget like that, you look at an actor and he looks right, and he's only got one line, so you book him, and he goes into makeup and comes out...and he can't do it. Now what are you going to do? Are you going to fire him and start all over again? You haven't got time. It happens all the time. You've miscast him. You've got it wrong. So Mike didn't always get it right. He frequently got it wrong."

Ian accepted that such defects are so minor that it does not affect the viewer's enjoyment of *Witchfinder*. This is in large measure because the performances of the principals, Ian Ogilvy, Vincent Price, Hilary Dwyer and Robert Russell are so brilliant, but Ian was critical of aspects of his own performance (unjustifiably):

> "To me, I nearly *killed* the end of that picture, because my screaming, 'You took him from me,' I think is just *awful*. It doesn't mean anything. It's just an actor screaming. He's got nothing behind it at all. Looking at it in retrospect, I just die of embarrassment, because I hate it. I think I'm very lucky I got away with that because I was tired, it was late at night, it was a bad, long day, and it was just technical. I loathe me and I just think, 'You're very lucky that the ending works because you could have killed that ending.' It doesn't strike you but I know it was shallow and didn't mean anything."

Yet it is quite attractive the way he begins, 'You took him away from me,' and then repeats more quietly, 'You took him from me,' which conveys despair. He laughed:

> "That was probably because I was tired and I couldn't bother to repeat the line exactly! I found it very hard and I didn't quite understand what Mike wanted, and I don't think he did either, really. So there are elements of all that, you look at your own thing and you think 'Ohhh...' The thing Mike was very worried about was the oath-swearing scene in the church. Because he said, 'Are we going to get away with this? Can you do it?' I said, 'Well, what do you mean?' He said, 'Well, it's awfully near the knuckle. What I've written, could be funny.' And I said, 'Well, I don't think it's going to be funny, if you let me do what I want to do.' Now, I don't particularly *like* it, but I think the fact of the matter is, we take some time over it and we don't try and hide it. We don't try and shuffle it under the carpet. We're quite open about it. And he was very *pleased* with that scene in the long run. I think it's a bit embarrassing now, but at the time we were all frightfully pleased with it. We thought it worked like a dream. We thought that the sincerity of it was right."

Diane Ogilvy remembered it slightly differently: "I still can't get over that *extraordinary* scene, because Mike rewrote that the night before and came and read it to us. We just sat there, because the way it read, it was so ghastly it wasn't true. We kept saying, 'You can't do that, you can't do that,' and they did it, and, thanks to Mike and Ian and Hilary, it was one of the most extraordinary scenes in the movie."

What is very convincing about the scene is that Ian is holding Hilary's hand while they are praying, but when he comes to swear the oath of revenge, he pushes her hand away, as if not to involve her in the guilt of what he's going to do. Ian commented wryly: "Well, actually, on a technical level, I've got to have two hands to hold the sword! Do you see? What happens is, I hold her hand and then the sword would come. Well, I've got to have two hands. It may *look* like it's putting her away. It's just a technical thing. I've got to hold the sword with two hands, so what do I do with her hand? I give it back to her."

This is remarkable because it adds to the truth of the scene. Ian agreed:

> "Well, that's right. That's again the happy accident of the technical side, and the other thing that you have to think about is that, in among all that nonsense, I am trying to capture the light with the sword. Coquillon said, 'Ian, there is one particular angle where the light will catch it.' So while I'm doing that, I'm slowly revolving that sword, hoping that sooner or later that light will catch it. So you're thinking of all that kind of nonsense. But Mike was very worried about that. He said, 'I'm not sure we can get away with this, but let's shoot it, and if it works, then that's fabulous, but I'm not sure it will work.' He was slightly embarrassed by having written it."

Of course, if *Witchfinder General* is a revenge Western (influenced, some critics have said, by Budd Boetticher's Randolph Scott films like *Comanche Station* and *Ride Lonesome*), then that scene explains the character's obsession. Ian commented:

> "Yes, but to formalize the oath of revenge, to make it such a formal thing, was what embarrassed him. He was slightly embarrassed by his own writing, but he left it in because he felt that it had worked, that the actors had brought it off. I quite liked the scene and I thought, 'No, the thing is to be brave about it and just do it and *not* be embarrassed by it, because in those days people actually might have done that sort of thing.' You don't know, but they *might* have done."

In this scene, there are little details like the word witch scrawled on the inside of the chapel, which add resonances that other filmmakers might not have bothered with. Ian observed:

> "That is a real church. Brandeston parish church. The village of Brandeston was very near where I was working up in Norwich on Anglia Television's *Menace Unseen*. I kept driving past and thinking, 'I'd love to go see it again.' It was called Brandeston and it *was* Brandeston. And that was a real church—I don't remember how we quite got permission to scrawl all over the walls and throw the pews around, but we obviously did."

(Benjamin Halligan found the location to be Newe House in Pakenham, a gentry house of the early 17th century.)

Ian did not know if the people living in the localities where the film was made were proud of it: "I would have thought people who lived in those villages would have seen the picture and thought, 'Oh, very nice' and forgotten all about it. They're probably bank managers, you see. They're not film buffs, I wouldn't have thought." Mike found some great faces among the local people in Lavenham for the close-ups of the crowd in the witch-burning scene. Ian said: "Lavenham were local people mostly. They weren't expected to say or do anything. Yes, he was awfully good at that sort of visual side, trying to get the faces right. He loved all that." Amos Powell appears as an execution assistant, dressed in green.

When *Cahiers du Cinema*, the French intellectual film journal, reviewed *Witchfinder General*, they said it was an hour and a half of emptiness redeemed by 90 seconds of content at the end. Ian Ogilvy remarked: "I wouldn't agree with that, but also I would be amused by the fact that the ending was an accident, wasn't planned." Although Ian's role in *The Sorcerers* seems larger

A local fireman puts out the witch-burning fire after the important scene was completed. (photo: Philip Waddilove)

than in *Witchfinder* ("Yes, there is a huge chunk I'm not in"), he enjoyed making *Witchfinder* more. This is despite the fact that in *Witchfinder*, his character's emotions are simpler—they are revenge motives—whereas in *Sorcerers* he plays this slightly neurotic character who abandons his girlfriend to be on his own.

Ian mused: "I suppose that's true. I think I enjoyed *Witchfinder* more because it was quite obviously a bigger budget and we were able to spend more time on it. It wasn't so scrappy. I was prouder of *Witchfinder General* simply because I think it's one of the *best* pictures I've ever made. I've made some pretty awful ones. I remember *Sorcerers* being quite fun. It was all in London, apart from the motorbike scene. I suppose it was quite dark."

Ian took photographs on the sets of all the Reeves pictures. He commented:

"I've even got a 16-mm film on *Witchfinder*, of Mike directing. Silent, of course. And always gagging. You'd only got to point a camera at Mike and he'd stick a cigarette up his nose. The 16-mm camera I had had been used by somebody who'd done 16-mm Cinerama! He'd had 12 of these bloody things mounted, and I bought one. I've got a 16-mm film of the making of *Witchfinder General*, which I shot entirely silently, but I cut it all together and you get an idea of the sort of atmosphere, the gags, the fun we were having, the general relaxation of it all. I just shot people having fun."

Possibly the most striking feature of *Witchfinder General*, aside from Mike's direction, is the extraordinary musical score by Paul Ferris. It was not Mike's idea to use the highly romantic, quasi-traditional music in a horror film. Paul recalled that Mike gave him complete freedom:

"He left me entirely alone to do it. It was originally going to be Donald Pleasance. Because we were determined to make *the* horror film, absolutely for real and a real knock-out, I was going to do the score using real Elizabethan instruments. It wasn't going to be a classical guitar. I wanted to use a lute,

171

sackbuts and so on, together with probably quite a different performance to Vincent's, which is why Mike had such fights with him, because Vincent started doing all this business and Mike said 'Down, down!'

"I met Samuel Z. Arkoff after Vincent had come onto the scene; the only time I ever met Arkoff. Mike had explained I was going to use these original Elizabethan instruments and he said, 'Now, listen, kid, don't want any of this original Elizabethan instruments crap. Understand what I mean?' He gulped and his cigar flicked up and he walked off. End of meeting. That's absolutely true!"

Diane Ogilvy said that Mike laughed that no one on the set ever paid any attention to Sam Arkoff. Tony Tenser commented on Paul's story:

"I can't remember that. As far as the music was concerned, Mike Reeves brought in Paul Ferris. I'd heard some of the stuff that he'd done. I said, 'Excellent. Let him do it.' Then, when he did the theme for it and we just heard the theme, I said, 'This is great.' Whichever instruments he used was up to him. I wouldn't get involved with a thing like that. You pay a professional person to do a professional job. Although you may know the parameters of the job, it's his soul that goes into it and, unless he's *completely* off track, like he's going to use jaws harps and steel drums or something, whatever he needed was right. I think Arkoff, through Deke Heyward, wanted a couple of changes, so we added them. We shot them in the film, you know, a bit more gore or whatever, but no problem. We got on very well."

Some people find the *Witchfinder General* love theme reminiscent of *Greensleeves*, which Paul regarded as a compliment: "But if they actually go through the melody, it is actually nothing whatsoever like *Greensleeves*. Totally different melody."

He revealed, however, that he did have *Greensleeves* in mind when writing it:

"Certainly did, yes, but what I was aiming for was my own *Greensleeves*, a feeling of *Greensleeves*. Because *Greensleeves* for England is like *Danny Boy* for Ireland.

"What I was trying to do was write a melody that gave that feeling and you have to follow the music of the time. You can't go too far away from the actual chord sequences, but in fact the sequences aren't the same as *Greensleeves* either. So, what I was trying to do was produce as close as I could to a feeling of *Greensleeves*, which I think I did, but it is nothing like the *Greensleeves* melody. Plenty of non-musicians have said to me—musicians don't, because they know—'It's *Greensleeves*,' and I've said, 'All right, sing both tunes.' They don't even harmonize together. They're totally different."

Baker felt Paul's score: "...is derivative music to an extent, and it's bound to be, but it's lovely, picking up as the movement comes." But what is so extraordinary is the use of this lyrical music to accompany *Witchfinder General*'s painful and violent images. It is the opposite of what one would expect and, said Paul, that was the point: "That's why I did it." Paul agreed that it brings out the pain in the characters: "Yes, that was the idea, and it does in the good ones. We were all aiming toward that. Scarifying pieces are usually just orchestral dissonance. Now they're realizing that is just a dead end. People aren't dissonant."

Mike's genius shone in realizing what an important part music can play in a film and designing *Witchfinder General* to let Paul's genius flourish. According to Paul, it was Elmer Bernstein's

Mike Reeves, Philip Waddilove and Keith Grant recording Paul Ferris' score in Olympic Sound Studios, early 1968. (photo: Philip Waddilove)

theme for John Sturges' *The Magnificent Seven* that inspired Mike when it came to preparing the *Witchfinder* script. Paul confirmed that Mike loved the film and had seen it "300 times":

> "He was thinking of *that* one when he did *Witchfinder*. That's why he said, 'I want to do a Western.' He was always playing *The Magnificent Seven* on the turntable. You look at their sequences and the music sequences—they're very similar to an awful lot of *Witchfinder*.
>
> "He said to me, 'I want it to be an English Western. I want you to do the music. I'm going to shoot it like a Western and leave you loads of footage to fill with English Western music.' I remember Mike and I did talk about getting it like *The Magnificent Seven*. It was one of the records he had. When you think of the moments in *Witchfinder* that work, it's exactly the same—just transpose it to the States or Mexico. It's the same as *The Magnificent Seven*, very similar. Mine is weaker, because their theme for the villains in *The Magnificent Seven* is excellent and has never been bettered.
>
> "I think *The Magnificent Seven* is virtually the perfect film score. The whole thing's been shot in a way you know the director's talked with Bernstein, just as Mike and I did with *Witchfinder*. He said, 'I've got this long sequence here, Paul.' Great. And you know—and he knows—that it's not going to be silent. It's no good doing a few feet: what are you going to do? The horse is riding, so have the horse riding and let the music run. Most people do a few feet and no music, and they think, 'Why hasn't he written a lovely theme? Why isn't the music so good for this sequence?' Because it's too short, usually. Literally, that is too short, so you don't get the chance to develop it as they did in *The Magnificent Seven*."

Philip Waddilove observes as Paul Ferris works on the score for *Witchfinder General*.

Elmer Bernstein has kindly clarified the process behind scoring *The Magnificent Seven* in the light of Paul Ferris' description of working with Mike Reeves:

> "I am not acquainted with Michael Reeves' work, and it is a sadness to find that the last three years of his life came at a time when I was spending a great deal of time in London. Needless to say I was most flattered by Paul Ferris' observations concerning my score for *The Magnificent Seven*. John Sturges was never invasive of the composing process. What he did was to invite me to either a morning or an afternoon at the studio or sometimes to his home to tell me the story of a projected film before it was shot. His purpose was never, nor did he ever make an attempt, to tell me what the music should be. His telling of the stories was so beautiful and inspirational that I began to have an idea of what I might do in the long run. When the film was completed, and I actually started to work on the score, I was left completely alone. It was my decision, on seeing the film, that the character of the music should whip the action along. The language of the score was clearly Western/Mexican, which relates to its locale, but its greatest function was to move things on. Sturges was a great supporter, loved music, and, most importantly, once he knew he could trust, he trusted, something which is not in great supply at this time."

There are obvious parallels here with the way Mike Reeves worked with Paul Ferris.

Although *The Magnificent Seven* and *Witchfinder General* can be said to spring from the same approach to scoring, one could argue that Paul's score is the more original, but he himself rated *Seven*'s as perfect, along with *The Third Man*:

"I can't think of any other movie, apart from *The Third Man*, where I'd not change a note. With every other movie I've seen, I'm sure whoever's done the music would change it afterwards. Every time I see and hear *The Magnificent Seven* and *The Third Man*, they're perfect. *The Magnificent Seven* love theme, the counterpoint melody, the strings, is beautiful. Marvelous, absolutely perfect."

Surprisingly, Paul was among those composers who would change their work in hindsight, as he explained: "I wasn't happy with all of *Witchfinder* and had arguments with Mike about that when we did it. He wanted it to be a Western, an English Western, and the score to be Western-type. All shooting and horses: It *was* like a Western. Certain parts of that score I thought were not right, but he wouldn't let me change them even at the time of recording, because he was so knocked out with the sound of things, but some of it I think is not right."

Paul was referring mainly to the scene where Robert Russell on horseback is fleeing and the score gets hyped up like a more conventional Western. Mike wanted that music to whip up excitement but Paul, looking back, later thought that was a mistake, as the music in the tracking shots of Ian Ogilvy riding is at a different pace and the counterpointing produces an indescribable effect. Paul agreed: "Right. That's why I wanted to change that bloody sequence, but Mike wouldn't let me. I hated it as soon as I did it. 'Oh, Christ, change it now!' Mike said, 'No, love it!' I said, 'Aarrgh, change it, we can do it now!' He wouldn't have it. That's his prerogative."

According to Paul, Mike even used to write his movie scripts with headphones on, listening to film scores (Maurice Jarre, et al.) and was "certainly" drawing moods from the music:

"This is why Mike was so good, you see. A lot of directors do not think in terms of music when they're either writing or directing. It's a thing that you add later to make up the deficiencies in whatever. Which is silly. If you say right at the beginning that this film has no music, as in *Rififi*, that's fair enough. Then you work from that. But knowing there's going to be music in there and ignoring all that and then expecting the dubbing editor to save the film is the wrong way round. Mike *knew*, in *Witchfinder*, there was going to be music in all those long sequences. A man or woman who doesn't think that way will shoot shorter sequences. I think this is where a lot of them fall down. Actually, while I think about Mike saying he wanted it to be an English Western and the music to be as from a Western, e.g., *The Magnificent Seven* or one of those, no one had shot that before, *in* England, *about* England. Most English movies still bore me rigid. They're very beautifully photographed but to me they're not movies, they're stillies."

Paul assembled a 55-piece orchestra for the first session, which was the important part. As the budget was not large, he used up his own salary in the pursuit of excellence:

"I did the same as I've always done on all the films I've worked on. They give you a lump sum out of which you have to pay yourself, the musicians and the copyists. They pay for the studio, all the tape and all other costs. I got excited, as you do in the middle of the night, and added instruments, which of course costs money. A lot of money. If you get excited and your fee isn't high, what happens is you start adding oboes and horns, which is what I always did. I did it consistently and Mike was *the only one* who reimbursed me for what I spent. The only one who did something about that. It was about 1200 quid extra, which was quite a lot just to make up a 55-piece orchestra, and he gave me the money back, out of the film. He twisted Tony Tenser's arm to get it back. The rest never did. The music's more important."

Tom Baker commented: "He didn't have any money at all, so he really cared about what he was doing. It's magnificent, really. It's great credit to Mike because it shows the kind of loyalty he induced in people for his projects. It's Mike's enthusiasm to get people involved and get them doing things." Ian Ogilvy was present at the dubbing and was knocked out:

> "Paul Ferris should have gone on to marvelous things. A marvelous composer. I think the *Witchfinder* theme is one of the most lovely bits of music I've heard for a long time. That counterpointing to all that galloping stuff I just thought was wonderful. He's quite brave that I'm actually galloping to try and get somewhere and he's still doing 'dee-dee...' I thought it was very clever. He only had a very, very small budget and Mike said, 'What can you do?' And Paul said, 'I'm not going to take a salary. I'm going to spend it all on the orchestra.' I watched them dub it. It was very exciting. And Mike was knocked out. He said this has made his picture sound *big*. It did, all those throbbing violins going."

Paul's score is unbearably moving at the climax of the picture when Hilary Dwyer's screams merge with the music after Mike Reeves' flash of genius in showing the screams echoing down the corridors. Paul Ferris acknowledged this:

> "Right. And those were his ideas, the screams echoing and echoing with the images and into the music. And also his idea was these out-of-focus stills at the beginning. The important thing is we all had the same desire to make it good. We were all movie-mad and we had the chance because Tony Tenser was inexperienced and we had the tremendous energy to actually do it. Now it wouldn't be allowed. The whole thing. Mike was 24, I was 26, Ian and Nick both a few years younger. Vincent was the oldest one, which is why the fights came with Mike."

Singles of the *Witchfinder* theme were released but Paul thought they "weren't right" and commented: "It's used quite a lot with the Wolfe music, who co-published it. They're a film library and at that time I didn't know anything about that sort of stuff. He said, 'You'll earn more from the library with this music than the film.' That's true, I have. But right at the end of the love sequence with the guitar and strings and harp, I bring in two trumpets when they dissolve through to Vincent. That's cost me a fortune. Wolfe said, 'If that bloody thing wasn't in there, this bloody thing would have been played all over the world.' But it's there right at the end, and nobody had enough money to re-do it! I like the irony of it."

Witchfinder General did have some awkwardness, harking back to *Revenge of the Blood Beast*. Wilfrid Brambell's little cameo as a horse trader is rather camp, agreed Ian Ogilvy: "I don't know what Mike thought of that. I think he thought it was funny." However, these defects are totally overshadowed by the brilliance of the music, the acting, the direction, and also the photography.

For one of the major elements that contributed to making *Witchfinder General* a masterpiece, along with Paul Ferris' score, was Johnny Coquillon's photography, a vast improvement on the photography of *The Sorcerers*. Stanley Long was reportedly in line to photograph the film, but withdrew as he did not care to work for Mike again after his experience on *The Sorcerers*. He apparently did not like Mike all that much. Johnny's background was mainly documentary, but it is again Alfred Shaughnessy we have to thank for suggesting him to Mike, as he explained: "I also recommended to him a good friend, Johnny Coquillon, the French Canadian cameraman, who had photographed my picture *The Impersonator*. Michael engaged him to photograph *Witchfinder General* and the result was superb. Typically, he thanked me for that idea, too." Tony Tenser recalled that Mike insisted on having Johnny Coquillon: "Mike did that. I remember him now,

One of the major elements that contributed to making Witchfinder General a masterpiece was the outstanding photography. (Philip Waddilove)

a smallish, dark-haired man. I remember discussions with him. He was a dedicated cameraman. He was really a potential director."

Nicky Henson was very impressed: "John Coquillon's superb photography contributed definitively to the final effect. He was a really clever guy. It was a big breakthrough for John, that movie. Lovely guy, too. He painted a sunset on one of the lenses for one of those shots in *Witchfinder.* I remember him being up all night in the hotel doing it for the next day."

Ian Ogilvy was equally impressed by Johnny: "Johnny was using filters and all sorts of things that Mike had never seen. Well, Mike *knew* about them, but it was wonderful. Johnny was putting in lovely skies and things and contributed an enormous amount to *Witchfinder.* And he was recognized, because he went on to work for Sam Peckinpah."

In terms of being perfectionists in their work, Johnny Coquillon and Mike Reeves were two of a kind and were therefore inseparable. Tom Baker remembered:

> "He was excited when he met Johnny. Perhaps he was very open-minded about what was possible and what could be achieved. I suspect it was Mike's enthusiasm. There's a shot where Ian and Hilary first go upstairs to bed. There's a shot where she goes up with a candle. I remember Mike saying, 'I'm bloody well going to make that so it looks like a candle and this guy will do it. He's got some idea, he says "Yeah, we can do that." ' Anyone else would say, 'Oh, no, we'll put a filter on, flood the place with light.' I remember him just being knocked out. He found that lots of cameramen would do it but, in his experience, here was a cameraman who didn't think he was just being tiresome by wanting to try and create candlelight. He thought this was wonderful. 'Here's a guy who's on for it as much as I am.' As everyone was. It's like his relationship with Paul Ferris, that's the same thing. He was keen to meet people who were 'on' for the fun of the movies as much as he was."

Tony Tenser was concerned about the effect of this perfectionism on his budget:

"There was always this question of the costs running up because we were working to a budget, even though we had a contingency. Although I wouldn't in any way or shape get involved or interfere with Mike's artistic license, when it came to what I thought was wasting money I thought we couldn't afford to waste, I had to say something.

"There were three or four occasions where Mike and I had words. We didn't really quarrel, but we differed and I had to put the foot down. He was a perfectionist in his way and I had my own artistry, even though in those days it was pounds, shillings and pence. We weren't a large production company with unlimited funds or vast funds.

"I remember one of the early scenes shot where there's a procession through a village and where a witch was going to be hung. I was there at the time. I remember they fixed the brace under her breasts and she really looked like she was hanging. The noose around her neck wasn't really fitting, but it looked like it was. The priest was walking down and before you saw them, you heard the intonation of the priest. It was *extremely* well done. They were going to shoot the scene where she was being hung and we were on the hill. It was a sunny day with fleeting clouds. Beautiful location. Everything was fine. I never had much to say to Michael. I left him to it.

"If he stopped filming for a while and was having a sandwich, it was no good telling him a joke or a story or asking him anything—his mind was full of what he was doing. So, unless he spoke to me, I wouldn't say anything to him, unless there was something which I felt had to be said. And the lighting cameraman there, John Coquillon, a very good up-and-coming cameraman, also was wanting to do things right. He was with Mike, they were like twins.

"We were ready to shoot this part of the scene and there was a set-up waiting and we were just standing around waiting. So I said to the in-line producer at the time, 'What are we waiting for?' And he said, 'The lighting cameraman's waiting for the cloud to come over a certain way, so that you get the scene where the cloud passes over as the woman is being hung,' or something like that. I said, 'Well, we'll wait for this cloud but, if he doesn't get it, I'm not waiting for any more clouds!' Because I *know* that the audience won't notice that. If all goes well, you'll see a shadow going across, which would be fleeting. So we missed that shot! They're waiting for the next one. I went to Mike and said, 'I'm sorry Mike, we can't. Please don't hang around.' I said to the lighting cameraman, 'Get the shot. Get it in the sun. The next cloud, that's it. The next cloud and that's it. If you haven't got it then, you haven't got it.'

"So they got the next cloud. They thought they'd more or less got it with the next cloud, but I wasn't going to wait any more. That was once. After that, we were pals again, but I think it rankled with Mike a bit and, of course, he felt there was some interference, but I was only concerned with the cost of it and what we were getting for the cost.

"There was another thing where we had a few words. No shouting or screaming, always quiet, very controlled. Paul Ferris had a part in the film as the husband of the woman who gets burned. His wife had been burned and he was upset and he'd got a knife. He goes to the inn where Vincent was and goes into the hall and shouts out to Vincent Price, who comes down the stairs, and he hurls abuse at him for what he's done to his wife. He's got his knife out and he's going to go for him with it. They were just a few feet apart. Vincent was up a few steps, thigh boots, his coat off, and he had a pistol. As

Reeves was a perfectionist, leading to some run ins with Tony Tenser. (photo: Philip Waddilove)

the guy comes in with the knife, he shoots him. And Mike wanted it to be realistic. He burst his own blood bag. It was worked by remote control. You pressed something and it burst the blood bag. You actually *saw* the whole thing. It had to happen at the same time, no question of cutting away and cutting back to see the blood.

"But Mike reckoned—he was quite right—that if somebody gets shot with a ball at that range, he's going to be hurled back a few feet. Nine hundred and ninety-nine people out of a thousand wouldn't *know* or expect that. What happened was he had a harness under his doublet, with a wire that was fed through a hole in the scenery behind him. As he was shot, he was pulled back slam-bang against the thing. So, he was pulled back, he activated the blood bubble in his chest, he activated the one in his mouth by biting on it, and a smoke pellet was activated at the same time: it all had to be simultaneous. They rehearsed it a couple of times and I said to Mike, 'I think you're really asking for too much, Mike. Yes, by all means the puff of smoke and all that, but by hurling back as well, you're going to pull him off his feet. He might not fall right and it might not *look* realistic.'

"But he insisted. I said, 'Okay, couple of rehearsals and one take. We're not going in for a second take of that. You should do one take of that.' The master shot had already been done. He got it in one take and I wasn't going to have him re-do it. He wanted to do it, but I said, 'No, you've got it.' It was not going to make any difference. Everything was fine. You could have spent a whole day just doing that one part of a scene with no dialogue, just him being shot and falling back! You can see how I was thinking: money. The whole crew there on location, being fed, watered, hotels, housed. We never quarreled over it. He accepted my say. But it was very, very rare that I had to become involved with anything."

Composer Paul Ferris turns to acting for his small role in _Witchfinder General._

It is clear from Tony's honest account of his entirely reasonable budgetary pre-occupations that Mike's artistry was definitely reined in by these constraints.

Paul Ferris was billed in the credits as Morris Jar, purely, he said, "as a joke, because I still think that Maurice Jarre is one of the best of them." Paul spent a couple of weeks on location in Bury St. Edmunds and watched Mike filming a couple of times. He explained how he came to have a part in the film:

> "I only did that because Mike said, 'If you don't do it, you bugger, I will,' and he was a worse actor than I was! Mike said, 'It's a small part. It's not worth seeing them. If you don't do it...' He said, 'I want you to do it.' I said 'No.' He said, 'All right, Ferris, if _you_ don't do it, _I_ will!' I said, 'All right, that does it.' The billing was a joke which we worked out and we were both tickled with: Morris Jar! Mike had a tremendous sense of humor. Just because it was all blood and guts, or a lot of it, it's not to say you can't laugh at a little bit of it."

For Ian Ogilvy, Paul Ferris' death is one of the moments of near-humor in the film: "You know why there's a puff of smoke comes out of his chest? The reason for this is that you have these exploding pellet things—I have it on 16-mm film—I think it happened _10_ times and the damned thing never went off! The special effects man said, 'Look, all I've got left is this little smoke pellet.' Mike said, 'Well, we'll have to have it.' If you look closely, there's a puff of smoke comes out of his chest, because we ran out of exploding pellets! That's the kind of thing

The critical witch-burning scene in *Witchfinder General*

that happened." Another example of Mike's ability to "make do." The scene where Rupert Davies claps Ian on the back after his long ride and clouds of dust rise up is also quite funny, Ian concurred: "Oh, terribly. Mike loved that. I said, 'Do you really think that we ought to do that?' And he said, 'It's funny, it's funny!' "

Paul Ferris recalled one occasion when Tony Tenser grew perturbed: "I do remember Tony Tenser going up in arms about the footage wasted when watching the rushes. The shot of the sea rushing in, telephoto I think it was, the waves crashing in. It was about a full can of film. And Tony Tenser was literally jumping up and down in the seat. He said, 'Mike, why are you doing this? Whole can of film on fucking waves! What was wrong with the first one?' "

Tony responded:

> "I wasn't there when he shot the waves. It was very effective the way he did it but there was a lot of footage wasted on his getting it, because you see what he was looking for—and in fact he got it, if you watch the film carefully—was that there was a wave that came in of a certain size and shape, which turned into fire. So it had to be a certain shape and size, as the flame. You couldn't muck around with the flame, so you mucked around with the wave to match it. You saw this *big* wave and before the wave had finished falling, it had turned to fire and you were in this next scene in Lavenham. Extremely well done, but it was costly for the effect it had on the public in general. The public doesn't notice things like that. Even the critics don't see that. I don't know to what extent it has an effect on the film in general. You can go on and on and on spending money. Polanski was the one for that. He really was the one for that. It would show. The effect would be very good."

Tony admired Coquillon's perfectionism for all that it was costly: "It was *his* idea to wait for the cloud. It wasn't Mike's. He was the *Mike Reeves of the camera*!"

There are a tremendous number of dissolves in *Witchfinder*, from a body into a campfire, and especially the famous one from the waves into the flames, which was actually scripted. (The shot of the flames is borrowed from the scene of the burning Jaguar at the end of *The Sorcerers*, which reminds us of the low budgets Mike was operating under.) Ian Ogilvy recalled: "He was very proud of that and talked about that a *tremendous* amount. He talked about it *before* he shot it." It was a very conscious thing:

> *Very*, very conscious thing. He said, 'Look at these waves.' Because they were gray. He said, 'Look at that. Well, we go straight from this into the fire. It's going to be a really slow lap dissolve into this fire.' That was very conscious. And the love scene, he said, 'What we're doing here is, I'm literally going to be shifting this camera around. I'm going to be picking it up and moving it and doing that.' He said, 'You just keep going if you can. Think of things to do and I'll think of things for you to do. I promise it'll all be very tasteful and very dark.' Because I was a bit worried. Because I think Mike was perfectly capable of shooting..."

What really caps that scene is the music which makes for an extraordinary marriage of image and sound, Ian agreed.

Diane Ogilvy characterized Coquillon's relationship with Mike:

> "Mike certainly knew which lens would be going on the camera. He knew it before he'd go on the set. I don't know where he acquired it, but he had it about everything apart from the music. Luckily, Paul spoke this extraordinary language. Mike would say, 'Can we have a *boom!* There?' and Paul knew what he meant...I think Mike would have said the whole time that he very much listened to what Johnny was saying. There was a box called 'Johnny's box of tricks.' I don't remember Johnny mixing in as much. There was a friendship afterwards, but Johnny didn't become part of what I would call the gang...but tremendous love and respect between the two of them."

Johnny Coquillon later recalled in a letter to director Jeff Burr (who made one of the final Vincent Price films *From a Whisper to a Scream*):

> "We made *Witchfinder* in the autumn of 1967 with not too much money, but hearts full of love. We shot the picture in five weeks on an Arriflex camera in Suffolk—great locations. The few built sets were constructed locally and put up in an unused World War II aircraft hangar we happened to find in the area. I think the rent was around £50 per week. We got lucky. Lighting was by courtesy and, to some extent, generosity, of the then small (now very big) Lee Electric. The generator was the noisiest and oldest piece of machinery imaginable. But it was all we could afford and it worked and made light for us and we were delighted. Happy and exciting filmmaking days.
>
> "As to my relationship with Michael Reeves—fabulous. Michael was 25 years ahead of his time. He used to say we both were. He would (and should) have been a powerful filmmaker today. Michael was 24 years of age at the time—and had the eye and imagination of a veteran. I still wonder whether we ever worried our producers about our way of shooting *Witchfinder*. We were determined to make it our way and not in the conventional, accepted, boring (to us), ways of those times...I will tell you how Michael Reeves and Sam Peckinpah and I used to work: Get in there. Get the shot/scene as *you* want it. Kick arse. Producers will howl (they did daily on *Witchfinder* and again on *Straw Dogs* and very much so on *Scream and Scream Again*—way ahead of its time at time of shooting). Ask Deke!"

The witch-burning scene was a happy marriage of image and sound.

Jeff Burr was a Mike Reeves fan while growing up in Georgia and as a student at the University of Southern California he even spoke to Don Siegel about Mike at a tribute to Siegel's work in the early '70s. He would later work with Ian Ogilvy on *Puppetmaster 5*. Mike's work would also influence other young horror filmmakers like student Roger Watkins (*Last House on Dead End Street*), whose film professor Paul Jensen would show *Witchfinder General* to his students and said (in *Headpress* 23): "It made them *feel* in rather complex ways. I know Roger respected that film and I think he probably also respected me for showing it to a class and defending it."

The bold dissolves in the film were, recalled Ian Ogilvy, very much planned and not the idea of Johnny Coquillon but of Mike Reeves:

> "It was very much Mike and he was very pleased about them. He liked all that. Like he enjoyed enormously the children eating baked potatoes in the fire. When it goes back to the fire and it's just the embers, there are children playing. The fire has all died down. You see children poking around in the fire. I don't think it comes over: They're eating baked potatoes! But I don't think it works quite, because I don't think the children quite knew what they were supposed to be doing. Maybe the potatoes were too hot. There's no close-up of a child picking it up and eating it. But Mike said, 'What they are actually doing is eating baked potatoes!' That was the way his mind worked, with sort of awful black jokes. 'Are they looking for the bones? No, they're eating baked potatoes!'"

Paul Ferris explained that what Mike was trying to show was that it was "a big day out." Though this does not come across well, it shows how there was thought and intention behind every shot in the film.

The locations in Norfolk and Suffolk are stunning and David Pirie argues that they contribute significantly to the film's thematic structures. Locations ranged from the village of Kersey at the start of the film to Lavenham, Brandeston, Bury St. Edmunds, Cuckmere Haven in Sussex, Kentwell at Long Melford (the dunking scene), Orford Castle (the climax), Langley Park and

Black Park. Ian Ogilvy confirmed that Mike had final say of locations selected by Philip Wad-dilove: "Mike would have picked the locations, of course. Philip Waddilove's job it was at the time, I think, to provide locations, and I think Philip did a lot of the ground work. Mike obviously would have approved it all. But it was *perfect*. Apart from the discomfort, it was marvelous. I think the locations were excellent. Philip was associate producer on it. He was there all the time. He was there with a walkie-talkie, being another sort of assistant director. He was doing all sorts of jobs on it. He was taking photographs of it."

For his work on the film, Tony Tenser promoted Philip to full producer status on the credits. Philip also got drafted in to cover for an absent actor and played a cameo as a Roundhead of-ficer opposite Patrick Wymark, and his wife Susi was persuaded to appear as one of the women in the animal pen because Mike felt there were not enough women in the shot. Diane Ogilvy commented: "This is why I don't think Mike was naughty about Equity, because it cost Philip a fortune to pay all his back Equity dues to be able to play that scene. Because he hadn't paid up for years and years."

Philip recalled his film appearance in his memoirs. This came shortly after a short strike by the technicians and was the most expensive day's shoot other than the witch-burning sequence:

> "This was on a Sunday, and we were filming a scene that involved Crom-well himself, played by the popular British leading actor Patrick Wymark. Our location was a beautiful old watermill where Cromwell had met for a conference with his officers. We only had Patrick's very expensive services for the single day, so we had to complete the sequence before we wrapped. As usual, shooting was to start at seven-thirty, soon after daylight. At about eight o'clock, I was taking care of some production details behind the mill, when Michael Reeves suddenly appeared and said to me: 'You've got to get into makeup—immediately! John Swift is lost or something and you're going to have to take over his role.' 'Michael, this is no time for practical jokes,' I replied. He responded tersely by handing me a piece of paper. 'It's no joke. These are your lines and we need you on the set in about 30 minutes.' John Swift, who was playing one of Cromwell's officers, had in fact had an automobile accident that necessitated him going to an emergency room, so he didn't show up until after we'd shot the scene. Luckily, I had only two lines to learn and our director said my performance was acceptable—barely!"

In fact, it seems Equity was quite hot about the use of non-Equity actors, even in small roles. Paul Ferris had been an established actor, of course, but Tom Baker wasn't and Equity objected when Mike tried to use him in a small role, as he recalled:

> "The back of the wig that is on my head is in *Witchfinder*, but once they found I didn't have an Equity card, they told me to come back next day. That's not even the back of my head, it's the back of the wig that's on my head. After the credits, when those guys are riding and they get off their horses and they're shot at, there's a guy rises up with a rifle from the bracken and the rifle is balanced on the shoulder of his mate, and the head of the mate is me! So I'm lying in the bracken with someone else behind me and I rise up. That day they only shot the shot from behind that, the guy firing at Ian and Nicky and people, but before I could come back the next day, Equity had sussed that I was the writer! I wasn't being paid, Mike said, 'Why don't you come along?' They asked Mike, 'What was the writer doing, when an Equity member could get a day's work?' So, quite reasonably, I wasn't included. A shame. Because the guy does get shot the next day. I thought that was gonna be great. I could be shot the next day. That's my claim to fame. I

was only pulled in the day before and that was because we were shooting outside London, that's the only reason I'm in there. That section for some reason was shot at the very end and money was running out. The leaves were coming off the trees. It was shot out in Pinewood somewhere. I remember we went to Pinewood to see some rushes after that day."

Lavenham was actually one of the places where the real-life Matthew Hopkins operated, noted Ian: "We were lucky to have Lavenham. They were very cooperative. All the TV aerials had to come down. It was nice to have that."

Deke Heyward had used Lavenham to enthuse Vincent Price about the picture in his letter dated August 12, 1967:

"We are shooting almost four weeks on actual location in Lavenham, which is the most marvelous *untouched* 14th century village. Exactly like it was in the old days (except we will have to take down four television antennae). Dirt roads, no asphalt, no planes overhead. No automobiles. Up to your navel in antiques. And yet for all this, it is only 12 miles from the swinging town of Boodle-on-Crile (pop. 12,000, which is the heart of the sheep country of England). They have free concerts every Monday, Wednesday and Friday in Boodle, from 7:30 to 8:30, and sheepmen come from miles around. To listen."

Some of the outdoor scenes in the film look cold and windy. Ian said: "It was, up in Norfolk, all around Thetford. It was bleak and cold and wet and windy."

When Herbert Lom played a witchfinder in Michael Armstrong's *Mark of the Devil*, an interesting variation on *Witchfinder General*, he later tried to dissociate himself from the film's violent scenes. Ian noticed that Vincent Price never questioned any of the violence in *Witchfinder*, such as the slow witch-burning at Lavenham:

"I don't remember him making any objection to it at all, no. There *was* a lot of excitement about that burning, because that's not historically accurate. They had never done that. That was Mike Reeves' idea, that one. 'Let's all do a nasty one!' And the poor stunt girl was burned. As she was being lowered—they only lowered her to about a 45-degree angle—the wind changed direction and, it wasn't too bad, but she had slightly burned wrists and so they dragged her down. So, there was an element of spectacle there, and it was curious that the next day several inhabitants of Lavenham, people who had taken part in it and lived around the square, said, 'You should have heard the clanking and the crying and the screaming last night.' That we'd woken a lot of the ghosts up. And they were being quite serious about this. 'There was a terrible, awful noise of wind, screams and moans.' It was strange."

Tony Tenser remembered this vividly:

"The girl that we had playing that part again was a friend of a friend. She was an actress and she was married to the Earl of Kimberley, Maggie Kimberley. Before this, I knew of John Kimberley, because when I was with Compton, he did some work for us and eventually we put him on our board. You've got Michael Klinger, Tony Tenser and the Earl of Kimberley, as a PR man. We had him for about a year. He didn't contribute very much. He was a belted Earl. She was his wife at the time. She was quite a good actress, but we had to use a double. It was a very, very hairy scene. What happened was she's tied to a ladder and the ladder's lowered into the flames. She was covered with asbestos and what have you. There was also blood put on her where she'd been beaten before it all happened. She was very well protected and then she was lowered into the flames. We were shooting it, getting all the sound effects as well. She was told, as soon as she felt she was getting too hot, she should change the pitch of her screams, so that we knew that she wasn't acting. She was doing fine. She changed the pitch of her screams. We got her out and what happened was that she should have changed it earlier, because the heat was melting the makeup blood and the blood was blistering her skin and she had blisters on her hands. It wasn't too bad, we stopped in time and got her off. Just her eyebrows were slightly singed."

Tony would not dismiss the ghost stories:

"Could well be, because there were some very old buildings there. Where Hilary looks out the window to say she sees him coming, very old building. Lots of very old buildings. In Lavenham Village itself, lots of them. The others that were more modern, we shot round them or covered them up. But the buildings that were there needed nothing done to them. They were of that period. It was a creepy place at night. The hotel we stayed in, the Lavenham Arms or something, it was again oak beams and things.

"I remember we had to shoot that scene in Lavenham when we were getting toward the end, because Vincent was booked for his next job and there wasn't much time between us by the time we had finished with him. There were about three days before he starts the next job and, really, he should have left and gone. We wanted an extra day. We'd have just about managed to do it if we'd got an extra day. We had to finish it that weekend. Vincent was seen in it. It had to be right.

"So I got a fellow called Raymond Greenberg, who used to do all our film insurance. He was a qualified barrister, but he made his living as an insurance underwriter. Raymond had me in the office and we had a chat about it. We were good friends, he was a charming man, and I said, 'Now, Raymond, we're going to do this scene next week or two weeks' time. All this has to happen over this weekend. If it rains and there's a light rain, you can shoot it, you won't see it, but if the rain is heavy, it will spot the camera and you will see it. People will get wet and you *will* see it. What can we do about it? It's going to be a very expensive thing if we go into an extra day or an extra two days, even if we get Vincent Price. It's very, very tight.'

" 'Well,' he said, 'we may get you a pluvius policy.' I must admit I hadn't heard of it. I'd heard of the god Pluto. I thought this sounds something to do with wet or the sea or something. It's to do with bad weather. And he in fact got us an extra pluvius policy. It was expensive and quite a bit out of our budget to get it, but we had no alternative. So we had a three-day pluvius policy. It did rain fine, for most of the time, but nobody really got wet. It was a very fine rain that started and stopped but it never landed on the lens and it didn't affect the film."

Territorial Army personnel were used as extras in this scene, Tony explained:

"We were going to shoot the scenes leading into where the witch gets burned. We had a three-day weekend to shoot it in, Friday, Saturday and Sunday. It

Local residents were used in the witch burning sequence of *Witchfinder General*.

meant the whole of the day, as well as going into some of the evening, that the aerials were down. We got the cooperation of all the villagers.

"All the shop signs, Smoke Players, and all those things were taken down and straw was put over the ground. It was made to look medieval and we needed a large crowd. All the villagers turned up for this big show for them, to see the witch being burned. There were no speaking parts, so you didn't need to have Equity players for it. It was just a crowd scene.

"So, rather than cast extras from London all the way up there, Arnold Miller went and saw the local Territorial Army man and they said, 'Yes, we've got about 150 men and they'll bring their wives and kids.' And we dressed them up. Those at the front had everything, the tall ones at the back had a hat, the short ones at the back had shoes, and those at the end had a sleeve. We bought a load of sacks, burlap bags, and we dyed them brown and cut the sleeves to wear as smocks. They all worked. It was to cut the expense.

"We had one or two who *were* extras, where the camera pans and they're watching the final burning. One woman genuflects, one man halts and spits, and these people were used to acting, I believe, but there were no speaking parts, just expressions. You saw some kids' faces, the kids were made to look down and it was a tracking shot with the camera passing."

Unfortunately, the execution scene was trimmed by the censor, John Trevelyan. Ian Ogilvy commented: "There was a point where, on the dummy of course, the wig burst into flames. There

187

was a great ball of fire, which was horrid. That was foul, that, and I think Trevelyan quite rightly got rid of it. That sort of thing went. Moments that might have been happy accidents!"

Tony Tenser too was remarkably sanguine about the BBFC interference: "They didn't want to see the wig actually burning. I didn't mind the censor very much in those days because, looking at it, he had a job to do, and he wasn't just doing it as a job, he was a very responsible man. And, in fact, Trevelyan came onto our board later on. We were quite good chums. He had an office upstairs and he used to sit on the production side board."

Tom Baker was not so tolerant of censorship, despite his personal aversion to violence: "The film censors were really going on about the violence, although it's historical. It's bizarre. I'd forgotten just what the world was like then. I think there was one remark, it must be from the notes on the script, where the Hilary Dwyer character has been raped by Price and she kicks him in the balls, and the censor says something like, 'We really can't have that, it's not playing by the rules.' It's just unbelievable! We lived in a very decorous age then, where it wasn't cricket to kick a man in the balls on the screen!" The censorship of *Witchfinder* would become a *cause celebre* in British film history.

Tim Miller reflected on the contrast between the content of Mike's output and his personal nature: "Mike had a great gentleness—a sweet nature indeed. I appreciated this since I understood the awful tension between the will to make films and the demands imposed by the business. I remember mainly Mike's kindness and the clash between that and the nature of Mike's output."

Certainly Ian Ogilvy confirmed that Mike never got furious with anybody on the set. He kept his temper when things went wrong and never fired anyone:

"No, we didn't have time to fire people. We just made the best of a bad job. If somebody couldn't do it, then he'd cut him out or give him less to do or keep the camera off him or something. That's the same with all movies. The whole thing is a compromise, all the time. A compromise with other people, a compromise with the time. And he compromised, best compromiser in the business. Budgets like that, you could do nothing else. And as long as it wasn't your fault...

"I remember there was a scene in *Witchfinder* where I thought he'd die with laughter, where there are a whole lot of us galloping along and I'm in the lead. We're all strung out. It's the first time we're all together. Now, I can ride. I've ridden all my life and I've been on the picture now for a fortnight and I know my horse. Nick has gone off and taken riding lessons. He's on rather a small pony. He's fairly okay. The other two characters behind, one of them could sort of ride, the other again had had about three lessons. And off we set. And my horse is so fast, it just—whoom! —overtakes this van and I can't stop it. Mike's on top filming away and then Nick's little pony gets the bit between his teeth and *he* overtakes the van, so Mike says, 'All right, all right, concentrate on these two behind me.'

"Neither of them could ride very well, so they're hanging on like grim death and they've got these helmets on. And very slowly both helmets slide over their noses like that and they're saying, 'We can't see where we're going.' At this point, Mike is lying on top of the van, choking with laughter, saying 'Keep running, keep running, it's too funny, keep running.'

"Nick and I are up ahead and I can suddenly hear Nick saying, 'Look out, there's an awful lot of rabbit holes...' and he's over, his horse is over. At which precise moment, Captain (my horse's real name) also caught his hoof in a hole and over I went. So we're lying there. I'm lying on my back and Nick is lying on his back, we're both laughing like a drain, our horses are disappearing over the horizon, these other two are still trotting up the road, not being able to see anything with the helmets like that, and Mike's helpless on top of this van!

"Now those are the kind of things didn't irritate him. As long as it made him laugh, it was fine. He said, 'I don't know how we're going to reshoot that. It's just impossible. How do we shoot this? It's too funny.'

"And I broke my foot on *Witchfinder General*, going over the table, in the bar fight. It was sort of halfway through the production. I was still able to walk just about, but I did sit on a horse rather more often than I would normally have done. Again, an accident, and you sit on a horse more! They collected 10,000 pounds insurance and were able to shoot three more sequences. What scenes they were I don't know, but Mike said, 'Thanks very much. I can now shoot three scenes I couldn't have shot before.'"

The pictorial composition in *Witchfinder* is striking; *Penthouse* noted that Mike surrounded himself with Turner prints. Ian commented: "I don't remember Mike ever going round an art gallery or anything like that. I don't think he had wonderful pictures in his house. He'd be much more likely to have a film poster up than he would a Turner print." Paul Vestey agreed:

"If it was a Turner, I would think it would have come from his mother's house and filled up the wall space. I doubt his mother had Turners. I'd have thought she'd have proper country scenes. I remember he was very keen on Andrew Wyeth, the American artist who paints in a very graphic way. He was very keen on him long before anybody else had ever heard of him. It wasn't Annabelle, I think it was Mike, because I remember one time when he came back from the States, he'd been introduced to the artist's work, because he had a book of prints. I certainly remember these Wyeths."

Tom Baker was of the same opinion: "His artist of choice was Wyeth and there was one of that girl who is or isn't crawling up the meadow." The Wyeth prints were also favorites of Annabelle and when Mike died, Paul Ferris took them and kept them at his house in Winchester. Later, he sold them, as he found a couple of them "fairly creepy" and they were a constant reminder of the loss of Mike Reeves. Paul recalled one print in particular was Mike's favorite, showing a crippled girl reaching up into the distance.

Nevertheless, as Ian pointed out, Mike had an innate sense of visual composition: "With that visual eye, he went out and found the location and—bang!—there we were. We were shooting all that on Army land, on the ranges, which meant you had perfect roads but not a house in sight, which meant you could do those great long tracking shots with very unspoilt open heathland-type countryside. Miles and miles and miles of it. Still there, all that, the ranges are." Paul Ferris agreed: "A great eye for the movies!"

Mike was a master at using tracking shots. The tracking shots in *Witchfinder* were done from the roof of a Dormobile and the tracking of the motorbike ride in *Sorcerers* was done, according to Ian, from "either the boot or the back" of a Jaguar: "Jaguars were very good camera platforms as far as Mike was concerned and, in fact, the camera platform for that motorcycle sequence was almost certainly the car we smashed up at the end. But he was always lying in the boots of cars, *endlessly* lying in the boots of cars."

Ian agreed that other British pictures of the time were static in comparison and "these things shift." The pace of Mike Reeves' pictures creates an element of excitement, he thought: "He loved all that. Some of his favorite sequences in *Witchfinder* were the horse riding sequences, with that *enormous* animal that I had, which was unstoppable. I used to say to Mike, 'I do need half a mile beyond when you say "cut." I need another half a mile, because I can't stop this animal.' He loved all that stuff. He really wanted to make Westerns, you understand. Because

Witchfinder, after all, was a Western. He *knew* it was a Western. Revenge Western, totally, in costumes."

Ernest Harris witnessed Mike's passion for Westerns:

> "I remember the scene that he particularly loved was in *Duel at Diablo* where James Garner is walking along holding the horse's tail, a hallucinatory sequence. The film's got some good things—the scene where James Garner falls off his horse in the desert and he's trying to get across the desert without water. He holds on to the horse's tail and just drags on behind the horse and he's going through a heat haze. I remember Mike talking about that scene. And Bibi Andersson had been living with the Indians, because she'd lived with them rather than let them kill her, and her husband rejects her; it was almost back to *Witchfinder* with this girl being persecuted for saving her own life. I remember that was the film he liked and I think he said he wrote to Ralph Nelson."

Mike's friend Peter Fraser commented: "I worked for Ralph Nelson, I thought he was the *worst* director in the world."

Fortunately for both *Witchfinder* and *Sorcerers*, Ian Ogilvy was quite experienced at riding both horses and motorbikes: "I'd ridden since I was about seven, so I'm an experienced horseman. Obviously, I had to be on a horse an awful lot of the time. I suspect Mike, knowing that, decided to use it. On the motorbike side, I think Mike knew I rode motorbikes, so he might even have stuck it in. 'As opposed to a car, let's have a motorbike scene.'" Ian seemed to be going very fast in that scene, as he agreed: "Yes. It was on the new M4 we were shooting that, again *completely* illegally. But then, you see, we had very little equipment. It was Mike Reeves lying in the boot of a Jaguar, no lamps because you didn't need them, maybe a sun gun on the side shots."

According to Nicky Henson, Mike on set created the "best atmosphere I've ever worked on a picture on." He elaborated:

> "There was always a wonderful atmosphere. Lots of jokes going on all the time. But anything that got in the way of the filming...In fact, I think the atmosphere *was* so good because of the jokes, that it actually speeded up the creative process. Certainly something I found *very* strongly when I was on it was that everybody felt free to offer advice, from Johnny Coquillon down to the grips. Everybody would say, 'Ere, guvnor, why don't we try so-and-so?' and he'd say, 'No, *that* doesn't work, but, oh yeah, *that's* a good idea,' only because everybody felt it was really like going out shooting a silent film. There was no improvisation because the script was there and his discipline with the camera was there, but it was very kind of freewheeling and a very, very good working atmosphere."

Tom Baker said: "Mike clearly had a leadership charisma, there's no question about that." Nicky put this down in part to Mike's rapport with the whole crew:

> "I think they all had a great regard for him. There was kind of some aura about him that made you know that you were working with someone who was kind of a bit hot. And we're talking about 1967. The last collapse of the British film industry wasn't until 1970. I remember doing a lot of films afterwards, toward the end of that British film boom, where the units would do anything for anybody because they were just desperately trying to hang on to their jobs. It wasn't *that* feeling at all. It wasn't, 'We've got to do this

one well, otherwise, the British film industry collapses.' Everybody talked about 'our picture,' which is very rare for English technicians. They were all talking about 'our picture,' as opposed to 'the picture' or 'your picture.' Everybody talked about 'our picture,' which is lovely. Everybody felt very proud of it, I think, while we were doing it."

Nevertheless, there was some friction between Mike and the film technicians' union ACTT, which was noticed by Ernest Harris when Mike invited him and his girlfriend, Jean, to visit the set. Ernest recalled:

"Jean met Vincent in Leicester Square. I was working in Miracle at the time and Jean had just left me at Miracle. She knew he was staying at a hotel just off Leicester Square and she came back an hour later—she'd actually met him! I rang Mike at his hotel in Bury St. Edmunds and arranged a visit to the set. It was 11 p.m. but he came to the phone and didn't mind. He said he'd arrange for us to have lunch with Vincent. When we arrived, Mike was involved in some problem with the union and there seemed to be a row going on. I opened a door at the end of the hall, saw what was happening and closed it. Mike had seen me and came out later. He apologized and explained that the whole unit was about to leave for Aldeburgh.

"I was told that Vincent had already left for Aldeburgh. He offered us a lift but we said we could do the journey easy enough. We didn't! We had this horrendous day of traveling all over East Anglia. We arrived at the hotel in Aldeburgh just as the entire unit was heading off to film at the castle! We had to get our bus back, so didn't go with them. We chatted to Mike for a few minutes and then he had to go. While we were waiting for our bus, Vincent turned up with his wife. When he got out of the car, I went over to him and said, 'Mr. Price, we're friends of Mike Reeves.' Because Mike had said he'd arrange for us to have lunch with him on that day, but the sheer chaos that was reigning when we got there...And when I said we were friends of Mike Reeves, he was getting this case out and he went 'What?' He just stood there like...We were unaware of the friction between him and Mike. But he said to us at that time, 'Next time I'm over here, write to us, come down to the set'—and we went down after that on virtually every film he made in England."

The union dispute arose when ACTT noticed Tigon's crew was too small. The technicians went on strike for two days until an extra man was hired. Philip Waddilove remembered the problem in his memoirs:

"The crisis came approximately halfway through principal photography. For the first two weeks, we'd been working a six-day week, but this was taking its toll on all concerned, so we made the following Saturday a rest day. The day before this, we were shooting chase sequences on horseback across wild open country. There is hardly any untouched open countryside remaining in England, but my army service came in handy with respect to this problem.

"The Stanford Battle Camp and Training Area near Thetford is one of the few parts of the country where there are no defined fields, few roads and no telegraph poles. A close friend of mine from my Royal Horse Artillery days was by then a senior officer at the War Office in London. In return for giving the Army an onscreen acknowledgment, my friend agreed to our using the entire training area for three days when it was not being utilized by troops—at no fee whatsoever. He also provided us with a unit of the Royal Signal Corps so we would have sophisticated radio communications!

"The first day on the Stanford area had gone wonderfully well and we'd gotten nearly all the material we needed. However, in certain well-marked parts of the battle area, there were hundreds of unexploded artillery and tank gun shells lying around. A rumor went through our unit that a member of the crew could easily tread on one of these unexploded rounds of ammunition and be maimed or even killed. One of the unit called their ACTT representative, Les Wiles. Wiles drove down from London immediately and, on the eve of our rest day, called a strike. In addition to the allegations about unexploded munitions, he claimed that we didn't have enough portaloos—mobile lavatories—on the location!

"Susi and I returned to the Angel Hotel from the Stanford location to be told by Michael Reeves that, under strict ACTT strike regulations, he as the director was forbidden to speak to me as the producer! Arnold Miller had already left to spend the weekend at home in London and Louis M. (Deke) Heyward was nowhere to be seen. In fact, Deke only visited the set twice during the entire six weeks of principal photography—once when we shot the bare-breasted sequences for the German market and once when our location was close to Newmarket racecourse on a major race day.

"So it was left to me to deal with the crisis. I immediately called Tony Tenser in London, but he'd gone home for the weekend and I wasn't able to reach him for a couple of hours. When I finally did get through to him, he repeated his mantra about my always worrying too much. I remonstrated with him. 'Tony! We've got a genuine strike on our hands here and if someone doesn't do something about it soon, we won't be shooting on Monday!' He agreed to come down to Bury St. Edmunds the next day, but suggested that I should try and resolve the problems myself.

"After a beer or two in the hotel bar, I approached Les Wiles, who was at the other end of the bar, and suggested that we should sit down and have a talk. He agreed to this and, with Susi—a trained stenographer—in attendance to take down notes of the meeting, we negotiated our way through the problems.

"Wiles agreed with me that the matter of the unexploded shells was blown out of all proportion, especially when all concerned were fully aware of where the danger areas were located and that these were clearly defined. I then conceded that we should rent a couple of extra portaloos and that they would be in place by Monday when, all being well, we would resume shooting. However, Wiles raised another issue, one that related to our sound crew.

"He pointed out that, according to ACTT requirements, we had been filming with one man short in the sound department. I said that it might be difficult to find an extra man by Monday, but Wiles replied that he actually had an easy solution for this. His ageing father Sid Wiles was an ACTT sound technician and just happened to be free if we would sign him for the remainder of principal photography. I of course accepted this generous offer and the strike was called off! In fact, all that Sid Wiles was required to do was to carry the battery for the sound recording equipment whenever it needed to be moved, a task that I had personally been performing up until that time."

Ian Ogilvy concurred that Mike was able to make a hard-bitten crew work as hard as they could for the benefit of the film:

"Mike did have this ability, so long as you liked making movies in the first place. Mike had an extraordinary ability to get crews to work under conditions they wouldn't normally work, and with enthusiasm. In all that time, I only remember one crew member starting to make a fuss about anything, and that was a stills man on *Sorcerers* who started to complain and the rest of the crew said, 'Ah, shut up! Come on, we're trying to make movies here!' On the whole, Mike was able to do that. I don't quite know how he did it. I think it was just because he was *so* enthusiastic and gave praise when it was due, rounds of applause in rushes for some of Johnny Coquillon's stuff. 'Oh, Johnny, that is marvelous!' All this was going on and people react to that and respond very well to it. So I think they did like working with him, because it was like making movies in the old days."

Mike had this ability from his earliest days as a filmmaker. It wasn't just something he had developed by the time of *Witchfinder*, Ian believed:

"Oh, that was true from the very beginning, because he was just enthusiastic about the business of making movies. I once said to him, because I learned an awful lot from him and I learned a lot about the technical side of film-making, 'I have a feeling I'd like your job,' and he said, 'Oh, you've only just realized that! Of course, it's the best job in the world.' I've changed my mind since. You've got to be a diplomatist more than an artist. I don't want to do it any more, but at the time I desperately wanted to, because it just looked like such fun. Mike did have fun. He had a lot of fun because he was smashing with you at making movies on a shoestring. He had nobody to answer to really. The budgets were so small, nobody was going to get *too* worried about this or that.

"Mike was rather clever, you know. He used to get away from producers by going to these out-of-the-way locations. Not so much on *Sorcerers*, but certainly on the first picture, although Maslansky was there, but Maslansky was so intrigued at playing a funny policeman, he forgot about being the brilliant producer! He was frightfully proud of his performance.

"On *The Sorcerers*, producers weren't really terribly evident, because we were zipping around London in funny locations and we never told anybody where we were going. And Tony Tenser certainly didn't want to come out onto the Norfolk flats, nor did Sam and Jim, happily ensconced in Los Angeles. So he was always fairly careful to get away from these people, because most of the time that doesn't happen."

This was no reflection on Mike's friendly relationship with Tony Tenser, of whom Ian said: "He was very nice. We all liked Tony tremendously, but he was one of those sort of little men who didn't *really* know the job and always thought too small. He never thought very big."

Arnold Miller also gets a producer's credit on *Witchfinder*, despite the fact that Ian Ogilvy said he had nothing to do with it, and even Mike Reeves queried the credit by putting a question mark alongside his name on his copy of the publicity literature sent out by Tigon. Tony Tenser explained: "Arnold Miller and Stanley Long were involved in in-line production. I brought them into that because of what they did on *Mini-Weekend* and then *Sorcerers* and Arnold Miller was delighted. He didn't do much, but I think what he did was when we needed horses and things like that, he did the deals on that. He acted as sort of a part-producer."

One might imagine from the number of popular television faces (*Maigret*'s Rupert Davies, *Steptoe and Son*'s Wilfrid Brambell, *The Power Game*'s Patrick Wymark) in subsidiary roles in *Witchfinder General*—and the casting of *The Saint*'s Ivor Dean again as a Police Inspector in

The Sorcerers—that Mike cast these roles by watching television, but Ian Ogilvy was dubious about this:

> "I don't know, again, this visual side of him. Mike did watch quite a lot of television when he wasn't watching movies, but I suppose, on the visual side, the reason why Ivor Dean was cast as a policeman was because Ivor Dean *looked* like a policeman. He looked like a policeman to Mike, too. Wilfrid Brambell *looked* like a tacky little horse dealer, possibly. I don't think he ever thought it might be cheap to do that.
>
> "He thought that Patrick Wymark was something of a coup, you see. He was splendid. He was very pleased about that, and he was a bit fearful, because Patrick Wymark only did the one day and Mrs. Wymark phoned and said, 'Now, you do know about Patrick, don't you?' Because Patrick was not easy. Mike said, 'No, I don't.' She said, 'Well, mustn't let him have a drink.'
>
> "This is from the wife, the day before they're going to shoot! As it turned out, he was fine. And Rupert was lovely. I think he was interested in getting a few names into it simply in order to sell it better. The idea of getting Wilfrid Brambell to do four lines I think appealed to Mike simply on the selling basis of it. I wouldn't have thought it occurred to him that what eventually came out might look rather cheap! To him it was necessity."

Paul Vestey recalled Mike's television viewing habits:

> "I remember we used to watch *That Was The Week That Was*. He certainly enjoyed it. Everybody did. It was hysterical, of course. I don't think that he was interested in satire for himself. I think he just thought it was good fun, like everybody else did. I think he certainly watched *The Avengers*, because that was sort of modern for the time. I don't know that he watched that much television because dinner would have happened about eight, half past eight, nine, and that would have gone on till eleven or later, by which time in those days television would have been finished. Of course, there weren't videos, so we couldn't record anything. He'd be hopeless now; he certainly wouldn't get any sleep at all. He'd have absolutely loved it."

Nicky Henson joined the picture two weeks after it began shooting, arriving in Aldeburgh, where his scenes set in Lavenham were shot, which meant he never did go to Lavenham, he recalled:

> "That was only the interiors, I didn't do the exteriors. There was one scene where we rode down past a bunch of soldiers, which was supposed to be either before or after a great battle that they couldn't afford to shoot. It was either Tigon or AIP, for the Battle of Naseby they were going to have us doing little bits on Hampstead Heath, about six or seven of us doing the close-ups, and they were going to use stock shots from *Genghis Khan*, the long shots, because they had red uniforms. They had red clothes in *Genghis Khan*. That was either Tigon's or AIP's idea. They said, 'We can't talk about the Battle of Naseby and not have it.' So they were actually going to take us up to Hampstead Heath and we were going to shoot little bits of hand-to-hand fighting and then they were going to cut to long shots from *Genghis Khan*, which AIP had the rights to or something."

This would be the montage sequence Tom Baker has described. Nicky noted that Mike Reeves vetoed this absurd suggestion

> "...pretty quickly. But it was talked about seriously for some time. We had some good laughs about it. It was late in the day anyway. We had already come back to London and we were having to go out shooting stuff near Windsor, because I was rehearsing a play, I remember. Stuff that we hadn't managed to get up there, like the very opening sequence where Ian and I arrive and we're riding down, our first chat, I seem to remember was shot near Windsor."

This was Black Park, used in Hammer horror films.

Nicky spent about five weeks on the picture in all and was sometimes the butt of Mike Reeves' sense of humor. Ian Ogilvy remembered one instance: "The scene where they run up the hill to Orford Castle, he made Nick do it three times with no film in the camera! That was the kind of gag Mike used to do. 'Go on, let's make him do it again!' 'Okay, ah, sorry love, could you...' We were all down there pissing ourselves. We were kids, really." Nicky looked back on this with amusement: "Swine made me do it again! He said, 'We've got to go again, there's a hair in the gate!' And they were laughing *so much* and I was so worn out, so tired! Can you imagine tooling up that bloody hill with all that stuff on and I was so tired that I couldn't hear the laughter. Ian's got a shot on his 16-mm film where I get to the bottom and Mike comes up and tells me. It's silent, it's a long shot and I just fall over backwards!"

Tony Tenser was not on set then but, looking back, was not too amused by Nicky's plight, bearing in mind the pressures of time and money they were under and the potential for accidents, which could have been a catastrophe for the schedule. He was mildly sarcastic:

> "Poor chap! I would have a theory about that. Because we're talking about a film that was made after *Cul-de-Sac*, and there was a scene in *Cul-de-Sac* where Lionel Stander carries the body of his bandit friend who's died and he carries him down the ramp of the castle to throw him into the thing. Polanski made him carry the body down and said, 'No, that's no good, you didn't throw him in right. Pick him up and then go up.' Lionel Stander said, 'What?' 'You pick him up and carry him and walk up there.' And each time he did that scene, he either threw him in too hard or not hard enough and the poor little Irish actor's head was getting banged, and in the end Stander got a rupture through it by the end of the film.
>
> "I said to Polanski later on, 'Why are you doing this?' And I knew what the answer was going to be. It was a silly question to ask. He wanted him to look clapped out so that he didn't have to act the part. When Henson reaches the castle, he's out of breath, he's been running, trying to save somebody's life. So Mike Reeves may have referred to the Polanski film, I don't know. But what Mike Reeves was doing, I would think, was really tiring him, so that when he shot the scene, it would be more realistic, although he never gave me the impression of being that kind of director. Polanski was. Mike Reeves respected his actors and got the best out of them. It may have been a practical joke or he may have felt that he really wanted Nicky to be clapped out. You'd never get to the bottom of that. But I wouldn't have objected to that as a practical joke *in that context*, fine, but if it wasn't in the context of the film, I'd have said, 'What the hell are you doing? He's going to fall over and then hurt his leg or something.' "

Tony Tenser listens to Mike Reeves talking to his idol Boris Karloff on the set of *The Sorcerers*. (photo: John Hamilton)

Diane Ogilvy said Mike talked "very little" about Polanski but would have known his film work: "Mike would indeed have seen it and it would have been a common talking point, as Tony knew his work, in the same way as two people come together and they've got that in common." Of course, Polanski's *Repulsion* shows an interest in obsessive violence, and Mike Reeves and Roman Polanski are unusual in British films in that interest in the dark side of the psyche, but Diane had "no recollection of any in-depth talking about Polanski's movies."

Remembering Ian Ogilvy's comment that Mike liked to get away from the control of producers, and bearing in mind Vincent Price's terse observation to the author that Mike "lacked discipline in his sense of life" in the same way that Orson Welles did (he was not referring to Mike's work), there seems no doubt that Mike's treatment of Nicky was mere diversion rather than a Polanski-style realistic method. Ian Ogilvy pointed to his 16-mm film as proof. He was adamant: "Tony's wrong. He's forgetting about continuity. We might not shoot the next scene until weeks after. Mike did admire Polanski's get-up-and-go and his pictures. Mike was mad about Françoise Dorleac, he liked *Cul-de-Sac* a lot, and the dark pictures. Mike was in awe of actors and didn't interfere with it too much. 'Faster' or 'slower' and sometimes 'a bit angrier,' but he wasn't Stanislavski."

For Diane Ogilvy, the atmosphere Mike engendered was not affected by the role of the producers. When Tony Tenser was not present, Arnold Miller was around occasionally, she recalled, "but it was almost like it was us and them, the producers. Like children. 'Duck, here come the grown-ups.' Nobody was very nice to Tony. He wasn't encouraged to be around. We were all charming to him, but he was a grown-up. He was being frightfully serious."

She said that Mike and Tony never fell out, "but Mike would have spent, I would think, quite a lot of time trying to avoid him. And Tony might have thought he was locking himself up having a gloom, but he would actually have been running away from him."

196

The question of Mike's general working discipline is interesting. Given Ian's description of Mike as "not much of a diplomatist," Vincent Price confirmed to the author that he detected signs in Mike of hypersensitivity: "Yes, and I think he was not in complete control of himself."

Vincent also commented to Lawrence French: "...had he been disciplined, he could have become a very good director. Believe me, this profession takes enormous discipline. You're out there at six in the morning, and you're up till midnight, and back at six the next morning, so there's no fooling around. If you want to last, you're disciplined." Vincent also told the author that Mike's "great potential" consisted of both technical ability (in terms of camera movements and cutting) and his future as a storyteller. Asked to whom he would compare Mike as a director, he replied: "He was more like Orson Welles—both lacked discipline."

Nicky Henson commented:

> "I can't imagine what he means by 'lacked discipline.' I don't think he did lack discipline. I just don't think he showed it. I think he did *all* his homework. The logistics, as we say, for that picture, to get *that* shot on that tight budget in that amount of time I think shows the opposite to a lack of discipline. I think Mike had a great, a great discipline, but didn't come across as a kind of Von Stroheim type, so therefore because he was kind of a bit young, and had long hair, and looked a bit gawky and strange, maybe he didn't look like he did."

Diane Ogilvy said: "Very occasionally, Mike would have an idea on the spur of the moment for shooting something. I would describe it as sheer genius. 'Let's try and waste just a few feet and see if we can do something.' No lack of discipline."

Tony Tenser's view was: "He was a disciplined man, but not military-disciplined. He was an *orderly* man. I wouldn't use the word *disciplined*. He was orderly." Tony frowned when asked about Mike's propensity to fool around: "I think if he did that, I wouldn't be about. But I know that they were his friends and they'd have a little giggle now and again. Nothing wrong with that, but I was never aware of any practical jokes as such, unless it was the sort of practical jokes where somebody puts a whoopee cushion under somebody's seat if somebody's a bit nervous, that sort of thing. Somebody else's time and money, you can have practical jokes!"

Paul Ferris thought that Ian's description of Mike rolling on the floor was a description of the euphoria that comes with manic depression and agreed with Vincent Price's comment that Mike was not in complete control of himself: "Exactly the truth." He agreed with Vincent that Mike lacked discipline: "Yes. Me, too. Exactly the same. All those things. It's called manic depression." On the other hand, Paul found no surprise in Mike's ability to marshal such a large production so efficiently: "You do, you're forced. When I say you're up and down, it's not a question when you're down that nothing can go on. All I'm saying is when it's on you, it's in you. When it comes on you, you have to fight it. It's biochemistry. He knew that."

Paul stated that neither he nor Mike was able to find a satisfactory treatment:

> "No. I went in to see a doctor in Winchester, where I was living then, and he prescribed largactil, which is what Mike was also prescribed years before. It helps, but it doesn't cure. The problem is that the knowledge of the biochemistry of the brain at the moment is so little. I was on largactil. Mike was on largactil. All it does is reduce you to that level. It does that for sure. You don't go up, you don't go down, and you're not particularly happy, you're not particularly sad, and in fact it just drains the life out of you. Which is what happened to Mike. We spoke about it together, after *Witchfinder*."

Nicky Henson explained how the classic and very disturbing climax of *Witchfinder General* came about:

"Every time it was on somewhere, *Time Out* used to say, 'The best British post-war horror film. The last three minutes say more about the nature of violence than all Sam Peckinpah's movies put together.' Actually, the truth of the last three minutes was: I was supposed to run through to try and find Ian and save him, I would come in, rush up to the thing, take out my pistol, shoot Vincent and he would say 'You took him from me, you took him from me,' rush at me, and I would shoot Ian and kill him. That was the scripted thing.

"We were in the middle of the night, shooting at Orford Castle, just outside Aldeburgh. We were doing an all-night shoot doing that section, because they had to let Vincent go quite soon. Incredible number of set-ups. Something like 83 set-ups in one night, with that wonderful lighting cameraman Johnny Coquillon doing brilliant stuff. During the running through the passages, which we did earlier, I'd already shot somebody with one of my pistols, and when we got to this sequence, I said, 'Mike, we've dropped a terrible clanger, continuity-wise.'

"He said, 'Why?' I said, 'Because I come in, I shoot Vincent now, I then shoot Ian with the other pistol. I've just unloaded it, I've just shot it, it's a flintlock, isn't it?' He went, 'Jesus Christ, that's the whole end of the film fucked.' He said, 'It's okay, we'll improvise. I'll tell you what we'll do, you kill Vincent, Ian runs at you screaming, 'You took him from me, you took him from me,' I'll put you behind some bars and I'll get Hilary to scream and scream and I'll freeze frame on her and bleed the color...and that's the end of the film. That's all we'll do with it.' And *that's* the last three minutes that say more about the nature of violence in film than all of Sam Peckinpah's films stuck together. It was improvised."

Ian Ogilvy confirmed Nicky's recollections:

"Yes, that's quite true. He only had one pistol and I think he'd done something with one. It *is* true, but it is actually much more than that. There were actually four or five pages in the script, following the book. I think in the book Matthew Hopkins ends up in a Gypsy encampment and I think the Gypsies kill him or something, I can't remember, but in the original script there were another four or five pages. We ran out of money, simple as that.

"Not only did we run out of money, but we had Orford Castle just for the one night and only till about one o'clock in the morning, and we had an awful lot of stuff to get through, a lot of set-ups, and we never finished it. I can't remember exactly what was going to happen but it went on from there. It didn't stop there. I think I rescued her and we run away together or something. He ran out of time and money and that was the end of the picture. That really *was* the end of the picture.

"Then he thought, 'Well, what are we going to do? Oh, yeah, I know what we can do, just end it really downbeat and the audience roll out!' For instance, at the very end when that scream is echoing round the corridors, all those shots of corridors are beginnings and ends of the scenes of us walking through. It's the camera running, and if it went on running, we would appear running through with our hands tied up. He just used the beginnings and ends of all those shots. It was a combination of a continuity mistake, of money and time; we just ran out!"

Tom Baker said of the final version of the film:

Gillian Aldham with Michael Reeves on the set of *Witchfinder General*

"Not too bad, really, it was pretty fair. The ending isn't of my choosing, but it's a correct ending, obviously, for the film, given who made it. Certainly correct for Mike to put that ending on. I pick up on the slightly doomy side of things. I think it's very doomy, this sort of transference from hero to villain in the last minutes of these films. He was certainly aware.

"I remember taking him to task that it was a slightly cheap trick to kill off people at the end of movies, because it slightly leaves the audience a bit stuck. They can't giggle. The director's suddenly thrown this thing at them. So, in a way, you have to be serious at the end of these movies. It's also a horrifying trick, the way he chooses to switch the hero into his culpability, Sara's cracking over the edge and realizing what her boyfriend's doing. That's why I was trying to have Gypsies hang them, and off into the sunset. I thought, clippety-clop, let's get off and let's go home and be optimistic about life. No, I can't pretend I was writing for *that*."

Nicky Henson testified that AIP wanted the film to have a happy ending in which Ian and Hilary escape together: "AIP wanted them to ride into the sunset."

In fact, there was an intermediate version, between Tom Baker's and the final version. Vincent was to meet death by fire. Ian Ogilvy was to throw a large pike at Vincent's chest, causing him to fall into a vat of coals and become alight. Philip Waddilove explains further below why this ending had to be abandoned in favor of the final version.

It apparently did not worry Mike that he falsified history, since the real Matthew Hopkins was not hacked to death, as Ian explained:

"No, he died in his bed, I believe, rather peacefully. That wouldn't worry Mike at all. *We're making movies here!* No, that wouldn't worry Mike at all. He *was* very proud of the fact that we actually shot it in Lavenham and we got the names of the witches, he was very proud of all that, but he had to have an ending. He couldn't have Matthew Hopkins dying in his bed, no!"

Ian remembered the problems in filming the climax, which has drawn praise as one of the great endings in the cinema:

"Yes, but that was also contributed to by John Trevelyan very much. Mike had me hit Vincent Price 14 times with an axe. John Trevelyan was a distant cousin of Mike's and they were very friendly, and of all the film censors, Trevelyan was the best, because he actually knew, understood and loved movies. Mike showed him the picture and Trevelyan said, 'Mike, it's a wonderful movie, but I'm sorry, you cannot. There are certain things that will have to go. I'll let you have Ian Ogilvy hit Vincent Price what, three times.'

"Mike said, 'You'll kill my picture!' Trevelyan said, 'No, I won't, I'll improve it.' And when Mike saw it, he said, 'He's right, actually, he's made it better.' So, this great ending, an awful lot of circumstances came into it. Vincent Price was fed up. He was *very* unhappy by this time, very miserable, he wasn't being cooperative. He was being, on that evening, deeply uncooperative. Very. He wouldn't wear padding, for instance. I had this axe made of hard rubber and if he'd worn padding I could actually hit him quite hard. He flatly refused to put the padding on. He said, 'Naaaah, you just don't hit me.' Mike said, 'Put it on, he's *got* to hit you. Doesn't make sense if he sort of goes like that [lunging feebly].' 'I'm not wearing the goddamn...' All this was going on. So it wasn't easy that night. It was a sod of a night to shoot. It was cold and it was uncomfortable. Everybody was in a state."

Ian was not well that night, recalled Diane Ogilvy:

"I remember Vincent being miffed, I don't know why, and my major concern that evening was that Ian was dying of flu and the doctor had been round and given him a mammoth jab of something. They were over budget and if Ian hadn't broken his foot and got that insurance money, they would have been over budget and not got it back. They did get it back. It was one of those evenings when Betty Reeves arrived with smoked salmon sandwiches for the whole crew and cast, just being round the corner. As far as I know that was the only time. I don't remember too much because my main concern was keeping Ian warm because he had a terrible chill. He had a terrible fit of shivers."

Despite this, she judged her by-then ex-husband's acting in the final scene as "brilliant."

Vincent Price told the author that he could not remember the prevailing conditions but confirmed that he refused the padding and suggested that Ian not actually hit him. Eventually, he put on some padding, but not all of it, and as a result, recalled that he *was* bruised.

Tony Tenser also told of the difficulties that night in Orford Castle:

"We were striving for a gloomy, brooding effect in this real castle with its winding stairs. I walked onto the location and found the makeup people mixing something in a bucket. I asked them what it was and they said it was guts for Vincent! They had arranged with a local farmer for some pig stuff but hadn't gotten it. I warned Mike that the censor John Trevelyan would never allow guts hanging out of Vincent, but Mike said, 'No, I'll get him to okay it.' Eventually, Mike didn't use the guts. The scene did go on a long time and was trimmed. Trevelyan later joined the Board of Tigon.

"I never interfered with Mike other than on policy. I never interfered with actual scenes, actors' performances and so on. We were going to shoot

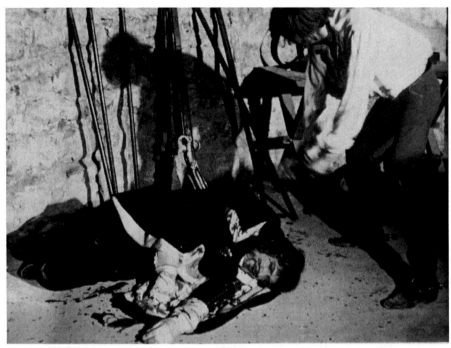

The difficult climax of *Witchfinder General* created a great deal of concern on all fronts.

this scene, which was going to be the end of the film, and we couldn't find Vincent and he'd had three or four glasses of red wine. He'd had a couple of bottles in his room and, for some reason or other, something had upset him. I didn't know what it was. He did this horrible shout! He was *happy*! He was slightly inebriated, but he wasn't *drunk*. He offered me a glass of red wine but I declined. We had to walk him round with coffee to get him right. But something had upset him, and we didn't really get to the bottom of it.

"It might have had something to do with Mike Reeves, but of course Ian Ogilvy took it to heart. He was a real pal of Mike Reeves. They were virtually like brothers. They were really two of a kind. He would really feel for him. If Ian felt anybody wasn't treating Mike right, it would upset him. He wouldn't go around fighting and shouting but he'd be upset. I felt that.

"Vincent was delaying the film because he'd had a few drinks or something had upset him, so when Vincent didn't want to put too much padding in and we insisted that he did, I think Ian must have lost his temper over that. He must have; it was very realistic! Nothing *wrong* in that. The scene looked extremely realistic. He hit him really hard and bruised him. It was a good thing he had padding on. If it had been a real axe, he would have killed him."

Philip Waddilove's memoirs have shed further light on this whole situation:

"These scenes were shot in the dungeon at Orford Castle on the Norfolk coast, a location that was riddled with problems because it came under the jurisdiction of the British National Trust. We had three nights' work at the castle and there was no question of going over schedule because Vincent had to leave for New York the morning after our last night at the castle. Later that same day, he was contracted to begin rehearsals for *Darling of the Day*, his first Broadway musical, and nothing could keep him in England.

"The first problem with the castle came when I was negotiating with the National Trust for its use. As it is open to the public every day from sunrise until sunset, no inducement could alter the Trust's ruling that we could only use it from six in the evening until two in the morning. At that ungodly hour the entire place was cleaned for the next day's sightseers.

"The fact that probably less than a dozen people a year visited the remote castle didn't make the slightest difference to the civil servants with whom I was dealing. The next difficulty revolved around the actual screenplay and the very final scene in the dungeon that involved the heroes killing the Witchfinder in a blaze of burning oil. During the first day's shoot at the castle, despite the National Trust representative having seen the screenplay previously, he said he'd been told by his superiors that there could be no fire in the dungeon, even though it would of course be a controlled FX.

"Tom Baker had long since completed his screenwriting duties, so it was left to Michael Reeves and myself to work out an alternative to the burning. There was a deep water well in the center of the circular dungeon and I suggested that we place a wooden cover on the well and convert the top of it into a sacrificial altar. Accepting the idea, Michael then contributed the main detail of the scene that ends in the Witchfinder being hacked to death with an axe.

"As I'd done on several previous occasions, I met Vincent's limo as he arrived at the location that final evening. When he and his wife Mary, paying her only visit to the set, alighted from their car, I could see that Vincent was somewhat inebriated. Although we'd been told before the movie that he enjoyed a drink or two, he was never anything other than totally sober throughout principal photography. I decided that it would be wise to overlook his condition that night and watch events as they unfolded. It wasn't long before Michael came hurrying up to me in a fury. 'The bastard's drunk—Vincent's drunk,' he yelled at me. 'How could he do this to me on the last night—I'll kill him!' 'Michael,' I replied gently, 'you'll do no such thing.' Michael's response to me was to turn on his heels and storm away in a huff."

Philip recalled for Bill Kelley that by the time Price's death was shot at 1 a.m., Mike had worked Vincent nearly 36 hours. He had been out for dinner and had some wine: "Michael was furious...He was really rough on Vincent. I took Vincent up the stairs as Michael was rehearsing the others and said, 'Vincent, I'm sorry, I don't know what Michael is doing.' And he said, 'Oh, that's all right, old boy.'"

In his memoirs, Philip revealed the extent to which he protected Vincent from Michael on that last night:

"The night was one I'll never forget. We had 35 set-ups to get through in just eight hours, all in the confined space of the dungeon—an unheard-of schedule. Our sparks (lighting technicians) were nothing short of brilliant and I've never witnessed a film crew work in such a disciplined fashion before or since. Pulling socks over their shoes, they moved the big lights from one set-up to another without a sound, while Michael continued to shoot. It all continued wonderfully well until the final set-up, when Ian hacks Vincent to death with an axe.

"I saw Michael talking suspiciously to Ian behind one of the equipment vehicles and I sneaked as close as I dare to hear what Michael was saying.

'I want you to give it all you've got, Ian,' he said. 'I don't care what you do to the bastard—it's got to look totally real!' I hurried over to the chippies' (carpenters') truck and asked one of the men for some sponge rubber padding. Then, running to the nearby pub where we'd rented some space as dressing rooms, I explained to Vincent that Michael was going to go for realism in the final set-up and persuaded him diplomatically that I be allowed to pad his costume with the foam rubber. That scene has become a benchmark in horror movies, but Michael wouldn't talk to me for days."

Philip also told Bill Kelley: "I remember the wardrobe girls kept running up, stuffing more foam rubber padding under Vincent's cloak, to protect him from the axe blows."

Ian did agree that he was angry with Vincent, but said that Tony confused realism with loss of temper, which he denied: "I wouldn't be so unprofessional. Mike did tell me, 'Hit him as hard as you can,' but I couldn't, even with the padding. The axe was rubber but it was hard. I pulled it a bit when I hit him, but I suspect he did get bruised. He didn't have all the padding because I suspect he didn't want to look fat." Nicky Henson commented: "I think Vincent did have fear, and understandably. I think he expected the sort of treatment where you get a stunt double in and, also, possibly not Ian doing it, either. You know, they'd all be sitting in the caravan telling jokes!"

Vincent denied that he was actually inebriated but confirmed to the author that he was upset and that it was Mike's doing: "Yes—it was Mike's inconsiderate treatment." His version of events differed slightly: "Ian didn't want to hit me. That's why he lost his temper. It did not bruise me." (Vincent was possibly being diplomatic, as he had already said he *was* bruised.)

For whatever reason, there is an extraordinary intensity in Ian Ogilvy's performance. *Village Voice* found his screen persona unique because he has a natural gentleness that suddenly erupts into violence in the Mike Reeves films. Ian commented laconically: "Well, I'd say that's the script." Pressed as to whether it was mainly the script, he said: "An actor's controlled by the script, totally. If the script says gentle one minute and violent the next, then that's something that I will do, but it's not something that I've been clever and created. Sometimes I think people read too much into what is after all just a basic job of work." Ian agreed that some great actors, like Robert Vaughn and Vincent Price, seem to subsume everything into something that is totally theirs, but he put it down to their being American: "Absolutely. That's very American, in my view. The American film persona is a very well-developed thing. We're not stars in England. We just go on being actors."

Of course, *The Sorcerers* and *Witchfinder General* contain many levels of similarity, such as the evil within each of the characters Ian Ogilvy plays, as if Mike Reeves were taking different story levels and bringing out what he wanted to emphasize. Tom Baker agreed: "The themes are unusually concentrated. It's not easy to see, 'Is this the real Mike Reeves?,' it's so concentrated."

Ian Ogilvy argued against the idea that Reeves was shaping a screen persona for him:

"I hadn't thought of it like that. There are similarities. The innocent girl. The erstwhile mate. It might be a paucity of imagination, of course, that he remade *Sorcerers* in *Witchfinder.* But I would not have gone on working with Mike. Mike would have become embarrassed eventually by the association that he could only work with one actor. And, indeed, *All the Little Animals*—it's a slim little book about a mentally defective young man of 34—Mike thought it was wonderful and wanted to make it. Big departure. It had moments of horror in it, but a very *sensitive* book written by a recluse who lived in Cornwall. That was his big project that he really, really wanted to make. He'd asked Arthur Lowe and Arthur was frantically keen to do it, and for the younger man he wanted I think David Warner, John Hurt or someone."

Ernest Harris recalled that Mike once said he'd like to tie Ian's hands down. Mike thought Ian tended to be florid in his acting sometimes. Mike himself had very long hands, Ernest thought.

Some writers have suggested that Mike Reeves made Vincent Price re-dub all his dialogue to make his performance more menacing. Ian Ogilvy was not so sure: "I don't know if that's true. I know we had to post-synch a tremendous amount anyway, for technical reasons." This was because of the hangar they were using for interiors, Ian explained, and the sound of rain drowned out voices: "Rain, the wind got up, rain, you could hear everything. It was a waste of time. It was a waste of money, but it was forced on us. Mike would have loved to have been in a studio." Tony Tenser commented that the hangar filming was not a great problem because they took a "wild track" for those scenes, a track used only for reference, and dubbing would be done later.

Ian identified which scenes were shot in the hangar:

"Things like the prison scenes. Rupert Davies all chained up. All the prison. The whole dungeon set was built in the hangar. All that was done there. The interiors of the inns were in this hangar too. They weren't real, they were sets. Innkeeper scenes, all the interiors were done in this bloody hangar. All the interiors were done on sets, you see. Robert Russell, who plays Stearne, was completely re-voiced. Completely. He had a rather high-pitched voice, and the man who re-voiced him is the fisherman, who says he didn't know there was a war on till you gentlemen told me."

Ian agreed that it is a remarkable job of dubbing, as the viewer cannot tell it has been re-voiced: "Yes, excellent, there's no way you can. Because he looks wonderful, but Mike said, 'It's ridiculous, he sounds wet.' So we re-voiced him. That was his biggest part ever, I should think. He was marvelous, marvelous, and all that nasty digging the stuff out of his arm!" Russell, a former stunt man, got a lot of television work subsequently as a result of his excellence in the film. Russell eventually attended the Press Show with Mike Reeves in Soho Square, to which Mike invited Ernest Harris and his girlfriend.

As Vincent's performance stands today, it is probably his most chilling because he is so dignified and never overacts. Ian Ogilvy said: "I think that's why Vincent was quite proud of the picture. Because he'd always specialized in high camp and Mike, having wanted Donald Pleasance, was determined to get Vincent doing a performance that was going to be *not* high camp."

Vincent denied to the author that in the post-synching made necessary by filming in the hangar, his performance was altered. Jack Lynn, who had a small part in the film as the innkeeper, was given the task of directing Vincent's post-synching, as this was mainly a question of timing and did not need Mike Reeves to supervise it. It was all done in a day or two before Vincent left the picture. However, Ian Ogilvy was sure Mike instructed Jack Lynn, a former Dean of the Pasadena Playhouse and former dialect coach to Gene Hackman, Dustin Hoffman and many other Hollywood stars, to get Vincent to bring his vocal performance down. Ian recalled that Vincent, knowing of Jack's experience, was happy to follow his instructions. Paul Ferris commented: "Mike absolutely hated re-voiced or dubbed performances and his ideal was to make movies with live natural sound."

Tony Tenser said:

"Mike felt that Bob Russell's voice didn't go with this macho part of the henchman, so he wanted to re-voice him and he arranged with Russell's agent that it was okay, so we got somebody to do that. Mike said, 'Whilst we're about it, there are some of the scenes where Vinnie's been hamming it up a bit,' (in Mike's words). Shakespearean stuff, throwing his voice on stage. I said, 'I don't think he'd be interested in doing that.' But we got a chap along who's a Professor of English and got him pally with Vincent and he talked him into spending a couple of days with us up at the studio, whilst we were re-voicing Bob Russell. We didn't re-voice Vincent Price, we re-dubbed his own voice. We did the two at the same time."

Tony felt that if Mike had not been going to re-voice Russell, he might not have bothered to re-dub Vincent. Diane Ogilvy observed: "Mike never let on that he was thinking of re-dubbing Vincent, but he must have guessed. I think Vincent re-dubbed that while Mike was still shooting."

Nicky Henson remembered Vincent's departure from the film set: "I know that they had a row that night and he walked off, having finished shooting what he was shooting. He left and he didn't say goodbye to anybody. Just got into a unit car and went. In his costume, I think. He couldn't *wait* to bloody get away! We never saw him again." Tony Tenser agreed: "I can't remember him saying goodbye to anybody."

It is somewhat surprising that Vincent Price, even after completing the dubbing, still had no idea that *Witchfinder General* would be for many the most important film of his career. Tony Tenser revealed this:

"I remember Vincent phoning me before he was going back to America. His schedule was very tight. 'Well,' he said, 'it ain't going to be much of a film,' or words to that effect. He didn't have high aspirations for the film. So I said to him, 'Vinnie, I think you'll find you've come out very well, especially with this re-dubbing and with the music on it.' He said, 'Will I be able to see a copy?' I said, 'As soon as I have a print, go in to Sam Arkoff. I'll notify him that you are to go to his first private screening of it. You'll see it first.' I said, 'I'm not a betting man, but I'll have a bet with you that you'll like it. I know I'm gonna lose now, because even if you do like it, you can say you don't like it. But, knowing you, I would say that you'll like the film. You will change your opinion.' I never met him, but Sam Arkoff said he was pleased."

Vincent sent Tony a note to that effect and, as noted earlier, Tony acknowledged his note on April 24, 1968.

Sam Arkoff was pleased too and later commented to Bill Kelley: "Michael Reeves brought out some element in Vincent that hadn't been seen in a long time. Vincent was more savage in that picture. Michael really brought out the balls in him. I was surprised how terrifying Vincent was in that. I hadn't expected it...There was a malevolence, a malignance about Vincent in that role." Vincent, as was his custom on completing a picture, also sent a note to Deke Heyward, who replied on April 22, 1968: "Thank you for your nice note. I am glad you like the film. I know that Jim thinks it is one of the best we have gotten from England. Everybody also thinks this is about the best production in the Poe series for the past few years. I do too. You were a thoroughly believable menace, not like the sweet lovable character we all know you are!"

Tony Tenser appreciated the fact that Vincent was proud of the picture in later years and of his performance in it:

"It's the *third good one* and *his* first good one, maybe. I always watched a Vincent Price film. I liked him, I liked the type of films he was in, I liked the way he acted. Having known him on the film, I can see him acting and some of the pleasure's gone, because I know his mannerisms. He deserved his money. Where he was hamming it sometimes on *Witchfinder General*, I think he was deliberately doing it, having a bit of fun throwing his voice. In those cases where we re-did it, we did it mostly with the voice. Mike made him shoot the scene two or three times and used the best of it to do it.

It would have been all right in the film in any case, but Mike managed to make his total performance be believable and accurate."

Vincent Price had fought Mike Reeves throughout the making of the picture, but it should not be forgotten what a huge Hollywood star Vincent had been and Mike had clearly done little to ingratiate himself or even be diplomatic. What he chose to do now, having seen the film, was something extraordinarily generous for a star of his magnitude, something possibly unique in cinema history where the star and director clashed bitterly throughout. He chose to include Mike in his round of thank-you notes to the key people, sending him a two-page handwritten letter on April 18, 1968, not only congratulating Mike but essentially apologizing for his behavior!

Mike's friends and colleagues much appreciated this gesture at the time and still did decades later. Paul Ferris said: "I thought it was very large of the man; good spirit to write afterwards." Nicky Henson found it "wonderful": "He was terribly thrilled. Vindicated, but not in a kind of triumphant way. He was very *moved* as well by it." Tom Baker agreed that Vincent did a wonderful thing: "It is good. You're a film star, you're taking a big chunk of the budget: that's very decent of him and very honest of him, I think."

Diane Ogilvy said: "It was an absolutely extraordinary letter and it was certainly one of Mike's treasured possessions. It was an apology." Ian Ogilvy remembered Mike's reaction too: "Mike was delighted by Vincent's letter. He showed it to anyone who might have been interested and I think he was wholly flattered that Vincent recognized the validity of his direction and that he had bothered to write at all. After all, there was no onus on Vincent to do so."

Some might imagine there was also an element of trying to get back into Mike's good books, as he was so obviously a red-hot talent with whom it would be good to work again, but Diane Ogilvy doubted it: "If there was any element of it, none of us picked it up."

Sadly, the original letter somehow got lost when Mike died. Paul Ferris cleared

Mike's flat and it was not among his effects. For many years, the contents of the letter were the subject of speculation, that Vincent was sorry that he hadn't worked harder for him, that he blamed his behavior on the fact that he had just given up smoking, etc. Fortunately, Vincent had kept a photocopy of the April 18 letter and the full text follows:

Dear Michael:

I saw "The Conqueror Worm" or whatever it's called, and I must say it is a very impressive, moving, and exciting picture! Congratulations!

The contrasts of the superb scenery and the brutality, the action of the hero forces against the inexorable, almost pedantic, inaction of the forces of evil make for a suspense I've rarely experienced.

I'm sure you have a big success and a long feather in your cap.

Thought it might amuse you to know there is a bad jumpy cut being made here in the tavern when I go out to keep my first tryst with Hilary—all because of the nude girls—as I remember you did two versions—too bad Tigon didn't send the other version—it's a bad cut.

So, my dear Michael, in spite of the fact that we didn't get along too well—mostly my fault as I was physically and mentally indisposed at that particular moment of my life (public and private)—I do think you have made a very fine picture and what's more I liked what you gave me to do!

All best ever,
Vincent
PS: My thanks too for the call! Sorry I missed you!

Asked to comment about his letter to Michael, Vincent said: "I sat down and wrote him a letter and said, 'I think you've done a brilliant job. It's a wonderful film.' And he wrote me back, saying, 'I knew you would think so.' He was a strange young man, and he would always have to end up any conversation saying, 'And God bless your soul.'" (Bill Kelley has rightly pointed out that the final line of *Witchfinder* is "May God have mercy on us all.") This was not the only odd Mike Reeves expression. Diane Ogilvy remembered, 'Gentlemen, let's make a movie!': "He'd say that, just before they'd start shooting, to anybody who was listening."

On another occasion, Vincent recalled: "He showed great promise. He was a wonderful director, but these problems he had. He called me after *Witchfinder General* was released in England, and it got very good notices. It was really a hit for him. He said, 'There, you see, I told you so!' It was a mad kind of thing to do."

As Robin Wood has written, one does not want to overvalue *Witchfinder* just because its maker has died shortly afterwards, but it does add a very poignant aspect, and *Witchfinder* is already an unbearably poignant work. Ian Ogilvy agreed that Mike's death added this tragic resonance to the film when he watched it himself: "Yes, I think it does, very much." Vincent Price confirmed to the author and others that Mike Reeves' *Witchfinder General* was one of the best pictures he ever made.

Chapter Seven: Aftermath

Violence is horrible, degrading and sordid. Insofar as one is going to show
it on the screen at all, it should be presented as such—and the more people
it shocks into sickened recognition of these facts the better.—Michael
Reeves, *The Listener*

The final cut of *Witchfinder General* was uniquely dark in the British cinema, but Tony
Tenser, with his enlightened respect for the artistry of his directors, did not tamper with it. The
attitude of the British film censors was a different matter, however.

Mike arranged a screening of the uncut final version, the answer print. David Austen and
Ernest Harris attended. Ernest Harris recalled that screening:

> "I remember when I saw it with Mike the first time. You know these endless
> shots of Ian riding across the countryside? It always seems that this scene
> starts with this great horse's rump coming into the picture. I remember Mike
> sitting there saying, 'Rump!' He said Wilfrid Brambell was like an old gar-
> goyle to look at. I remember turning to him at the end of the film. He was
> sitting two rows in front of me, and as the film ended with that screaming
> and the music comes in, he just turned round and looked at me like that. I
> said, 'You bastard!' Mike seemed pleased that I found the film disturbing.
> That end is so memorable as it is now, because from the moment that Vincent
> knocks at the door of their room and the first time that Ian says, 'I'm going
> to kill you,' the film is just a roller coaster. You just sit there and you're
> waiting for it to get worse and worse."

Tom Baker agreed that the film cranked up toward the end: "It does. We were trying to fit
all this damn stuff in, apart from anything else. There's an awful lot to get through, because we
were quite hooked on the coming and going from place A to B."

Ernest's first impressions are valuable because he had not been intimately involved with
the production, as had so many of Mike's friends, and came to it with a fresh eye. He revealed
how he came to be invited to the screening:

> "All that happened that day was that I was getting ready to go to lunch and
> Mike came in with David Austen and said, 'Do you want to see a movie?' I
> went, 'Okay, what is it?' He said, '*Witchfinder.*' I said, 'Yeah, right, let's go.'
> We went up to a viewing theater in St. Anne's Court, opposite the entrance
> to Film House, which was the back entrance to Columbia Pictures. It was
> directly below there. We went down there and there was just the three of us
> in the theater and it was a shattering experience. I was certainly unprepared
> for the intense violence and the almost casual brutality of the film.
>
>   "I remember it being an incredibly intense sort of feeling watching the film
> for the first time, because the only similar time I had that feeling was when I
> saw *The Wild Bunch* in the cinema. I thought, 'They can't be doing this on
> the screen.' I'm sure the bit where Ian chops Vincent was much longer, and
> the pricking of Rupert Davies. I remember vividly the witch going down
> with her hair on fire, which was actually in the trailer. When I saw the film
> in the cinema, it was gone then. I'm glad that was cut out simply because
> it was one of those things you get in a film where you feel someone's just
> being clever. Having seen both versions, I can't really see that the cuts did
> a lot of damage to (or really improved) the film."

Ernest noted Mike's particular satisfaction with some aspects of the finished film: "I remember him praising the music for *Witchfinder.* Somewhere I have an audio tape that Mike gave me of somebody (I have no idea who) playing the 'Love Theme' on a piano. He turned up at Miracle and gave me this soon after I first saw the film and expressed my own admiration for the music. Somebody else he singled out for great praise was Robert Russell. He was also very pleased with the American title *The Conqueror Worm.*" Mike was quoted in *Penthouse* as saying "Changes of title are nothing."

This was not the first screening of the film, as Mike and Paul Ferris showed an early rough cut to film censor John Trevelyan. Nicky Henson told the sorry history of the censorship of *Witchfinder General*:

> "Mike knew Trevelyan and didn't want any trouble with cuts in the film later because, you know, you put it together and score it. So he showed him the film—a rough cut without the dubbing and without the score. And Trevelyan said, 'Fine.' Mike said, 'Do you mean that? Because if we put the score in and then I've got to put the scissors in, we get those terrible jumps and stuff.' He said, 'No, that's absolutely fine.' And they took it back to him six months later, after Paul had written the score, and he said, 'I'm sorry. I had no *idea* what difference dubbing and music makes to a picture. I've *got* to put cuts in.' That's an extraordinary story."

Paul Ferris said that Trevelyan's interference caused minimal damage to his score:

> "There's one minuscule jump right at the end. The torture sequence with Rupert Davies was what worried John Trevelyan more than the end. He for sure trimmed the end, because there are parts of that without music. I talked to John Trevelyan. He came when we showed the answer print. And he was horrified. (Not literally!) 'Christ!' After the score had been added, it was all quite terrifying and that's why he chopped out quite a lot of it after the music had stopped. He didn't cut the music, which shows you how good he was, really. I mean, he knew his job was indefensible. I must say, he did do his job. *Before* that, he spoke to me just to find out what was going on and see what our intentions were. He certainly spoke to Mike, too, and after it he said, 'Christ, I've got to cut something here, because it's a little bit over the top.'"

Trevelyan said he had never known background music to heighten screen violence so significantly.

Mike Reeves did not take the censorship of his film lying down. After an abortive telephone conversation with John Trevelyan, an exhausted Mike went on a short holiday to Jamaica, where he wrote an extraordinary letter to Trevelyan to ask that they not ruin the whole point of his film with ill-advised censorship. From the Bay Roc Hotel, Montego Bay, he wrote on April 7, 1968:

Dear John,
First of all, please forgive the various lapses of spelling, grammar and typing that will occur in this letter; for like most writers I am proficient at none of them.
Anyway, with regard to Witchfinder: *I am sorry our talk the other day was so brief; to be honest, I was so damned nervous, I have a feeling that I probably made no sense at all. There were so many things I wanted to say about the picture, and there was so little time, that I in all probability made a complete idiot of myself. In any case I thank you for your forbearance, and hope that a little of what I was trying to say permeated through my sea of incoherence! I thought*

The shocking brutality of *Witchfinder General* caused problems with censors and critics.

I'd write you this letter to try and make plain to yourself and Lord Harlech what I was a) trying to do with the film, and b) my feelings on your particular problems with it with regard to cutting.

First of all, let me say that I fully appreciate your difficulties, and realize what they are: 1) it is a film that, by very fact of starring Vincent P., and being distributed by the firm that it is (I am not in any way knocking Tony—I like and respect him) it may get seen by sections of society that maybe (though I must add that in my opinion, a mere 25-year-old though I may be, it won't) it might have some detrimental effect on; 2) whilst I myself may have certain admirers amongst our illustrious press corps, I have the overall image of a maker of cheap horror films—and this is not going to help matters (by the way, this is said in the probably conceited assumption that I have any image as a filmmaker at all!)

So—to the film itself, and by the way, you will certainly gather from what follows that I would like you to hold this letter in strictest confidence—please!

Despite its pedigree, as outlined above, Witchfinder is a serious picture; that is not to deny its legion of faults—I am only too well aware of them, believe me. However, I think the end result is pretty powerful, as you yourself said—more so even than I thought it was going to be, and I knew what I was aiming at, despite the multitude of AIP-inspired iron manacles that were perpetually descending vice-like on my shoulder. Its overall message (though I loathe the word) is as anti-violence as it can be. Violence breeds violence, and that end-violence in itself is insanity. To put that over to a paying audience, particularly one who is paying to enjoy a vicarious thrill from once-removed sadism, surely this cannot be anything but moral?

And for what it is worth, I think this is what Witchfinder does, whether that audience is consciously aware of it or otherwise. If, as AIP wished me to do, I had dissolved from the final close-up to a shot of Marshall and Sara riding blissfully into the sunset, I would agree with you that the film should be cut—and to be honest I would have had a troubled conscience for quite a while at having made it. However, its present ending, I feel, is salutary, moral, highly depressing (it may even cause the film to lose money, and knowing this, and allowing me to keep it, is one of the reasons I admire Tony): AIP I never consulted, so that's their hard luck—in fact, feeling as I do about that bunch of ponces (and I mean that almost literally) I hope devoutly that it will in the States!

From the point of view of actual cutting, I have as you know, voluntarily made three cuts myself in the places where I feel the film in fact does descend into merely gratuitous sadism. (I ask you to excuse their initial inclusion on the grounds of directorial nerves, a desire to keep the film up to feature length by including all dramatic impact of any value at all in the cutting stages, and the usual problem of not realizing one's mistakes till one sees a fully dubbed, color, consecutively projected print.) Literally the cuts I have made are as follows: The cell scene: I have shortened it by half, removing the two most obviously vicious blows to the woman's face. The burning scene: I have cut the final C.U. of the Elizabeth Clarke character's bleeding face—in fact, in terms of dramatic cutting rhythm, this makes the whole sequence better constructed! Apart from these I am not willing to make any further cuts, and from what I remember of your office's rejection slip, I will try and outline why below.

Generally: In order for the film to retain its point, there must be a level of brutality through-out; thus, by seducing the audience into accepting it, we prime them for the ending, where the stool is whipped right from under their feet, and they are left looking at themselves, and their involvement with the foregoing violence, with, I hope (and am in fact sure) the sense of self-loathing one invariably receives when one has been momentarily involved in a flash of sadism—however slight it may be, no matter be it verbal or physical. If the film is cut to an 'acceptable' level of violence, this ending will lose all point and become merely 'horror-comic,' and that is what both you and I so desperately wish to avoid. If the picture is reduced, it could well become just an exercise in gratuitous violence (assuming you didn't cut about 35 minutes, in which case we are all wasting our time, and a lot of Tony's money!), and would have exactly the reverse effect it is intended to have, i.e., an audience having a lovely time reveling in their nice censor-protected 'safe' brutality. (I am of course admitting that it is an extremely brutal film whatever you, I, or the projectionist at the Rex, Solihull, do to it!)

In particular: the torture of Lowes—one only sees the pricker (don't laugh, that's what they used to call it apparently...) actually go into his back twice, and on both occasions extremely briefly. If this is removed, the scene will become nonsensical, as well as dramatically ill-con-structed, and thus point us on our way to the drastic error of moral judgment outlined above. As far as screams go, what is he supposed to do? Suffer magnificently with just a faint moan or two? Surely this would nullify the point that suffering is horrible, degrading and as far from what one could call 'Hollywood glamorous' as it could be?

The beating up of the girl in the cell: As I said, I have already halved it, but it must remain in order to keep the vital level of brutality, which for reasons mentioned earlier, has to permeate the whole film.

The moat-drowning sequence: same thing applies, though at this point I in all honesty can-not see where the objection to this lies. In my opinion, and due to lack of time, weather problems etc., this scene is so undershot that I only just managed to cut it together at all, and in fact, with reference to my whole thesis with the film, is what I would consider a regrettably tame sequence. For the record, apart from one extreme long shot, there are only four cuts to the victims in the water, and each of these is only 18 inches long. The fact that anyone should even consider cut-ting the scene at all seems to me incomprehensible—but a considerable tribute to Paul Ferris' music and my editing! (For which, thank you—or Mr. Croft, or whoever even envisaged the idea of even partly cutting the sequence!)

The burning scene: As I said, I have cut one of the shots of Elizabeth Clarke sans eye, and it improves the scene a lot. It was gratuitous in the first place, and destroyed the momentum. As for the rest of the sequence, there is only one other really horrifying shot, that where she *actually catches fire: This is a) necessary for the 'level of violence' thing, and b) occurs in a very fast long shot. The rest of the scene is entirely built in terms of effectiveness by the girl's fear, and Paul, and the crowd, and Hopkins' reaction to it. I do not see either how or why it should be cut, to be honest, scaring though it may be. (By the way, though this is obviously not an anti-cutting ploy, did you know this scene is entirely factual? Tom Baker and I reconstructed it from, I believe, a New Statesman article about witchcraft in the Middle Ages). As far as level of screams go, the same comments apply here as to the torture of Lowes. This girl is suffering horribly, and I want the audience to suffer with her—not enjoy the sequence for its meretricious thrill value (if it has any).*

The final sequence: This pertains particularly to my general remarks about the aim of the film. If cut, and just suggested, it will just be an exciting (though probably nonsensical) finale of the "Will the dashing hero escape and kill the dastardly villain, rescuing the fair maiden on the way?" department. Then, instead of deeply disturbing the audience at the finish, the whole thing will merely become ludicrous, enlivened by some suggested sadism—and as I said earlier, I don't want my name associated with anything of that order, any more than I understand you and your office would. Marshall's madness at the end must be motivated, and strongly motivated, to have any effect; so also must the final image of Sara screaming hysterically. And if the sequence in the castle is cut down, this will not be the case. As I say, the morality of the film lies in its whole content; and the fact that in the final 90 seconds the violence explodes utterly in the face of the 'sympathetic' protagonists (by their own participation in it) is the core of all that is good (morally good) in the film.

Destroy the film and you render its denouement of complete despair meaningless: do that and you might as well ban the whole thing, for it would become just another exercise in 'terror for kicks.'

I don't want that to happen; financial, 'artistic' or career considerations apart. Surely you have to agree with me on this?

I'm sorry this is so long and involved. I trust it makes some kind of literary sense—I'm afraid I can get a bit involved when I feel fairly deeply about a difficult subject. When I get back from here, I'd like very much to talk with both you, and, if you wish, David Harlech about the situation. Believe it or not, I have lots more to say! (Particularly regarding advertising, Tony's probable hostile attitude toward your office—which I beg you to disregard, though as you certainly know better than I do, with him it is just a manufactured phase! —and the best way to generally cope with this situation. Believe me, John, I have tried to be as honest as I can in this letter; I hope none of it sounds rude or unreasonable; I hope also you'll believe one thing about Witchfinder; whatever its demerits, it has at least one or two things going for it—it's an honest film, and the audiences I have tried it on have all emerged from it well shaken, and with the overall point of the movie embedded in their not always too-sensitive brains. I think it will do the same for general audiences too, whether or not, as I said earlier, they are all able to put it into words.

Yours—Michael

N.B. Please-also-forgive all the underlinings etc. in this—I write better screenplays than letters, tho that may not be saying much!

What are we to make of this? We know that the ending of *Witchfinder* came about accidentally, but Mike clearly realized it gave the preceding film an immediate moral justification. Ian Ogilvy believed Mike then developed his case about the film's moral purpose from there, and it may well be he talked himself into believing it after a while. Tom Baker was skeptical:

> "Mike had this notion that he tried to pull the wool over Trevelyan's eyes. This letter he sent from Jamaica: 'The film is violent because I am trying to put people off violence.' Ha! I can't remember if that was a heartfelt belief on his part. It may have been, but I don't remember him saying that when we were 16 years old! 'I'm screwing the bottle into the face so that people

down the council estate will never be violent again!' That's why it would have been so delightful to see him progress, to find out, once he'd learnt all the tricks, would he just go on with tricks or did he have more to say? It would have been fascinating. It's a great shame, I must say."

Unfortunately, Trevelyan did not buy Mike's argument, though his reply was cordial enough. He wrote to Mike on April 29, 1968:

Dear Michael,
I am very sorry that we had to make cuts in your picture Witchfinder General, *and feel that I owe it to you to explain our reasons for this.*
First, let me say that I have no doubts about your integrity in making this picture, nor about the validity of the theme. You set out to show that violence is horrible, especially when associated with sadism. Unfortunately in doing so you presented us with serious problems, as follows:

(1) We have for some years taken a strong line about scenes of violence, which we believe to be often harmful, and if we passed your picture without cuts this would, to many people, appear to be a complete reversal of this policy, which has been widely publicized in the Press and on television. Whereas some people no doubt have felt that in the context of what you were saying such extremes of violence were justified, we believe that a large number of cinemagoers would not only be revolted by the violence, which indeed you would want them to be, but would be unlikely to appreciate the point that you were making through it.

(2) We believe that, while many people deplore violence, there are some who not only accept it but actually enjoy it. This is something that we do not want to encourage, and I believe that in passing your picture we would be taking a substantial risk of doing this.

(3) There is reason to believe that the continuous diet of violence through screen entertainment, both cinema and television, may be conditioning people to its acceptance, so that they are becoming indifferent to it. While you can argue that this justifies what you have done, there is an equally strong argument that we should maintain our present policy.
As I have told you, we have not only cut scenes of violence in many films, but have totally refused several films on these grounds. As a result I often have to justify our actions. I believe that if we passed your film complete it would have been more difficult for me to do this.
In conclusion I would like to express regret that I underestimated the impact of this film when I saw an early assembly or rough cut. I now know the film well, and I believe that I am justified in saying that the impact was immensely heightened by color, sound effects and music. The picture in its final form was very much stronger than I had anticipated, and it will have the effect of making me more cautious in future in making preliminary judgments on films of violence.
With good wishes,
Yours,
John Trevelyan

THE STORY

It is 1645. Civil War tears England asunder. Whatever conventional law there was has collapsed, to be replaced by the whims of local magistrates. In the Parliament-held, embryonically Puritan Eastern sector of the country, one particular man is making full use of his natural talent for opportunism. This chosen man is Matthew Hopkins, a lawyer from Ipswich, and his chosen profession (though he might be capable of convincing himself that it is a vocation) is Witchfinding.

East Anglia being almost entirely rural, is still heavily enamoured of age-old superstition and it is on this that Hopkins capitalises, along with his assistant John Stearne. Riding from village to village, they seek out those who arouse the local peasants' suspicions—for whatever genuine or manufactured reasons—and having proven their helpless victim's guilt, briskly hang, burn or mutilate them; all at the current going rate of three guineas a head for each execution. It is against this background that one Richard Marshall, a young and comparatively innocent Roundhead soldier, rides home on leave to visit his sweetheart, Sara.

Sara is the niece of John Lowes, the elderly cleric of the village of Brandeston. Lowes himself, a kindly old man, has leanings towards a rather high Church kind of Protestantism—and as such, in this Cromwell-held area, is regarded with distrust and even hatred by his parishioners.

Having secured Lowes' permission to marry Sara, Richard leaves happily, to rejoin his regiment, but Hopkins and Stearne, unknown to him, have been sent for by the Brandeston villagers.

They arrive in the village. Lowes is tortured and thrown into a cell. His life is only temporarily spared by the efforts of Sara, who submits to Hopkins' inherent sexual inadequacy, seduces him—and successfully. For a while—short while—all seems safe for Lowes. Possibly Hopkins, though he might have few other virtues, could be induced by his essential self honesty into sparing the priest. But then events occur that permit the inevitable.

Whilst Hopkins is temporarily absent the brutish Stearne rapes Sara. Hopkins hears of this—and exacts the cruellest revenge he can, not on Stearne but on Sara. He orders the immediate execution of Lowes. A few days later Richard learns of the events at Brandeston from an army farmer. He rides furiously for the village, to find Sara, shattered and stunned, hiding in the desecrated church. Marshall, a man living within his own carefully outlined code of simple honour, swears total vengeance. And it is in his achievement of such that he eventually destroys not only himself but Sara as well. The only "survivor" of the ensuing orgy of violence is possibly Hopkins ... for Matthew Hopkins, though outwardly an ogre of sadism and materialism, has others involved, lack—personal honesty, and he dies still in possession of it.

213

One's abiding impression of this situation must be, how sad that a filmmaker prepared to make such a passionate and articulate defense of his work (however specious the argument, though even that is debatable) should be prevented from exhibiting his work of art in the form he wanted. The growing international reputation of *Witchfinder General* over the decades must demonstrate the wrong-headedness of the film's initial censorship. However, Trevelyan noted in his memoirs *What the Censor Saw* that Mike Reeves strongly resisted the censorship of his film and took no part in the cutting, but was agreeably surprised when the censored print was shown to him and thought the cuts were very well done.

Still, the censorship of a masterpiece like *Witchfinder* was an artistic crime, but even in its censored form it seemed to be a picture of great maturity, because of the nature of its ending and its consistency with the outlook on human nature in all Mike Reeves' work. Ian Ogilvy testified that it wasn't *simply* a matter of happy accidents: "He very much wanted to make the point that my character, Marshall, becomes *as bad as* Hopkins in a way, that we're all capable of foul deeds, and that the hero ends up by being just as vicious and foul as Hopkins. He very much wanted to make that point."

For critic Robin Wood, it is a very intense point to make but perhaps not a totally mature one. Ian Ogilvy felt that in later years Mike Reeves would most likely have modified his pessimism. For Ian, that degree of maturity sat in Mike's personality not inconsistently with his impulsive streak:

> "I suppose he was impulsive with *some* things. You say somebody's impulsive, you automatically assume he's going to be impulsive about everything. He was impulsive about things he just suddenly wanted to get up and do. I suppose in film he did give it rather more thought. Maybe he reserved his impulsiveness for just ordinary everyday life when he was bored. Buying a toy gun for himself was boredom, I suppose. But in film I suppose he had thought about it. He certainly gave a lot of thought to it. He was very good about other people bringing ideas to it. He wasn't a svengali, at all."

Tony Tenser was not surprised that Mike made the film so dark and pessimistic or, as he described it, 'foreboding': "This is what the story was. People were being hunted as witches. The mark was put on them and they would be killed even if they were innocent. Remember the scene where the people were being drowned: If they drowned they were innocent, if they lived they were guilty. It was a terrible, terrible period to be in, based on history. This was not a tongue-in-cheek horror film. This was classical. It came in the horror genre but it wasn't a horror film. It wasn't intended to be a horror film."

Tony said that there would have been even more vociferous disapproval of the film's violence if they had not toned it down a bit, but he argued that the violence was inherent in the story:

> "I remember the argument between Mike Reeves and John Trevelyan, and subsequently with me being involved with Trevelyan. Trevelyan wanted to be stronger with the cuts that were made and I was the piggy in the middle. Mike said, 'He's not going to touch that. That's going to stay there.' Trevelyan said, 'No way I'm going to allow that.' I had to sort of try and mediate. I remember explaining to Trevelyan, 'Look, by all means, if you have to cut that and that, I'll go along with it and convince Mike Reeves of it, but you have to bear in mind what Mike Reeves is trying to do.'
>
> "He hadn't told me this, but I *knew* what he was trying to do. It relates to something I knew before with Polanski. Somebody was once interviewing Polanski and I was there. They're asking about the type of films he makes. Why does he make films of this terrible, horrifying sort? Polanski, who still spoke with quite an accent, halting for words, said to this man, 'If you

were walking down the street on a nice sunny day and on the left there's a wedding and the bride and groom are coming out, and the church bells are pealing, there are flowers and family and snapshots and children playing, and 50 yards further up on the other side of the road, a bus has just run over a woman's head, which one are you going to watch?' He didn't wait for an answer. So we're talking about film having this sort of effect.

"People in general may not admit it or want to be but they're attracted by terrible scenes far more easily than they're attracted to happy scenes. From my experience of dealing with people like Polanski, I realized Mike was trying to get people to really *hate* this man for the horrible things he was doing, and hate him to such a degree that when they came out of the cinema, they were ashamed of themselves. It would shame them out of wanting to see the violence and out of wanting to seek revenge. That's what he was trying to do. The only way to do that was to really make people go for it.

"I was in the town of Southport later on and we were making the film *What's Good for the Goose* with Norman Wisdom. We managed to get the rushes shown at the end of the evening performance at the local Classic Cinema. So, when everybody was out, there was a half-hour break, we'd go along there and we'd see not the previous day but the day before that. I said, 'If you come up, you'll see the rushes there,' and some people went to see it, some not. I was always referred to as Guv by the crew, and somebody said 'Guv, why don't you let people here see one of your films? What about *Witchfinder General*?'

"So I said, 'If it's a rainy day and we're off, we'll stay in the cinema, see the rushes and stay on and watch the film and then we'll all go and have a pint and something to eat.' Everybody said, 'Oh yes, we'd like to see it.' So I arranged to have a print sent up. My wife Diane hadn't seen it. She was sitting next to me and people were dispersed. Diane had a friend there and she was with another chap and this chap was a Southport man. He was an educated man, came from a good family, a quiet, intensive man, who appeared to be a managerial type. He was sitting behind us with Diane's friend. We had about 100 people in the cinema. The crew brought their girlfriends. It was freebies. It was after the show. The manager himself sat and watched the film. He hadn't seen the film.

"And when we got toward the end of the film, when Ian was hitting Vincent—there were murmurs all the way through and the girls were closing their eyes at these terrible things (if they hadn't averted their eyes, they wouldn't have been so terrible, but averting their eyes made it more terrible)—suddenly, as the axe was falling, someone behind me stood up and shouted, 'Kill the bastard, kill the bastard! Kill the effing bastard! Smash him! Kill him!'

"I turned round. This intelligent, educated, quiet managerial type was in a rage! He was in a rage at the film! And when the film was over, he sat down and was deeply embarrassed. He was ashamed of himself. Seeing that in real life showed me that Mike achieved the effect he wanted. To get them to be so much involved in it that they would be worse than the Witchfinder and then feel ashamed afterwards. It works.

"Trevelyan was helpful and I managed to keep as much of those parts of the film as were *necessary* to do that. Because there was one part I wouldn't even show to the censor, when they were mixing the entrails. I thought, 'There's no way he's going to pass that. There's no way I can say to him, "Look, it's necessary to see his entrails hanging out." No way.' That wasn't necessary."

The contemporary reviews of *Witchfinder General* were mixed (later reviews were considerably more adulatory, in publications ranging from *Time Out* to *Village Voice*) but included some raves. Felix Barker (London *Evening News*) said: "Michael Reeves, a very talented young director...carries us magically back into the 17th century. There is a real feeling for period." Tom Milne (*Monthly Film Bulletin*) praised "Reeves' subtle use of color." The stunner was the attention accorded it by John Russell Taylor in *The Times* in his review of May 11, 1968:

> "For the encouraging thing about Mr. Reeves, one of the youngest of the new wave of British cinema, is that he is a very good director. He has a sharp sense of pace, a sophisticated eye for possible absurdity...(and) that vital gift in a filmmaker, the instinctive ability to make anything he trains his camera on look interesting...there is much in *Witchfinder General* which would win Michael Reeves an important reputation if he were dealing with some more pretentious, but fundamentally no more serious subject...Mr. Reeves is no longer merely promising. He already has real achievements behind him: not merely good horror films, but good films, period."

Diane Ogilvy recalled that this review, in particular, shook Mike Reeves and may have done more harm than good: "There it was in black and white and it shook him. He didn't want to be a genius. He wanted to be very good but he didn't want to be a genius. Ian probably remembers the excitement that Mike went through that *Films and Filming* were going to come and interview him. He was a young filmmaker. He didn't know how any of his films were going to be received." David Austen, in *Films and Filming*, cited Bertrand Russell on the nature of fear and deemed the film "very frightening."

Tom Baker doubted Mike was shaken by Taylor's review: "He wrote quite a nice review. We stayed up half the bloody night. We went round to the Air Terminal in Cromwell Road, it's a Sainsbury's now, and grabbed the first editions to see what was going to be said. I remember it was quite polite, friendly. I think he did say it's got a literate script! I can't imagine Mike being overawed by that too much."

Sarah Reeves remembered one critic did annoy him: "In *Witchfinder*, when everything had been shot, perfect, with soldiers riding along, he realized all ought to be wearing white gloves. He had to set up again, everything, all shot again. Then some critic said, 'Oh, that shot of the white gloves!' Mike was furious! The expense. But he was a perfectionist over little details you'd hardly notice."

Other critical responses were predictably horrified. Dilys Powell (*Sunday Times*) found it "peculiarly nauseating." Margaret Hinxman (*Sunday Telegraph*) wrote: "*Witchfinder General* is an exercise in sadistic extravagance, all the more repugnant for being ably directed by Michael Reeves." David Wilson (*The Guardian*) concurred: "The film is less concerned with narrative than with exploiting every opportunity for gratuitous sadism."

The Universe, a Catholic newspaper, wrote a lucid appraisal, marked in Mike's scrapbook: "The young director's object seems to be to shock his audience into a recognition that violence breeds violence and especially violence born of religious fanaticism. The point is taken, but it seems somewhat exaggerated." Not much recognition there of what Mike argued was "morally good" in the film.

But the critic who really got under Mike Reeves' skin was dear old Alan Bennett in his Views column in *The Listener*, a column of personal opinions and, significantly, not a film-reviewing feature. Bennett's appalled reaction to the film gave rise to the strongest condemnation of the film (and, by implication, its maker) that ever appeared in print, prompting Reeves for the only time to reply to a critic of his work in a public way.

Bennett complained of "a ground bass of beatings, shootings and torture, all weltering in blood" in the May 23, 1968, issue of *The Listener.* After listing various incidents of violence, he continued:

EDGAR ALLAN POE'S
THE CONQUEROR WORM
FROM AMERICAN INTERNATIONAL IN COLOR

"Of course blood and guts is the stuff of horror films, though, as with Victorian melodrama, what makes them popular and even healthy are the belly laughs which usually punctuate them. For these one can generally rely on the film's star, Vincent Price. There are no laughs in *Witchfinder General*. It is the most persistently sadistic and morally rotten film I have seen. It was a degrading experience, by which I mean it made me feel dirty. I would not have wasted space on such a shambles had not the film received serious and favorable critical attention in several quarters. Mr. John Russell Taylor in the *Times* emphasized its subtlety, imagination and camera-work over three columns. Mr. Tom Milne in the *Observer* commended it for showing intelligence and talent, real style and presence. This seems to me pernicious rubbish. The world of film is not an autochthonous world: Sadism which corrupts and repels in life continues to do so when placed on celluloid. It is not compounded by style nor excused by camera-work. Hitler had a film made of the death throes of the plotters of July 1944. I wonder what Messrs. Taylor and Milne would make of that. Purely, of course, in terms of film."

A stunning put-down, and one that obviously stung Mike into an immediate reply, as his letter was printed in the following week's issue:

"In last week's issue of *The Listener*, there appears a somewhat vitriolic condemnation of my film, *Witchfinder General*, and of two of the critics who were kind enough to praise it. Mr. Alan Bennett takes the film to task for 'making him feel dirty' due to the extent of the violence presented in it. I have no desire to quarrel with him over the film's merits or demerits as 'art' (whatever that may mean); but would like to make a couple of my own points in answer to his review. First, I think Mr. Bennett and I are at least in agreement over one thing—that violence as such is more horrible than can be adequately described on paper. However, Mr. Bennett implies that violence on the screen is perfectly acceptable so long as it is 'punctuated...by belly laughs.' Not only does he state this, but also indicates it may even be healthy in such circumstances. With this I would quarrel most vehemently.

"Surely the most immoral thing in any form of entertainment is the conditioning of the audience to accept and enjoy violence? Is this not exactly the attitude that could lead to more and more *casual* indulgence in violence, starting with individuals, and thence spiraling nauseatingly upwards to a crescendo of international blood-letting? To sit back in one's cinema seat and have a good giggle between Mr. Bennett's bouts of 'healthy' violence, as he so strangely advocates, is surely immoral to the extent of criminality. Violence is horrible, degrading and sordid. Insofar as one is going to show it on the screen at all, it should be presented as such—and the more people it shocks into sickened recognition of these facts the better. I wish I could have witnessed Mr. Bennett frantically attempting to wash away the 'dirty' feeling my film gave him. It would have been proof of the fact that *Witchfinder* works as intended."

Ian Ogilvy reflected that Mike overstated his case in this letter: "It's writing of a very young man, isn't it? It's unsophisticated. Also, I get the feeling that was *very* much written in the heat of the moment. 'Oh, well, I'm going to dash off a letter to them.' I don't think he thought about that very much. 'Nauseatingly spiraling to international blood-letting...' I think probably on rereading that, Mike would be somewhat ashamed of it."

Mike developed his case further later that year in the only interview he ever gave to a popular non-film publication. He was featured in the Shows column of *Penthouse* and explained to their reporter: "I'm interested in the depths of human degradation. Just how far you and I can sink. I think violence and murder are quite justifiable. All you have to do is bring it down to an acceptable level. Then you can make points about the aggressiveness inherent in everybody."

This is certainly a lucid piece of self-analysis of the themes of his films. Both *The Sorcerers* and *Witchfinder General*, of course, *are* about people sinking to the depths of depravity, and people who viewed those films without knowing anything about Mike Reeves might well attribute a neurotic personality to their maker, and even critic Robin Wood said the films had neurotic elements. Ian Ogilvy was not entirely convinced that Mike really held these views: "Sounds a bit pompous, coming from Mike, that. I don't really know where that came from, to be honest. He wasn't *really* like that most of the time I knew him. There *was* a neurotic element to Mike. But he was not without a sense of humor. He had an enormous sense of humor and laughed like a drain a lot of the time. But I do think that there was a neurosis there, because he was so obsessive. His interests really lay only in one area. You've got to have interests elsewhere as well."

Ian Ogilvy said that Mike "had a very strong attitude" about the violence in his own (and other people's) pictures. There is a paradox in Mike Reeves' work, though, because he does seem to go beyond showing how horrible violence really is to exploiting it to make an exciting picture. He gets the audience's adrenalin flowing, so there does seem to be an ambiguity in his attitude in that he was aware of the commercial appeal of violent events. Ian Ogilvy was in agreement with this analysis:

"Absolutely right. Indeed, I would suspect—remember how young we all were—that Mike's explanation to *The Listener* was right off the top of his head, to be honest. He did say this. He did say that he found John Wayne-sort of bar fights *wrong* and immoral, because a) they glorified a saloon bar fight, and b) they didn't tell the truth about what happened when you hit somebody in the face. He did say this and he said this quite a lot. At the same time, you're probably right. He was much more interested in making an exciting movie than in posing moral questions of the treatment of violence, much more."

Censors apparently believe that screen violence stimulates violence in viewers, though the evidence seems to deny this, and Ian did not believe it: "I wouldn't have thought it does, either. No. I don't think Mike thought too deeply about that kind of thing. He certainly didn't in the early days. His passion was, let's make a movie, let's make an exciting movie and as well as we can. That's what he wanted to do. Mike loved shooting fight scenes. He loved doing them. But he also wanted them to be rough and tough."

Then again, later rip-offs of *Witchfinder General* like Michael Armstrong's *Mark of the Devil* lacked Mike Reeves' sense of pain and leered rather more. Ian Ogilvy commented: "I don't think Mike Reeves leered at all. Also, since *Witchfinder General*, there have been movies that made *Witchfinder General* look like a vicar's tea party! It was only of its time that it was violent."

On the substance of Mike Reeves' theory about the screen presentation of violence, Ian Ogilvy reflected:

"I know it was a case he developed. Whether or not he believed it beforehand or whether it was something he developed in the course of all this criticism, he certainly stuck to it absolutely passionately. I think he was rather excited by the kind of furor that this picture had created. I think it took him by surprise, frankly. The more I talk about it, I just wonder how much effect the criticism of it, and then the implied criticism of his mental state, maybe got to him. I wonder how badly *Witchfinder* did eventually affect him. The fact that he was criticized personally for the violence might have affected him and might have contributed to his misery a bit. I just don't know, it's only supposition."

Mike had gone to see Dr. Blaikie in April 1968. The doctor referred him to a psychiatrist. Mike was also using narcotics to help him sleep. He was also given antidepressants and sedatives. Betty would eventually become concerned about the amount of drugs he was taking. Some wondered if Mike's personality was a little fragile to cope with the pressure. Ian agreed: "Yes, I think that's quite true. There was a certain fragility in his personality. I think I might have pushed too hard the cynicism. The only cynicism Mike had was in order to be looked upon as a very, very successful film director, as opposed to being a man who wanted to make a lot of money. He was passionate about movies. He simply had a streak of realism in him about what kind of movies were going to be successful."

On the other hand, Paul Ferris did not believe Mike was adversely affected by the criticism of *Witchfinder*:

"No, I don't think so. I'm sure he knew that the film was, given the circumstances, as good as he could have made. Violence is not attractive, and that is what Mike was trying to do with that, I know. He hated violence himself. He would never have been involved in a fight. What he was trying to do, as Siegel does and all the good ones do—unlike *The A-Team*—was, if someone is hurt, it is a horrific thing. Which is what he was aiming at, I'm sure, in *Witchfinder*. He spoke about this. It's no use saying, 'Bang, you're dead!' and they go 'Aaahhh!'...all that shit, that's a nonsense. But people do get upset. Why Alan Bennett should, I don't know. I'd have thought he was more sensible than that."

Most unusually for a film censor, John Trevelyan felt moved to justify his decision to pass the film at all, writing to *The Listener* on June 13, 1968:

"In your issue of May 30, your film reviewer criticizes this Board for pass-ing 'atrocities' in the film *Witchfinder General*. From what he writes I get the impression that he may have seen this film before substantial cuts had been made at the Board's request. Even in its cut form it remains a violent film, but the excesses of its sadistic brutality were removed before a certifi-cate was issued for it. It would be fair to the filmmaker, Michael Reeves, to say that it was his intention to show that violence was repellent, but the Board did not feel that his intention justified the exhibition of this film in its original form."

Paul Ferris offered a defense of the film's near-unrelieved intensity: "Yes, but that's what it was (in those days). What are we saying? That's not what it was at all, it was much worse. It was *much* worse!" He confirmed that Mike had not worked out his position on violence beforehand and would not have read up on the issues involved:

"No, he was no great intellectual. But, does that matter, you see, for the truth of things? Twenty-four years old, movie mad, but what he did have in him was he wanted to make good stuff to the best of his ability. Movie mad, as we all were, so in that he's a bit like Hitchcock. I don't think Hitchcock went to university first and then thought, 'Right, I'll do some movies now.' He was movie mad. It's the wrong way round. It tends to be a bit tired if you come at it literally the other way round—no passion. Mike was passion, passion, passion, movies, movies, movies."

It is fascinating, but perhaps not totally unexpected, that Alan Bennett's vitriol somewhat declined over the years. Asked if he still felt such antipathy to *Witchfinder* and whether he felt Mike's argument about shocking people into 'sickened recognition' had any validity, he replied: "It's all so long ago. I remember being very shocked by the violence of the film then. Whether I would be now is a different thing. The presentation of violence on the screen in the intervening years hasn't done much to sicken people of it, it seems to me, but the arguments on the subject are so complex I'm reluctant to get into them. I hate theorizing anyway." Ian Ogilvy, told of this response, quipped: "Has he seen *RoboCop*"? [Paul Verhoeven's extremely violent com-mercial success.]

Ian Ogilvy reiterated: "Mike was extremely generous about what Trevelyan had done to the picture. His attitude was John had simply tightened it up, he'd made it leave-it-to-your-imagination, and Mike was distraught at the idea of four minutes taken out, but when seeing it, he was as happy as a sandbag." Paul Ferris agreed that Trevelyan's interference didn't spoil the film: "I thought it improved it."

Tony Tenser commented: "I believe in some countries like Japan where they wanted the extra cuts in, they'd be put in to that negative for that country, where they'd dub it into their own language. They'd put it into the negative." This is what enabled a video company, Redemption, to patch together a restored version of *Witchfinder* in 1996, using cut-in scenes from overseas prints (not always seamlessly). The main additions to existing U.K. prints were some minor scenes of female nudity in tavern scenes, four more seconds of the pricking of Lowes, 19 more seconds of Elizabeth Clarke being lowered into the flames, additional shots of the ducking, nine seconds more of Sara being tortured by Stearne at the climax, and four more seconds of Marshall attacking Hopkins with the axe.

The move in the later years of the 20th century was toward greater censorship. Ian Ogilvy did not think Mike could have made *Witchfinder* then, but not necessarily for reasons of censor-ship: "All those sort of movies have their day, haven't they? He would love *Aliens*. *RoboCop* he would adore. Excessively violent. I think he would think they are absolutely wonderful movies. I don't see any move. They are much more violent than *Witchfinder*. More gratuitous."

There was certainly a move against violence on television then, with the appointment of William Rees-Mogg at the Broadcasting Standards Council, a conservative dubbed 'Switchfinder General' by the tabloid press! Ian Ogilvy argued: "But Mike would have hated to have worked for television. He didn't like television. He *watched* it. He'd have loved the video business. Of course, this was years before videos and things like that. He'd have had the most enormous collection of movies you'd ever seen, but I don't think he'd have liked working for television very much." Indeed, Mike was to turn down an opportunity to direct a television show, as Tom Baker will explain.

Ironically, over the years, television has occasionally butchered *Witchfinder* worse than the censors did. When Thames Television in London showed *Witchfinder* in 1983, they cut out Ian's oath of revenge, purely to fit a time slot (they later explained). Ian reacted mildly to this mutilation of his superb performance: "Well, it is kind of important that you see that I make some kind of avowal of revenge!" That scene is actually the pivot of the film, so we may suppose that Mike Reeves would have been very distressed at that.

Ian said: "Yes, he would have hated that, but then he would have hated anything that didn't make sense in telling the story. The story was very important to him. More than any moral implications or anything like that, is it a good story and will it hold an audience and is it going to be fun to make and fun to shoot and fun to watch, really." So, Mike Reeves clearly didn't want to dispense with strong narrative. Ian commented: "That was a leaf from Don Siegel's book." *Witchfinder* was actually banned at the ABC Cinema at Sale, near Manchester. Ian Ogilvy was amused looking back at that, but doubted Mike would have been amused at the time: "I think he'd have hated that."

The film is such a work of all-out passion and intensity that one almost feels the filmmaker has emptied himself into it and was left at a loss to top that. Ian challenged this view: "But it wasn't even original, that. A man wrote a book and he read the book and said, 'Oh, this would make a good film.' It's not even *his* concept, he's just read a good book, sat down and cobbled together a script and it worked!" One must also remember that Mike was pleased by the good reviews *Witchfinder* received, as evidenced by the obvious pride with which he contacted Vincent Price to show him he had been right to resist his usual mannerisms.

Ian Ogilvy confirmed that Mike showed a lot of interest in the fate of the film after making it and "was a passionate promoter of it all, really." He retained a Tigon publicity sheet for the film, on which Mike had made comments in his own hand, expressing disagreement and disapproval of much of the contents of the leaflet. Ian described Mike's inscriptions as "furious writing," even though the leaflet was "quite glossy for those days." Mike scribbled all over the story synopsis "because it's rubbish as far as he's concerned, absolute rubbish, so he scribbled all over that." It seems to have been the attempt to portray the film as a serious historical account of the Civil War period that attracted his fury, but he also fulminated at minor inaccuracies, such as the description of the character played by Wilfrid Brambell as a "horse-stealer" when he is in fact a "horse-dealer." Mike wrote, "Rubbish" beside this inaccuracy.

He also put a question mark by the names of some of the extras, and against 'Music,' 'Screenplay,' 'Producer Louis Heyward' ("Rubbish, you see," said Ian Ogilvy) and 'Co-Producer Arnold Miller' ("Arnold Miller had nothing to do with it," said Ian). Against 'Assistant Director' Mike has written, "Who?" Ian Ogilvy laughed: "All this going on. I always thought this was quite funny." A typographical error has Rupert Davies as 'Rupert Daview.' Mike has circled 'Daview' angrily and written, "Typical!" Ian commented: "He felt anything being published like that was no good being inaccurate." Indeed, Maggie Kimberley's name is spelt 'Kimberly' on the credits of the print and camera operator Gerry Anstiss is "Gerry Anstice."

Ian recalled that AIP did not know what to do with *Witchfinder*: "Their first, initial reaction was, 'My God, we've got a bloody art movie on our hands! What are we gonna do?' And they put it out as a second feature to a Tommy Sands–Annette Funicello beach movie as far as I remember." It was apparently Jim Nicholson's reaction that it was an 'art movie' rather than Sam Arkoff's. Although he admired it, he was concerned how they would be able to market it.

Tony Tenser said: "All I know is that Deke Heyward said, 'Sam thinks we've got a great winner here. He's going to change the title, because people haven't heard of Mike Reeves.' They had heard of Vincent Price and Sam wanted to have an Edgar Allan Poe connotation to it. So he used the quotation from Edgar Allan Poe and apparently *The Conqueror Worm* was a good title for America." Vincent was hired to recite at the beginning and end of the film a few lines from Poe's poem. Although Ernest Harris has recalled that Mike liked the title *The Conqueror Worm*, Mike was upset at further interference, but soon shrugged and told Ian Ogilvy: "Oh, what the hell. It's still our movie. They haven't changed that."

Vincent Price later commented:

> "They just picked a title that they thought would sell. I thought *Witchfinder General* was a wonderful title, because that's what Matthew Hopkins was, but *The Conqueror Worm* was the title of a poem by Poe, so they could sell the film as Edgar Allan Poe in America. I didn't really know where the poem came from, until one day I was rereading *Ligeia*, and in it is the poem, *The Conqueror Worm*, which I had completely forgotten about."

Undeniably, the film made a fortune in America. Ian Ogilvy recalled: "It was a sleeper. They started getting little mini-queues around the block and they realized it wasn't for Annette Funicello. It was for this really weird English film, and then they upped it and started selling it, but before that they had no idea what to do with it. None at all." Tony Tenser thought Sam Arkoff made a mistake in changing the title: "It went on the art circuit. I think if he'd have called it *Witchfinder General* to start with, he would have done better. Far better. Because *The Conqueror Worm* didn't appeal to any particular audience; the title didn't. I'm a great believer in titles. I don't say that the title makes people go and see the film, but it's a tremendous asset to a film if you've got the right title." *Variety* noted *The Conqueror Worm* "doing fairly brisk biz...$97,000 in 17 spots."

Witchfinder General was an enormous financial success and grossed over eight million pounds in its early years of release. Tony Tenser regretted that Tigon did not benefit financially to that great a degree due to AIP's share in the film: "AIP took credit for their side of it. They had Vincent Price in the Western hemisphere and they had the whole of the Western hemisphere.

They put half the money up. They did well. We did well. Yes, we had people coming to us with more deals and things like that, but mostly Mike Reeves was the beneficiary, and he was entitled to be." Mike went to visit AIP in Los Angeles to capitalize on the success and discuss possible future projects.

Chapter Eight: Yeoman's Row

"One of the perennial arguments Mike and I had was about altruism vs. selfishness. Mike said, 'All human behavior is self-interested.' And I, as a general sort of liberal student-type, would say, 'No, no, no, people are more than that, people can do things altruistically. People *can* help each other.' But Mike was insistent—and I think he may be right—that all behavior was initially motivated by self-interest. If you believe that, perhaps you do get a bit down." —Tom Baker to the author

Ian Ogilvy described the social life that centred on Yeoman's Row around this period: "There was a great long period in the '60s when we would say, 'What are we going to do tonight?' 'Oh, well, let's go round to Mike's.' You don't phone up beforehand. The door was always open. In the winter it was shut but you just pushed it. In the summer the door was wide open. And you just pushed the door and could just walk in."

Diane Ogilvy did not find it surprising that the door was left open: "It was easier than getting up and opening it. One knew that at a certain time people were going to start coming in. When I say it was open house, it was a meeting place. It was there that one met and it would always be the same people."

Some of Mike's wide circle of acquaintances in the film world would visit him there—people like Alfred Shaughnessy, Lee Marvin, and even Don Siegel. Ian Ogilvy confirmed this:

"Yes, I think he worked quite hard at it. But then I think a lot of people who pushed the door were nothing to do with it. Paul Vestey was one of those who pushed the door, Jock Russell, a great friend of his, pushed the door, their respective girlfriends, odd bods. Nicky Henson for a little bit was able to push the door. Nicky intrigued him. Nicky became for a while part of the set because of *Witchfinder.* He was my other best friend. We were, and are, bosom buddies. It was very odd but I'd always just *gone.* And we used to go out, we might get a take-away, sit around, talk, watch a movie or go out to a movie, or we'd do something like that, but we'd do it as a great group. We used to sponge off him dreadfully, because it was his house, because he was richer than any of us. We'd drink there and all the rest of it."

According to Iain Sinclair, Mike had never had a meal in his own house. Tom Baker agreed this was almost true:

"I moved into the house when Jock Russell moved off to his own house. I was given the spare bedroom and I did live there for some months at a time and I was just thinking, 'What did Annabelle as the sort of resident girlfriend think of me? Was I a bit of a pain?' And then, I thought, 'Well, there wasn't any problem in the kitchen, because no one else was ever in the kitchen!' Totally undomestic in that sense. Might have had coffee, might have had a bowl of cereal, but I don't remember any of that."

Diane Ogilvy commented:

"Mike was incredibly generous. One had to fight very hard to be able to pick up our share of the dinner bill. He knew that we were surviving on whatever Ian was earning. He would nearly always make the gesture of paying for the movie tickets. One would yearn for Thursdays, when the new movies came out. One would be eating together often during the week and he would always make the gesture, but he *knew* that we wanted to hold our heads up, as we thought we were doing. The only time I ever remember accepting any money from Mike at all was when Ian went over to pick up the award for *The Sorcerers* at the Trieste Film Festival and Mike was too ill. He was with me the weekend and he spent the whole weekend on the telephone, which did outrageous things to our telephone bill, and we did say to him, 'Yes, all right, you *can* pay for that!' Yes, he was very generous, certainly."

Tom Baker described Mike as "a phone man, always on the phone."

Mike's money did not seem to be a barrier, Diane testified: "No, he never lived a lifestyle that we couldn't keep up with, or very seldom. Perhaps with other friends one might have occasionally taken a bottle round if one was going round that often, and maybe we didn't as often as one would have done with someone that was broke or broke like we were, but I certainly remember Mike writing out a cheque for me for a million pounds once. I'm sure he hadn't got that much money in the bank, but it was a joke. I don't know where it is. I wish I'd still got it."

Paul Ferris also recalled life at the house: "We saw movies. I remember seeing *The Killers* and another Siegel film, *The Line-Up*, with Eli Wallach, about drugs in dolls, also very good. I saw that about half a dozen times. We saw *Invasion of the Body Snatchers* a few times. Nearly all the life there, whenever I was at the house, was movies. That was the all-pervading atmosphere. The music of movies, seeing of movies, talking about movies. Games. Drink. And that was about it."

Paul confirmed that Mike had no film director friends: "There was no time. I can't describe the atmosphere there, but it was incredibly intense, the whole thing. When you went there, which I did a lot, it was incredibly intense, almost always about the movies. He didn't stop to think, 'Oh, I've got to invite somebody or other round.' I mean, there just wasn't time. It was all whatever with the movies."

One might be surprised that Mike did not bring in anyone from the British film industry he admired, but Paul Ferris argued: "I don't think there was anyone he did." Yet there were other interesting filmmakers of the time like Peter Collinson, but Paul said: "I doubt if Mike would have found him interesting. He had one idol only and that was Siegel." Paul recalled too that Mike was "always talking about" Corman and trying to "turn on us lot" to him, too. He remembered Mike showing Corman's brilliant psychedelic movie *The Trip* (banned by the U.K. censors) on 16-mm at Yeoman's Row. Paul Vestey commented: "He would have been more interested in someone established, whose work was there for him to see. He might have been fairly self-involved."

Young filmmaker Michael Armstrong, another Tony Tenser discovery with *The Haunted House of Horror*, and himself a very promising talent who would make a brutal but impressive reworking of *Witchfinder General* after Mike's death, became friendly with Mike in the final months of his life. Benjamin Halligan reports that they began talking about setting up a production company together.

Paul Vestey found the atmosphere at Yeoman's Row increasingly not to his liking:

"I think it *became* intense. The first year or so, it was less so. Then I think that's exactly the time I started seeing less of him, because I do think it became rather one-track. I think I went more motor racing or whatever, and he went more film. We sort of saw each other but not every day, as it would have been before. I think I'd got to the stage of thinking, 'It's no good me being with these people who just talk about nothing but films. I must go and do more things of my own.' "

Jock Russell, who lived for a while at Yeoman's Row, was a long-time friend of Mike's, said Paul Vestey. "I think his father and Mike's father had been friends or in business or something. Jock and I were in business together for a long time. The garage I owned, we owned it jointly, back in 1965–1966. Mike must have introduced me to Jock." Again, Mike would generally talk cars with Jock rather than movies. Jock had been to Eton but was not a contemporary of Ian Ogilvy, as he was older than Ian.

Tom Baker also pictured the social scene:

> "Amos Powell, all the way from Sussex. 'Knock, knock.' 'Oh, Amos, well come in, nice to see you.' 'We've driven up.' Then, one o'clock, 'Time we went home.' Driving off. I've just got to go upstairs to go to sleep, but Amos and his girlfriend have to go off to Sussex. So, yes, people would just drift in, but that was part of the charm of it. That's the buzz. There was someone whom I remember being there a bit when I was there, but he was very much a 'yes' man and wouldn't challenge Mike on anything, would sit at Mike's feet saying how wonderful Mike was and how he was the answer to the world's cinema. Whereas the rest of us were arguing away our own corners about everything."

This is a reference to critic David Austen. "I think we overlapped a little in the house. I wasn't Mike's best friend, but I was perhaps the closest hanger-on of those years before and perhaps this bloke superceded me as the hanger-on. I remember friends Peter and Pam Fraser, they couldn't stand him. I remember when they went round once or twice, saying there was that sort of bloke, almost to suggest there was an element of flattery which the rest of us didn't give Mike at all. We didn't need to. He was the charismatic leader of the group."

Peter Fraser confirmed Tom's account:

> "I never liked the guy. He was a sycophant. Once he was saying to Mike how directors make certain kinds of movies and say certain kinds of things and praising Hawks and so on, but I think these directors were just employees. The business didn't operate in that way. I had to get up and leave. Yeoman's Row was always packed with people. It was untidy, there were stacks of papers all over the place. A lot of people there who were not friends. People who thought that Mike could do them some good. Mike wasn't stupid, he must have known that. I dropped in once at Yeoman's Row about nine and said, 'Let's go and eat,' so we went out to eat at an Angus Steak House to get some peace, the house was so full of people."

Diane Ogilvy could not agree that David Austen was sycophantic: "He wasn't a sycophant, his knowledge of movies was almost as good, if not as good, as Mike's and they enjoyed each other's company both socially and writing together. He was a good and kind friend to Mike."

As the Mike Reeves household began to attract more actors, Paul Vestey and Jock Russell felt increasingly out of things, as Paul explained: "I suppose they talked more and more about movies, and we both thought we'd better go and do something else, I think. When he was first starting, he was a lot of fun about it, when he went out to see Siegel, it was all new and he was tremendously enthusiastic. And, then, I think he got more serious, obviously because he wanted to really get on, and then he did get a bit obsessive about it all, I think." Jock Russell eventually moved out when he got married and moved to Jersey.

Betty Reeves would occasionally visit Mike, but Paul Ferris confirmed that Betty Reeves never visited the house when Mike had his friends there. She would not have appreciated the atmosphere as described by frequent visitor Diane Ogilvy:

Annabelle and Sue, wife of Jock Russell (photo: Paul Vestey)

"He had every catalogue of every movie that could be hired in London. There would be a weekend when there would be 16-mm reels all over the place. Occasionally, he'd phone up and say, 'I've got such-and-such,' to people, I suppose, or one would turn up and there would be a movie session going on. I've seen all sorts of extraordinary movies there. One never quite knew what you were going to get. *San Francisco*, that was the first movie I ever sat through at his house. He just liked movies and the better they were, the more he liked them. But, obviously, I think at that time he had a great respect for anybody who could make cheap good movies, because that was what he was going to do."

Diane confirmed that he liked Humphrey Bogart pictures, for instance: "Yes, yes, yes. He knew who wrote them, who produced them, who lit them. There wasn't anything he didn't know. He really was encyclopedic." Of Roger Corman, she said: "I think he admired him. I'm not sure how much. I knew he admired him, but Siegel was something different. He really was."

As one might expect from a man so obsessed with movies, Mike did not have many friends outside the business. Ian Ogilvy also pointed out:

"He didn't have many friends *inside* the business; he didn't have many friends. Not because he wasn't a friendly man. It's just that he was quite a shy man. His friends were school friends from the same background as him, probably from the same money as him. Paul Vestey was very rich, a member of the Vestey family. Mike had a very, very small, close circle of friends. Nicky very nearly became a good friend because of *Witchfinder*, but there was something so flamboyant about Nick that Mike loved having him round, and Nick would make him laugh a lot, but he'd take him in small doses. It was that kind of thing, and if you weren't interested in movies..."

Oddly enough, Paul Vestey and Jock Russell weren't particularly interested in movies, they were just old friends and I suppose they could talk about cars a bit. And he felt easy with them. He didn't have an enormously wide circle of friends, not at all. There was a hard core of us: me and my wife at the time Diane, Jock and Paul, Annabelle of course...Then odd bods would drift in and out."

Diane Ogilvy did not agree that Mike was shy:

"Ian is an actor, so is very used to putting himself over, so I think he thinks anybody else that isn't, and doesn't, is shy, whereas I think Mike was more retiring than Ian, but not as strong—he wasn't as good at making himself heard as Ian. He had a great understanding of people. He *could* go up there and hustle in Wardour Street, which is a tough thing to do, but he had this understanding, too. There are some things which he spoke of to me person-ally and that was because he didn't want anybody else. He didn't talk to a bunch of people. He didn't want anybody to talk about it much. So I think it will remain with me."

Nicky Henson gave his view:

"We weren't like close bosom friends, not like Ian and he obviously were, and I suppose Paul Ferris and he became very close later, because Paul was psychologically very complex as well. I just remember those evenings that he liked having me around, because he thought I was an idiot, and I could kind of sense that. I remember he had a dodgy script sent to him once, a really naff horror script. We were at Yeoman's Row and it was a really, really bad script. He said, 'I've been sent this script,' and I was so keen to do anything, I went, 'Anything in it for me?' He said, 'You want it? It's absolute rubbish.' And he gave it to me and I read it. And I read the whole script through and I read all the parts and he was crying with laughter. I've never seen anybody laughing so much, and he wouldn't let me stop! I had to read the *whole* script from beginning to end, reading *all* the parts of this terrible script."

Diane Ogilvy was there that evening: "We were all laughing so much, it was terribly, ter-ribly funny. He played every part." She agreed that Mike might have been thought boring if you weren't interested in films: "I always thought that that was why Mike and Nicky were never *great* chums. They didn't not get on, but they were not great chums because Nicky, at that time, I don't think was desperately interested in movies. He was a great theatergoer and did most of his work in theater and so there wasn't a great talking point. Nicky was and is quite knowledgeable, there's very little he doesn't see, but not in those days."

Nicky explained: "In those days I was really kind of stupid and extrovert, young and keen. It was the '60s. I didn't go to sleep in the '60s in case I missed anything. I was so overexcited and he found that terribly amusing. The more of a fool I made of myself, the more he would just sit there quietly watching this bloke make an absolute tit of himself. He just thought it was great."

Another time, Nicky commented to Jonathan Rigby (*Shivers*):

"Looking at pictures of Mike now, I'd forgotten how good-looking he was. But to us, he was a real nerd; we just thought he was the world's most un-attractive geezer and we all used to feel sorry for him. He had girlfriends

Portrait of Michael Reeves photographed by David Farrell

and all that but he was socially inept. What he did have, though, was an encyclopedic knowledge of movies, and when he walked on the set he was a completely different man. He knew exactly what he was doing and he was a wonderful referee: He'd listen to ideas from everybody."

Yeoman's Row was where Mike worked as well as entertained. Tom Baker wrote there with Mike: "Sometimes we would write at night, but we wrote pretty quick. It's not difficult to write the actual physical stuff. Not many words in a script the size of *Witchfinder*. To actually physically write it down doesn't take very long."

Diane Ogilvy described the house: "The house was a drawing room downstairs with a kitchen (if there was a dining room between the kitchen and drawing room, one never used it), then upstairs was his bedroom and bathroom. Then, on the floor above, was a spare bedroom with a separate bathroom, which Jock Russell had, and Mike's little study. It would have been built as a bedroom but was completely decorated as a study with built-in bookshelves." Diane thought Mike had all his own movie posters up in the study, either on the walls or folded away on the shelves. It was in the study that Mike wrote his scripts.

It was the success of their collaboration on *Witchfinder General* that cemented the friendship between Mike Reeves and Paul Ferris, as Paul confirmed: "Not the commercial success, because you don't know initially, do you? But it was the happiness of the collaboration. I wasn't at all happy with the music of *The Sorcerers*. I hated it. I still do. *Witchfinder* was about 60% there and he'd done a fantastic job on the film, and he was knocked out with the music. Before that, we were sort of dancing about, but after that we knew we were on the same wavelength. That's why."

Paul Ferris agreed with Nicky Henson and Ian Ogilvy that Mike Reeves wanted to have a regular team on the pictures he made:

> "He did. It's funny—just as Siegel does. You look at his films; virtually a stock company over the years. And Clint Eastwood's done virtually the same. Mike was the same. It's sensible. Movies are an enormous amount of money, which generally go wrong. You do two bombers now and you're gone. So that's what Siegel's done. Eastwood's not stupid either. Mike had picked that up: Why take chances?"

Paul, who saw *The Killers* at Mike's house only about 10 times (!), revealed that Don Siegel visited Yeoman's Row after the release of *Witchfinder General*: "After *Witchfinder*, it may have been his mother who wrote or called, but Don Siegel came over. He did contact Mike and say he was worried about his obsession with violence and that it was bad for him. I did meet him later at Annabelle's flat. He wanted me to do the music for a film which didn't happen. I'm sure it was his mother who actually contacted Siegel, because Mike was so besotted with Siegel. Siegel, for sure, was in contact with Mike. He'd seen *Witchfinder*." Paul confirmed that Siegel was impressed by *Witchfinder*: "Oh, sure, he was, he was. I saw him later in Annabelle's flat, years later." Paul found Siegel surprisingly humorous, "like Walter Matthau."

Diane Ogilvy confirmed that Siegel visited Yeoman's Row: "I remember meeting Siegel there for two minutes once. Turning up and finding out Don Siegel was there and thinking, 'Oh, we'd better move ourselves because this isn't the right time.' I remember meeting him very, very briefly." Don Siegel later recalled Mike's condition:

> "Directing is very frightening, and you physically have to be in excellent health. It's very demanding. I don't think Michael was well, with all his bouts of depression, either through drugs or whatever. I knew he took drugs. I don't know to what degree. I know he smoked pot—and why not? I know he'd had pneumonia. I think he was just terribly nervous about getting up to bat, as any person who's talented is. It's only the pods and the peasants who get up there and aren't afraid. I'm always very nervous. I always think each picture I'm going to do is the last one."

Tom Baker was there and found the evening most entertaining:

> "Don Siegel was in London and came round for a visit. It came up in conversation that Don's son had recently admitted to smoking dope and to Don saying he wished he had too, so he would be better able to tell what his son was on about. 'Well,' said Mike, 'we can help you there.' And set to roll up a joint. Don had a joint. Not that drugs were a significant part of Mike's

life at that time and certainly nothing harder than cannabis. Cigarettes and alcohol and film film film film were what drove life on. Though I think sleeping pills had already put in an appearance."

It is, of course, an amazing reversal from the time when Mike knocked on Siegel's door in Hollywood as a fan to Siegel wanting to borrow Mike's composer for one of his own films. He was also instrumental in borrowing Mike's lighting cameraman, which is a further tribute to Mike from a talent like Siegel. Johnny Coquillon, who went on to shoot Sam Peckinpah's *Straw Dogs* (a film often bracketed with *Witchfinder* in commentaries on modern screen violence), later revealed that Siegel's fascination with *Witchfinder* was what brought this about: "The film was to be a turning point in my life. Who is to know these things? About two years after the film was made, a Don Siegel in L.A. called his good friend—a Sam Peckinpah, also in L.A. —inviting him to see '...an interesting number a couple of kids have made in Britain.' The 'interesting number' was *Witchfinder*. Sam Peckinpah was about to embark on *Straw Dogs*." A great irony is that Sam Peckinpah began his career as a dialogue director for Don Siegel, just as Mike Reeves later did.

The demands of making *Witchfinder General* had put further strain on Mike's relationship with Annabelle. They had separated before the shooting. They had been having rows for some time over Mike's dedication to his work and his fear of being tied down. Paul Vestey explained: "I suppose the trouble was at that stage he was at home quite a lot with writing and whatever, and I suppose she was too. He was quite his own man, really. I think there were moments when he thought he ought to have a girlfriend, then there were moments when he sort of thought he didn't want anybody around. She just got used to him, I suppose." Paul Ferris commented: "They had terrible arguments."

Ian Ogilvy was unsure of the precise circumstances, as to whether she got fed up with the way he was treating her or just his general lifestyle:

"In those senses, he was a very private man. He'd be open to anything about movies but one never quite knew. And yet I knew him so well, and Annabelle. Annabelle had finally got bored and pissed off and Mike couldn't really understand this, which is terribly unfair on Annabelle, because he'd thrown Annabelle out about four times, and then begged her to come back. He hadn't behaved toward her terribly well. Again, we were what, 22, 23 or so. I think she just left and Mike found this very hard to take. He went into a great gloomy thing and had a minor nervous breakdown. Diane was much more around and she sort of nursed Mike a bit. I wasn't really around much. I was working. I was probably away doing a television series or something. I was away in Persia, making a movie called *The Invincible Six*—a remake of *The Magnificent Seven*, same plot with Iranian actors.

"I do think Mike's attitude to women was slightly peculiar. Not a hint of homosexuality, I'm not talking about that. I just think that he wasn't terribly easy in the company of women. I think he was happier in the company of men. But there were always very pretty women around. For instance, Dani Sheridan, who plays the singer in the nightclub that I kill in the alleyway in *The Sorcerers*. She now calls herself Sally Savalas, because she spent years with Telly Savalas and has a son by Savalas. She used to pop in around that period."

Diane Ogilvy recalled: "Mike was desperately cut-up when he and Annabelle separated and, because of my loyalty to him, I was cross with her. She probably had just as much reason to make her decision as he had to make his decision, but my loyalty was 100% with Mike." Mike's Aunt Joan commented: "I would never say that they were well-suited. He was very much in love with her, but basically I wouldn't say very well-suited." Mike's cousin Sarah agreed that Mike was terribly upset when it all finished and she went to see Annabelle, who said, "No question, it didn't work."

Baker didn't learn about the split until later: "When I got married to Bridget in November 1968, I wanted them to come to our party, and to my surprise I found that Mike had left Yeoman's Row and it took me a while to find out where he was living. I finally got through to Annabelle and then she told me they *had* split up, but that was the first I knew they had really split up. It was pretty acrimonious because Mike wouldn't come to my party, because I mentioned that Annabelle had said she was coming and he said, 'Well, I won't come if she's going to be there.' "

Diane Ogilvy did not feel that Mike was shy with women:

"No. There weren't many other girls around. Dani was around a tremendous amount in the last few months of Mike's life, in the last few months when he was living in Yeoman's Row. Then she moved in. Not to look after him. To live there. I think that Dani was all very much part of that sort of scene. That's where the nightclubbing came in. He met her through *Sorcerers*. For some time before I met him, he had an established relationship with Annabelle, which was unusual at that age. So perhaps the other young men that didn't have established relationships might have thought it a bit odd."

The enormous artistic, as well as financial, success of *Witchfinder* posed a problem for Mike as to how to follow it. Paul Ferris, then very close to Mike, described his desperation for a good subject by way of illustrating Mike's awareness of his privileged situation:

"I had no money at all, but Mike's the only one I've ever met, who has money, who felt guilty an awful lot about having money, which he did. He didn't take a holiday except from money he'd earned. Now, after we'd finished *Witchfinder*, he was desperate for a film script and he said to me at one point, 'Do you think it would be all right if I use the money to buy a good script?' Because he was also very keenly aware of the charge that had been made against him, 'It's all right for him making these movies, he's using his own money.' He was very aware that charge would be made against him.

"He asked me seriously if I thought it was morally right to buy a script. I said, 'Mike, you're kidding!,' but he never did spend the money. He was very wary about using money he hadn't specifically earned and didn't do it. I don't think he thought about politics. But of course it is politics, isn't it? What he was saying was, to me, very political. He *knew* I had no money whatsoever—from a completely working-class family. He was to all intents and purposes *loaded*, but to actually rebel against that and say, 'I don't want people to think that I've done it just because of the money, so I won't use my own money'—that is in itself political and moral. To me, he was completely without any sense of class superiority or inferiority or snobbery. He felt guilty about being privileged, which is in itself political. He wasn't a saint, but why did he say and do all that? He *did* say and do all that then, that's the point. He didn't have to. He could have said, 'Fuck you lot. Right, one is setting up one's own film company and one is going to make the films one wants to make.' He didn't."

Diane Ogilvy was in agreement with much of Paul Ferris' account:

"I was never aware of Mike ever having a holiday as such. He would certainly be leaping around but always because he would be trying to set something up. He would get on an airplane, he would pick up the telephone. I think what Mike was saying, and I think what he said often, was that he wouldn't use any of his own money on a picture, because he wanted to know that he was all right without it and could do it without it. But he certainly lived on the money. He would have had to. He exhibited absolutely no snobbery at all. He had been poor, very poor. Not poverty, of course not, but it was very much, I believe, living in the lodge gates of the rich family that lived up at the end of the drive."

Diane was not surprised that Mike asked whether he should use his money to buy a script: "I can see that he would have suffered the agonies of the damned trying to work it out. He did think about it, but, certainly by the time I met him, he'd got it all worked out. He wasn't going to use it for anything. And he wasn't extravagant."

Neither Paul Ferris nor Ian Ogilvy remembered Mike ever talking about politics. Ian said he never expressed any political leanings:

"I would imagine he was Tory. I don't remember him having any simply because, again, I can't stress too often how obsessive he was about his one subject. I even used to say to him at the time, 'You know, you would be, to somebody who's not interested in movies, quite a boring man.' He would have been quite a boring man to talk to. And if the conversation turned, well, he could talk about cars, that sort of thing. But if it went on to something he hadn't really thought about, he'd be bored very easily and want to get back to *his* subject.

"But he loved actors, because he was entranced by what they did. He didn't understand them and thought that was wonderful. He wasn't at all the sort of Hitchcockian director who despises them. He didn't despise them at all. But he loathed the theater. Hated going to the theater. 'Oh,' he said, 'something could go wrong.' He was convinced. He said, 'I can't bear the embarrassment if something goes wrong, if the actors don't triumph.' He said, 'I can't bear it.' So he *loathed* the theater. Didn't like going at all. He said, 'Films, nothing ever goes wrong in them.' It was this *safety* thing he'd got."

Nicky Henson was not one of the group who went to see movies with Mike, he explained:

"No. Because I was always in the theater and so I never did. He used to go a great deal. There was a bunch of them used to go, and they used to try and take him to the theater. He *hated* the theater. He was terrified of it. It frightened the life out of him. Because he *knew* that something could go wrong, so he couldn't relax, in case one of the actors actually dried. In a cinema, he could sit and watch it and he knew that, apart from the film breaking, nothing could go wrong, so he could just get on with coldly, analytically watching what was happening. He came to see me in the theater and he'd sit cowering in case I dried or a piece of scenery fell down or something, because he couldn't say, 'Cut!' and go again. He came to see two or three things at the Young Vic. I think he saw me in *Look Back in Anger*. I played Jimmy Porter. He certainly saw the Wakefield Nativity Plays, I don't know why—bizarre thing!"

Diane Ogilvy, who never went to the theater with Mike, said: "I would suppose that if he did go and see those, it would be because he was either thinking of casting Nicky or about to have his first meeting with him or something like that." She did not think it was just because they were friendly: "He would have had to have been backed into a corner to have gone just for that reason. It made him physically ill, the thought of anybody being up there with egg on their face because they couldn't remember what to say and nobody was going to shout, 'Cut!' "

One criticism one could levy is the lack of any political awareness or attitude in Mike's films. Ian Ogilvy said: "He wasn't interested in that at all. He was quite selfish. Of course, he might have *developed* political ideas and thoughts, but at the age of 23, his obsession was movie-making. 'Well, politics, listen, so long as they let me make good pictures...' That's really the way he was."

Yet Paul Vestey stressed Mike's great generosity: "He was certainly capable of doing almost anything, really. I don't think he was interested in money, in a funny way. I don't say he didn't want to have it—he did—but I don't think he was avaricious in any way or wanting to pile it up. The fact that he had 200,000 or 300,000 wouldn't have mattered." Paul was skeptical about Mike's supposed guilt over his wealth: "He used to buy a lot of expensive cars without feeling too guilty about it!"

Mike did feel that spending earned income was all right, according to Paul Ferris: "He told me he had only ever had one holiday and that was in the Bahamas from money he had earned, from work he had done." Tom Baker commented: "After *Witchfinder*, he went to the Caribbean a couple of times. It must have been when he split with Annabelle, because there was clearly talk of girls in the Caribbean and stuff." The letter to John Trevelyan was from Jamaica, and it seems he went to the Caribbean again with a girl after he had become ill. Peter Fraser recalled: "He actually did say he'd met some air hostess. Maybe that's where he'd been. That's what I'd do if I had the money and I was fed up because nothing was happening."

John Hall, who had once gone on a short holiday to Paris with Mike, pointed out that although Mike "wasn't averse to the company of young ladies," he "would probably talk to them about films."

Chapter Nine: Final Projects

The films are almost existential in their deadness and alienation at the soul of them.—Iain Sinclair

AIP finally recognized Mike's artistic—and, more important to them, financial—potential and offered him a number of other projects they had in development. None of these projects were, therefore, of Mike's own origination and, even if *Witchfinder* had not been either, at least he created the script with Tom Baker from scratch. Now he was being asked to direct scripts written by others, where his creative input would be limited to rewrites. Clearly, Mike Reeves flourished better under a producer like Tony Tenser, who would involve Mike in the creation of the script from the idea stage, as with the next Tigon film they would soon be preparing. It is not entirely surprising, then, that things did not work out smoothly over the AIP projects.

Mike was reportedly inundated with scripts. Deke Heyward, continuing as AIP's London Director of Overseas Production, recalled in *Filmfax*: "I gave Mike a copy of Shelley Stark's *When the Sleeper Wakes* script (from the H.G. Wells novel), which he returned furiously annotated. I never really got around to reading it as we went into meeting after meeting about *De Sade*, which he very much wanted to direct." *When the Sleeper Wakes* had been around as an AIP project since 1965 when it was going to star Vincent Price and Martha Hyer and it was even announced to the trade as 'H.G. Wells' *2267 A.D.—When the Sleeper Wakes.*'

De Sade was, of course, a film biography of the Marquis de Sade, conceived by Deke Heyward as a lucrative AIP project, but scripted by the great fantasy writer Richard Matheson. Deke told Tom Weaver (*Fangoria*) of his admiration for Mike's work:

> "He was wonderful. He saw pictures in his head, which is what good directors do; he knew what the pictures would be before he shot them. *Conqueror Worm* was made for $175,000, and it didn't look like it; at the time, it looked rich and full and complete to me. That was thanks to the genius of Michael Reeves. Michael and I started talking, post-*Conqueror Worm*, about doing *De Sade*. I had a vision of *De Sade* and I wanted to do the picture desperately, to accommodate the vision. I described scenes that I would like to have written and scenes that I'd like to have shot, and I could get very enthusiastic about them. Also, I was interested in experimenting on a number of time levels...Reeves was never really in the picture 'cause there was no script when Reeves was alive."

Mike was initially keen to make another cinematic statement about sadistic violence but this coincided with a difficult period in his personal life. The break-up with Annabelle had depressed him and he was worried that he would not be able to follow *Witchfinder* with something as good. Paul Ferris actually believed that the *De Sade* project made Mike even more depressed: "He went down and down with that damn thing. There was something sinister about the script. I read it. It was very depressing and he said everyone who had been involved with it, something bad had happened to them. Orson Welles tried to get funding for it. It could have been a great film. That script—it scared the shit out of me. Brilliant script. They killed it. He was a good writer, whoever wrote it." (Paul actually remembered the title of the script as being *Implosion*, but this was actually another script by Richard Matheson, which was never made but regarded by its author as his best; it seems therefore that Mike had a copy of *Implosion*. As it was never made, though, Paul's comments—specifically, 'They killed it'—appear to be about *De Sade*, and he simply conflated the two projects.)

AIP, however, saw *De Sade* as a great example of their "philosophy of unrequited sensationalism," as writer David Will has put it, and insisted on blood and guts and nudity. Ian Ogilvy explained that this was not what Mike wanted to do at all:

> "After *Witchfinder General*, for a start, the AIP Studios that had before thought merely, 'Well, we could use him,' wanted him to be their star director. He had endless invitations. 'Please, please, come out, come out, if you can do that, you can do it here.' But he was just being offered all the crap that he refused to shoot in *Witchfinder General*. He was offered those kind of exploitation movies. He just didn't want to do that. But he was quite pleased with the fact that all of a sudden the AIP Studios thought he was a star director. I think the chances are that all of a sudden he was quite 'hot' and all the rest of it and all he was being offered was a load of shit. And if he wanted to try and get something off the ground himself, they'd say, 'No, *we've* got something for *you*.' They wanted him to do *their* stuff and he really wanted to do his own stuff.
>
> "He used to say, 'Let's make shit, but let's make really good shit.' That's the point. He didn't want to make bad shit. And I think he thought *De Sade* was going to be bad. I think *De Sade* did affect him somehow, slightly. I never read the script. I don't know anything about it. I just have the *feeling* that he was quite affected by that. He did some location work on it, went off abroad to France or wherever it was to look for locations, and then he just walked away from it, just turned his back on it, and I'm not sure why. I never really knew."

Of course, Sade's reputation has been restored by intellectual critics as an original pre-Surrealist thinker, someone who challenged the morality and conventions of his day. His life itself was fairly harmless, it was just his writings that were controversial, so it would be possible to make an interesting film without being cheap. "But that's not what he was being asked to do," explained Ian Ogilvy; and, indeed, the film eventually made by Cy Endfield was trumpeted with a nude photo spread in *Penthouse* magazine!

As 1968 wore on, Mike's depression worsened and in the summer he had a virtual breakdown. Toward the end of the year, he went to see his doctor again and as a result, he went to a private clinic in North London, which specialized in sleep therapy. Betty visited him there while he was under heavy sedation and later recalled that he did not like it there. Part of the treatment was electroshock therapy for his anxiety.

Under the circumstances, he could not cope with the violent and depressing nature of the *De Sade* script. AIP had brought the young filmmaker Gordon Hessler in to produce the film. He reportedly had meetings with Mike in West Germany and London and he recalled in *Fangoria*:

> "*De Sade* was a film that was going to be the biggest production that they had ever made; they had asked me to produce it and Michael Reeves was going to direct it. Michael was having severe mental problems at the time. He was a wonderful man who would have been one of our most brilliant directors. I flew to England to talk with Michael about *De Sade*, but he was sick. Michael was not able to do *De Sade* because he was getting mental treatment—electric shock and all those horrible things. They put another

director, Cy Endfield, on it. I got *fired*, virtually, on that picture, and I thought my career was over."

Mike made a voluntary decision to withdraw from *De Sade* and Diane Ogilvy accompanied him when he went to tell AIP. She recalled:

> "He was really quite ill at the time, he was in hospital during the week being put to sleep and then spending weekends with us and then he went back to Yeoman's Row. He found the subject very, very depressing and was very worried about how he would cope with it mentally and I went up with him, literally because he was nervous of saying no, he wasn't going to do it. I went up with him and waited outside the office while he went inside. He went to see Deke Heyward."

Intriguingly, the film would be completed by Mike's hero Roger Corman when Cy Endfield caught flu, though Corman refused credit.

Mike was also considered for another AIP script, Robert Thom's gangster picture *Bloody Mama*, of which Diane Ogilvy remembered: "He was very excited about that, definitely. He *was* keen to do it. It was his first sort of real big-budget movie." Corman directed it after Mike's death, starring Shelley Winters, and it was one of the best of his later films.

Mike's health and well-being were increasingly an issue. Throughout his life, Mike had kept in touch with his Aunt Joan, "tremendously" in her description: "He would always ring up. I think more [often] phoned me and came to see me more than writing long letters." She testified that he remained close the last year of his life but did not burden her with his troubles, which she assumed were due to the same problems her brother Derek had had. She did, however, know that he was on medication: "That he certainly was. I think basically that was all this circulatory trouble. I don't think he ever brought me any of his problems." Mike also had full support from Betty, as always.

One interesting thing is that it seems Mike's manic depression was easily concealed, even from people who were close to him. His cousin Cherida was to say: "I firmly believe that Mike was not a manic depressive. Like all men with a mission, he thought only of the job in hand and not of himself at the time." (However, she was married and living in Costa Rica when Mike died and was out of touch with him then.)

Even Diane Ogilvy could not believe it: "I still do not believe that Mike was manic depressive. He suffered from the most awful depression and it is not at all uncommon for clinically depressed people to feel suicidal and to attempt suicide. When he was having the sleep treatment, in North London, he was allowed to come and stay with us for some weekends. The only pills he had with him were Nembutal, to help him sleep. Mike got no more elated than any one else I know that works in the film, television and theater world." It seems that Mike was more willing to confide in male friends about something so personal. Both Paul Ferris and Philip Waddilove had no doubt that Mike suffered from manic depression.

So Mike withdrew from *De Sade*, which was made by Endfield with a cast including Keir Dullea as the Marquis de Sade (Paul Ferris recalled that Orson Welles dubbed the actor 'Keir Dullea, gone tomorrow!') and John Huston, and released to zero critical acclaim. "Pretty tepid stuff" wrote Leonard Maltin (*TV Movies*).

Screenwriter Chris Wicking has recalled that Mike's pet project was a film about Christ's return to earth, which is intriguing; Peter Fraser thought this was probably just an idea. Even more intriguing, but difficult to believe, is a claim Johnny Coquillon made in 1985:

> "After the release of *Witchfinder*, Michael was swamped with scripts. Very few appealed to him and at times I dismayed at the number he rejected. In retrospect I see his point now. One subject in particular nearly happened. But

then conditions began to be imposed—script, cast, crew approvals, location approvals. Approvals here, there and everywhere—except, it seemed to Michael, to the color of the socks he wore. He could not accept and rejected the project. He went to the United States where he had spent some time at U.C.L.A. One day he called me, full of excitement. He'd found *the* story. We were going to ride around the U.S.A. (non-union), shoot in 16-mm and shoot every which way into the sun and out of the sun—on motorcycles. For the first time since *Witchfinder* Michael Reeves was excited. The lead actor was to be a long-time L.A. buddy—a completely unknown son of an actor—name of Peter Fonda. The film was to be called *Easy Rider*. It was while he was planning this movie that Michael Reeves died. I still mourn the man and miss him. Always will. One doesn't get to meet many people like him."

FOR THE FIRST TIME...
the classic tale of the restless dead and their unspeakable hungers!

EDGAR ALLAN POE'S
THE OBLONG BOX
COLOR

Vincent PRICE
Christopher LEE

Coquillon is the only person who has ever suggested a connection between Reeves and *Easy Rider*, and the chronology does not seem to hang together. Mike was still involved in post-production on *Witchfinder* when *Easy Rider* started shooting in February 1968. Tom Baker was skeptical: "It seems most improbable to me." Corman biographer Beverly Gray did not believe it, pointing out that Sam Arkoff's autobiography indicates that Dennis Hopper was the intended director from the start. It is unclear whether Mike did ever spend time at U.C.L.A. or know Peter Fonda, though with his freedom to travel he was capable of turning up in unexpected places such as La Jolla, California, and knew many of the Corman circle such as director Daniel Haller. It is strange that he would be keen on a motorcycle picture, given his fear of motorcycles. An extraordinary conundrum.

Deke Heyward persevered with Mike Reeves. One must give him his due. The next script he was offered was *The Oblong Box*, another in the interminable Edgar Allan Poe series, starring Vincent Price again and also Christopher Lee. The original script about a family curse, revenge and disfigurement, which has been described by David Pirie as "banal," was by Lawrence Huntington, and Mike set to work rewriting it, with input from David Austen. Originally, it was planned that Vincent Price would play both the brothers in the film, Sir Edward Markham (actually played in the film by Alastair Williamson) and his brother Julian. Peter Fraser said:

"*The Oblong Box* was a piece of shit. Same field, horror again. Mike wanted a change of direction. A new concept that would open a lot more doors for him. He wasn't being offered what he wanted. You can't make fantastic art out of crap. In movies, it is not so much what *happens* as how it is presented, but there is no room for you to exploit that if the material is no good and I think he felt *Oblong Box* was no good."

Mike was not, in fact, the original choice to direct. On October 16, 1968 producer Deke Heyward wrote to Vincent Price that Lawrence Huntington was going to direct, but by the time Vincent arrived in London on November 12, the picture was to be directed by Michael Reeves and Vincent had a meeting with Mike that day after costume fitting.

Ernest Harris commented: "I recall talking to both David Austen and Mike about Mike's planned version of *Oblong Box*. Mike hated the Lawrence Huntington script and had rewritten it with David Austen and Christopher Wicking and had included lots of in-jokes, such as the witch-doctor chanting an incantation which invoked the name 'Namroc, Namroc' (read it backwards) and one of Christopher Lee's entrances being preceded by the line, 'Give me another faggot for the fire.' " Ernest explained this joke: "When I first heard this joke, I'd met Lee once or twice. David Austen always used to swear that both Lee and Price were gay. He said that Mike referred to the fact they were both in *The Oblong Box* as 'Fifteen foot of faggot laid end to end.' But that sounds more like David than Mike." None of this rude schoolboy humor (Lee was certainly not gay) survived into the film.

Gordon Hessler was relieved when AIP again asked him to produce, with Mike as director. Many of the *Witchfinder General* team were reassembled in the obvious hope of emulating the success of that film (and Deke had written to Vincent, "hope we have another *Conqueror Worm* on our hands"): Vincent Price, Hilary Dwyer, Rupert Davies, Johnny Coquillon and so on. Paul Ferris stated he would have done the music if Mike had directed the film: "I'd have gone on working with Mike because I loved working with him." The film was originally going to be shot in Ireland and filming was due to begin on November 18, 1968.

However, Mike was now in a downward spiral, possibly due to taking too many prescribed pills, and could not cope. Gordon Hessler recalled that Mike was "terribly sick." Things came to a head when the weekend before shooting was to begin, Mike took four or five Nembutal capsules with some alcohol and was found unconscious at his flat—he had moved from Yeoman's Row—by his daily woman. He was rushed to the hospital and made a good recovery. Dr. Blaikie, his physician, thought it was "some form of gesture" that Mike had made on that occasion. Dr. Blaikie said: "The gestures were made to draw attention to himself because he was unable to cope." But Diane Ogilvy did not believe it was a deliberate overdose: "I can't believe he wouldn't have told me."

Chelsea News later stated: "Asked by the coroner if he was a man who made dramatic or theatrical gestures, the doctor said Mr. Reeves was very histrionic." Ian Ogilvy's view on the description of Mike as very histrionic was simply: "To a doctor, maybe. To a doctor he was histrionic." He did agree about coping, though:

> "I think he was finding it hard to cope. What he was finding it hard to cope with I don't know. Not being privy to Mike's black dog moods and not really understanding them. It's quite hard to understand why a man like that should be depressed about anything. He had all the money he needed. He had super girls. Plenty of women who found him very attractive. I slightly lost touch with him at the end. He was very close to Paul Ferris. They were doing a lot of soul-searching, drinking, and I know Diane helped him through a nasty little breakdown. I was away and I wasn't around to help at all and I would get reports from Diane saying, 'God, he's so depressed and I have to go round there and hold his head and cuddle him and things like that.' I don't know what it was about."

Patrick Curtis commented to Pete Tombs: "He was a delight to be around but he was be-devilled by something." Tom Baker agreed, telling Tombs: "He certainly became un-talkable to, or not easily sociable with. He would shut right down and that was probably about three or four months before he died."

Chris Wicking shared his memories of *The Oblong Box* with Kim Newman in the *Monthly Film Bulletin* in 1988:

> "I went into the business to direct, and was kind of side-tracked into writing. The first thing to be made was *The Oblong Box*, which was an additional

239

dialogue job. It was going to be Michael Reeves as director; I knew Michael vaguely and we had the same agent. Michael needed some extra scenes, or so they thought, and they couldn't afford anybody better, or anybody more expensive than me. It would have been several steps back for him after *Witchfinder General*, of course. They were trying to rush something into production to take advantage of Michael's talents and they had that one standing by, and I think they promised him *When the Sleeper Wakes*. Also he had a project about Christ's return to Earth now...or rather then, in 1968. *The Oblong Box* was like the carrot. But the weekend before the picture was due to start, he rang Gordon Hessler, the producer, saying, 'I just can't go ahead tomorrow.' Apparently he had all sorts of problems with doctors. He was on uppers and downers and XYZ and shock treatment, which was all pretty awful."

The immediate effect of Mike's overdose, which was generally believed to be a suicide attempt, was that AIP got cold feet and asked Gordon Hessler to replace him as director of *The Oblong Box*. Vincent Price had renewed his relationship with Mike by this point and things were now very different between them, as Vincent realized what a wonderful filmmaker Mike was:

"That poor boy! He was going to direct *The Oblong Box* and *Scream and Scream Again*. But he had this terrible problem of suicide. He tried it about four times and finally they thought they had him cured. When we got together on *The Oblong Box*, I said, 'Well, I think you were wonderful. You made a marvelous picture. Now let's get along on this one...' We got along very well during the preparation. But when we started to do the costume tests, he tried it again—I was told—and the company couldn't afford to take the chance. They just said, 'He's too unstable.' It was a shame. He couldn't control himself. He was on the flip and then his girlfriend ditched him because she couldn't put up with him. He was just completely determined to destroy himself."

Mike walked off *The Oblong Box* the day before shooting commenced on November 20, 1968. Ernest Harris stated: "I would agree with Vincent that Mike was replaced on *Oblong Box* because of his first overdose. This was confirmed to me at the time by Dennison Thornton, who was doing AIP's publicity, who told me that Mike was 'going the right way about wrecking his career.' I am sure that Mike never directed any scenes on *Oblong Box*."

Gordon Hessler now took hold of the production and abandoned plans to film in Ireland. He revamped the script with Christopher Wicking, to whom Mike introduced him. Wicking wrote additional dialogue for Vincent to improve his role. Mike's contributions were abandoned and he received no credit on the finished film. The production moved to Shepperton Studios in Middlesex. Gordon Hessler recalled: "AIP was so worried about their big production *De Sade* that they didn't pay any attention to us. We just made the film we wanted to make, they were very happy with it and we got a contract to make another three pictures."

Although he had been replaced, Mike did visit the set at Shepperton in the early days of filming, which may seem odd, but Ernest Harris, who was invited along to Shepperton by Mike to observe the production on one occasion, said: "I suspect that he was not entirely unhappy to be disassociated with the script." Ernest in fact visited the film set twice. The first time was actually at the invitation of Vincent Price, who invited him and his girlfriend Jean to the set of all his British pictures. After the overdose incident, Mike telephoned Ernest and said he had not been very well, but did not elaborate. Ernest thought that, as they were not close friends, Mike wanted to play it down and didn't want to discuss it. He told Ernest he was going to the *Oblong*

Michael Reeves planned to visit Vincent Price on the set of *The Oblong Box*.
Box set to see Gordon Hessler. Ernest told him he'd been invited down by Vincent and Mike said he'd see him there.

Ernest recalled:

> "We got to the studio only to find that Vincent wasn't there that day. As we knew nobody else on the set (except a passing acquaintance with Chris Lee), we decided to leave. Before we did so, Mike turned up and took us onto the sound stage where he introduced us to Gordon Hessler, who was kind enough to invite us to stay and watch the shooting. Also present at the time were Sally Geeson, Chris Lee, Alastair Williamson and David Lodge (the latter was visiting to have lunch with Lee). After lunch, Jean and I joined Mike and Chris Lee in a quiet corner—we were later joined by Sally Geeson—where we chatted about movies (Lee, of course, chatted about Lee). Sally Geeson was falling asleep. The tea lady said, 'Poor love, she must be bored stiff.'
>
> "Mike didn't particularly like Chris Lee and got up and left. I recall that after Mike left, we stayed on for a while and Lee, not realizing that we knew Mike, made some quite rude remarks about him to the effect that he (meaning Mike) thought he knew everything and that he had actually done very little of value on *Castle of the Living Dead*, yet was taking credit for it to further his career. This was, of course, nonsense. Certainly, Mike never claimed any credit for the finished *Living Dead* while I was around. I got the impression that he had generally helped out during a chaotic situation—maybe doing a bit of rewriting and second unit work. My later brief conversation with Maslansky certainly suggests that whatever his contribution was, it was of value and was appreciated. Lee is often happy to run down others, while promoting himself (ad nauseam). When we pointed out that, on the contrary, Mike had never tried to claim any credit for *Castle of the Living Dead*, Lee didn't like it, said, 'Oh, you would know, would you?' and tried to change

the subject...My impression of Mike on that day was that he was relaxed and happy and certainly not sorry to be off *Oblong Box*. My girlfriend Jean, however, tells me that her most vivid memory of Mike on that day was that when she shook his hand, he felt terribly weak and ill— 'like a twig.' At the time Mike was talking about future, more personal projects.

"The second time we went, it just seemed there was absolute chaos on the set. One of the cameras came down some stairs and crashed through a wall. They were doing a scene with Rupert Davies in his studio. They must have done it 20 times, over and over again, and everybody was getting really fed up. Vincent Price had just heard that Fred Clark, the actor, had died. He was a friend of Vincent's and he was pretty upset. He'd just had news of his death. We were talking to Gordon Hessler about the art of movies and Gordon said, 'Oh, I don't think there's ever been any artistic movies.' Vincent just looked at me and rolled his eyes and he said, 'Oh now, come on, Gordon!' And he said, 'Well, unless you count the Olivier films,' and I thought, 'It's the old English thing that you equate quality with content.' In other words, it can only be art if it's filming some other art. Vincent was a lovely man, one of the nicest people I've ever met."

The Oblong Box emerged, predictably, as a very average Hammer-style horror movie, entirely lacking in Mike Reeves' intense vision of evil, and certainly no successor to *Witchfinder General* despite some of the same cast and crew. But producers would continue for a couple of years to try to plunder the *Witchfinder* gold mine with rip-offs like *Mark of the Devil, Cry of the Banshee, Mark of the Devil II* and *Blood on Satan's Claw*. One of the better rip-offs was the great Jess Franco's *The Bloody Judge*, a biography of the "Hanging Judge," Judge Jeffreys, played by Christopher Lee. Jess Franco confirmed that he had seen *Witchfinder General* before making *The Bloody Judge* and had admired Mike Reeves' work: "Of course. He was the *first*! But the producer said he wanted it (*The Bloody Judge*) to be more *historical*." Some shots are almost a direct copy of *Witchfinder*, but even the talented Jess Franco could not equal Mike's masterpiece.

When one looks at *The Oblong Box* and *De Sade* as finally made by others, they are both mediocre films and it is hard to imagine how Mike could have transformed the material. Perhaps it was the realization that he couldn't that led to his willing abandonment of them. Paul Ferris was unsure how Mike would have coped with directing a big flop at this stage: "Maybe that's what he was afraid of. He was not lacking in self-confidence, but he didn't have the fantastic natural ebullience of someone like Orson Welles, and even *he* went slowly down after that (*Citizen Kane*)."

According to Vincent Price, AIP also had Mike in mind to direct *Scream and Scream Again*, a horror fantasy written by Chris Wicking which was a distinct improvement on *The Oblong Box*—it was not another Poe adaptation—and brought plaudits to Gordon Hessler when he eventually directed the film. Based on a novel by pulp writer Peter Saxon, the original script was by Milton Subotsky but was not to Hessler's liking and Chris Wicking completely rewrote it. Vincent said of Mike: "I had looked forward to knowing him better on *Scream and Scream Again*, etc."

It is a pity that AIP was not more sensitive to Mike's artistry; as Diane Ogilvy has pointed out, they did not know what they had. With AIP's backing, Mike might have cranked out pictures like a British version of the young Roger Corman. Ian Ogilvy agreed:

"Oh, yes, he would have cranked them out. He didn't want not to be making movies, but the fact was that he was doing it on his own reputation as opposed to anything else. We didn't have an AIP over here and, of course, when AIP did discover him, they wanted him to crank out movies along the lines of *De Sade*. They'd gone downhill then. And he didn't really want to make Edgar Allan Poe pictures, but they'd finished, and they wanted him to make sleaze pictures, really. He just didn't want to know. So, all of a sudden, he had backing. He had people wanting him to make pictures, but they were *too* far that way. They were just tacky. I think that's what he felt about the *De Sade* script and the whole atmosphere. AIP just wanted a lot of naked girls and a lot of screaming. That's all they wanted and he just didn't want to do that. Because, although he was accused of gratuitous violence, he would always draw the line somewhere."

Unfortunately, the prospect of a major British film company like Rank funding a movie-maker like Mike Reeves was beyond the pale, even in the late '60s. Ian Ogilvy commented:

"They wouldn't have much call for him. But, again, he *was* aiming for that. Steve McQueen made a film called *The Blob*. There's no *shame* in doing this, because we're doing them as well as we can, but he said, 'The point is, the day will come when I've got enough reputation for being a very successful filmmaker in financial terms—and, with any luck, they like the pictures as well—that I'll get these things and we can break out of it.'

"But he didn't see any way of sitting down and writing a script—apart from *All the Little Animals*, which he was very, very enthusiastic about, and I can understand why, because he didn't really need a script, he could just start on Page One and shoot it—he didn't see how he could *guarantee* to make money. That's what he wanted. He wanted to guarantee the producers to make money. *Guarantee*. Back in the early days. Later on he'd have relaxed a bit. And indeed the whole idea of making *All the Little Animals* meant that he must have relaxed, because there was no guarantee of making any money on that. Small-budget picture again."

In this vein, Mike explained to *Penthouse*: "I worked with Don Siegel in Hollywood and I guess he's my great god. Followed by Roger Corman. I admit I'm all for commercial films. If you don't make money you can't make your next film. But there's no reason why successful films shouldn't be good ones."

Similarly, he told *Vogue* magazine around the same time: "Too many people now want to be a film director rather than direct films. One's ambition should be to establish a reputation for professionalism and establish one's freedom that way."

During the trip to Shepperton Studios, Mike told Ernest Harris of a script he was writing called *Razor*. Diane Ogilvy remembered Mike talking about it and he did actually mention it to *Penthouse*, which reported: "He plans to shoot *Razor* with a new company formed by himself, composer Paul Ferris, and actor Ian Ogilvy, in October...His next film is going to be more of a thriller." This film later meant nothing to Ian Ogilvy nor to Paul Ferris, who also both had no knowledge of a production company, other than as Paul reported: "All he said to me was, 'We must form a company together.' "

Presumably, Michael Armstrong would have been involved too. Paul stressed that Mike's motive was greater control over the pictures and not financial: "Mike had no interest in money whatsoever, of making money for himself. I never have." As for *Razor*, Ernest Harris remembered: "He told me how he planned the title shot: a flesh-colored screen, an open razor slashes across, seemingly cutting the screen. Blood begins to seep through and form the word RAZOR. I can't swear to the subject matter but think it may have featured a psychopathic lesbian." This does seem to confirm Paul Ferris' belief that the intense Mike Reeves vision would still have come out in a non-horror thriller: "I'm sure it would have come out. I'm sure."

Ian Ogilvy confirmed that *Razor* "means absolutely nothing to me at all" and denied that he was consulted about having a production company: "He might have had it in mind vaguely. But the one thing I knew he was much more interested in was this *All the Little Animals* and, indeed, when I worked with Arthur Lowe *years* later when we did the film of *No Sex Please, We're Brit-ish*, he suddenly said to me, 'My God, Mike asked me to do that. Whatever's happened to that picture?' And I couldn't tell him."

Arthur Lowe had agreed to play the lead if the finances were raised. Writer/producer Philip Mackie of Granada Television did approach Mike via Ian Ogilvy about making the film for its new film division, but Mike discovered that the rights to Walker Hamilton's novel had already been acquired. Ian knew Mackie because he had starred in Mackie's amusing television series *The Liars*. Discussions between Mike and Mackie went on for some time. Mike prepared a treatment and both men scouted locations, but the film never came off. At the end of the day, the bizarre subject matter was too uncommercial; indeed, when it was finally filmed nearly 30 years later by Jeremy Thomas, it was not well received by critics or public.

And they all lived happily ever after, whenever possible.

COLUMBIA PICTURES Presents The WHITNEY WADDILOVE Production of a ROBERT ELLIS MILLER film

The Buttercup Chain

HYWEL BENNETT · LEIGH TAYLOR-YOUNG · JANE ASHER
SVEN-BERTIL TAUBE · CLIVE REVILL as "GEORGE" Music composed by ROBERT RICHARD BENNETT

Mike, of course, had other films to turn to. Diane Ogilvy commented: "He was always going on about Westerns, big machin-ery movies, he was going to do it all: I wish he'd made *All the Little Animals*." Another film Mike was very keen to make was *The Buttercup Chain*, which was later made by Robert Ellis Miller. Philip Waddilove owned the rights to the book and promised Mike he would direct it. Philip had married Susi shortly after the end of filming *Witchfinder*, even using the unit catering and publicists. Mike attended the wedding. Philip chose *The Buttercup Chain* as his next project. "He was *most* excited about that," recalled Paul Ferris. "It wasn't a bad script. The film I thought was awful. I saw a bit of it. Twaddle. But the script was better than the film. I was going to do the music. No big deal to me yes or no, but it was important to Mike."

Ian Ogilvy remembered Mike telling a story of how he tried to get Columbia Pictures to back it and said this illustrated Mike's pitch to producers:

"I think his main thing was, 'Look, I make pictures that make money for no money. I'm not going to cost you very much.' Mike had *The Buttercup Chain* at one point and he went to Columbia with it. He said, 'Here's the book' and all the rest of it. And they said, 'How much?' This is Mike Reeves' story. And he said 'Oh, 750,000 pounds. Quite a lot.' And Columbia said, 'I'm terribly sorry. We don't *make* pictures for that sort of money.' Mike said, 'What do you mean?' They said, 'Well, you know, three million.' And he said, 'I couldn't use three million. This is a very small story.' They said, 'Well, I'm sorry, we're not interested. *You've* come *here*.' And he came back and he said, 'I just can't believe that attitude. It's just potty, isn't it?' And the picture eventually got made, probably for *five* million. But Mike could have made it for 750,000."

Ian did not think Mike dressed up—in business suit and tie—when he went to see potential backers like Columbia: "I don't remember Mike dressing formally for business meetings. He didn't wear clothes particularly well and wasn't interested in them—they were just things that kept you warm and modest. We *all* wore ties more often than we do now. I have photographs of myself at RADA as a student, wearing a tie. I suspect Mike would have made an attempt to spruce up a bit. The attempt would have failed." Diane Ogilvy agreed: "He would have put a tie on if he'd thought he had to, but it wouldn't have gone with anything. It would have been enough to have got into the dining room or whatever would have been required."

Paul Ferris recalled that the business of Mike directing *The Buttercup Chain* "went on, it seemed to me, for a long time." Then Philip Waddilove bowed to pressure to do the film with the older, more experienced Miller and, according to Paul, "dropped Mike at the last moment and that knocked him right down." Philip Waddilove did not remember it quite that way, though he did tell Bill Kelley that Mike was "terribly depressed about losing that."

Philip's memoirs explain the background to Mike losing *The Buttercup Chain*:

> "Production work on *Witchfinder General* accounted for almost 12 months of my life. Soon after the last day of principal photography on *Witchfinder*, John Whitney suggested that he and I team up again to produce a movie. He had read Janice Elliott's novel *The Buttercup Chain* and had heard from his agent that Columbia Pictures might be interested in making it as a motion picture. He asked me to read the novel and to give my opinion on it. Soon after doing so, and after both of us agreed that it would make an excellent movie, we jointly purchased the rights. Within weeks, we were invited to meet with Columbia Pictures executives at their offices on Wardour Street to discuss the possibility of our producing the movie under the Columbia Pictures banner. Our meeting took place in Maxwell Setton's elegant office suite and was the first of what were to become regular early-evening appointments. Max, a Hungarian expatriate ex-film producer, led the somewhat eclectic studio team to whom John and I would be responsible. The other team members were ex-actor John Van Eyssen, David Niven, Jr., son of the actor, and Erika Lees, their attractive story editor. We were also introduced to Kenneth Maidment, Columbia's low-profile managing director, who came by to greet us. Then, as John and I were invited to seat ourselves on the opulent office settee, we were each handed gin and tonics from the drinks cabinet.
>
> "From across his large mahogany antique desk, Max beamed at us and, in his cultured Hungarian accent, opened the meeting: 'OK boys—let's see your list of writers!' John and I glanced at each other nervously. We had already agreed between ourselves that Peter Draper, an extremely successful television writer who had worked with John on *The Plane Makers*, would write the screenplay. 'Well, Max,' I stammered, 'we don't actually have a list, because John and I are pretty well committed to Peter Draper...Peter's brilliant...Oh, and we're hoping we can persuade Michael Reeves who's just finished shooting *Witchfinder General* to direct for us.' My pronouncements met with horrified stares. 'Draper's only written for television, and nobody's seen *Witchfinder General* yet,' Max growled at us. 'Anyway, Michael's not ready to direct a two-million-dollar movie. Have you boys thought about Jack Clayton?'
>
> " 'But, Max,' I responded, delicately ignoring his question, 'John and I believe that with Michael directing, we can produce the movie for one million dollars.'...I anticipated a warm reception to my statement but my words went down like a lead balloon."

Philip and John decided to dig in their heels about Peter and then fight for Michael. Eventually, Columbia agreed to use Peter:

"While Peter had been busy writing the first draft, John and I had spent considerable time with Michael Reeves, consulting with him on many aspects of the production. By then, *Witchfinder General* had opened to considerable critical and popular acclaim plus healthy box-office figures. We therefore believed that we would now be able to convince the Columbia Pictures executives that Michael was the right choice to direct our picture. From Michael's point of view, it was also his first chance to break into big-time movie-making and escape from low-budget horror films. At my urging, John agreed that we would dig in our heels at Columbia believing that, with Michael, we could repeat our coup with Peter Draper.

"However, it would take almost nine frustrating months before John and I finally signed a director. Despite the fact that we had persuaded Ken Maidment and his figure-crunching production department that our one- million-dollar budget with Michael Reeves directing was feasible, Max Setton and his colleagues wouldn't agree. Their total filmmaking budget for the U.K. that year was 10 million dollars, but they didn't want to make 10 one-million-dollar films—they wanted to make five two-million-dollar ones for half the effort. More realistic than us, Michael finally told John and me that Columbia would never relent on our hiring him, and that we should now accept the fact. He also told his agent to call Columbia and confirm formally that he no longer wished to be considered for the job."

Directors then considered were John Schlesinger, Roman Polanski, Brian G. Hutton, and Robert Ellis Miller, who got the job.

Philip had also begun looking for his cast:

"The first actress who came into our sights was Raquel Welch. This came about because Michael Reeves had been a guest at her wedding to producer Patrick Curtis some months previously. While he was still officially with our project, Michael had told Raquel about the film and had slipped her a copy of the screenplay. She loved the material...However, the Wardour Street gang responded to our submission with absolute derision!"

Mike clearly had a problem in following *Witchfinder General* and Ian, Diane and Paul Ferris all felt this had a lot to do with the depression he fell into. One wonders what his next film would have been like. Paul Ferris speculated:

"Well, it may have been awful. Where do you go from there, you see? What Mike wanted, I think, was a damned good thriller. He nearly made that *Buttercup Chain* and he was depressed, I think, mainly because Philip Waddilove let him down and promised him until the last moment. That was just personal let-down. And this *Implosion*...I think he actually didn't know where the hell to go from *Witchfinder*. He may have felt himself it was it. I think he did in a way, you know. It was weird. He was terrified of the next one. Absolutely terrified of where to go from *Witchfinder*."

Mike didn't want to make a flop, recalled Paul:

"He said that. We had many conversations about that, and he's right. They're horribly expensive things to make. What's the point of making them in exile, make one and then nothing? And he wasn't pretentious, artistically. You can say he wasn't very deep, at least verbally, philosophically. That doesn't mean someone isn't there instinctually, which I think he was. He didn't say so. What he said was, 'I want to make commercially successful movies.' He wanted to be known as a great commercial filmmaker like Don Siegel."

Ian Ogilvy thought Mike's inability to get backing for *All the Little Animals* also depressed him. Nicky Henson commented:

> "He couldn't get that together, but that was a very difficult subject to get a picture going, and I think he would have gone to America. I think he'd have worked in America because they actually appreciated filmmakers there at that time. In this country at that time we're talking of, it's the crumbling of that last kind of '60s resurgence in the film industry, and they were only interested in things like *The Oblong Box* and stuff like that. But, in America, he would have made proper movies, because he wanted to make proper movies. He didn't want to make shit. If he'd held his act together, we'd all be film stars! I can't believe it! He'd have taken us all out with him."

Paul Vestey agreed: "Mike was very sort of loyal like that, in a funny sort of way; if he liked someone, rather like Tom Baker I suppose, they'd certainly be put in everything or asked to help or whatever. I think he liked having people he knew around him."

Ian Ogilvy did not think Mike's depression was mainly to do with personal problems such as the break-up with Annabelle:

> "No, I think he had a certain fear. John Russell Taylor wrote, I think, four columns on *Witchfinder General* and gave the new Bond picture, I think, four lines, and Mike got frightened, I think. He said, 'You know, they're starting to call me genius, and it's very nice, but really it's a bit stupid, and I'm getting frightened. I think I'm going to have the most terrible crash one of these days.' I don't know where it came from, but I certainly think he began to query his own mortality and he got rather fearful about death and the meaning of life, which is where he and I parted company. Not in any unfriendly way, but if Mike wanted to talk about that, I didn't want to know. I'm a cheerful sort of chap and I couldn't really help him.
>
> "This is where he and Paul got to be very friendly. He and Paul Ferris, who always had that same sort of slightly Celtic melancholic streak about him. But what his depression was about...? He was always mildly depressed, oddly enough, about having all this money. He said, 'You don't understand the problems that are attached to it.' I said, 'Give it to me, see if I've got problems.' Annabelle leaving; the fact that he couldn't quite get himself together on the pictures. I really don't know the answer to what it was about. I think maybe it was just a natural depression. He could be very depressed, Mike."

Ian was sure Mike was determined to escape into quality films and the fact that he was only being offered horror was depressing him:

> "He would have left all that behind, you see. He always said, 'The only reason we're making these pictures is we can raise the money on them easily and we can sell them easily and by doing that I'm going to get myself a reputation as a man who makes money. Now the moment you make money, people offer you other films. The trick is to try to get them to offer you things other than horror movies.' That was his big thing. He wanted people to say, 'Use Mike

Reeves, he comes in, he does small-budget pictures and they make a fortune and they look good.' And he said, 'Slowly I can build my reputation up until one day we can really make the art movies. We can really make the movies we want to make.' He used to say, 'We'll make the art movie later on.' He didn't want to push that at the backers yet. He wanted to have a reputation as a money-maker. Yet Nicholson of AIP thought *Witchfinder* was an art movie. Mike laughed at the idea that *Witchfinder* was an art movie. It was a Western, a revenge Western."

Paul Ferris illustrated something of the nature of the suffering manic depression can impose and how this shared experience drew him and Mike closer together:

"In that period after *Witchfinder General*, I had also tried to commit suicide. It's of no interest, except that it matters in understanding Mike and that he *knew*. I just wanted to stop living. Obviously, I was in a terrible down, and took elaborate precautions to kill myself, which I was actually looking forward to. It sounds crazy, but it's true. I went up to Hyde Park. I was happy. It was a sunny day. I could see the trees, which I love. I went back to my flat on the second floor in Broadwalk Court in Palace Gardens Terrace and took 60 Mandrax ground up in milk to kill myself. I'd told everybody else I'd be away for the weekend and drank this stuff. The mistake I made—or *not* mistake—I left the door open. It was a bedsitter, kitchen, balcony, hallway and bathroom. Susan Waddilove, Philip's wife, came by about two days later. I'd left the door open, otherwise she'd never have heard me breathing. I was off the bed, lying on the floor, and they whipped me into hospital. I was in there for two and a half months and Mike came to the hospital. And we made a joke: We made a bet as to who was going to kill themselves first. 'Gruesome luck,' he said that."

Michael Reeves suffered another drug overdose in December. Paul Ferris commented that he thought, in retrospect, that his depression could have affected Mike and contributed to his gloom:

"I'd just get depressed about the world being unfair. Mike was of the same cast of mind. When the depression comes on you, it's not something you can reason your way out of, so I damn well know that he would have killed himself at some time anyway, as I tried to. It grabs hold of you and you go down. Mike went down. He was depressed with, first of all, losing *The Buttercup Chain*. He was also worried, just as you are with any work you do, that he wouldn't be able to do it again. He was terrified of that. His next one had to be the right one. I'm sure that's a lot to do with it, too."

The deepening friendship led to an extraordinary gesture on Mike's part, which Paul revealed:

"When I came out of hospital, I was going to get married for the first time. Mike took us to the Carlton Tower Hotel. I was tired of living in Broadwalk Court and London generally. I wanted to move and live in the countryside. I had my eye on a house in Hedley, Hampshire, which was then £6,700 and something. He took us along to the Carlton Tower and we had dinner there. He said, 'How are you going to buy the house?' I said, 'Well, a mortgage, usual way.' 'How much is it?' I told him. He brought out a cheque book and said, 'I want you to have this as a wedding present.' I said 'Whoa, stop right there.' He said, 'No, look, got tons of it, I want to give it to you.' And I couldn't accept it. It's now probably £200,000 that he was going to give us.

"It absolutely knocked me sideways. I was too mean-spirited to accept it. It takes a hell of a thing to give that, but to actually accept it is a hell of a damn thing and I refused point blank. He was absolutely choked. I hurt him by not accepting it. Hurt him a lot. We had this argument. He said, 'You damn well know I can afford it and you won't accept it. Why?' Pure pride, nothing else. Not largesse of spirit, just silly pride, and I know that hurt him, because what I'd said was locking him out, because we did love each other. We both know he's loaded and he knows I need a house which he can easily afford. It wasn't as though it was all of his money. He knew that I knew what the percentages were. I think he also for sure thought I was an obstinate sod and I've always regretted that I didn't have the grace to accept it. He was right and I've always regretted it."

Diane Ogilvy commented: "He made these sort of generous gestures to anybody that was down and out. I don't know anybody who picked him up on it."

On the other hand, his social circle was beginning to include people outside the film business who were simply out for a good time at Yeoman's Row. Diane recalled: "After Annabelle left, he was mixing then some of the time with very different people that I didn't have much interest in. He was a nightbird. My opinion was that there were a lot of people wanting to stay in the house. Mike had a cheque book that seemed to go on for ever. That's one of the reasons his mother desperately encouraged him to sell the house."

Paul Ferris agreed, remembering a wealthy aristocrat and playboy: "William Piggott-Brown, he was there. Mike hated him." He said Mike found him priggish and had no time for these people who did nothing and swanned around with the attitude, 'I've got the money.'

Mike went to stay with Betty for Christmas 1968 and brought with him what he called his collection of pills. As a result of taking some of the pills, he slept for the greater part of the Christmas holiday. Betty was alarmed and wrote to his psychiatrist and said she thought her son was taking too many pills and they were making him increasingly depressed. She kept Mike's problems to herself in every other way. Diane Ogilvy said: "She was the sort of woman, she wouldn't have kept it *secret*, it wouldn't have been talked about. That very aristocratic type of English society."

Virginia Scholte saw Mike the summer of his nervous breakdown and observed: "Almost the last thing I remember about Mike is staying with Aunt Betty one summer when they'd moved to Little Bealings. I'd married Owen and we had the other little boys. Mike was going through a nervous breakdown at the time and he was there. He was just dreadful. He'd just sit at the table and wouldn't eat anything and he'd smoke endlessly. Not drink, but smoke. Or lie upstairs in a sort of depression. In a dreadful state. Ghastly. He couldn't speak."

Paul Ferris recalled Mike's period of decline and said he was drinking "a lot" and did concede his death "could have been a mistake" due to his drinking. He described the unhappy treatment Mike received in the private clinic: "There was an Australian girl, dark-haired, on the nursing staff, who tried to get him to sign a covenant to the hospital. She went round to the flat a few times—that's why we got him out, because Mrs. Reeves found out too. There was a girl trying to recruit donations. She was a nurse pretending to be a patient."

Paul knew because he had seen her working at the home. "That's what crunched it. She turned up at the flat, still pretending to be a patient, when we knew she was a nurse. That's when all the alarm bells went." Mike suggested to Paul that he should perhaps make a covenant to the home. Paul was appalled and realized that she had been persuading him. Mike said lots of people made a covenant and that it was a good idea.

It was clear to Paul that Mike was being fleeced: "I couldn't even talk to the doctor there about what was going on. I could just feel it was all wrong. Pile of pills by his bed and the place was in shit order. His mother took him out of the hospital in North London, which was awful and cost a damn fortune a week. They gave him pills and pills and the weekend we took him out, the man was going, 'Oh, he's got to be in here for at least a year,' and all he was thinking was money, you could see it. His mother knew it. We took him out and put him in a flat."

The flat was on an upper floor at Cadogan Place Court, 19 Cadogan Place (number six), opposite one of Mike's favorite haunts, the Carlton Tower Hotel. It was rented. The Yeoman's Row house was sold. Paul Ferris said: "His mother wanted him in a flat, away from Yeoman's Row and all the people." Paul Vestey agreed:

> "His mother was always very worried about him. I think she thought film people were a bad influence, not suitable at all. I do remember talking to him about it and I do know that he sold the house, really, because he had a number of hangers-on that he found difficult to get rid of or to keep at arm's length, so I think it was thought easier to sell the place and go somewhere else. I think he thought a flat would be a better idea, because it was more sort of anonymous."

Iain Sinclair said to Pete Tombs: "I think he felt that he was responsible suddenly for this whole crew of other people and he wanted to push them back." Diane Ogilvy linked the move to Annabelle too: "I thought it was because he was trying to get rid of a whole lot of unhappy memories that he wanted to put behind him."

Paul Vestey agreed that Yeoman's Row had become open house: "People were wandering in and out and I think there were beginning to be people who were taking advantage. I don't know who they were." John Hall felt Mike never knew how to say "no." There does not seem to have been any suggestion of a flat being easier for a single man to manage, given that Annabelle had left, if only because Paul Vestey said he "can't imagine Mike managing anything himself" and the flat was almost as big as the house. Nevertheless, the strategy worked insofar as people did not call round as much, as Diane Ogilvy testified: "Not as much, no. I think there probably was about the same amount of room, but certainly not all the extra bedrooms."

Paul Vestey did not go round there terribly often: "I probably only went round there half a dozen times or something. I used to go round and have a drink and then we'd wander over to the Carlton Tower and have dinner." Paul remembered the flat was on the third or fourth floor and recalled the exterior's "strange sort of Tudor architecture." Peter Fraser said it was a "completely different" atmosphere to Yeoman's Row. Only Mike was there, no one else, it was decorated in a "laid back, upper class" style, quiet, neat and tidy, unlike the chaos at Yeoman's Row.

Mike had had just the one session of electroshock treatment to cure his depression. Paul Ferris recalled one effect of it: "What it did, apart from anything else, was it gave him the most awful stutter. Terrible stutter at the end there, after the shocks. Talking about horror, that to me is horrific. It's wrong, whatever the troubles are. Criminal, for Christ's sake. Mike ended up with a most awful stutter. He could hardly speak back in that flat." Nicky Henson remembered seeing the marks on the side of Mike's head after the treatment, and Diane Ogilvy just remembered that he was "very miserable and he was being a bit stuttery."

Mike's next picture for Tony Tenser in fulfilment of his Tigon contract was a surprising choice, an IRA thriller originally to be made at British studios and on location in Southern Ireland! Tony dreamt up both the idea and the title, which he considered commercial: *O'Hooligan's Mob.* Ian Ogilvy found it a very amusing title. Tony Tenser told the story:

> "Mike and I were working on *O'Hooligan's Mob* straight after *Witchfinder.* As long as he did one film a year for me, he could do the other films. I had the idea of doing *O'Hooligan's Mob* and Mike had this chap Amos Powell

who wrote a precis of it. Mike liked it and I liked it. We then did a long precis, almost at the script stage. It was a good title, I thought. One of my fortes was titles. Mike cowrote the script with Amos Powell, a very good writer he brought in.

"It was about a nonpolitical young fellow who joined the then-IRA and he got involved in it. He was a farmer's boy. There was some gun-running and he got involved in that. The Black-and-Tan were after him. Then he was going to be publicly executed by firing squad. I can't remember the ending of the film, but he managed to free himself, got out a machine gun and shot as many people as he could before he was gunned down, shouting, 'Long live Ireland!' or something like that. Mike had arranged to send a second unit out to Dublin to find locations. We saw an old prison there which we were going to use. There was going to be a part for Ian Ogilvy in it. I don't think he was playing the lead. I think he was playing the part of his friend. It was too flamboyant a part for Ian Ogilvy. Although he could act the part, his presence wouldn't be believable. It was more of a Nicky Henson part. We were going to get a name in it.

"We were then going to start to put the money together to make it. It was going to be like another *Witchfinder General*, but modern and dealing with the Irish problem as it was at the time. This was before we had all these terrible happenings. It jumped the gun, because the film had machine guns blazing and explosions and a firing squad. It would have been a highly successful, high-quality film with a lot of action. It was going to be a bigger film than *Witchfinder General* in money and budget and scope, because there were things in a film of *Witchfinder*'s nature where you could cheat. You could get a sack and cut holes in it and it could be a smock for somebody. In a modern film, you'd have to have traffic, you'd have to have taxis and buses and cars. It's got to be more real.

"So then, it would have had to have been a bigger budget. We were going to get American International. I had already discussed possibilities with them and we were going to go from there. We didn't even have a full, proper working script on it, but I had a series of pictures taken on the locations where we were going. We were also doing a deal with Ardmore Studios. I went over there. I was treated quite well. I was met and taken to this big hotel in Dublin. I stayed the night there and was taken to Ardmore Studios in a limousine and shown round. The boss of the studio showed me the facilities to encourage me to do the studio work there. It was several months after *Witchfinder General*, but we were working on it then.

"Mike's potential was being realized. He had pictures lined up, but this was going to be *our* next film, which was going to be done the following year. AIP definitely would have come in with *O'Hooligan's Mob*, but it wasn't to be. Deke stayed on and did a couple more films. They used to chat to me about it, but we didn't get involved in anything else after that. I may have sold them a film later on, but I didn't get involved in that degree. They would certainly have been in with *O'Hooligan's Mob* and the only reason that wasn't made was because Mike died."

Diane Ogilvy commented: "I thought it had been shelved before that, because I thought *Bloody Mama* was the one that was in the forefront."

Ernest Harris had a memory of Mike describing a scene he wanted to realize in *O'Hooligan's Mob*: "He described to me a cobble-stoned street at night, rain swept, illuminated by a street lamp and a wounded man staggering along it with a submachine gun." Unfortunately, *O'Hooligan's*

Mob caused Tom Baker and Mike Reeves to fall out a little bit, as Tom was initially going to be the writer, as he explained:

"After *Witchfinder* was made, Tony Tenser said, 'We must make something else!' *Bonnie and Clyde* had just come out. Tony says, 'Got to make a machine gun movie, this is what's making the money. Who's got ideas about machine gun movies?' It seemed to me the only time machine guns figured much in our history was in Ireland in the Troubles, because in those days there was no trouble in Ireland at all. I'd been in Dublin four years, there was nothing, total peace. It didn't start again until 1969. It didn't seem an outrageous idea. I had vague memories of newspaper articles. In the 20s or something, there was odd machine-gunning going on, and possibly in the Civil War, possibly with the English irregulars and the Irish revolutionaries, and so there was various stuff.

"Tony said, 'That's good, that's interesting, we can fit machine guns into an Irish story. I'm very busy at the moment, but in a few weeks, I'll get back to you and we'll sort this out.' Then I went to Malta. My father died, I came back to England, stayed with Mum in the country and thinking as soon as Tony says, 'I want to talk to Tom about this,' Mike would say, 'He's down at his Mum's, here's the telephone number.' Nothing happened at all. And because my Mum's a widow and my sister's gone back to Hong Kong, I stay down there two or three months to help her out and when I come back to London, to stay with Mike I guess for whatever reason, I say, 'By the way, did Tony ever say anything about the machine gun movie?'

" 'Oh,' says Mike, 'that's been written, by Amos Powell. Amos has written that.' And I said, 'What the hell do you mean?' Amos was a bloke who lived in Sussex, an American, possibly had some filmwriting connection, a member of Mike's circle, penniless also. He would arrive, play poker, drink drink, drive away into the night back to Sussex, but—this is classic film world—he was at someone's elbow when the notion of the script arose. And, unfortunately, I rather took against this. I have to say, I was pissed off at this thoroughly. I felt that Mike had been disloyal to me. He may have been unaware totally that I felt that that was my property or my idea or whatever. I have no idea, because I never got cross with him to his face about it, terribly, but I just felt, why didn't he pick up the phone? Why did he say, 'Well, Tom's not here, but Amos might do the job for you?' I felt he should have said, 'Tom's at this number.'

"And, in a way, I got a bit estranged with him over that. And so, from that period, I didn't see very much of him. Partly, I then went off to Hackney to live with a group of friends in a flat and Mike wouldn't come and visit us in Hackney. It's not he *wouldn't*, he just didn't do that sort of thing! From that period, March 1968, I hardly saw him. I saw him once or twice down in Yeoman's Row, and then when I was doing rewrites at Borehamwood. He wouldn't come to my wedding party in November 1968, and then I went to his flat a couple of times to ask him about TV stuff."

Peter Fraser agreed that Mike was reluctant to venture out of Yeoman's Row: "He came once to my place to eat. He liked being in his own home."

Peter did say that in the six years he had known Mike, from the runner on *The Long Ships* to the acclaimed film director, "he didn't change, to me, he was just the same." Peter felt that Mike remained optimistic that a good project would come his way: "Something could have been happening, that's what kept Mike going."

Chapter Ten: Decline

It sounds crazy, but he could have been the English Spielberg, he understood the vocabulary of film so well.—Paul Maslansky

The last time Ernest Harris saw Mike Reeves was at the corner of Baker Street and Marylebone Road. Ernest was walking when a taxi drew up and Mike got out. They discussed, of all things, *Citizen Kane*, which Harris thought was playing at the Times Cinema nearby. A fitting last memory of the man who was the Orson Welles of his day, in the view of colleagues such as Paul Ferris, Vincent Price, Patrick Curtis and various critics. In Mike's scrapbook is a letter he pasted, from Ernest to *Films and Filming* magazine, answering in two words a reader's letter asking who was there to put the cult cinema scene on the map: "Michael Reeves."

There was now a short-lived improvement in Mike's physical well-being. His mother had been worried about the amount of prescribed drugs he was taking and, after he left the clinic, he was still taking a large number of pills. Ian Ogilvy was away working abroad, but Nicky Henson and Paul Ferris kept in touch with Mike and were alarmed at how much medication he was taking. Nicky and Paul said, "This has all got to stop, Mike." Paul Ferris went round to the flat one day and persuaded Mike to throw the pills away. He recalled: "I flushed all of his pills down the damn toilet. His doctor had him taking six different pills a day. There were hundreds of them. I went over there and flushed them all down the toilet, literally….whole hundreds of them…with his assistance. I said, 'Mike, you've got to stop this.'"

Nicky Henson commented: "I wasn't there, but there was the grand pill throwing-away ceremony, where he chucked everything away. By that time, he had pills to sleep, pills to get up, uppers and downers. On prescription, from the doctor. We've always felt very, very strongly that he was under the control of the doctor. He lived his life through those pills. There was no reason why he should, as far as I could see." Nicky was not around as much as Paul Ferris, he explained: "I wasn't. I saw Mike occasionally but, again, life was lived at nights with those people and I was always in the theater. I was always working in the theater, so I wasn't around. Paul would be around a lot more." Philip Waddilove also grew concerned and spoke to Mike's psychiatrist and encouraged Mike to throw away his pills.

Mike's mother later told the coroner that she had never seen Mike so happy after he threw the pills away. He was eating large meals and sleeping well on his frequent visits to her house. However, Paul Ferris believed that he subsequently went down again, due to the manic depression from which he suffered. He thought Mike did develop a fear of mortality that overcame him: "When you go into what I used to call the black deeps, the depressions, it tempts you as well. It's almost seductive how far you can go down. I can see that in Mike. You go down that road."

Paul Ferris attributed Mike's death to a temporary depression, although he could not be sure it was suicide. Accordingly, he blamed himself for not doing more to prevent it:

"I flushed all the pills away and a few days later, it seemed—I can't remember the time span now—I was living in Broadwalk Court then, not too far away—I said to Mike, 'Come stay with me in Broadwalk Court.' Which is what Nicky did for me years and years before, when I was going through a bad period. He just took me home. Mike said 'No, no. I'll be all right.' And his mother was coming on Monday and all that. His mother found him. I *bitterly* regretted that ever since, not taking him home. As with me, it was temporary, probably temporary. It's the luck of the draw. Susi Waddilove found me. I was totally intent on just dying. Mike wanted to die, I know."

Paul tried to reconcile this with Mike's wanting to be a great filmmaker: "Why does it have to be one more than the other? It's not something you choose at any one time. One time you'd be up and do your work, which is what I did with music or whatever, but when you're down, it's not that you don't want to write music or make movies, it's just that you're down and want to die. It's not that you're being silly and someone's saying, 'Don't. You're thinking these bad thoughts.' It grabs you and you do go down. He did go down. He *did* die, that's the point. *He* did, I didn't. I wanted to die. Tired of the pain of living."

Some people felt being on his own made it harder for Mike to cope with these feelings. John Hall, who had been in Vietnam, said Mike was "a fairly lonely character." Paul Ferris said:

> "Yes, I'm sure, and Annabelle, I know, feels bad about that, but you are engulfed with this depression which grabs you and takes you down. Now, if you're lucky, you're with people who can bring you out. Mike wasn't. I left him that Friday, and went home for the weekend. If I'd have taken him home...I was within an inch of it but, being undemonstrative and not wanting to push things with him, because, Christ, he was as much an adult as I was, I didn't. But now I see I should have actually taken him back to Broadwalk Court, exactly the same as Nick did with me when I was in Broadwalk Court. He took me out to his place for 10 days."

Iain Sinclair wrote: "He was using a lot of pills: Valium, lithium, barbiturates. He had trouble sleeping and trouble talking about anything except his own problems—and Don Siegel. Any new faces that came into his orbit were given a forcible induction course in *The Killers*." Tom Baker was mystified by Mike's rapid decline: "He was shedding friends left, right and center. My friend Peter Fraser went round with Pam to see him in that flat. He said Mike was just sort of sitting in this chair hugging his scrapbook to his chest. I just think, 'How could you possibly?' Yet Peter thought, 'Well, why are Pam and I in the room? Who have we come to see? We've come to see him and all he can do is sort of hug his scrapbook.'

"I don't think he was overawed by the success of *Witchfinder*. He's not George Lucas. I think, 'Why didn't he gather folks around? Why didn't he say, what are we going to do next?' It wasn't his style. But if he was aware that he needed support, he could have done that. But I think it's a shedding of the friends through some depression or something. I think the circumstances closed in on him in some way and that prevented him from staying in touch with people, certainly with Peter and me." Figures from Mike's beginnings, Paul Maslansky and Mel Welles, visited him and found him a changed man. Benjamin Halligan attributes to Mike a loss of confidence in his ability as a film director, as if *Witchfinder General* had never happened.

Peter Fraser revealed that Mike was not on his own that time he visited him in the flat. David Austen was there and they were chatting. Peter commented:

> "When I last saw Mike, he'd just come back from America. He was always quiet; he was even more quiet then. He seemed a bit down. It wasn't that he wasn't communicative, they were just sitting there blathering. Mike was hugging his scrapbook to his chest. I look at the body language. Look at *how long* it was since he made a picture. Most people are in the business for ego, for money, for fame. Mike liked pictures. He didn't want to do things for money. He wasn't being offered anything good."

Tom had the same feelings as Paul Ferris in wishing he had been more insistent about taking care of Mike just then:

> "He fell apart, but also why did his relationship with the team? I mean, he was, in a sense, creating a team. With hindsight, it's easy to see that when someone's having those sort of difficulties, that's when you have to stay close

to them, even if they don't want you to be close. I've found that since. He never suggested that I work with him again after that."

Tom did try to be of some practical assistance, since none of Mike's projects were getting off the ground. He got a job doing script rewrites at Borehamwood Studios for an ABC TV/Hammer/20th Century-Fox television series *Journey to the Unknown*, produced by Hitchcock's television producer Joan Harrison. He went to see Mike to suggest he could direct one of the episodes of this short-lived (seventeen 50-minute episodes, in color) series of weird paranormal tales. Mike dismissed the idea. Tom commented:

"I was so shocked when I suggested he could do one of these TV things. The Mike that I knew before, if he'd have had the time, would have grabbed that, just for the fun of getting a camera and having a few actors and trying. Even if it wasn't film, it was big budget and just for that fun. And all his other projects...*Buttercup Chain* he wasn't taken up because they didn't trust him as a director to handle that subject, but it puzzles me as to why his previous 10-year enthusiasm which would bubble anyone along sort of evaporated later. Perhaps depression came upon him."

Peter Fraser thought it *might* have been arrogance on Mike's part to dismiss the idea of working in television, "but Mike loved *movies!*"

Tony Tenser had also tried to cheer Mike up by inviting him to the Cannes Film Festival to help him get over the break-up with Annabelle. Mike went down there on his own and Tony recalled: "He was depressed. I tried to fix him up with some bird, she was a minor actress, and she told me the next day he spent all night making love to her *ear*. He wasn't interested. He was only interested in one thing, films." It was all he lived for.

Others of Mike's circle would not agree with Paul Ferris' view that Mike wanted to die. Paul Ferris agreed that whether he could have saved Mike was "imponderable." Tom Baker accepted that Mike was in train of shutting his life down:

"He had been pretty ill. Tales of him going to the Caribbean with some girl, he seems to have been a bit spaced out at that stage. In a sense, it must have been suicide on one level, from the shutting-down of his life. His life was clearly shutting down. Peter's image of him clasping his scrapbook, that is shutting your life down. Your friends come to see you and if all you can do is just hug your scrapbook of your career in silence, you have in a sense withdrawn within yourself completely, and in a sense that is shutting your life down."

Peter Fraser said: "I saw him within a couple of weeks of his death. He needed to break up the things he was sitting upon. 'I'm fed up here, nothing's happening.' Or he was a bit down, he got into depression. How *long* had he gone without making a movie?"

Michael Reeves was found dead on Tuesday, February 11, 1969. The precise circumstances will probably never be known.

He went and had lunch with Ian and Diane Ogilvy that Sunday. Diane recalled: "He was with us in our little house in Putney. He was fine at lunchtime on the Sunday. He was playing cowboys and Indians with my daughter. When I saw David Austen a couple of years ago, we were talking about Mike and he said he saw him that evening, after he'd had lunch with us, which I never knew until a couple of years ago."

Deke Heyward claimed to have had a visit from him on that Monday. Without a definite project to absorb him, Michael had taken to dropping in on Deke at the AIP office. Heyward

recalled in *Fangoria:* "After the picture was completed, he'd come to my office and just sit on the floor. He'd say, 'I just like being here. I like being with you. I like to be around. Is it all right? Am I bothering you?' It was sad." Clearly, this was the effect of Mike's illness, as Diane Ogilvy testified: "I never saw any signs of lack of confidence ever, either on the set or off, ever."

On the Monday, Deke found him sad and uncommunicative, he told Bill Kelley: "We weren't close, but I felt like a father watching his son and unable to do anything about the state he was in. I didn't think he would commit suicide, or I would have done more. I don't know whether he did commit suicide or not. No one does, really." Tom Baker commented: "That's sad. Mike didn't like him, anyway. He wasn't a nice man. He'd insist on these sex scenes, girls with their breasts exposed, so he could sell it better in America. Sounds as though Mike was losing touch with everything, really."

Benjamin Halligan notes that Mike had lunch with Hilary Dwyer at the Carlton Tower that day, discussing a new script. It hardly suggests a man with suicide on his mind.

Cadogan Place apartment where Michael Reeves was found dead.

Betty Reeves had arranged to have lunch with Mike that Tuesday. Virginia Scholte recalled that she turned up early and so she went straight to the flat at Cadogan Place, arriving at 12:30 p.m. She was greeted by Mike's daily woman, who looked distressed and said that Mike was unconscious. Betty went into Mike's bedroom and could see that he was dead. The police were notified. Police Constable Brian Bowden-Brown of Chelsea Police Station came to the flat and found Mike lying on the floor at the side of the bed. He was partly dressed in day clothes and partly in pajamas. The Constable searched the flat and found a number of bottles containing capsules, including two beside the bed. These were Mike's prescribed drugs. (Nicky Henson thought Mike had found an old prescription to get these.)

Betty Reeves informed Ian Ogilvy by telephone that Mike was dead and he confirmed that it was a great shock:

> "Oh, frightful! Absolutely dreadful. Well, he was my closest friend, you see. I mean, bar none. And yes, it was dreadful. Appalling. Hard to believe. And ever since I have vigorously defended him against people who have said to me, 'Oh, he committed suicide!' and I have said, 'No, it's *not* true.' Because I don't like the idea that he did, and I don't think he did, anyway. I really

don't. The official verdict was accidental overdose. Based on the fact that he was only about a few grains over. It was the mixture of barbiturates and alcohol. If you're going to kill yourself, take the whole bottle. And I know what he was doing. He always did take sleeping pills and toward the end he was drinking very heavily, and I suspect he just came back one night out of his mind and took one pill too many and said, 'Oh, get a good night's sleep,' and naturally they were more powerful. That's what I like to believe."

Diane Ogilvy was pregnant with her son Titus Michael—named after Mike Reeves—and Betty Reeves had thought she should not be told Mike was dead, as Diane recalled: "Mrs. Reeves spoke to our nanny and told her to tell Ian. There was a lot of hush-hush going on in my household. Mrs. Reeves told Ian not to tell me and Ian thought that was ridiculous." Diane was not surprised that Betty had this presence of mind: "She was a very upper-class woman who had strong opinions about how one should behave, so she would have done the stiff upper lip."

Betty Reeves did not want anyone to go to Mike's flat, but Paul Ferris insisted and he and his wife went round there. Betty then gave them many things, including some of Ian and Diane's belongings, which they later saw in Paul's house. Paul took Mike's 8-mm copy of *Carrion*, his film splicing machine, and the Andrew Wyeth prints to his house in Winchester. This later caused some resentment among other friends of Mike's. The original of Vincent Price's letter to Mike somehow got lost.

Mike's death came as a great shock to all his friends, who thought he had recovered from his breakdown quite well. He had put behind him the AIP pictures about which he had had misgivings and was sleeping and eating well again. He was back working with the genial Tony Tenser on a film that just might have been as good as *Witchfinder*. Whether he was really getting over the break-up with Annabelle is not known, as he rarely discussed his private feelings about her. He was having some social life, though, with Dani Sheridan and her set.

Diane Ogilvy said: "I think he was doing some clubbing the last few months." Paul Vestey observed: "I must say I had thought he'd got better, because I hadn't seen him for a bit and then I did see him only a couple of weeks before he died. I think it did come as a great shock to everybody. I don't think anybody expected anything like it, really. I shouldn't think it was suicide. I don't know, you can't tell, can you? I wouldn't have thought he was suicidal by nature."

Philip Waddilove was in Stockholm scouting locations for *The Buttercup Chain* when he heard the news. He doubted it had anything to do with Mike's break-up with Annabelle, he told Bill Kelley: "Michael had these liquid sleeping drops, and he never measured anything. It was a tragic accident, but not a suicide. Michael was too involved with motion pictures to be concerned with deep personal relationships. I believe he was also too ambitious in his movie-making to take his own life." Ernest Harris recalled meeting David Austen a few days later. Austen could not even discuss Mike's death.

Tony Tenser told a version of Mike's death he believed to be true, although it did diverge significantly from other versions. He had certainly been aware of Mike's psychological problems and use of prescribed medication:

"They were prescription things. I don't know why. He could get quite depressed and, at times like that, we just used to talk about happy things, try and get him out of it. He could still work. I should think at times it manifested itself in a scene to its acceptability rather than to its detriment. I know Annabelle, his girlfriend, was aware of that, and I was concerned when I knew that he was taking aspirin-type of drugs. I told him, 'You really ought to try to manage without them if you can.' And she actually got him off them. If she hadn't done that—it's not her fault, because she loved him—it may never have happened. Because he didn't commit suicide. He didn't, he didn't."

"The housekeeper came there and what he'd done is, he'd taken some aspirin or something to sleep, and he woke up in the middle of the night, wanted a glass of water or something, and wanted to get off to sleep. He forgot he'd already taken some. He wasn't drowsy enough, so he took some more and he just went to sleep. I don't know if he'd been drinking, but he wasn't a heavy drinker, not to my knowledge. Glass of wine. He wasn't a boozer. Yes, he could feel down at times and you'd try and cheer him up and say, 'How do you feel?' But that's the story I got. That's what happened. The woman who does the daily for them came one morning and he was just asleep in bed. From what I remember, there wasn't an empty bottle there; some had been taken. So, if you commit suicide, take the whole lot! He took a second lot to get off to sleep again. This is what the general feeling was."

Tony got this story from the housekeeper herself when he phoned upon hearing of Mike's death.

Ian Ogilvy regarded Mike's death as "the loss of a very close friend and I think quite a loss for the British industry," but never dwelled on the films that might have been for him as an actor if Mike had lived:

"I honestly have no memory that we were going to have a production company. None whatsoever. I also know perfectly well that the picture he was really keen on, this *All the Little Animals*, I really was *not* going to be in. He said, 'I'm sorry, Ian, but there's three parts and none of them fit you.' I read the book and I thought it was the most charming and wonderful thing and very, very 'Reeves,' a new departure, but he would make it wonderful, and I knew there was no part for me. I knew that this *gold mine* had to stop."

Asked by the author in 1988 how he heard of Mike's death, Vincent Price said: "I don't remember, but did hear it was a suicide." He thought Mike's "broken romance" was partly the cause. He was later quoted as saying: "He had a lot of problems, really mixed-up problems, one of them being dope, another being an unhappy romance, and he killed himself. It was a great loss to the cinema."

Paul Vestey recalled that Annabelle came round to his house in Cheval Place the night after Mike died: "She was so upset. I don't think she was blaming herself. It was a bit on and off."

Don Siegel was notified of Mike's death in Mexico, where he was shooting *Two Mules for Sister Sara*. Later he reflected: "I think he committed suicide. I couldn't figure out why. I couldn't understand why a young man who had achieved very quick recognition would do that. I guess in a fit of depression, he just made the decision." Siegel wrote in a letter, quoted by Benjamin Halligan: "I saw in Michael many of my own faults and I had hoped that, without being fatuous, I could be of some help to him." He briefly considered if a film could be made of Mike's tragic story.

Nicky Henson was terribly shocked to hear of Mike's death, though he had not seen him since the *Witchfinder* preview:

"Oh yes, obviously. I remember April 1968 going to the preview of *Witchfinder*—I remember it being April 1968 because it was the morning after, I had the most terrible hangover. I opened the night before in a musical called *Canterbury Tales* which was a disaster, we stayed up all night because we knew it would come off at the end of the week, and it ran five years! So we all stayed up all night, and then I went straight on to the preview of *Witchfinder* (at Denham?) and I don't know if that's the last time I saw Mike but anyway he was there."

Alfred Shaughnessy commented: "I was shattered to hear of his death and used to discuss him and his great promise with Ian Ogilvy when we were working on *Upstairs, Downstairs* some years later."

Tom Baker learned of Mike's death from a newspaper appreciation drawn to his attention while he was on a plane:

> "I rang up somebody in the local police station to find out what had happened and my memory is that a policeman said, 'I can't really tell you, you'll have to come down, but I can tell you that it was accidental death or considered to be an accident.' That must have been the result of a coroner's hearing. What puzzles me is, were we such a scattered group of people? At the time, it didn't seem so surprising to me. I wrote to Betty and got a slightly unhappy letter back from her, partly because she'd always felt there were a number of us who'd sort of hung around Yeoman's Row, just feeding off Mike's largesse both financially and spiritually, or creativity, or whatever, and I think there'd been some trouble before and she may have felt I was in that category, I don't know. She wasn't rude to me, but I think I said, 'Why is it, when so many of us loved him, that he didn't seem to be able to stay in touch with us?' and she referred to 'rats leaving the sinking ship.' She wasn't happy. I knew her quite well, she was always very kind to me and very friendly and hospitable."

The inquest was covered by *Chelsea News*, which reported:

> "A 25-year-old Chelsea film director, Michael Leith Reeves, who was found dead in his flat at Cadogan Street [*sic*], died from taking an overdose of barbiturate, the pathologist, Professor Donald Teare, told the assistant deputy coroner, Mr. Christopher Stone, at the Westminster inquest last week. Prof. Teare said that the blood barbiturate level in the body was not high, and the dosage was consistent with an injudicious overdosage rather than an attempt to commit suicide...Mr. Stone said it was clear that Mr. Reeves had been working under a strain and obviously had some psychiatric problems for which he had been receiving some treatment. He may have been a person who was used to taking tablets and thought that it had become necessary to take more in order to get a good night's sleep. The coroner said he was not satisfied that it was a deliberate case of Mr. Reeves taking his own life, and he recorded a verdict of accidental death."

The Daily Telegraph reported Betty saying at the inquest that Mike had become depressed after completing *Witchfinder*, which had "taken a lot out of him" and that he had "girl trouble."

The frequently asked question about Mike Reeves is: Did he commit suicide? A biography cannot avoid this unfortunate question. Vincent Price thought he did, but then that is what he was told. No one will ever know for certain but, purely from the circumstances as investigated by the coroner, the overdose does appear to have been accidental: He was in the act of putting on his pajamas when he died. Seemingly a tragic effect of Mike's carelessness. Diane Ogilvy commented: "Mike had a trick for when he couldn't sleep. He would get up, get fully dressed, lie on his bed and then he could fall asleep. Now, having read what the coroner's report said about him being half dressed, it is obvious to me that this is what he was doing and that he took just one pill too many while he was getting dressed."

What is more likely than a deliberate act is that he would have died soon in any event. Clearly, as Tom Baker eloquently put it, Mike's life was closing down around him—the abandoning of offers of film and television work, the shedding of friends, his withdrawal from normal social interaction to someone "cloaked in an air of sweet desperation," as Deke put it, and hugging his scrapbook of his career to his chest. Paul Ferris has revealed that Mike wanted to die and expected to soon. The biochemistry of his brain was allowing his manic depression, not in evidence until after Radley, to worsen.

Mike was aware of his condition. He was taking largactil for years and wrote a script called *Manic Mind*. He must have known his father Derek was a manic depressive, although Betty tried to hide it from him, because Paul Ferris knew and discussed the problem with Mike, including the fact that Paul's own father was a sufferer. Virginia Scholte said her side of the family all knew that Mike was manic. If it is true that Derek Reeves committed suicide (although it probably isn't), Mike's death becomes more understandable. It was in the genes. Michael Reeves was clearly a very sensitive man and his depression was doubtless worsened by losing Annabelle, who had been so supportive, and by his fear of being unable to sustain the critical acclaim enjoyed by *Witchfinder*, but these were minor contributory factors. Inappropriate medical treatment can hardly have helped, either.

In the author's view, the very mania that lent a stark intensity to all Mike's work was what eventually killed him, in the sense of shutting down his life as a film director and social being. It cannot be too surprising that, in his befuddled and desperate state of mind, he could not administer his dosages correctly and accidentally overdosed. This seems the likely explanation, although there will always be a mystery at the heart of what killed such a talented and brilliant creative force. "Just snuffed out," said Paul Ferris with feeling.

It is interesting to note that *one* of the interviewees for this book referred obliquely to a suicide note: "And then there was that whole business with the note that the doctors took, but we can't get into that...That's very heavy, isn't it?" He would not be drawn any further. However, it is difficult to lend any credence to this, as he was not present at the scene and it was most likely a rumor that he accepted as true. Neither the coroner nor Paul Ferris, who was so close to Mike during this period, had any knowledge of a note. Of course, there are some people who look on the final minutes of *Witchfinder* as the longest suicide note in history, but that is just romanticizing a pragmatic, if downbeat, ending to a low-budget film that had run out of time and money.

Dr. Blaikie described Mike at the inquest as an uncooperative patient who would break appointments. Ian Ogilvy was unsurprised: "I'm sure that was true. Mike was somewhat *cavalier* in a way with his treatment of people—in the nicest possible way, but he was a careless man. Because his mind wasn't there. He was the archetypal absent-minded professor, if you like. He didn't really think about things. If Mike said, 'I'm coming round, be with you in half an hour,' three hours later he would turn up!"

This may well tie in with Vincent Price's description of Mike's approach to people as "impersonal," and Nicky Henson detected the same when Mike was at work: "I used to put it down very much when we were filming to the fact the guy had so much on his brain. You'd be talking to him and he'd be a bit distracted-looking, but I didn't find that strange in any way."

Michael Leith Reeves, one of the greatest natural born filmmakers England has ever produced, was cremated on February 20, 1969, at Ipswich Crematorium, on Cemetery Road, Ipswich. His ashes were strewn on the February Lawn in the Garden of Rest near the old fish pond at the front of the green-domed Temple of Remembrance. There was no memorial stone, nor was there a memorial plaque in the Temple of Remembrance—nothing to indicate the passing of this great artist. Paul Ferris remembered masses of flowers, but was too grief-stricken to be able to take it all in. Virginia Scholte went with her mother and her brother Miles Huddleston and his wife. She remembered seeing some film people there. (By some weird coincidence, Boris Karloff died that same month.)

Tony Tenser was certainly there and it was the first time he met Mike's mother, the only one of Mike's relatives he ever met. He recalled: "I only knew his mother. She came down for the funeral and we went out and had coffee somewhere and she took it quite well, externally. I remember saying to her he was like a son to me." Diane Ogilvy believed Tony really did feel like that. Diane was also full of praise for Betty: "She did this wonderful thing at the crema-

The Ipswich Crematorium where Michael Reeves' ashes were spread on the February Lawn in the Garden of Rest by the fish pond.

torium. We were all in the little chapel and usually the coffin goes out and you see it go out. She wouldn't allow them to take the coffin through where the flames were until everybody left, which I thought was a wonderful thing to do. Why doesn't everybody do it? You just don't want to see those flames."

How did Betty Reeves react to Mike's death? Virginia Scholte said:

> "Aunt Betty would *never ever* accept that it was suicide. He certainly never committed suicide in her eyes. But one doesn't know whether that was just because she couldn't bear the thought. She always swore that he didn't, but to everybody else it seemed he had, because he was on drugs for that. We always were just sure that he had committed suicide. There was absolutely no question that she ever thought he had killed himself. It was an accident. He fell and hit his head on the wall or something. She always maintained that the psychiatrist gave him far too many pills. She always said they said, 'He's a rich young man. Let's get hold of him and screw him for what we can.' But she was absolutely shattered by his death. He was everything she had left. Suddenly, that was taken too. She was incredibly brave. And very religious. She got a lot of strength from that."

Pamela Hoare recalled: "I remember my mother saying that Betty said at least she wouldn't have to be perpetually worrying about him. All so sad, really. I remember a portrait of Michael in the house when Betty was still there, after his death." The portrait was acquired by Cherida Reeves when Betty died.

Paul Ferris told an incredibly poignant story of Mike's final days:

> "After Mike died, his mother came to me and said that one of the last things that he was most concerned about before he died was that he wanted to buy this house for us and that I wouldn't accept it. He kept going on and on in his flat the last few days: Could she persuade me to accept the money for the

house? It's incredible. And I still couldn't. I said, 'I'm sorry, Mrs. Reeves, I can't do it. I couldn't do it then, even less now somehow.' It's like robbing the grave. I couldn't do it. She said, 'All right, will you accept a mortgage?' I said, 'Yes, all right.' "

The mortgage was duly arranged through Mike's solicitor Gerald Whately.

Paul's story seems to indicate that Mike sensed the end was near. Paul himself thought it was so: "Yes. He was all alone. If I'd just taken him home to the flat, it could have been all different. Who knows? Again, if I'd taken him home, nursed him through, who knows? He may have gone out next week and killed himself. You don't know."

Of the effect of Mike's death on his mother, Ian Ogilvy commented:

> "I would assume she was absolutely shattered by it, because that left her totally alone as far as I know. There must have been other members of the family, but I didn't know any of them. I would imagine it would have shattered her. I was *very* busy at the time. I was being abroad an awful lot and I just went on with my life and assume she went on with hers. I'd known her, but I suppose the difference in age and everything like that, what I was doing, what she was doing, I just didn't keep in touch at all. I sometimes feel rather bad about not keeping in touch with her."

Paul Ferris said that, to his astonishment, she told him after Mike died that her ambition was "to hurt as few people as possible for the rest of her life." He described her as a "most delightful and charming woman." Diane Ogilvy said: "I remember going down to stay with her two years after Mike had died and the garden was full of things like swings and slides for the local playgroup that they had." Diane was unsurprised that Betty went on to have a thriving social life: "I'm absolutely convinced she would have done and a lot of it would have been for the local community. I always called her 'Mrs. Reeves.' She was a very grand lady. She talked about him a tremendous amount, although she automatically stopped when the children came into the room, although they weren't that big. She seemed absolutely fine, but then I was very young at the time. Maybe she wasn't, underneath all this."

Betty continued living at Galleon House until about four years before she died. She was finding the house too big for her. She moved to what Virginia Scholte described as "that grotty, nasty little house she hated" for a year, but "the one she ended up in was a lovely little Queen Anne town house at Woodbridge." Galleon House she sold to her friends Eustace and Judy Miller. She would drive herself to see Virginia and Owen Scholte in Kingston, Canterbury, but then gave up driving and went in a private taxi through the Dartford Tunnel. Virginia commented: "I saw her a lot really. I was a god-daughter and in fact after Mike died, Miles, my brother, and I were her sort of closest relatives and, although older, were rather like her children, because she was the same age as my mother, because she had Mike so late, you see. She used to come here and spend most Christmases. She drove me mad, but I was very devoted to her." Owen said: "We were practically adopted, really." Eventually she had a couple of falls. She fell in the street once and broke her elbow. She needed a walking stick.

Betty was agreeably surprised to have a visit in 1985 from an American Mike Reeves fan called Randy Everts, who was a student. He recalled:

> "I did have a rather splendid all-day visit in 1985 with Michael's mother, who showed me several photo albums of him and his movie-making. I had gotten her address from a friend of Michael's and the address was Little Bealings, where I drove and, being rather pushy, went instantly to the Postmistress of the little town, since the address in Little Bealings was a name, not an address. She informed me that Mrs. Reeves had removed to Woodbridge. I

262

found her at home and we had lunch and much talk. I arrived with my dark glasses on, resembling one of the Blues Brothers, and when she opened the door, she said, 'You are from Hollywood!,' which in fact I was (having been spawned there) but, as I explained, was on a scholarship to and back from New Delhi, India. She had gone out that day shopping for a coffin! Talking about Michael was enormously painful for her still."

Owen Scholte confirmed that Betty was pleased by this visit: "I remember Aunt Betty telling us when we stayed with her latterly that somebody just knocked at the door and asked her if he could come in and talk to her about Mike Reeves. She welcomed it, he came in and talked away, said how marvelous he was, extraordinarily talented person. I remember her telling us that." Betty was certainly proud of Mike's reputation. Owen said: "She was aware of the fact that he was extremely gifted, and was highly thought of. There were fans and people who, often in the profession, asked after him and thought he was the cat's whiskers, the best."

Virginia Scholte qualified this slightly, because of the nature of the films:

"She certainly took an interest in what all the papers said and she had them all stuck in these scrapbooks and photographs of him and everything. She never actually brought those books out and showed them to us. She kept them meticulously, she must have done because they were all stuck in in sequence, with photographs that were relevant and all that, but she never brought them out and said, 'Look, this is what they say about Mike,' which is strange in a way, really. I do think she wished always that they didn't have to have been those sort of films. I think that was a slight sort of regret in a way. Although she was so proud of him, I think she wished they could have been lovely, sort of romantic films. She hated anything to do with violence."

Randy also witnessed Betty's anger with Annabelle: "Mrs. Reeves always referred to Michael's fiancee by the nickname 'that bitch.' She was a feisty old lady, she was." Virginia agreed that Betty blamed Annabelle for Mike's depression: "Certainly his mother did. Aunt Betty hated her. She hadn't a good word for her. I think because she dropped him." Apparently Betty and Annabelle had gotten on all right before that, Virginia believed: "I think reasonably, yes. I never met Annabelle, so I never heard her side of the story, and Mike can't have been easy, can he? With a chap like that, couldn't have been easy. I'm sure it wasn't all her fault at all. Aunt Betty would obviously be biased, wouldn't she?"

Other friends of Mike's tended to cast blame on Annabelle for leaving Mike. Diane Ogilvy was antagonistic toward her, though she later realized that was unfair. Paul Ferris agreed:

"I *know* that's unfair. At the time she was shunned by everyone. She thought I was shunning her too. All I was doing was just keeping away from it all. I went completely off the scene. Annabelle used to frighten the life out of me. I told her that when we spoke about Mike over the last few years. We became very close friends, but she thought I disappeared off the scene on purpose against her, because everyone else was against her, which wasn't the truth."

It is a sign of the high esteem in which Mike Reeves was held that on January 17, 1970, the National Film Theatre in London honored him with an all-night retrospective, a virtually unprecedented tribute to such a recent filmmaker and, especially, to one with such a short career. They showed, in sequence, *Castle of the Living Dead, Revenge of the Blood Beast, The Sorcerers* and *Witchfinder General*. Ian Ogilvy was invited to give an introductory talk. (Vincent Price told the author: "I didn't know anything about it!")

Peter Fraser was also present. Ian found it an interesting experience, as it showed him something of the cult interest Mike had already become:

> "Well, there was enormous interest. I was very surprised because the National Film Theatre did a starting-at-midnight retrospective, at which I gave a little introductory talk. What fascinated me was who was there. Yes, there were the young, the long-haired, you know, but there were also elderly colonel types. The cross-section! If you'd look at this audience, you'd think, 'Are you *all* fans of Mike Reeves? What an extraordinary cross-section of people you are!' There were the obvious movie buffs, and also what was obvious was that every person in that audience had seen each one of those films four or five times, because they would begin to tense *before* the thing happened. So there was enormous interest but, again, it was such an odd cross-section."

Ian's observation about tensing is interesting, because the remarkable thing about certainly *Witchfinder* is that its power does not diminish on repeated viewings, as David Pirie has pointed out. You do still tense before the scenes in which you already know what is going to happen. Ian commented: "I suppose so. Having been in it, I don't find that, of course. I remember all the things that went wrong and the stupid things that happened." Tom Baker said something similar when it was put to him that the films had an unsettling quality: "It's difficult for me to sort of see it really, because I'm so used to the guy and how things are set up and how things come about." It is a phenomenon especially true of the ending of *Witchfinder*, which never fails to chill the blood, and Ian agreed with this: "Yes, but it is odd that that was more a happy accident than planned. It certainly wasn't planned at all."

Paul Maslansky also attended the NFT tribute. Ernest Harris had known him slightly when Ernest worked for Columbia Pictures and spoke to him there, confirming that Maslansky was full of praise for what Mike did on *Castle of the Living Dead* and scotching the rumors that Mike did very little on the picture: "He was very grateful for what Mike had done on the film. He really admired Mike and valued the work Mike had done on that film."

An even more remarkable testimony to Mike's impressive talent is the tale told by Nicky Henson, especially when one again bears in mind how few films Mike made:

> "Quite soon after Mike's death, I met Siegel and Corman. I went to see Siegel for *The Black Windmill* and I went and saw Corman for *The Red Baron*, which he was shooting over here, and I realized when I got to *both* the interviews that the only reason they wanted to see me was to talk about Mike. They asked to see me about small parts—I didn't get either of them—and I got in, and, each time, when I'd got in the room, they said, 'You were in *Witchfinder*, right?' I said, 'Yes.' 'How well did you know Michael?' 'Well, pretty well.' They said, 'Tell me about him.' An hour I did in each office, I remember, talking to both Don Siegel and Roger Corman about Michael. They were fascinated by him. Corman would watch everything and he was just fascinated. If Mike had been American, he'd have been working for Corman. And Mike was heavily slated to do *Bloody Mama* and then he died. He was going to do *Bloody Mama* after the *De Sade* picture and then he died, so Corman did it. Whether Corman knew that, I don't know. But, again, he was absolutely fascinated. The moment I walked in that door, he said, 'Tell me about Michael Reeves.' "

Considering that Don Siegel and Roger Corman were the two filmmakers he idolized since the days of his sneaking into movies through the exit as a schoolboy, there can be no finer tribute to what Mike Reeves achieved in his short career in the cinema.

Epilogue: Mike Reeves' Legacy

His name can be added to the all-too-short list of real craftsmen like Fuller, Corman and Siegel who have brought real qualities of imagination to low-budget and basically stereotyped works, turning restrictions and conventions to advantage, so that the end product not only belies its humble origins, but can also stand as an independent achievement of importance.—Julian Bamford, *Films in London*

Critic Robin Wood wrote a fine appreciation of Mike's career in *Movie* magazine shortly after he died, noting that in Mike's work, "One is aware of far more promise than achievement." It is probably futile, but still interesting, to wonder what would have become of Mike Reeves as a movie director if he had lived. Ian Ogilvy said Mike would not have been satisfied with the cult reputation he presently enjoys, but was aiming for a career like Steven Spielberg's:

"I think the closest filmmaker today to Mike Reeves is Spielberg. I am convinced that he saw Mike Reeves' pictures. *Duel* is a total and pure Mike Reeves picture, to me. That's absolutely *pure* Mike Reeves. I'd love to meet Spielberg one day and say, 'Have you ever seen Mike Reeves' pictures? Do you know who I'm talking about?' I'm probably wrong, it's just I *feel* he's seen them. Mike Reeves would admire what Spielberg does tremendously and he would have liked to have done that kind of thing, and maybe he would have had the opportunity, except that he would have had to take himself through the terrible doldrums of the '70s in movie-making. But, again, he had the money to buffer himself. He would have been able to survive it."

Of course, one wouldn't necessarily see a film and say, "That must have been directed by Steven Spielberg," but one can readily sense Reeves' personality in all of his work. Ian Ogilvy concurred:

"Yes, but I wonder whether that wasn't because of the restraints imposed on him that his personality comes through more strongly. I wonder if, given a really large budget, he wouldn't simply have used all the toys available to him in their best possible way, which then would have submerged that personality. You would have then just had a marvelously well-made film. You would have said, 'Good Lord, it's a beautiful film, it's well-made, but I don't recognize Reeves in it.' Because he's got all the money he needs and he's got all the toys he wants. He loved toys, you see. He loved cranes and booms and was always frantically anxious to have these toys on the set. Because they're fun to play with. He actually loved the equipment. He loved all the bits. He knew his lenses. He was one of the *last* directors who walked around with the viewfinder. Not many directors do that, but Mike did it because it was a toy.

"He also knew his lenses. He would look and he'd work it out and he'd say, 'Yeah, I want a 50 on there.' In those days, we didn't really use the zoom lens all that much, we'd stick a 50 on as opposed to putting a zoom on, because there was an awful lot of light loss on a zoom, and if light was a bit low, Johnny Coquillon and people like that didn't want to use the zoom. So Mike would say, 'Okay, we'll have a 50.' *Now* on a film, a director will say, 'Go in a bit, go in a bit, go in a bit, yes, that's lovely, what is that?' And they'll say, 'Well, I suppose it's about a 36 and a third.' In those days, we actually used the real lenses. We knew all that, and he was very good on geometry."

Ian was sure Mike would have adored technical developments like the Steadicam:

"It's a device that's been around for a bit now. I think a cinematographer invented it. It's a harness that the camera operator gets into. It takes quite a lot of time. The camera is mounted on the harness and it's got a system of gimbels and gyroscopes, which means that you can have the man literally run down the stairs and go through corridors and things. Every movement is compensated for, which means that, although you don't get a perfectly smooth image, it's virtually smooth. Now Mike would have *loved* a technical development like that, because he really loved hand-held stuff. The more hand-held stuff, the better. He'd have said, 'We don't actually have to mount it, we could actually be free with it.' The Steadicam actually allows you to do that, but it *looks* like it's on a dolly. So those kind of technical developments he would have liked."

Tony Tenser also believed Mike was in the Spielberg mold: "I feel that Mike had the dedication and the talent and, with the experience that he was getting and the way he was doing it, he would have been in that scheme of things by now. I believe that if it had been done gradually, Mike would have graduated. If he'd made *O'Hooligan's Mob*, it would have had to have been a bigger budget and he would have gone on to bigger things from there. He was definitely in that mold."

Recognition of Mike's talent came internationally. Perhaps the most extraordinary example was given by Ian Ogilvy:

"When I did *Waterloo* with Sergei Bondarchuk, it was for Laurentiis. I *assumed* I got the part because I had done two film tests for Laurentiis. One I hadn't got and the other picture was never made, but he'd spent some money on me, flying me out to Rome, and I thought it was Laurentiis. It wasn't really a big part, but it was a nice part. *Not a bit of it!* Bondarchuk had seen *Witchfinder General*. And he wanted to talk to me about Mike, and I had to say, 'He's dead.' And Bondarchuk, this great Russian director, went white. 'But,' he said, 'he was one of your *great* directors!' It was nice that Bondarchuk recognized Mike's extraordinary work. He said, 'It's one of the great films of all time, *Witchfinder General*. It's a wonderful film.' "

Not only film directors responded to Mike's direction. Nicky Henson recalled actress Susan Hampshire's reaction to *Witchfinder General*: "Some time after it came out, it was showing again somewhere. I was living with Susan Hampshire, who knows an awful lot of film directors and knows a lot *about* film directors. She lived with Jan Troell for some time and was married to Pierre Granier-Deferre. She really does know movies inside out and backwards. I took her to see it and she came out and said, 'Jesus, that boy was a genius!' I said, 'Why did you say that?' She said, 'He absolutely had the instinct of where to put a camera. There is a right place to place a camera and there is a wrong place, and he absolutely instinctively put it in *exactly* the right position every time. Visually stunning director.'"

Nicky Henson once put Mike second in importance to Nicolas Roeg. Ian Ogilvy commented:

> "I think that's a bad comparison, because my admiration has always gone out to filmmakers who make great films on tiny budgets. Roeg went on from cameraman and, even on his early pictures, he had much bigger budgets than Mike ever had. I do admire David Lean, but if you can't make a good film on his budgets, then you should have no business being a film director. If you'd given Mike Reeves one of those budgets, he wouldn't have known what to do with it. Or, at least, he would. Mike really worked on a shoestring. Real shoestrings. And I think one of the *great* things about Mike, regardless of what you think of his pictures, is that he produced three movies at all for a total budget of under £200,000. Three movies! That's one of the *great*, remarkable things about him, I think."

Nicky Henson was no longer so sure about putting Mike Reeves second in importance to Nic Roeg: "It's hard, isn't it? I was obviously obsessed with Nic Roeg at the time and I'm not quite so much any more. Mike is unique, and I've done 25 films, and that's the most important filmic experience that I've ever had, working on that movie. Unfortunately, it was very early in my film career, so I didn't appreciate it as much as I would have done if it had been now. I'd love to get my teeth into a lovely script again, a proper movie. I've never done a *proper* movie apart from that! It's the only *proper* movie I've ever done."

Nicky enthused over the fact that Mike made *movies*: "You see, the equivalent nowadays would have been television. He'd have been working in television, and he would never have been able to work in television, because he went to the *movies* and looked at the big screen. He would have hated all this scanning and panning, the way they sell movies on video nowadays, because he really was a widescreen man."

Ian Ogilvy, however, thought that if Mike had not gone to live and work in America in the '70s, when the British film industry collapsed, he would have readily turned to television, as feature film directors like Jeremy Summers did:

> "I think yes, he would. I think he would have enjoyed it, too. In between his own projects. One of the things he would have appreciated was that someone would have wanted to use him for his own sake, as opposed to him taking a project. Someone would say, 'Oh, we'll use Mike Reeves, he's a good director.' He would have enjoyed all that. I think he would have adapted to television and he'd have made episodes of *The Saint* or whatever. Yes, I think so.
>
> "It's awfully hard to wonder and hypothesize as to what he would have been like. I think he would have had to get over this neurosis business. He'd have had to calm down a lot and work out his problems and go to a psychiatrist. I know he did go to a psychiatrist, but I don't think he enjoyed it all that much, really. Some people say he was burnt out, or something like that, but that is assuming he wouldn't have got himself together. If he'd got himself together, I suspect he would have adapted."

It is more likely, however, that he would have heeded the call of Hollywood, Ian thought: "He'd have gone like a shot. He had no great love for working in England. Perfectly happy to work in Rome or anywhere. He just wanted to make movies. *Where* the movie was going to be made, to hell with it!" Nicky Henson commented:

"It was such a short time, and I know he got depressed and all that, but I can't believe that he wouldn't have gone on and made movies, and been a proper movie-maker. Somebody would have taken him in hand. One of the things I do think about the *Oblong Box* syndrome, and things like that, I think he had a built-in defense mechanism: 'I don't want to become known as one of those naff English horror film directors.' I think he'd have wanted to go into different areas. And it would have been interesting to see how his writing developed."

Paul Ferris paid tribute to Mike's instinct for direction:

"He was a great eye for the movies. Fantastic damn talent. He was a *great* film director and loved movies at the age of 24. Extraordinary damn talent. I can't think of any others. Sure eye. At that age. Wonderful eye. No trick movements for their own sake. You can't think of anything to do with the actors, move the camera: He *didn't* do that. There were the most involved damn movements in some of *Witchfinder*. There's a beautiful movement which, if it hadn't been done properly, would have been a complete disaster, when Ian comes into the room with Rupert Davies for the first time. Rupert Davies says, 'Glad to see you,' and all that business, and he does a complete turn round him and then turns back. The camera follows him round. That's just dead right and, when you watch it, it doesn't feel like the camera's doing all that, but it is. He's turned right round. Brilliant eye, that he did have."

John Hall did not consciously think of Mike Reeves as a great talent. "He was just 'Mike'." But he would not have been surprised if Reeves had gone on to become a big name. Paul Vestey said Mike's friends did not at this stage realize that he would become a lasting figure of the British cinema, written about on a par with Alfred Hitchcock: "I wouldn't have thought so. He was very single-minded in wanting to get into films and wanting to direct, so, certainly from that point of view, you can't imagine anybody being more positive in the way he went about it." Of course, if Reeves had Hitchcock's budgets, his work would not have lost some of its original quality.

Ian Ogilvy agreed: "That's quite true. On the other hand, Mike loved toys and games, and, after all, a film set is just a big toy. If you've got an awful lot of money, you can buy a bigger and more expensive toy. I think he would have handled it very well. To have been allowed to play with some of these special effects, I think he would have adored. I really do."

When Mike Reeves died, no one really succeeded him in the sense of being a young British filmmaker of artistic promise combined with commercial success. Ian Ogilvy said: "Michael Armstrong tried to. He couldn't do it." Ian only partly put the lack of a successor down to the failure of the British film industry at that point:

"That. Styles changed. I wrote a sort of Mike Reeves picture for Nicky Henson and for Vincent Price, a horror movie all set on a deserted lighthouse: *Nichtophobia*. Very Mike Reeves. Nicking stuff all over the place, but it was a sort of Mike Reeves picture. I finished it and it was goodish of its type, with a nice part for Vincent. Vincent never saw it. Nice part as a demented pirate called the Admiral. Called all his men by the names of parts of the ship. I was quite proud of the script. But styles had changed. They just weren't making movies like that any more. Things like *The Exorcist* were beginning, *big*-budget horror movies. All of a sudden the style changed. And the industry just died. In 1972, they just pulled out. It was like the Israelites leaving!"

Nicky Henson remembered *Nichtophobia*:

"It was the film that Mike Reeves would have shot. It was going to be. It was going to be our tribute to Michael. Wonderful script. We nearly got the money together and all that. We got a guy who said he could get the money together. It would have been wonderful. He'd written it because he worked out the cheapest set that he could think of was a lighthouse. For all the different floors, you just change the furniture. You have the one floor built and then you just change the furniture, so you're on the next floor. Use a different lens and make it look a little bit smaller. It was great."

Ian Ogilvy would forever live with the legacy of his work in the Mike Reeves canon: "There is always fascination. I still get letters to this day. The interest comes always from movie buffs. And *Time Out*. *Time Out*'s a great one for *Witchfinder General*. Every time it comes on, it's 'Hurrah!' Which is curious, considering there's no great political statement. It's mildly anti-authoritarian, or showing authority at its worst. And it liked Cromwell!" From the '70s onwards, *Witchfinder* played a lot on television:

"It does, and it's popular, but nobody knows who made it, only film buffs. Actors say, 'God, that was a great film,' but they don't know why. They don't know who made it. Or they're vague. They say, 'What was his name? What happened to him?' It's no more than that. So when you think [about it], the vast general public has no idea who this guy was and has little interest.

"Also, you know, people *are* divided about *Witchfinder*. I've met a lot of people who loathe it. 'Bloody awful film. Awful, stupid, terrible thing. Badly made and everything.' They just didn't rate it. Couldn't see what all the fuss is about. It's not universal. Highly intelligent people. Alan Bennett is no fool. Very intelligent man. So is Bernard Levin. Total rubbish, as far as they're concerned. 'Walk out, go out, can't be bothered with it, I've got better things to do.' *I* don't agree with that, but you have got to respect the opinions of not-stupid men."

The tragedy of Mike's early death is that he was denied the chance to create an oeuvre as large and extensive as that of the filmmakers to whom colleagues have compared him, Alfred Hitchcock and Orson Welles. Confirming Paul Ferris' comment that Mike never thought about the future, Diane Ogilvy said: "If Mike ever did think about being a 'Hollywood great,' that would be something he would be leaning toward *one day*." It was not to be. Patrick Curtis commented to Pete Tombs: "It's a desperate shame that Michael's not around. I think the film industry as a whole has really lost something because of it."

Betty Reeves died on April 3, 1986, really of old age. She was 84. Virginia Scholte recounted what happened:

"She had a heart attack. She had pneumonia in the winter and we all thought, 'Well, this is it, really,' because she was so ill, but she recovered from that and then, about a couple of months later, she had a heart attack, was taken into the hospital, had another one and died. So she didn't have too lingering an end. She was a very courageous woman, really, considering she'd had a sad life. She'd had a miserable childhood, married late, had this one precious boy, lost her husband after only 11 years and then Mike, so she had a very sad life."

Betty is buried in the churchyard at Little Bealings. Sadly, Virginia decided that she could not keep the masses of photos in Betty's photo albums and chose a small selection of the photos of Mike and Betty that most intrigued her and disposed of the rest. Grateful thanks to her for some of the nicest photos in this book.

Many of those who worked with Mike Reeves on *Witchfinder General* found it to be the best working experience they ever had. Despite a distinguished career, Ian Ogilvy always regarded it as one of the very best things he had ever made. Vincent Price regarded his performance in it as one of his very best. Hilary Dwyer's film debut remained the high spot of her acting career. Without Mike Reeves to direct his work, Amos Powell found no opportunities in London and returned to the States, where he sought out his friends Brett Halsey and Chuck Griffith. Brett recalled: "Amos and I spent a good deal of time together after he returned to the States, but he seldom talked about his professional association with Mike. Amos' inability to get his writing career going made him very bitter and a bit paranoid."

Chuck Griffith commented: "Brett Halsey and Amos Powell were best friends for some years, until Amos dumped Brett in a fit of pique. Amos fired everyone, including yours truly, after a brother of his died. He did a guest shot for me in *Doctor Heckyl & Mr. Hype* in 1980. A brother of his was a stuntman for me in *Eat My Dust*. When another brother died, Amos' bitterness became terminal." Brett revealed the terrible tragedy that befell the author of *Revenge of the Blood Beast* and *O'Hooligan's Mob*: "He ended up shooting himself in the lobby of St. Joseph's Hospital in Burbank, California, as a result of being refused admittance because of inadequate insurance."

Chuck Griffith continued to work in the film business as a writer and director and, with a settlement from Corman over *The Little Shop of Horrors* when that was remade as a successful stage musical and big-budget Hollywood movie, tried his hand at novel-writing. All he had ever seen of Mike's work was a cut of *Revenge of the Blood Beast* during the editing, until he visited Philip Waddilove many years after Mike's death and saw *Witchfinder General* on Philip's TV set.

Philip Waddilove himself, after producing *The Buttercup Chain*, which premiered in 1970, tried to set up a film with Don Siegel, whom he had met through Mike at a screening in London. The film was to be *Paradise Mountain* and star Clint Eastwood for Universal in 1974. Philip had a three- or four-day script conference with Siegel and was put up at the Beverly Hills Hotel, "car, bungalow, the lot." He recalled that Siegel talked about Mike "all the time." The film did not happen, but Philip and his family moved to Los Angeles in 1977. Philip went into a general business career and became a member of BAFTA L.A., where he would encounter Vincent Price again:

> "Until Vincent's death in 1993, I invariably bumped into him at the annual BAFTA garden party held at the British Consul-General's residence. Vincent's

opening remark to me was always along the same lines: 'Of course Michael just hated me because he never wanted me in the part!' Diplomatically, I of course always refuted this, but Vinnie would come back at me: 'His suicide was such a pity and he had so many problems, especially the drugs.' Unfortunately these were basic fabrications that were to a large extent originated and perpetuated by Vincent himself. I said to him, 'Vincent, *you* are responsible for this.'"

The most extreme after-effect of working with Mike Reeves was reflected in the subsequent career of Paul Ferris. He eventually gave up music professionally, after scoring more horror movies and having a violin concerto performed at the Wigmore Hall. He then invented a new method of making clay pipes! Next in this extraordinary life, he went to sea as First Mate on a tug, eventually getting his Master's Ticket and becoming captain for Jackson Marine in the Persian Gulf, involved in general supply to oil rigs. He grabbed this as an escape route from working in the film industry and did this for five years. In the mid-'80s, he came back to England and started trying to write music again and, said Ian Ogilvy, "bought himself one of these enormous great machines." He went back to his then ex-wife and settled in Leamington Spa, investing in a fish-and-chip shop in Tipton: "It seemed like a good idea at the time. I got robbed."

At the time of interview for this book in 1988, he was negotiating to go to Libya to run an expatriate village for Swedish engineers! This did not come about and Paul went back to sea. Eventually, the work dried up and he relocated to Bristol because he loved the sea. He took his HGV license and drove delivery lorries. One day, he fell backwards off a lorry he was unloading and realized his sense of balance was deserting him. Sadly, he had come down with Huntington's chorea, which is a hereditary disease, and died in 1995.

Paul explained the reason for his checkered life since working with Mike: "The trouble is you get spoilt. Maybe that was the problem with Mike, too. I started too high. Orson Welles, in the same way, went down after almost the first moment. And that was so exciting, it was so exciting, I was completely spoilt. *Maroc 7* was a pain in the ass, but *Witchfinder*, because of Mike, we all loved. It was like a fantastic paid holiday."

After that, it all seemed an anti-climax: "*The Creeping Flesh*, parts of that were as good as anything I've ever done. Movie was absolute crap. I stopped doing them eventually because of that. I love music too much, and the movies too. I got tired of all the bullshit. I stopped stone dead with a movie called *Persecution* produced by Kevin Francis." Paul detested Kevin Francis for his treatment of his father, cameraman and director Freddie Francis, who worked for his son.

Unfortunately, in 1988, Orion (located in the United States), which had taken over the AIP catalogue, removed Paul Ferris' essential score from the U.S. prints of *Witchfinder General* and substituted a synthesizer score to save on royalty payments. Nicky Henson explained it was "because he was the only one left that they would have to pay any money to. So they pay a composer a lump sum, $8,000 or something, to write a score which he does on a synth, and that's it, then they have no further payments to make out."

It was Philip Waddilove, by phone from Los Angeles, who first alerted Paul that the version put out on Home Box Office in the U.S. featured a new score. Ian Ogilvy found Paul's attitude to the "desecration" of *Witchfinder General* "remarkably philosophical." Paul confessed to being "pissed off" about it. He recalled Philip's telephone call and his feelings about the news:

"He thought it was awful, so he said. He didn't think it was all that good. If it was better, I don't mind. If it's worse, that's what chokes me. They've got their own man in, paid him a fee, and kept the royalties for themselves. There's nothing you can do. You have no rights. I have no rights. Legally, no rights at all. That's what they work on. That's why I gave it up. There's nothing I can do about it. If it had been an improvement, I wouldn't mind. If it lessens it in any way, that's an artistic crime.

"That's why I left the whole damn business. They're all doing it all the time, they have no love of movies. It's not what I want to be involved in, and I wasn't prepared to carry on just doing rubbish. I love the movies and music too much still, so I thought, 'Stop. Do something else I can earn money at and still keep a love of the movies.' To work with these prats, I can't stick into it. Some people do, I can't do that. I want to do only good work in it or not work in it at all. Ian says, 'You're wrong, stick in there.' Not me, no. That's why I got out of it."

Tom Baker in 1971 (photo: Tom Baker)

The composer of the new score was Kendall Schmidt. He commented to Tim Lucas (*Gorezone*): "I pretty much like what I did with the film. I took an acoustic approach, used mostly strings, did a contrapuntal kind of score. I think it fits dramatically, but if you've seen the film 20,000 times the way it used to be..." To be fair, Schmidt's score could have been worse. It is slightly reminiscent of Paul Ferris' work, albeit much less effective. Overall, it does reduce the impact of Mike's masterwork, but it still does not destroy it. Nevertheless, the removal of Ferris' score is as unthinkable an action as the removal of Bernstein's score from *The Magnificent Seven*.

The trouble with Schmidt's defense of his work is that it ignores the moral question of interference in the work of a deceased artist, especially given that *Witchfinder* was Mike's one masterpiece and he strongly conceived the film with the music as an essential ingredient of the revenge Western, just like *The Magnificent Seven*. Tom Baker confirmed this: "There was definitely an element of an awareness of trying to do that, of trying in some sense to make movement through the landscape relevant, and that comes across." To remove such an outstanding element of the original conception, particularly one so brilliantly realized by Paul Ferris, was little short of criminal in that it was likely to damage Mike Reeves' lasting reputation in the United States as an artist of great power.

Tom Baker gave up the commercial film industry and turned to agricultural pursuits. He had not made much money from *Witchfinder*: "Tony just paid us £500, split down the middle, and that was that. Little did I know it would ramble on all these years." He got no residuals from the various reshowings and video and DVD releases. He was paid only £17 per rewrite on *Journey to the Unknown*. He eventually found people would recognize his important contribution to the Mike Reeves canon.

In 2003 he was invited to a public discussion with Iain Sinclair on the use of landscape in *Witchfinder General* at Cecil Sharp House in London, which the author attended. Tom praised Paul Ferris' music for adding "tremendous gentleness" to the landscape. Iain asked if the emphasis on landscape came about due to the influence of Western movies, since the film has been described as a Suffolk Western. Tom said there was "a touch of that," but it was also "*necessary* for people to be moving a lot" and, as well as this, the landscape provided a "good opportunity to be outside, away from the claustrophobic interrogations."

Annabelle Webb went on to work in movies as a P.A. She worked on *The Mackintosh Man*, *Outland* and *They Shoot Horses, Don't They?* and went out with the latter's star, Michael Sarrazin. For years she worked with Elizabeth Taylor. Later, she married an airline pilot, Captain Bill Steele. Paul Ferris attended her wedding. She went to live in Hong Kong for some years and remained friendly with Philip Waddilove and Ian Ogilvy.

Tony Tenser gave up the film business in 1972 and relocated to Southport, where he followed property and mail order interests. He was unhappy that Roman Polanski's memoirs barely mentioned him, but would eventually find his association with Mike Reeves bringing him long-overdue recognition, including a biography by writer John Hamilton.

Ian Ogilvy and his wife Diane were divorced in 1989. Ian had grown dissatisfied with his career in Britain. This was despite the major publicity he had attracted playing The Saint in *Return of the Saint* on television in the '70s. Ironically, this was a role that Vincent Price had played on U.S. radio in the 1940s. When Ian worked on a *Maigret* television movie with Richard Harris, Harris advised him to move to Hollywood. So Ian took the route Michael Reeves might well have followed 20 years before and emigrated to Los Angeles, landing a Hollywood movie and starting a successful American stage career. He also did a lot of U.S. television, often as a guest villain, and did more writing. He

had already sold a play and he wrote a series of comic novels. He got married to producer Kitty Boxleitner, another person who has considered filming Mike's life.

When Nicky Henson, Paul Ferris and Ian Ogilvy, all great friends, met in the years after Mike's death, they never mentioned Mike. Nevertheless, they were all most happy to be interviewed by the author about him individually. Ian Ogilvy was later interviewed on the phone by the late Bill Kelley and on film by writer/filmmaker Pete Tombs for a Channel Four U.K. television documentary on Mike Reeves, part of the *Eurotika* series on cult filmmakers. This documentary did more to spread Mike's fame than all the writings on him to date.

Interestingly, Tombs had a link to Mike's past, as he explained upon reading the British edition of this book:

> "When we were kids, we lived for a brief while near Mrs. Reeves just outside Ipswich. I was too young to really know what was going on, but I remember my sister used to deliver newspapers to the Reeves' house. This would have been in the late '60s, so I guess Mike Reeves was still alive at that point, although not living in the house at the time. I remember my parents talking about his death, which was widely considered at the time to be suicide."

Pete then formed his own DVD label and began investigating the possibility of freeing the negative of *Revenge of the Blood Beast* from the film laboratory where it had been mouldering in Italy due to unpaid storage bills, with a view to an eventual DVD release of the original widescreen print.

In the new millenium, *Witchfinder General* was voted one of the hundred greatest British films of all time in a poll by the *Daily Mail* in conjunction with the BBC. In August 2000, the American Cinematheque honoured Mike Reeves with a special tribute evening at the Egyptian Theatre in Los Angeles, organized by Philip Waddilove and with Ian Ogilvy in attendance. And in 2003 finally came serious critical recognition of the genius of Michael Reeves with the publication of "Michael Reeves" by Benjamin Halligan at Manchester University Press, a beautiful critique of the value of Michael Reeves' short but unique career.

Filmography

Films realized by Mike Reeves as director, writer, assistant director or runner, amateur and professional:

Amateur Movies

Untitled 8-mm Short; Featuring Joyce Grenfell; Filmed at Cold Ash; Michael Reeves: Writer/ Director

Untitled 8-mm Short; Featuring Tom Baker; Filmed at Cold Ash; Michael Reeves: Writer/Director; Plot: features a thrown bomb

8-mm Short (Title Unknown); Featuring Tom Baker (with a broken leg); Filmed at Cold Ash; Michael Reeves: Writer/Director

8-mm Short (Title Unknown): Filmed at Radley College; Michael Reeves: Writer/Director; Plot: Featuring a freshly dug ditch

Down (8-mm b/w): Filmed at Radley College; With Ken Brookman; Cameraman: Alex Waye (unconfirmed); Michael Reeves: Writer/Director; 1958/9; Plot: Chase scene on Radley College parapets

8-mm Short (Title Unknown): Filmed at Radley College; Cameraman: Alex Waye; Michael Reeves: Writer/Director; Unfinished; Plot: Horror movie featuring a boy's hands sliced off by the wheels of a train; Also a devilish laboratory; Lab scene exposed over train scene

The Ballad of the Battle of New Orleans (8-mm b/w); Filmed at Radley College; Produced by Ken Brookman; Michael Reeves: Assistant Editor/Assistant Sound Editor); 1959

Carrion (8-mm silent b/w); Filmed at Foxbriar House, Cold Ash; Starring Ian Ogilvy, Mike Reeves; Sound: Diana Tetlow; Cameraman: Tom Baker; General Assistant: Paul Vestey; Michael Reeves: Writer/Director

Tale of the Artist (nominal title); Written by Tom Baker; Michael Reeves:Director

Intrusion (16-mm sound b/w, remake of *Carrion*); Filmed at Foxbriar House, Cold Ash; A Leith Production; Starring Ian Ogilvy, Mike Reeves (under pseudonym Martin Reade), Sarah Dunlop, Desmond Bane, John Hardy; Cameraman: Tom Baker; Production Manager: Paul Vestey; Grip: Bob Armstrong; Michael Reeves: Writer/Director; 10 mins.; 1961; (Soundtrack lost)

8-mm Short (Title Unknown); Filmed at Mr. Phelps-Penry's flat, Montagu Square, London W.1; Cameraman: Tom Baker; Michael Reeves: Writer/Director

Professional Movies

Fun In Acapulco: Directed by Richard Thorpe; Starring Elvis Presley, Ursula Andress, Paul Lukas, Alejandro Rey; Tests by Don Siegel; Mike Reeves: Dialogue Director (on Siegel tests); 1963

The Long Ships: Director: Jack Cardiff; Producer: Irving Allen; Associate Producer: Denis O'Dell; Second Unit Director: Cliff Lyons; Assistant Director: Bluey Hill; Screenplay: Berkeley

Mather and Beverley Cross; Based on a Novel by Frank G. Bengtsson; Photography: Christopher Challis; Editor: Geoff Foot; Assistant Director John Hoesli; Production Manager: Paul Maslansky; Costumes by Anthony Mendelson; Sound: Paddy Cunningham; Technical Adviser: Erik Kiersgaard; First Assistant Director: Derek Cracknell; Produced by: Warwick Films (London)/Avala (Belgrade); Mike Reeves (a runner); Starring Richard Widmark, Sidney Poitier, Rosanna Schiaffino, Russ Tamblyn, Oscar Homolka, Beba Loncar, Edward Judd, Clifford Evans, Jeanne Moody, Colin Blakely, Gordon Jackson, David Lodge, Paul Stassino, Lionel Jefferies; 1964.

Castle of the Living Dead: Director: Warren Kiefer; Screenplay: Warren Kiefer; Assistant Directors: Fritz Muller and Michael Reeves; Executive Producer: Paul Maslansky; Production Manager: Roberto Dandi; Photography: Aldo Tonti; Cameraman: Luigi Kuiviller; Editor: Mario Serandrei; Art Director: Carlo Gentili; Music: Angelo Lavagnino; Makeup: Guglielmo Bonotti; Sound: Fiorenzo Magli; Costumes: Martin of Rome; Hair Stylist: Paolo Borselli; Producer: Serena Film (Rome)/Francinor (Paris); Starring: Christopher Lee (Count Drago), Gaia Germani (Laura), Philippe Leroy (Eric), Jacques Stanislawski (Bruno), Mirko Valentin (Sandro), Antonio de Martino (Neep), Luciano Pigozzi (Dart), Ennio Antonelli (Gianni), Donald Sutherland (First Policeman and Witch), Louis Williams (Second Policeman), Renato Terra (Forge); 90 mins.; 1964

Genghis Khan: Director: Henry Levin; Producer: Irving Allen; Associate Producer: Euan Lloyd; Screenplay: Clarke Reynolds and Beverley Cross; Based on a Story by Berkley Mather; Technicolor Photography: Geoffrey Unsworth; Second Unit Photography: Tony Braun; Second Unit Director: Cliff Lyons; Action Sequence: Bob Simmons; Editor: Geoffrey Foot; Supervising Art Director: Maurice Carter; Set Designer: Toni Sarzi-Braga; Art Directors: Heino Weidemann and Mile Nickolic; Special Effects: Bill and David Warrington; Music: Dusan Radic; Costumes: Cynthia Tingey; Sound: George Stephenson and Hugh Strain; Co-producer: Irving Allen, CCC (Berlin)/Avala (Belgrade); Mike Reeves (a runner); Starring Omar Sharif, Stephen Boyd, James Mason, Francoise Dorleac, Telly Savalas, Woody Stode, Kenneth Cope, Michael Hordern, Robert Morley, Eli Wallach, Yvonne Mitchell, Roger Croucher, Don Borisenko, Patrick Holt, Suzanne Hsaio, George Savalas, Carlo Cura, Gustavo Rojo, Dusan Vujsic, Jovan Tesic, Andreja Marcic, Thomas Margulies; 1965

La Sorella di Satana (Italian title))aka: **The Revenge of the Blood Beast** [U.K.]; **The She Beast** [U.S. title]); Director: Mike Reeves;Pproducer: Paul M. Maslansky; Second Unit Director: Charles B. Griffith; Screenplay: Michael Byron (Mike Reeves and Charles Byron Griffith, from a Treatment by Amos Powell); Production Company: Leith; Photography: G. Gengarelli; Camera Operator: Mario Cimino; Script Girl: Claudine Mallet; Makeup: David Pollack; Set Dresser: Annabelle Webb; Property Master: Pete White; Editor: Nira Omri; Music: Ralph Ferraro; Sound: Lars Bloch; Sound Editor: Nick Alexander; Eastmancolor-scope: Technostampa; Starring: Barbara Steele (Veronica), Ian Ogilvy (Philip), John Karlsen (Count Von Helsing), Mel Welles (Innkeeper), Jay Riley (Vardella), Lucrezia Love (rape victim), Richard Watson, Ed Randolph, Peter Grippe, Tony Antonelli, Kevin and Woody Welles; 76 mins.; 1965

The Sorcerers: Producers: Patrick Curtis and Tony Tenser; Executive Producer: Arnold L. Miller; Director: Michael Reeves; Assistant Director: Keith Wilkinson; Screenplay: Michael Reeves and Tom Baker (Based on an Idea by John Burke); Photography: Stanley A. Long; Editors: Ralph Sheldon, David Woodward and Susan Michie; Art Director: Tony Curtis; Music: Paul Ferris; Songs Performed by Toni Daly and Lee Grant and the Capitols; Continuity: Doreen Soan; Production Secretary: Sheila Miller; Camera Operator: John Mantell; Camera Assistants: Don Lord and Gordon Thornton; Sound Mixer: Ken Osborne; Boom Operator: Mike Payne; Gaffer: Maurice Corcoran; Construction Manager: Jack Palmer; Makeup: Geoff Rodway; Producer: Tigon/Curtwel/Global Productions, copyright Tony Tenser Films Limited; starring Boris Karloff (Professor Monserrat), Catherine Lacey (Estelle), Ian Ogilvy (Mike Roscoe), Victor

Henry (Alan), Elizabeth Ercy (Nicole), Susan George (Audrey), Dani Sheridan (Laura), Ivor Dean (Inspector Matalon), Peter Fraser (Detective), Meier Tzelniker (Snack Bar Owner), Bill Barnsley (Constable), Martin Terry (Tobacconist), Gerald Campion (Customer), Alf Joint (Ron), Maureen Boothe; 85 mins.; 1967

Crescendo (originally **Apassionata**): Director: Alan Gibson; Writer: Mike Reeves (uncredited cowriter of original script with Alfred Shaughnessy); Starring Stefanie Powers, James Olson, Margaretta Scott, Jane Lapotaire, Joss Ackland; 1966; Released 1970

Witchfinder General: Executive Producer: Tony Tenser; Producers: Philip Waddilove, Arnold L. Miller and Louis M. Heyward; Production Manager: Richard Coward; Director: Michael Reeves; Assistant Directors: Ian Goddard and Iain Lawrence; Screenplay: Michael Reeves and Tom Baker, Louis M. Heyward (From the Novel by Ronald Bassett); Photograpy: Johnny Coquillon; Camera Operators: Brian Elvin and Gerry Anstiss; Camera Assistants: Tony Breeze and Chris Reynolds; Grip: Freddie Williams; Construction Manager: Dennis Cantell; Film Editor:Howard Lanning; Assistant Editor: Marion Curren; Art Director: Jim Morahan; Assistant Art Director: Peter Shields; Props: Sid Davies and Fred Harrison; Set Decorator: Andrew Low; Special Effects: Roger Dicken; Music: Paul Ferris; Sound Recordist: Paul Le Mare; Dubbing Editor: Dennis Lanning; Sound Mixer: Hugh Strain; Location Manager: Euan Pearson; Continuity: Lorna Selwyn; Production Secretary: Pat O'Donnell; Casting Director: Freddie Vale; Publicity: Jack Daw; Set Dresser: Jimmy James; Still Photography: Jack Dooley; Makeup: Dore Hamilton; Hairdresser: Henry Montsash; Wardrobe: Jill Thomson; Gaffer: Laurie Shane; Production Company: Tigon British in association with American International; Starring: Vincent Price (Matthew Hopkins), Ian Ogilvy (Richard Marshall), Hilary Dwyer (Sara), Rupert Davies (John Lowes), Robert Russell (John Stearne), Patrick Wymark (Oliver Cromwell), Wilfrid Brambell (Master Loach), Michael Beint (Captain Gordon), Nicky Henson (Trooper Swallow), John Treneman (Trooper Harcourt), William Maxwell (Trooper Gifford), Tony Selby (Salter), Beaufoy Milton (Priest), John Kidd (First Magistrate), Peter Haigh (Lavenham Magistrate), Hira Talfrey (First Old Woman), Ann Tirard (Second Old Woman), Peter Thomas (Farrier), Edward Palmer (Shepherd), David Webb (Jailer), Godfrey James (Webb), Paul Dawkins (Farmer), Jack Lynn (Brandeston Innkeeper), Martin Terry (Hoxne Innkeeper), Lee Peters (Infantry Sergeant), David Lyell (Foot Soldier), Toby Lennon (Old Man), Maggie Kimberley (Elizabeth Clarke), Bernard Kay (Fisherman), Gillian Aldham (Young Woman in Cell), Paul Ferris as Morris Jar (Paul), Alf Joint (Sentry), Dennis Thorne (Villager), Michael Segal (Villager), Michael Culver (Villager), Maggie Nolan, Sally Douglas, Donna Reading, Tasma Brereton and Sandy Seager (Wenches in Inns), Amos Powell (Execution Assistant in Green), Tom Baker (Soldier), Philip Waddilove (Roundhead officer), John Kidd, Susi Field, Derek Ware; 87 mins.; 1968

The Oblong Box: Executive Producer: Louis M. Heyward; Producer/Director: Gordon Hessler; Associate Producer: Pat Green; Screenplay: Lawrence Huntington (Based on the Story by Edgar Allan Poe); Additional Dialogue: Christopher Wicking; Photography: Johnny Coquillon; Music: Harry Robinson; Starring: Vincent Price (Julian Markham), Alastair Williamson (Sir Edward Markham), Christopher Lee, Rupert Davies, Sally Geeson, Hilary Dwyer, Godfrey James, Ivor Dean, Hira Talfrey, Martin Terry; 1969; (Michael Reeves did script rewrites, which were abandoned when he was replaced as director) [Note the number of Mike Reeves' players and crew in the finished film.] Although not a Mike Reeves film, it is included because of his degree of involvement and influence.

Savage Justice: Director: Michael Reeves; an extract from *Witchfinder General* released on 8mm to the home movie market by Walton Films.

Erroneous Credits

The Whisperers: Director: Bryan Forbes; Starring: Edith Evans, Eric Portman; 1966; Mike was reported by the *Oldham Evening Chronicle* (May 4, 1968) as having assisted Bryan Forbes in Oldham. (Ironically, *Witchfinder*'s Jim Morahan was a draftsman on the film.) The cutting is in Mike's own scrapbook and, strangely, he did not mark the passage, as he did with other significant quotes in clippings in the scrapbook. Philip Waddilove said: "I never heard any mention of Mike ever working with Bryan Forbes." Bryan Forbes told the author: "I've checked with my Production Manager at the time. To the best of our knowledge, neither of us can recall Mike Reeves acting in *any* capacity for me on *The Whisperers*. I could be wrong, but I'm sure I would have remembered. Certainly I had nobody assisting me. I know who my First Assistant was, a man called Christopher. In any case, it wasn't 1968, it was 1966.

Tell Me Lies: Director: Peter Brook; Starring: Glenda Jackson, Patrick Wymark; Michael Reeves is listed as 'Musical Director' of this theatrical anti-Vietnam piece in some sources, which is almost certainly incorrect); 1968

Easy Rider: Director: Dennis Hopper; Starring: Peter Fonda, Dennis Hopper, Jack Nicholson; Michael Reeves allegedly slated to direct, very unconfirmed; 1969

Unrealized Projects
(an incomplete listing)

Blood Moon/Flame in the Blood: script offered to Compton; Michael Reeves: the writer, proposed director; 1966

The Crooked Cross: Written by Peter Myers; Producers: Gerald Fernback and Richard Gordon; Michael Reeves considered to direct; 1966

Roman epic (Title Unknown): Starring: Brett Halsey; Michael Reeves was rumored to have been considered to direct; 1966

Manic Mind: a Fernback project; Michael Reeves writer, proposed director; 1966

Roman project (Title Unknown): Producer: Michael Klinger; Michael Reeves scouted locations with Tom Baker, project abandoned by Klinger; 1966

Devil's Discord: Written by John Burke; Starring: Edd "Kookie" Byrnes, Peter Cushing; to be shot in Rome; Michael Reeves was the proposed director, Patrick Curtis, the producer, a Curtwel-Compton co-production; never produced; 1966

Don't Look Now: Director: Nicolas Roeg; Starring: Julie Christie, Donald Sutherlan; Michael Reeves tried to buy the rights to direct the film; 1973

All the Little Animals: Director: Jeremy Thomas; From the Novel by Walker Hamilton; Starring: John Hurt; Michael Reeves wanted to direct this story; 1969

De Sade: Director: Cyril Endfield (completed by Roger Corman); Starring: Keir Dullea, John Huston; Michael Reeves did the location scouting; project abandoned; 1969

The Buttercup Chain; Director: Robert Ellis Miller; Starring: Hywel Bennett, Leigh-Taylor Young, Jane Asher; Producer: Philip Waddilove; Michael Reeves originally intended as director; 1970

Bloody Mama; Director: Roger Corman; Starring: Shelley Winters, Don Stroud, Robert De Niro; Michael Reeves originally slated to direct; 1970

O'Hooligan's Mob: Written by Amos Powell; From an Idea by Tom Baker; Starring: Ian Ogilvy; Michael Reeves to direct; never produced; 1969

Christ Project (Title Unknown): a film about the return of Christ to Earth in 1968; Michael Reeves was to direct; 1968

2267 A.D.—When the Sleeper Wakes: Script:Shelley Stark; From the Novel by H.G. Wells; Producer: Deke Heyward; AIP; Originally intended to star Vincent Price and Martha Hyer when first announced in 1965; Michael Reeves was to direct, annotated the script; 1968

Razor: Starring: Ian Ogilvy; Music: Paul Ferris; Michael Reeves: Writer/Director; 1968

Scream and Scream Again: Executive Producer: Louis M. Heyward; Director: Gordon Hessler; Screenplay: Christopher Wicking; Photography: Johnny Coquillon; Starring: Vincent Price, Christopher Lee, Peter Cushing; According to Vincent Price, Michael Reeves would have directed had he lived; 1970

Kill Me Kindly: a Tony Tenser project

The King's Shilling: From a Book by Ronald Bassett; a projected Tenser follow-up to *Witchfinder General*

Mistress of the Seas: a Hammer project to star Raquel Welch

The Instrument: From the Novel by John O'Hara

Television

TV commercials and TV films: Assistant Director:Michael Reeves; probably false credit printed in Tigon publicity sheets and *The Sorcerers* pressbook; 1964

Journey to the Unknown: 20th Century-Fox/Hammer/ABC TV; Michael Reeves proposed to direct one episode, however, he refused; 1968

Late Night Line-Up: BBC-2 TV; Screening of *Carrion* 8-mm by Philip Jenkinson as tribute to Mike Reeves after his death; 1969

Eurotika!—The Blood Beast: The Films of Michael Reeves: A production for Channel 4, U.K.; Half-hour career profile directed by Andy Starke and Pete Tombs; 1999; Featured on the new U.K. DVD releases of *The Sorcerers* and *Witchfinder General*

Film Appearances

Castle of the Living Dead: Michael Reeves makes a "Hitchcock" appearance as a dashing musta-chioed officer in suspended animation, and his hand doubles for Christopher Lee's hand; 1964

The Revenge of the Blood Beast: Michael Reeves appears in a brief close-up as one of the mob that executes Vardella; 1965

The Sorcerers: Michael Reeves' hands double for Ian Ogilvy's hands in the crashed Jaguar; 1967

Ian Ogilvy's 16-mm home movies show Michael Reeves at work directing *Witchfinder General;* 1967

Suggested Reading

In Memoriam: Michael Reeves by Robin Wood; *Movie* 17; 1969

A Heritage of Horror: The English Gothic Cinema 1946-1972 by David Pirie; Gordon Fraser, 1973

Lights Out for the Territory: 9 Excursions in the Secret History of London by Iain Sinclair; Granta Books; 1997

Vincent Price: A Daughter's Biography by Victoria Price; St. Martins Press; 1999

Cinefantastique Special Double Issue: "Vincent Price, Horror's Crown Prince," Vol. 19 Nos. 1 & 2, January 1989; magazine

Cult Movies No. 15: article "Backstage with Vincent Price: An Interview Conducted by Bob Madison"; magazine; 1995

Roger Corman: An Unauthorised Biography of the Godfather of Indie Filmmaking by Beverly Gray; Renaissance Books; 2000

Michael Reeves: Horror's James Dean by Bill Kelley; *Cinefantastique* magazine, Vol. 22 No.1; August 1991

A Siegel Film: An Autobiography by Don Siegel; Faber and Faber; 1993; no mention of Mike Reeves unfortunately, but contains a chapter on making *The Killers*

Caligari's Children: The Film as Tale of Terror by S.S. Prawer; Oxford University Press; 1980;

Young and Bipolar by Jeffrey Kluger with Sora Song; *Time* magazine; August 19, 2002

Penthouse Magazine, Vol. 3 No. 10; U.K. edition; 1968; "Shows" column entitled "Horror Clicks"

Michael Reeves: British Film Makers; by Benjamin Halligan; Foreword by Philip Waddilove; Manchester University Press; 2003

Beasts in the Cellar: The Exploitation Film Career of Tony Tenser by John Hamilton; FAB Press; 2005

The plots of the main Reeves movies have been reprinted from the *Monthly Film Bulletin* (copyright British Film Institute, reproduced with kind permission) rather than contemporary Miracle and Tigon press handouts, which usually left the ending unknown. Other brief comments from Leonard Maltin's *TV Movies* (Signet Books).

Fun in Acapulco: "Scenery outshines story of Presley working as lifeguard and entertainer in Mexican resort city." (Maltin)

The Long Ships: "Fairly elaborate costume adventure of Vikings battling Moors for fabled treasure has better-than-average cast to recommend it." (Maltin)

Genghis Khan: "Laughable epic with gross miscasting and juvenile script, loosely based on legend of Chinese leader. No sweep or spectacle, but radiant Dorleac and earnest Sharif." (Maltin)

Castle of the Living Dead: 1820. In a small Central European kingdom a troupe of strolling players—Laura, Bruno, Dart, Gianni and the dwarf Neep—are invited to give a performance at the castle of Count Drago. In a village tavern they meet Eric, a former cavalry officer, who joins them after Dart has stolen his horse. Their journey to the castle is interrupted by an old woman, who warns them that danger awaits them, but they press on and are welcomed at the castle by Drago and his sinister manservant Sandro. At the climax of the troupe's performance for the Count—a mock execution—Bruno is accidentally hanged; later that evening Dart, who has by now reached the castle, is hacked down with a scythe by Sandro. Next morning Sandro disposes of Gianni with a poison dart and knocks out Eric. Their suspicions aroused, Laura and Neep wander through the corridors looking for Eric and stumble on the mummified body of Drago's wife. Sandro appears and throws Neep over a parapet, and Drago tells Laura and the revived Eric that he intends to add them to his collection of preserved corpses. But Neep, who has recovered from his fall with the help of the old woman, tricks Sandro into killing himself and manages to distract Drago long enough for Laura and Eric to flee. Their escape is cut off by the local police sergeant and his deputy, who arrest them on Drago's orders, but the old woman appears and during a struggle with her, Drago is pierced by a scalpel dipped in his own mummifying poison.

The Revenge of the Blood Beast: Two hundred years after the people of the Transylvanian village of Vaubrac get rid of an evil old witch called Vardella by impaling her on a spike and dumping her in the lake, Philip and Veronica, a young English couple on holiday, arrive in Vaubrac. After spending a troubled night in the local inn, harried by the innkeeper's voyeuristic habits, they move on but are involved in a crash which plunges their car into the lake. The distraught Philip is taken back to the inn by a passing lorry driver, with a dead body which proves to be not Veronica but Vardella. An eccentric old man, Count Von Helsing, explains that Vardella had put a curse on the village, promising to return, and has obviously seized this opportunity to do so; he also explains that the only way to get Veronica back is to revive Vardella and exorcise her, properly this time. They revive the witch, and after some trouble when she rages through the village on a bloody spree, manage to exorcise her and cast her back into the lake. Whereupon Veronica reappears, apparently none the worse for her experience. But as they leave Vaubrac with some relief, Veronica suddenly remarks (with a sinister gleam in her eye), "I'll be back."

The Sorcerers: Ruined by the ridicule poured on his experiments in medical hypnosis, Professor Monserrat has lived for years in poverty, perfecting a method of obtaining control over the human mind. Urged on by his wife Estelle, he determines to try it out, and lures a bored youth named Mike back to the flat with the promise of an exciting psychedelic experience. Afterwards Mike leaves, with no recollection of what has occurred; but by concentrating together, Monserrat and Estelle can make him do their bidding. They will him to go for a nocturnal swim, and realize to their excitement that they share his sensations as though they themselves were in the water. Monserrat plans to use his discovery to allow elderly people to relive the experiences of their youth, but Estelle has different ideas: tired of poverty, she persuades her husband to make Mike steal a fur coat for her. Monserrat is forced to admit that he enjoyed the excitement of the robbery, and allows her to move on to other experiences. But when she makes Mike beat up his friend Alan, Monserrat realizes they have gone too far, only to discover that Estelle's will is stronger than his own. Having immobilized her husband by removing the stick without which he cannot walk, Estelle proceeds to satisfy her cravings by making Mike murder two girls, Audrey and Laura. By now the police are on Mike's trail; so are Alan and his girlfriend Nicole. Mike escapes by car, and Monserrat, summoning his last ounce of willpower, causes the car to crash. It bursts into flames, consuming not only Mike, but Monserrat and Estelle.

Witchfinder General: 1645. In an England torn by the Civil War, an obscure lawyer from Ipswich named Matthew Hopkins is able to roam the country with impunity and very profitably, instigating local witch hunts. His assistant, John Stearne, ensures by a judicious use of torture that anyone accused of witchcraft eventually confesses his or her guilt, and gradually Hopkins builds a reputation as Witchfinder General. In the village of Brandeston, one of the accused is the vicar, John Lowes, whose niece Sara makes a despairing attempt to save his life by offering herself to the witchfinder. Hopkins accepts. But Stearne discovers the bargain, rapes Sara, and so poisons Hopkins' mind against her that he orders the arraignment and execution of her uncle. When Sara's fiancé Richard Marshall—a soldier in Cromwell's army—returns on leave and learns what has happened, Hopkins and Stearne are already far away. Richard marries Sara and returns to the army after swearing vengeance on Hopkins, whom he proceeds to hunt down relentlessly in the months that follow. Hearing of his pursuer, Hopkins decides to take the initiative by arraigning both Richard and Sara as witches. Just as some of his army colleagues burst into the prison, the frenzied Richard breaks his fetters to prevent Sara from being tortured, and strikes Hopkins again and again with an axe. Aghast, one of the soldiers shoots the dying witchfinder.

The Oblong Box: England in 1860. After Sir Edward Markham is hideously mutilated by an African voodoo ritual, he is kept under lock and key back at the family estate by his brother Julian, his unspeakable face hidden by a crimson hood. When Sir Edward finally escapes, he seeks revenge on those he feels betrayed him, especially his brother, for whom the hideous torture was actually intended as retribution for the horseback hit-and-run of a native child. Edward is eventually killed, but not before he passes the curse on to Julian, who will henceforth bear the same disfigurement.

Crescendo: "Tiresome chiller has grad student traveling to France for some research on a dead composer, becoming involved with his crazy family." (Maltin)

The Buttercup Chain: Incest drama. "Cousins are raised together and find they needn't stop at kissing." (Maltin)

Bloody Mama: Gangster drama. "Sordid story of Ma Barker and her ugly brood." (Maltin)

Scream and Scream Again: "Distinguished cast does their darnedest to enliven (no pun intended) tired, confusing plot concerning mad scientist's organ/limb experiments and race of emotionless beings he creates." (Maltin)

For more information about books from
Midnight Marquee Press, Inc.
or
Luminary Press
Write to:
Midnight Marquee Press, Inc.
9721 Britinay Lane
Baltimore, MD 21234
USA

www.midmar.com